Equipped to Tell the Next Generation

Equipped to Tell the Next Generation

Donna R. Ryan

WIPF & STOCK · Eugene, Oregon

EQUIPPED TO TELL THE NEXT GENERATION

Copyright © 2020 Donna R. Ryan. All rights reserved. Except for brief quotations in critical publications or reviews, no part of this book may be reproduced in any manner without prior written permission from the publisher. Write: Permissions, Wipf and Stock Publishers, 199 W. 8th Ave., Suite 3, Eugene, OR 97401.

Wipf & Stock
An Imprint of Wipf and Stock Publishers
199 W. 8th Ave., Suite 3
Eugene, OR 97401

www.wipfandstock.com

PAPERBACK ISBN: 978-1-7252-6150-1
HARDCOVER ISBN: 978-1-7252-6149-5
EBOOK ISBN: 978-1-7252-6151-8

Scriptures marked (ESV) are taken from the Holy Bible, English Standard Version (ESV): Scriptures taken from the Holy Bible, English Standard Version ® Copyright© 2001 by Crossway, a publishing ministry of Good News Publishers. Used by permission.

Scripture quotations marked (NIV) are taken from the Holy Bible, New International Version®, NIV®. Copyright © 1973, 1978, 1984, 2011 by Biblica, Inc.™ Used by permission of Zondervan. All rights reserved worldwide. Used by permission.

Scripture quotations marked (NLT) are taken from the Holy Bible, New Living Translation, copyright ©1996, 2004, 2015 by Tyndale House Foundation. Used by permission of Tyndale House Publishers, a Division of Tyndale House Ministries, Carol Stream, Illinois 60188. All rights reserved. Used by permission.

Scripture quotations marked (NRSV) are taken from the New Revised Standard Version Bible, copyright © 1989 National Council of the Churches of Christ in the United States of America. Used by permission. All rights reserved worldwide.

David Ruis, "Spirit Is on Me," © 2007 VINEYARD SONGS CANADA (SOCAN) ADMIN. IN NORTH AMERICA BY MUSIC SERVICES o/b/o VINEYARD MUSIC USA. All rights reserved. Used by Permission.

Sections of this book have been adapted from the book *A Place of Healing* (copyright 2015) by Joni Eareckson Tada. Used by permission of the author and David C. Cook. May not be further reproduced. All rights reserved.

Excerpt from *Concerts of Prayer* by David Bryant, copyright © 1984, 1988. Used by permission of Bethany House, a division of Baker Publishing Group.

Manufactured in the U.S.A. 04/09/20

To my husband, Joseph Ryan, with love and appreciation.

O my people, listen to my instructions. Open your ears to what I am saying, for I will speak to you in a parable. I will teach you hidden lessons from our past—stories we have heard and known, stories our ancestors handed down to us. We will not hide these truths from our children; we will tell the next generation about the glorious deeds of the LORD, about his power and his mighty wonders. For he issued his laws to Jacob; he gave his instructions to Israel. He commanded our ancestors to teach them to their children, so the next generation might know them—even the children not yet born—and they in turn will teach their own children. So each generation should set its hope anew on God, not forgetting his glorious miracles and obeying his commands.

(Ps 78:1–7, KJV)

Contents

List of Graphs and Tables | ix
Preface | xi
Acknowledgments | xv
Abbreviations | xvi

Introduction | 1

Chapter 1: Where in the World Are We and How Did We Get Here? | 11
Chapter 2: The Computer Age and Where It Is Taking Us | 27
Chapter 3: Contextualization or Capitulation: A Struggle Gone Awry | 38
Chapter 4: The Compromise of Theology with Culture | 57
Chapter 5: More Consequences of Compromising with Culture | 73
Chapter 6: Understanding Holiness | 89
Chapter 7: Is It Reasonable to Expect Holiness in People? | 104
Chapter 8: The Beauty of Holiness | 118
Chapter 9: Holiness Brings Wholeness | 137
Chapter 10: Wholeness and Healing | 151
Chapter 11: Biblical Love Is Holy Love | 163
Chapter 12: Practical Concerns | 175
Chapter 13: Holy Grace | 189
Chapter 14: Absolute Truth | 201
Chapter 15: The Necessity of Prayer | 212
Chapter 16: Prayer for Revival and Reformation of the Culture | 229
Chapter 17: Earmarks of Revival | 243
Chapter 18: Final Thoughts on Telling the Next Generation and Revival | 260

The Wrap-Up | 273

Appendices

    Appendix 1: Timeline | 287

    Appendix 2: Joni's Wisdom | 288

    Appendix 3: Images of Love from Our Culture Vs. Scripture | 291

    Appendix 4: Refining Gold and the Firing of Porcelain and Ceramics | 294

    Appendix 5: Prayers of the New Testament | 295

    Appendix 6: Start Your Own Concert of Prayer | 300

    Appendix 7: Put on the Armor of God | 304

    Appendix 8: An Overview of Matthew 18–20 | 307

    Appendix 9: Prayers that Will Change the World | 310

    Appendix 10: Equipped to Tell the Next Generation Study Guide | 312

Bibliography | 341

Graphs and Tables

Figure 9.1: Bifurcation of the Gospel | 144

Figure 9.2: Holy, Holy, Holy God | 145

Figure 11.1: Possible meanings of "God is love" (1 John 4:8, 16) | 165

Appendix 1: Timeline | 287

Preface

The seeds for this book were sown in my early childhood. Even then, I was concerned about the spiritual state of Christianity in the United States. I can remember agonizing over why churches kept sending their best and brightest workers to foreign lands. My instincts were yelling, "But what is going to happen here?" I also remember the knot in my stomach when the day came that we could no longer pray the Lord's Prayer together or hear Scripture read in school. One day it was okay; the next it was illegal—with just the stroke of a pen. I felt like something precious was being ripped away from us.

A little later, I recall some Christians trying to warn of the problems that the increasing divorce rates and rise of single-parent families would bring on the children, but the media countered that there was no statistical data to support their concerns. Many years later, we have all of the statistics we need, but they are rarely used to promote change in these behaviors.

Within the decade of removing Bible reading and prayer from our schools we had riots in our streets, tanks in our cities to keep the peace, and abortion on demand. Still, the removal of Christianity from our public life was never part of the discussion of cause and effect. As a young person I watched as one major pillar of Christianity after another was knocked down and waited for leaders to rise up to defend the faith authentically and convincingly, but only a few isolated individuals were willing to connect the dots (whether in the church or in government). Christians built their own ministries and were more like voices crying in the wilderness than a unified force to be considered and followed. We, the culture and the church, kept drifting further and further from God and Truth. It was incredible to me how desperately this nation wanted to be deceived. I was deeply troubled as I watched the church I love bow to the culture that had lost its way.

Later in life I discerned a call to become a pastor as a second career. One day about mid-way through my MDiv, I was praying for our nation when suddenly, I sensed that God had impressed upon my mind that even the best of us had "missed it." There was no condemnation or anger; there was only sadness. I could not convince God that he was wrong, so I began asking him to show me how the best of us, his people, have missed it. By now I understood that to "miss the mark" was the literal meaning of the Greek word for sin. I kept wondering, "How are Christians in the United States sinning?" This book is an outgrowth of that question.

After graduation from seminary, a Christian friend asked me what I wanted to do with my degree. When I told her that I wanted to preach and teach the Bible, her immediate and honest response was, "We had better send you overseas! No one does that in America! You will not find any church here that will want you." This is a sad commentary on the state of Christianity in twenty-first-century America. This book identifies things that are needed to recover our vitality.

A few weeks later, I was sitting in my home office watching an ice storm form a truly beautiful pattern all over the windows. As I admired the beautiful patterns, I found myself being drawn into the scene so that it seemed to become a world in itself. The thought then came to me that while it was beautiful, it was not real. In fact it obstructed the view of what was real. I could no longer see the trees, the road, or the field that I knew were on the other side of that glass. It came to me that this is exactly what American culture has done to our Western Christianity. We see only the things of this world held up to us as beautiful and glorious (like the ice on the window) and ends in themselves so that we cannot see beyond the immediate. We no longer have an eternal perspective on everything (the reality beyond the window). Therefore, we have less and less ability to distinguish what is truly beautiful and lasting. Our fixation on the present and temporary things of this world is obstructing our view of the ultimate goal of eternity and of taking the gospel to all people so they can enjoy eternity with God too.

I am convinced that until our eyes are opened to the ways that American culture has evangelized, disciplined, and transformed the church to its image, all the prayers, Bible studies, and programs to win the culture to Christ are destined to fail or, at best, will have only limited success. This book challenges American Christians to be revived as Christ's new creation by looking first at what needs to be changed in us, so that we can be transformed to be about God's work in God's way carrying out the ministry of reconciliation in others. If we are not aware of what the problem is, it is difficult to deal with it. Often when a problem is discerned, we tend to ignore it and to hope it goes away. Then we wonder why things are not getting better. In the meantime we keep perpetuating the things that got us into difficulty in the first place.

Scripture is clear: we are to go into the world and make disciples for Jesus. There are multitudes of excellent books, seminars, teachers, preachers, and speakers who tell us what we must do to tell the next generation about him, but something is holding us back. There is a gap between our knowing what we should do and actually doing it. *Equipped* bridges that gap. For the reasons laid out in this book, I have become convinced that the solution is to recover the holiness of God in our lives and churches because it informs everything we are[1] and do.[2] I feel totally inadequate to describe the holiness of God. It is like trying to explain the ocean when the largest body of water I or anyone else has seen is a pond. How can someone with human limitations explain the unlimited? How does a finite being explain the infinite God? I do so with fear and trembling, with humility, and by God's grace.

Another reason for my hesitancy is the disregard of holiness by our culture where nearly everything is tolerated and accepted, and nothing is to be judged. However, holiness implies boundaries, purity, and a definite standard of morality which frequently runs contrary to current cultural beliefs. It is risky to take such an unpopular stand because political correctness and public opinion severely judge people who even hint at putting limitations on what is perceived as individual freedom. Nevertheless, God says, "I am holy," and commands his people to be like him. Therefore, holiness must be important for the church because it is important to God.

My hope is that this study of holiness will contribute to revival in the church in our age because it is aimed at the core of who we are and not just at what we need to do. It is about how to examine the messages rushing at us at the speed of light so that we may realize biblical, life-changing transformation reflecting God's new DNA that he infuses in all who come to faith in his Son, Jesus. God's people are to be holy; only then will we see the changes around us for which we long. Revival begins with us, but how do we become revived so we can tell the next generation?

---

1. Holiness informs our morality and emotions, our love and righteousness, and how we show mercy and grace. It brings beauty and wholeness to our lives. It is the basis of justice and judgment, to name only a few things.

2. This would include everything from personal relationships to ecology and includes marriage, education, caring for the poor and oppressed people of the world, and how we treat our neighbors and our enemies.

Acknowledgments

I WANT TO THANK my mentors, Garth Rosell, Robert Mayer, and Timothy Laniak, who walked with me through this journey and helped me see the path. Bob, thank you for all the behind the scenes help. I want to thank the "Holiness 880 Club," Sue Black, Dorothy Watson, Amy Chapman, and others for the many hours they spent struggling with the raw material to help me make sense of it. I greatly appreciate your patience with this math major who avoided every writing class she could and whom God with his great sense of humor has called to write a book. Finally, I thank my husband, Joe, for his love, patience, encouragement, and support through this long and difficult road. After Jesus, you are my love and my rock.

Abbreviations

WJE   Works of Jonathan Edwards
RA   Religious Affections

Introduction

CHURCH ATTENDANCE IS ON the decline,[1] and our best efforts to tell people about Jesus have minimal effect. Folks, especially younger generations, know little about Jesus or the Bible. The question on the minds of many Christians is echoed by Peter Gillquist when he asks why, although there are church buildings all around us, and there have been many decisions for Christ brought about by evangelists in America, the church "has not even begun to slow the world down on its godless rush to inevitable self-destruction."[2]

Why was it that at the peak of regular church attendance in America, the Supreme Court banned Bible reading and praying the Lord's Prayer from the public schools? What has taken place in the churches and the American culture that has relegated Christianity to the periphery of society? How can we, the church as the bride of Christ both individually and collectively, recover the influence we once had to speak with authority on issues of life, death, and morality? We pray for revival in the churches and reformation in the nation but see only pockets of God stirring things here and there. Might there be something holding us back from seeing God move mightily as he did in the Protestant Reformation or the First and Second Great Awakenings?

What the church teaches and Christians believe today has often been syncretized to conform to cultural beliefs. Psalm 37 might help us understand this blending of

---

1. Attendance is relatively easy to measure as opposed to spirituality or religious interest. See Gallup's "Religion" for an analysis. Gallup polls show that in the period of 1992 to 2018 among those reporting there was a decline of 20 percent of those claiming church membership from 70 percent in 1992 to 50 percent in 2018. There was a corresponding decline of 12 percent of folks who claimed to attend services weekly while the "almost every week" and "about once a month" groups fluctuated but remained stable. What is significant is that the percentage of those claiming never to attend religious services has doubled from 14 percent in 1992 to 28 percent in 2018. See Pew Research Center's "The Age Gap in Religion around the World," question 1, subsection 4. Pew reports that around 1960 over 50 percent of Americans of all ages attended services weekly. During the 1960s attendance among the under-thirty group began to decline. Since that time the decline has spread to all age groups. The sixty and over group has declined only slightly to about 45 percent while the forty to fifty-nine age group declined to about 38 percent. The younger groups dropped dramatically and more rapidly in recent years. The thirty to forty-nine age group dropped to around 30 percent, while only about 25 percent of the eighteen to twenty-nine age group attended weekly.

2. Gillquist, *Why We Haven't Changed*, 17.

Christian and cultural beliefs. When I taught that we are commanded to trust God and to do good, some parishioners asked, "Doesn't everyone do that? We each have the right to decide what is good in our own eyes." When I preached the command to commit our ways to God's way in righteousness, some asked, "Everyone has the right to make his or her own truth and the freedom to live it out. Isn't it judgmental to limit truth and righteousness to a book written thousands of years ago? Why would that have any bearing on our highly technological world?" When I told them that we are commanded to delight in God, many asked, "How can we be delighted in something we can't see when we are constantly bombarded with the horrific and hurtful things we do see happening in this world?" These are valid questions. It is apparent that cultural thinking has become intertwined with our biblical thinking and must be identified and removed (the ice must be melted) before we can find the answers to tell the next generation about Jesus. God wants us to see his eternal world beyond the transitory beauty of the iced glass window the culture wants us to see.

Not everyone falls for every deception; we will find ourselves in varying degrees in the various sections. Those things in the church that have been adopted from culture that contradict the word of God must be identified and eliminated in order for us to experience the transformation needed to become the people God is calling us to be if we are to reach the people of this age for Jesus.

This transformation usually takes time, which is why the Bible calls it a journey, but the journey has become bumpy and twisted. Watching even thirty minutes of national and international news leaves few people doubting that these are difficult, maybe desperate, times. A shaking is happening. We feel this shaking in skyrocketing debts, rising nuclear threats from countries like North Korea and Iran, increasing terrorism around the world (including the United States), and collapsing moral standards of secular and Christian culture of Western nations. It is like everything we think, believe, and do is being shaken apart.

This shaking does not surprise God. It is not evidence that God is no longer in control or that he has stopped loving us. To the contrary, there are good reasons why a just and loving God would allow people to experience this quaking. The writer of Hebrews records that God "has promised, 'Once more I will shake not only the earth but also the heavens.' The words 'once more' indicate the removing of what can be shaken—that is, created things—so that what cannot be shaken may remain" (Heb 12:24, NIV). The things of the world will pass; only what is of God will remain. This shaking is designed to reveal the temporary nature of the things of this world so that we will let them go for the eternal ways of God, and God's ways are holy.

After much prayer, research, and wrestling with God, I am convinced that recovering God's holiness is the key to seeing God work powerfully in our culture in this age. I agree with Gillquist that any "religious action . . . apart from holiness and righteousness, is futile in effecting change in the world in which we live."[3] This is the biblical

---

3. Gillquist, *Why We Haven't Changed*, 20.

perspective. Nearly two thousand years ago, the apostle Paul wrote, "As the truth is in Jesus . . . put off your old self, which . . . is corrupt through deceitful desires, and . . . be renewed in the spirit of your minds . . . put on the new self, created after the likeness of God in true *righteousness and holiness*" (Eph 4:21–25, ESV; italics are mine). This short passage is a call to God's people to be renewed in thought, action, and speech and to recover the holiness, righteousness, and truth that are just as much a part of the new self, created in the likeness of God, as love, grace, and mercy.

However, these things (holiness, righteousness, and truth) are foreign to many sitting in churches today, including many pastors. Thankfully, there are those who are resisting the cultural pressure to conform, but even the best of us have missed it. We have been transformed into our culture's image through the ever-present media. We are constantly bombarded with the culture's message of right and wrong through advertising, music, and entertainment of all sorts on iPads, smart phones, and the internet. It invades our thinking unnoticed, sets up residence in our subconscious, and becomes a part of us so that any biblical messages that do not conform to the culture sound strange, even to Christians.

A Few Obstacles to Holiness

The first and the biggest obstacle to holiness is our misconception of what it is. Hear what Jonathan Edwards has to say about holiness, "We drink in strange notions of holiness from our childhood, as if it were a melancholy, morose, sour and unpleasant thing; but there is nothing in it but what is sweet and ravishingly lovely. 'Tis the highest beauty and amiableness, vastly above all other beauties. 'Tis a divine beauty, makes the soul heavenly and far purer than anything here on earth."[4] If you are a typical Christian in the twenty-first century, this probably comes as a surprise to you because we have been conditioned to see holiness as legalistic and hurtful. What did Edwards know that we have forgotten?

A second obstacle to holiness is that it requires transformation, and change is often perceived as pain and suffering. The apostle Paul describes it as a shaking that gets rid of the temporary things of this world so that we have hold of the eternal. The apostle Peter explains the shaking as trials that are refining the faith of God's people like gold is refined in fire. Then he reminds his readers that God is holy and that his people are also called to be holy. Only God's holiness can melt that ice in which the church has become trapped and set her free to resume her journey to be about God's work of making disciples of all nations, including the United States.

A third obstacle is the pendulum of extremes. From morality to the way we make decisions, the journey of Western beliefs seems to be on a pendulum that swings from one extreme to the other. People keep trying to get it right while ignoring the one thing

---

4. Edwards, "The Miscellanies," 163.

that can make it happen. God's holiness provides answers and brings stability. However, the church has all but jettisoned the concept of holiness and has also been swinging on this pendulum of extremes. She does this when she rationalizes and relativizes her great doctrines such as separating the characteristics of God into opposing categories. Some argue for the gifts of the Spirit over the fruits of the Spirit or vice versa. Some have argued that the reasoning doctrines of righteousness, justice, and judgment are more important than the emotional ones of love, grace, and mercy, while others argue for the opposite. Preachers used to pound pulpits and preach hellfire and brimstone; today the true test of successful preaching is how well he or she makes people feel happy and satisfied about themselves. Biblically all of these qualities and others exist in God, and because they all belong to God, it is not either/or but both/and.

In order to see how this looks, let us quickly examine two verses in Psalms (we will look at others later). Psalm 89:14 (NIV) states, "Righteousness and justice are the foundation of your throne; love and faithfulness go before you." Psalm 85:10 (NIV) boldly declares that "righteousness and peace kiss each other." The Bible forever links those qualities of God that we often find incompatible in the twenty-first century. Love goes forth from the foundation of righteousness. For an example of how righteousness and peace kiss, imagine you are driving on a divided highway within the legal limits of the law. When you drive past a speed trap your heart will not race or your blood pressure rise. Additionally, you will not have to face your spouse to tell him or her that the new vacuum cleaner or golf clubs he or she wanted will have to wait because you were speeding. Righteousness informs love and brings peace.

It is time for the church to get off this pendulum of separating the characteristics of God that she feels are incompatible such as righteousness and love, justice and mercy, and judgment and grace. She needs to live in the tension of both/and where she must talk about the necessity for God's mercy because of the requirement for God's justice and where the true meaning of God's grace frees people from God's righteous judgment (that they truly deserve), and this happens only when they believe in Jesus. Recovering the concept of God's holiness is the only way to accomplish embracing all of God's qualities at the same time, to keep them in balance, and to recover those things lost to the church over the past sixty to a hundred and fifty plus years.

A fourth obstacle to holiness is the morality, or lack thereof, that we have come to cherish in the past several decades. In the past, while people may not have lived it (hence the need for revivals), most folks commonly agreed that morality was based on the Bible. In recent times it seems to be selected by what is "acceptable" in the moment and is often determined by individuals who rationalize behaviors as good according to what is perceived as beneficial to him or her in a given situation regardless of outcomes or consequences. It is commonly referred to as relative truth. However, ask yourself, "What happens when one person or group is utterly opposed to another?"[5] Rationalization and relative morality become disconcerting when we consider the

---

5. I will address this in chapter 2.

extremes of human nature that have been seen throughout secular and church history—the holocaust, terrorism, the Crusades, and Jim Crow to name only a few. Add to that the pendulum effect of swinging from one extreme to another in our personal situations, and we have a recipe for disaster. Think about how often the oppressed becomes the oppressor, the abused becomes the abuser! Consider how easily people rationalize and justify their actions, and the immensity of the problem becomes apparent. As the culture has changed there has been a definite swing in the way both the culture and the church decide what is moral.

Rationalizing moral practices is the outgrowth of the different approaches Western nations have used to process information and to decide what is important. Beginning with Providence, we will examine the effects that the Enlightenment, Modernity, and Postmodernity[6] have had on the doctrines and practices of the church and which have brought us to what is often called the post-Christian age. We will track the move from faith-based beliefs through reason and scientific principles to emotional philosophies and technological influences and examine what is needed to get the church back on track and equipped to tell the next generation.

A fifth obstacle to recovering God's holiness is the unpopularity it has in American Christianity. There are several reasons. First, when people understand the holiness of God, they are forced to face the reality of their own sin. People hear that they are not as "good" as our culture leads them to believe and become upset, accuse the preacher of legalism, and usually reject him or her. To those who believe all people are basically good, Henry Blackaby warns that "there will be no revival without holiness in the leadership. . . . Pull together all the phrases that revivalists of other generations have all quoted, and it will not make an ounce of difference to the heart of God. God is looking for holiness!"[7] Without holiness there will be no power to change lives. The best that can be expected is to maintain the status quo, which never happens.

Second, some feel overwhelmed by the enormity of their sin and feel that it is hopeless to work towards holiness. These folks may feel intimidated and shy away from trying. One way to begin the quest for holiness is to check what is going on inside you by asking God to show you what he wants you to work on. Whenever you are convicted about something, confess it and ask God to help you with your transformation. Remember always that Jesus died for your sins; you are forgiven when you confess and repent, and let God lead the change. He is always gentler than you anticipate. Holiness brings conviction to change but does not relentlessly accuse you or send you on a guilt trip.

Third, many people think holiness sounds boring. These folks believe holiness means they cannot have any fun. C. S. Lewis writes, "How little people know who

---

6. For more information on postmodernism, see Grenz, *A Primer on Postmodernism* and Lyon, *Postmodernity*.

7. Blackaby, *Holiness*, 72.

think that holiness is dull. When one meets the real thing, it is irresistible."[8] What did Lewis know that the church of the twenty-first century has forgotten? Chapters 6 to the end will answer this question.

Why Is Holiness Essential?

How often people talk about something (or write about it) frequently reveals how much it dominates their thoughts. In God's word, the Bible, the term for holy is found over 880 times. Taken together, the words for love, mercy, and grace combined appear about 850 times.[9] Combined, the words righteousness, justice, and judgment occur about 850 times.[10] The single quality of God that emerges dominant over all the others is "holy." It is used more often than either of the two groups mentioned above, and about twice as often as "love," "mercy," or "grace" taken individually. Furthermore, it is a requirement for heaven. The writer of Hebrews commands, "Pursue peace with everyone, and the holiness without which no one will see the Lord" (Heb 12:14, NRSV).

Scripture declares that God's name is holy; his Spirit is holy. In the Old Testament we discover that everything dedicated to God's service is holy. The temple and the tabernacle contained the holy place and the most holy place where God's presence dwelt. The Most Holy Place, the Holy of Holies, in both the tabernacle and the temple was open only to the high priest once a year on the Day of Atonement. The garments the priests wore were holy. Things like anointing oil, the altar, the place where they offered sacrifices, and the vessels and utensils used in that service were considered holy or set apart for the Lord. The assembly of the people gathered in worship was holy. Even the ground where God's presence dwelt was holy, such as around the burning bush and on Mount Sinai where God talked to Moses. Mount Sinai was so frightening when God was there that only Moses and Joshua dared to go on it. The people and the animals were forbidden to set foot on the mountain on penalty of death. In Amos 4:2 God "swears by [his own] holiness" that a certain thing will happen, which implies that holiness is God's innermost essence. Otto Procksch writes, "Amos . . . causes Yahweh to swear by His holiness (4:2), and therefore by His innermost essence, which is different from everything creaturely,

---

8. Lewis, *The C. S. Lewis Index*, 285.

9. All searches were done using BibleWorks 8, electronic ed. (2009). I used Greek for the word searches for consistency with the original texts throughout the Old Testament and the New Testament. All searches were done with the lemma for each word. For "love" I used ἀγάπη, (~355 occurrences) for God's love is strictly ἀγάπη. I used ἔλεος (~275) for "mercy" and χάρις (~220) for "grace." In the English translations, these three words are frequently used interchangeably. Ἔλεος is frequently translated, "unfailing love," "steadfast love, or "loving kindness" as well as mercy. Grace and mercy are sometimes translated interchangeably.

10. I used δικαιοσύνη (~360) for "righteousness," κρίσις (~270) for "justice" and κρίμα (~225) for "judgment." As with love, grace, and mercy, these three are often translated interchangeably. I used ἅγιος (~880) for "holy."

INTRODUCTION

let alone unclean or sinful."[11] Holiness cannot tolerate sin, which is entirely different from contemporary humanistic views on morality.

In the New Testament, Jesus, in his high priestly prayer on the Mount of Olives, called God "Holy Father." In the Sermon on the Mount Jesus commanded, "Be perfect, therefore, as your heavenly Father is perfect." The apostle Peter adopted God's personal revelation in the giving of the law when he quoted "I am holy. Be holy; for I am holy."[12] God's people are called "ἅγιος," the "holy ones," more commonly known as "saints." This term was first used of Jesus' followers in the Book of Acts by Ananias when he was sent to restore Saul's sight.[13] Later Peter went to visit the saints in Lydda. Many of the apostle Paul's letters were addressed to the holy ones.[14] Philemon is commended for his "love for all the saints" and that he has "refreshed the hearts of the saints." Peter describes the saints as "a chosen people, a royal priesthood, a holy nation, a people belonging to God that you may declare the praises of him who called you out of darkness into his wonderful light" (1 Pet 2:9, NIV). Martyn Lloyd-Jones describes saintliness as a "certain uniqueness" that is given by God.[15] This uniqueness implies that we are "essentially different from the world . . . cleansed from the guilt of . . . sin . . . . [and] brought into the presence of God . . . by the blood of Christ."[16] Furthermore this "quality of saintliness" is "something that is full of grace and charm, a faint likeness to the Lord Himself . . . because we are a holy people."[17] Saints are commonly thought of as "ones who are separated," but R. C. Sproul points out that there is much more to being a saint than being separated. "The saint is to be one who is *in a vital process of sanctification*. We are to be purified daily in the *growing pursuit of holiness*. If we are justified, we must also be sanctified" (italics are mine).[18] Justification, sanctification, and a working description of holiness and major doctrines of the church will be addressed in chapters 6–7.

Furthermore, how the church views holiness will determine her service and worship to God. Scripture gives two glimpses of heaven through Isaiah and John—both men saw the same thing. Isaiah was a priest who served God in the temple and who had a vision one day of God seated on his throne (Isa 6). The seraphim were circling him crying, "Holy, Holy, Holy is the Lord of hosts. The whole earth is full of His glory." The triple repetition of the word "holy" is the Hebrew way of elevating this quality of God to the superlative. Nothing else in Scripture but the temple is

---

11. Procksch, "ἅγιος," 91.

12. Lev 11:44, 45; 19:2; 20:7, 26; 21:6; 1 Cor 1:2; Eph 1:4; Heb 12:14; 1 Pet 1:15–16.

13. But Ananias answered, "Lord, I have heard from many about this man, how much evil he has done to your saints in Jerusalem" (Acts 9:13, NRSV).

14. Rom, 1 Cor, 2 Cor, Eph, Phil, and Col.

15. Lloyd-Jones, *God's Ultimate Purpose*, 25.

16. Lloyd-Jones, *God's Ultimate Purpose*, 26.

17. Lloyd-Jones, *God's Ultimate Purpose*, 33.

18. Sproul, *The Holiness of God*, 249.

elevated to this level of importance. Love is not. In fact, nowhere in the heavenly scenes is love specifically mentioned.

Isaiah was a priest and considered what we would call a "good" person; yet when he came face to face with the thrice-Holy God, he was instantly overwhelmed with his sin. In response, he cursed himself and confessed his guilt and the guilt of his nation, "Woe *is* me! . . . for I am undone; because I *am* a man of unclean lips, and I dwell in the midst of a people of unclean lips: for mine eyes have seen the King, the LORD of hosts" (Isa 6:5, KJV). When he encountered the Holy God of Israel, it did not take him but an instant to see his sinfulness and the sin of his people, God's chosen people. He understood that the best of us miss the mark; we sin against God and our fellow humans.

In this heavenly scene we see that the biblical view of people is far different from the humanistic view that all people are good. Sproul describes it this way, "In the flash of the moment Isaiah had a new and radical understanding of sin. He saw that it was pervasive, in himself and in everyone else."[19] In fact, it is our low view of the sinfulness of sin that causes us to question God's goodness when we see people suffer. God's holiness enlightened Isaiah and was a precursor to his volunteering to serve God. God asks, "Whom shall I send? Who will go for us?" Isaiah answers, "*Hinani*. Here am I, send me" (v. 8). He did not care what it was; he only knew that he wanted to serve this Holy God with all his heart, mind, body, and soul.

Additionally, our understanding of holiness affects our worship. About eight hundred years after Isaiah had his vision, John was also given a revelation of heavenly worship. He was in the spirit on the Lord's Day, and when he saw the Lord, he fell on his face as if dead. When he passed through the doorway into the throne room, what he saw was essentially the same as what Isaiah saw. The seraphim were circling the throne declaring, "Holy, holy, holy, the Lord God the Almighty, who was and is and is to come" (Rev 4:8, NRSV). The twenty-four elders knelt down and worshiped God. Later John saw a great multitude doing the same. God is "holy, holy, holy."

Holiness is not only God's "innermost essence," but it is the quality of God that holds every part of his being (righteousness and love, justice and mercy, judgment and grace, the gifts and the fruits) in perfect balance. Holiness is the means by which God avoids the imbalances (the pendulum) that we so frequently experience, such as legalism or licentiousness (as if one is better than the other), reason or emotion (as if humans are not both), and judgment or peace (as if we must reject one to have the other). Without it no one sees God. Without it, the church will not be equipped to tell the next generation about Jesus and bring them into his kingdom of light.

---

19. Sproul, *The Holiness of God*, 45.

INTRODUCTION

The Invitation

Os Guinness describes our culture as "powerful... pressurizing, and... pervasive... [with] speed, scope, and simultaneity... acceleration, compression, and intensification" as reasons why it is so difficult to tell people about Jesus.[20] He cites three things essential to the church's mission: "we need deep biblical convictions"; "we need a sure grasp of the history of ideas"; and "we need a skillful use of the sociology of knowledge."[21] Chapters 1–5 will examine the historical and sociological changes that have brought us to where we are today, how the culture has transformed the church, and how this has become a major obstacle to telling the next generations about Jesus and to making them disciples. Chapters 6 and 7 will explore the biblical meaning of the major doctrines of holiness, justification, sanctification, and what it means to be created in the image of God. Chapters 8–18 will suggest ways in which we can begin to experience this same balance in our lives and how this equips us in body, mind, and spirit to encounter others for Christ. Although I strongly identify with the church and the Christian faith, for the purpose of clarification I will refer to the church as the bride of Christ with the pronoun "she" instead of the first person plural "we," and Christians as "he," "she," or "they." I will refer to the culture as "they" simply to identify people and actions that are independent of the church. For "they," the reader will have to let context determine whether it refers to Christians or culture. The pronoun "we" will most often refer to myself and the reader or culture in general to which everyone belongs. Also, as you read, be thinking of how the information could be used to connect with people and to engage them in a way that might cause them to examine their own beliefs and be open to the gospel. The questions for each chapter at the end of the book will help guide you in this.

We are all on a journey; each of us is simply one more traveler passing through this world wanting to go to a better place that is eternally good and without suffering. However, a Holy God reigns there. The good news is this Holy God invites us to join him, and he has made the only way for this to happen. Jeremiah (6:16, NIV) instructs us, "Stand at the crossroads and look; ask for the ancient paths, ask where the good way is, and walk in it, and you will find rest for your souls." Isaiah calls it the "Highway of Holiness." Jesus calls it the "narrow road" and "the narrow gate."

Of this ancient way, David Ruis has written a song entitled "Spirit Is on Me." The opening words attribute this deep shaking and rumbling we are experiencing to a move of God in the earth. Ruis sees it as an invitation to God's people to respond to his holiness and reveals the benefits of saying yes,

> I can feel the wind in the Western sky, blowing on ancient ruins
>
> I feel the rumblings beneath the earth, speaking of old things renewing...

---

20. See Guinness, "Found Faithful," 102.
21. See Guinness, "Found Faithful," 102.

Come, take my hand. Walk with me to the ancient lands.

Come, take my hand. Run with me and dance again, and we'll be free.
We'll be free.[22]

The winds of change are blowing. The earth is rumbling; it is being shaken and only the things of God will remain. Three questions the people of God should be asking are, "How did the journey bring us to where we are?"; "How is it different from the biblical view?"; and "What can we do tell the next generation about Jesus and to bring about positive change?" History will help us to answer the first two questions. Recovering the holiness of God in the church and in individual lives of Christians is vital to enable us to answer the third. Come; walk with me on this ancient pathway of God and discover the beauty, wholeness, freedom, and fullness of his holiness. Then we will be free to be Jesus' disciples in every sense of the word. Who knows? God is on the move, and we may yet experience another Great Awakening or Reformation.

---

22. Ruis, "Spirit Is on Me," lines 3–9.

Chapter 1

Where In the World Are We and How Did We Get Here?

> As the Gospel is longer in the world and makes its way more widely across the earth, God entrusts men [and women] with more knowledge and more mastery of their environment. He does this fully aware of the risk that He is taking, realizing that some will pervert His gifts.
>
> —Kenneth Scott Latourette, *A History of Christianity*

THE MORE KNOWLEDGE WE gain, the less moral we seem to become. Allowing a child to go to the neighbor's house unattended could be risky if the wrong person happens to drive by at the wrong time. School shootings, terrorist attacks, human trafficking, and the like have become far too common. Many are asking themselves and others how we got to where we are. In the first five chapters, beginning with the invention of Gutenberg's printing press in 1439, we will examine events that produced major shifts in how we think and in what we believe, called paradigms, and the effects they have had on Christianity in Europe and the United States. The remaining chapters will draw on historical events and beliefs in order to rediscover biblical solutions for how we tell the next generation about Jesus in the midst of the current turmoil of this journey we call life.

From Providence to Progress to Postmodernity and Beyond[1]

Providence is the paradigm that believes God is the ultimate authority in the world who defines morality, beauty, love, and all that constitutes life and culture. He is the Provider of all things needed for existence. Providence in the form of Christianity has been at the foundation of Western civilization since the Roman Emperor Constantine's conversion in 324 CE. The Roman Catholic Church existed as the sole keeper of the faith for the

---

1. For more background of these events see Ahlstrom, *A Religious History of the American People*, and Latourette, *A History of Christianity*.

next 1200 years. However, all institutions become rigid with time, and although reformers challenged the church's authority, they had limited success.[2]

This began to change with the invention of Gutenberg's printing press in 1439, which made the Bible and other literature readily available to the general public and brought many changes.[3] Aided by this newly found source of spreading news to people who formerly were illiterate, the Reformation began in earnest in 1517 when Martin Luther nailed his ninety-five theses to the door of a Catholic church in Wittenberg, Germany. The Protestant Reformation[4] was established on the essential doctrines that the church must function according to the Bible alone (not human reason), and salvation is by grace alone (that comes directly from God and cannot be bought), and by faith alone (as opposed to any works people can do trying to earn it) through Christ alone, who is the only Lord and Savior, and to the glory of God alone. The Reformation also recognized the priesthood of all believers. Additionally, God was viewed as the Provider of salvation and all the spiritual, physical, and emotional needs of all people.

About a century later, many Christians felt the Reformation needed a reformation. As the form of the new Protestant churches became dominant over the continent they began to be steeped in their own polity and evangelists/pastors began to call them back to the original beliefs. New denominations emerged like the Moravians, Puritans, Methodists, and Baptists. Like their predecessors a hundred years earlier, the new reformers felt convicted to worship God according to the biblical standards of the Reformation as opposed to the established traditions of the church structures. Unfortunately the established churches, rather than be reformed, made life difficult for these new reformers. Just like Luther, Calvin, and the multitudes who had followed them, their beliefs were deeply ingrained. Many left their homes and risked their lives for a new life in the new world where they could worship God freely.

Many of the first settlers to arrive in this land that we now call the United States came from Europe to escape this religious persecution or to evangelize those already living here. There were Puritans, Presbyterians, Reformed, Baptists, Quakers, Congregationalists, Methodists, Moravians, and even Roman Catholics, to name a few. Throughout the colonies, questions of morality were deferred to the Bible for answers. Even those who had no direct religious affiliation often believed in Providence, a higher power that guided matters and provided the things we needed.

2. Some of these men include Peter Waldo, John Wycliffe, John Hus, and William Tyndale. Many sacrificed their lives. Others were driven into isolation. For more background of these events see Latourette, *A History of Christianity*.

3. For a timeline for these events see appendix 1.

4. Many Protestant movements came from what has historically been termed the Protestant Reformation: Lutherans, Reformed, Anabaptists, and Anglicans. These were the sources of many denominations such as Presbyterian, Baptist, Mennonite, Methodist, Quaker, and others. They all agreed on the basic doctrines presented in this chapter, but differed in how they were to be worked out. Many geographical areas specified their beliefs in confessions of faith such as the Scots Confession of 1560, the Belgic Confession of 1561, and the Bohemian Confessions of 1575. I acknowledge them all and will refer to them by the historical reference of Protestant Reformation or simply the Reformation.

A hundred and fifty years later, in 1776, the Declaration of Independence approved by all the colonies began with allusions to God and the rights that he endows to all people as their Creator and closed with firm reliance on Providence for protection. Providence was woven into the fiber of our being. This Supreme Being was involved in the well-being of all people for freedom, happiness, and life. The overwhelming majority of the population broadly held a Christian view of the world. For them, this Supreme Being was the God of Christianity. However, another paradigm was already emerging.

The Enlightenment was ushered in by philosophers of the seventeenth century like Locke, Hobbes, Descartes, Pascal, and Leibnitz. Contrary to the Protestant Reformation and the biblical witness of human sinfulness, the Enlightenment declared that all people are basically good and believed in the unlimited ability of the human mind to solve every problem with a new doctrine called modern science. Because of the reliance on the human mind, this time period became known as the Age of Reason. Truth was still understood to exist, but now the agent for discovering truth was the human mind and not God or the Bible. These ideas were advanced by philosophers of the eighteenth century such as Kant, Rousseau, Voltaire, and Hume. They "advocated freedom, democracy and reason as the primary values of society" which were based on the premise that "men's minds should be freed from ignorance, from superstition and from the arbitrary powers of the State, in order to allow mankind to *achieve progress* and *perfection*."[5] The result of these beliefs was "a further *decline in the influence of the church, governmental consolidation and greater rights for the common people*. Politically, it was a time of revolutions and turmoil and of the overturning of established traditions" (italics are mine).[6]

The American and French revolutions were outgrowths of these ideas. The deconstruction of faith in God, religion, and governmental authority that had begun with the philosophers expanded to the universities and through them to the educated elite. With faith in the power of the human mind and armed with the truth of science, the Western nations began to "move forward" using the tools of technology. In the view of the philosophers and the educated elite, God, religion, and governmental authority were found to fall short of the perfection the human mind could produce, but the people in the streets and sitting in the pews of the churches were not yet seeing it that way, as was evidenced by the references (to God) and Providence in the Declaration of Independence.

Ironically, Gutenberg's printing press which made literature cheaper and more readily available to the public and helped Luther's cause in the Reformation now enabled a new paradigm shift by making the philosophies of the new age readily available to all people. Using newspapers, flyers, and tracts, three new views of

---

5. Mastin, "Age of Enlightenment," lines 3–6. We will see how these italicized issues brought about dramatic changes to our journey.

6. Mastin, "Age of Enlightenment," lines 7–10.

God, religion, and government held by the modern intellectuals were now being promoted to everyone who could read and talked about with those who could not. These were: 1. Providence was nothing more than another superstition; 2. religion was synonymous with ignorance; and 3. government was to be mistrusted. A new or modern age had begun based on science and the power of the human mind. The paradigm shift had occurred.

The Modern Way

The change in the culture was nearly imperceptible at first but with the advent of the inventions produced by science during the Industrial Revolution (1790–1850) all of society could see what humanity could create and had heard the new philosophies.[7] New and better equipment enabled farmers to produce an abundance of food with less help. Advances in milling and weaving made food and clothing more readily available. This freed people to move to the cities where they found employment in the new industries popping up. The necessities of life were being produced in abundance, and easier conditions were guaranteed as machines did more for people. The promised good life was at hand.

Providence could still be found running concurrent with the Industrial Revolution in the strong Puritan work ethic and the Second Great Awakening (1790–1850) in which notable evangelists like Charles Finney, along with countless circuit riders, called the American people to faith in Jesus. During this time, a French aristocratic lawyer, Alexis de Tocqueville, visited the United States in 1831 to study its penitential system. After hundreds of interviews of political and social leaders coupled with astute observation, de Tocqueville discovered that while there were many different denominations found in America, each with its unique observances, there was only one morality preached by them all by which people were to relate to their fellow citizens. He later wrote, "Each worships God in its own way, but all preach the same morality in God's name . . . all sects in the United States are encompassed within the overarching unity of Christianity, and Christian morality is the same everywhere."[8]

Furthermore, de Tocqueville saw democracy in the United States as being both a moral as well as a materialistic force. This moral force was directed by "only one power, one source of strength and success, and nothing outside it" which erected "a formidable barrier around thought."[9] He reported that Americans saw their religious beliefs as "necessary for the preservation of republican institution . . . [This] is not the opinion of one class of citizens or one party but of the nation as a whole. One

---

7. For further reading on this era see Wood, *Empire of Liberty*; Howe, *What Hath God Wrought*, and McPherson, *Battle Cry of Freedom*.

8. de Tocqueville, *Democracy in America*, 335.

9. de Tocqueville, *Democracy in America*, 293.

encounters it among people of every rank."[10] In fact he quotes them as having said, "It is in our interest that the new [democratic] states should be religious, so that we may remain free."[11] Such was the pervasive influence of Christianity on democracy in the early to mid-nineteenth-century United States.

De Tocqueville saw Christianity as essential to democratic freedom, for it counteracted unrestricted materialism in which people were free to "extract from this world all the goods it has to offer . . . and daily make life more convenient, comfortable, and mild . . . [with] wealth and excessive love of material gratifications."[12] He wrote that in the pursuit of happiness and pleasure alone "there is reason to believe that they [Americans] would gradually love the art of producing them and end up enjoying them *indiscriminately and without progress*, like brutes" (italics are mine).[13] He warned that without Christianity's influence, "There is reason to fear that [Americans] may in the end lose the use of [their] most sublime faculties, and that, while bent on improving everything around [them], [they] may ultimately degrade [themselves]. There, and nowhere else, lies the peril."[14] Christianity was considered an essential part of American freedom.

De Tocqueville discovered in America that the religious belief of the immortality of the human soul was the greatest benefit any democracy could have. Without it, people are left to pursue only material goods, which would lead them to become something less than human. Consequently, he warned that "when any religion . . . has sunk deep roots in a democracy, beware of disturbing it. Preserve it carefully, rather, as the most precious legacy. . . . Do not attempt to deprive men of their old religious opinions in order to replace them with new ones, lest they should, in passing from one faith to another and finding itself momentarily devoid of belief, prove so receptive to the love of material gratifications that this love comes to fill the void entirely."[15] These words would take on fresh meaning 130 years later.

At the inception of Modernity, de Tocqueville insisted that "Christianity must be maintained at all cost in the new democracies."[16] He cautioned that while equality brings much good, it also opens the door to some dangerous human instincts such as isolation, individuals thinking only of themselves, and the inordinate vulnerability to material pleasure.[17] De Tocqueville saw the function of religion as the tempering force keeping egalitarian tendencies from plunging into self-made tyranny. Religion prevents this by raising people's vision beyond themselves to far more superior goals

10. de Tocqueville, *Democracy in America*, 338.
11. de Tocqueville, *Democracy in America*, 339.
12. de Tocqueville, *Democracy in America*, 634.
13. de Tocqueville, *Democracy in America*, 638.
14. de Tocqueville, *Democracy in America*, 634–35.
15. de Tocqueville, *Democracy in America*, 635–36.
16. de Tocqueville, *Democracy in America*, 637.
17. de Tocqueville, *Democracy in America*, 503.

than material goods and people's own senses. It turns people from continual contemplation of self and focuses them on their duties towards others. He concluded, "Religious people are therefore naturally strong precisely where democratic people are weak, which shows clearly how important it is that men retain their religion when they become equals."[18]

De Tocqueville also warned Americans that they had no safeguards against tyranny except for their Christian faith. The law did not keep tyrants from ruling; it was the mores and circumstances existing in every class of people that unified them and kept them safe from despotism. He observed that in the United States the churches held much power over the thinking of the people not through political action but through those things described above. The church was the "force that is moral as well as material, which shapes wills as much as actions and inhibits not only deeds but also the desire to do them."[19] He foresaw that to remove Christianity from the dominant form of life in America would open this nation up to tyranny of the self and material pleasures and warned, "When a society really reaches the point of having . . . a government equally divided between contrary principles, either revolution erupts or society dissolves."[20] In subsequent chapters, we will look at how this has played out 150 years later.

In the mid-nineteenth century, de Tocqueville admired Americans for how their Christianity intertwined with liberty such that one was needed to maintain the other for the preservation of the republic. However, he noted that the intellectuals of his day were already opposing his view, to which he responded, "That is how Americans see it, but obviously they are wrong, for every day men of very considerable learning offer me proof that all is well in America except for precisely the religious spirit that I admire."[21] From these intellectuals he learned "that the human race would have everything it needs to enjoy liberty and happiness . . . if only it could accept Spinoza's belief . . . or Cabanis's assertion."[22] De Tocqueville did not try to answer them on their ground, but responded with what he witnessed to be true and wrote, "To that I truly have no response other than to say that the people who make such statements have never been to America and have never seen either a religious people or a people that is free."[23]

---

18. de Tocqueville, *Democracy in America*, 503–4.

19. de Tocqueville, *Democracy in America*, 291–93.

20. de Tocqueville, *Democracy in America*, 289.

21. de Tocqueville, *Democracy in America*, 339. Spinoza and Cabanis were philosophers who promoted rationalism, materialism, and the modern ideas of self, and who laid the groundwork for biblical criticism.

22. de Tocqueville, *Democracy in America*, 339.

23. de Tocqueville, *Democracy in America*, 339.

Winds of Change Are Blowing

De Tocqueville was sensing the pull of the intellectual battle that was coming. He foresaw the dangers of materialism and unbridled pleasures and was convinced that Christian thought was the means to freedom. He warned that when a nation becomes truly divided in its principles, then that nation dissolves and falls into mobocracy.

Christian thought still had great influence in the mid-nineteenth century; nonetheless, the new paradigm shift arrived. By 1850 optimism in the future ran high. Many thought this new belief system would usher in the Utopia described in the Bible, and it would all be brought about by human ingenuity. Modernity, as it came to be called, with its faith in Progress and the human mind to find truth, promised answers to all of our problems. Unfortunately it left us with more questions than it answered.[24]

The journey through Modernity (1850–1950) brought us good things, but it also had unforeseen consequences. Management styles were developed to maximize efficiency and company profits, often to the detriment of their laborers. Men, women, and children worked long hours in these sweatshops. Instead of a utopia and unity, it brought the Civil War as well as meaningless and mindless work as the assembly line emerged and people were required to focus on one skill, resulting in monotonous repetition. Boredom increased as skill sets narrowed; specialization emerged, bringing isolation, and the satisfaction of producing a car or engine or dress with your own hands disappeared. A similar fragmentation occurred in the intellectual realm.

Through science and continued technological developments such as the telegraph and photography, information increased so rapidly that it became impossible for a single person to absorb all of the new knowledge. Just as the assembly line brought specialization in factories, so professionals became experts in a given field of study. People no longer went to a doctor or a surgeon, but to an internist, a pediatrician, an ophthalmologist, a podiatrist, a cardiologist, or a neurologist, to mention only a few. No one would venture into another's field of expertise. In mathematics, the purest of all the sciences, there was no one geometry that explained our observable universe, but there were many, like Euclidean geometry, analytic geometry, differential geometry, non–Euclidean geometry, plane geometry, solid geometry, and even one called "Thurston's Geometrization Conjecture."[25] Our world has become split into isolated specialties that can be seen clearly, for example, in the realm of science that was supposed to provide us with solutions and to unite us.

This fragmentation into specialized fields of expertise could be seen in the church as well. In response to the emphasis of the mind and the scientific process in Modernity, the church produced propositions in an attempt to reason with people and to show them how the Bible, and the church, followed the truth. Systematic theologies were developed. Theologians specialized in Old Testament, New Testament, or one

---

24. For more information on this era see Brands, *American Colossus*.
25. Weisstein, "Geometry," paras. 1 and 6.

book or one author of the Bible and wrote volumes of words setting forth their concept of what Scripture says. In an attempt to find the truth many tools were developed to study ancient documents and specifically the Bible.[26] Scholars began to deconstruct the texts for the noble purpose of getting back to the original meaning.

Unfortunately, many of these scholars brought to their study preconceived assumptions that the Bible was nothing more than humans writing about how they understood their circumstances. Some scholars refused to believe that God was the author or that miracles or prophecy could occur and automatically rejected all such references. It is not surprising, then, that they found thousands of alleged errors and inconsistencies that, in their minds, made the Bible nothing more than another mythology.

From scholars to business tycoons, some of these educated classes used their knowledge to debunk Christianity. Julius Wellhausen (1844–1918) was one such scholar who used higher criticism (now more commonly called historical criticism) to uncover the sources of ancient documents. This led him to propose that Moses did not write the Torah, but that it was nothing more than a compilation of many people writing well after the events.[27] He ignored archeological evidence and thousands of verses that contradicted his theories to arrive at his conclusions.[28] In a similar way, Kirsopp Lake (1872–1946) attempted to explain away the resurrection by proposing that the women simply went to the wrong tomb.[29] Darwin's *On the Origen of Species* provided an alternative to the biblical idea of creation that enabled people to reject God and the Bible.[30] In response to Darwin, steel magnate Andrew Carnegie (1839–1919) had what could be described as a conversion experience and wrote, "I remember that light came as in a flood and all was clear. Not only had I got rid of theology and the supernatural, but I had found the truth of evolution. 'All is well since all grows better' became my motto, my true source of comfort."[31] Faith in Modernity, people's ability to find truth through reason and the scientific method, was high, and many used it to absolve themselves from the need to believe in God through Jesus Christ because it was ignorant and superstitious.

Neil Postman has observed that in their search for truth the scholars "did not entirely destroy the traditions [of church and government] . . . [but] subordinated

26. These include form criticism, source criticism, redaction criticism, and comparative religions criticism. For a brief and reliable resource see Soulen and Soulen, *Handbook of Biblical Criticism*.

27. See Wellhausen, *Prolegomena to the History of Israel*. He proposed that the first five books of the Bible, known as the Pentatuch, were not written by Moses but were a compilation of groups consisting of Jehovists, Elohimists, Priests, and the Deuteronomist (JEPD).

28. Smith, "Critical Assessment of Graf-Wellhausen," para. 44. Also see Cardozo, "On Bible Criticism and Its Counterarguments." Since that time additional archeological finds have proven him wrong and his theories have lost favor among all but the most progressive scholars. (Same sources.)

29. Lake, *Historical Evidence for the Resurrection*, 246–48. He proposed that the women misunderstood the young man (who told them Jesus was not there) when he told them they were at the wrong place. They wrongly inferred the resurrection.

30. See Darwin, *On the Origin of Species*.

31. Andrew Carnegie as quoted in *Herbert Spencer*.

these worlds—yes, even humiliated them—but . . . did not render them totally ineffectual"; the concept of sin and regional pride still existed in nineteenth-century America.[32] Although less prominent in cultural thought, the influence of Providence could still be seen in evangelists like Dwight L. Moody, A. W. Tozer, and Billy Sunday. The first half of the twentieth century witnessed other outpourings of the Holy Spirit in the Azusa Street Revival which launched the Pentecostal Church and in the successes of Evangelist Billy Graham.

Modernity may have rendered church authority ineffectual but the promise of continual improvement of the human situation failed to happen, and faith placed in human reasoning or science was not always rewarded. All was not well. In addition to tedium, boredom, specialization, and fragmentation, the first half of the twentieth century brought World War I with the horrors of gas warfare, World War II with the Holocaust in Europe and the atomic bomb in Japan, and the Great Depression. People's faith was severely shaken in Modernity's ability to find absolute truth and to improve their lives through reason, science, and knowledge.

In this shaking another paradigm with a new center for authority emerged. It was called Postmodernity, which placed authority in the autonomous self. Just as the philosophers of Modernity deconstructed Providence, so the philosophers of the mid-twentieth century deconstructed Modernity. Modernity had continued to look for truth through the use of science and human wisdom. Postmodernity stopped looking for truth outside of what seemed true to the individual in a given circumstance. Truth became relative; ethics and morality were situational.

The key tool that the new philosophy used to deconstruct Modernity and truth was declaring that the meaning of words was found in the words themselves. Any preexisting meaning the author intended was impossible to know. This set individuals free to assign their own meanings to words and ideas and severely limited the possibility of authority coming from outside of the autonomous self. By the mid-twentieth century, philosopher/teacher Michel Foucault was promoting the idea that words are the vehicle of knowledge and knowledge is power; therefore whoever controls the language also controls the power.[33] History and knowledge are driven by "the desire to domesticate and control the past in order to validate present structures."[34] Youth and the media were at the forefront of this revolution

---

32. Postman, *Technopoly*, 45–48.

33. Erickson, *Postmodernizing the Faith*, 86. Erickson summarizes Foucault's philosophy of history and ideas as interpretations that are made by people in power, and every interpretation of experiences does "violence to that which is named. Social institutions similarly do violence by imposing their own interpretations on the flux of experience . . . every assertion of knowledge is an act of power." Knowledge is power and is conveyed in language; therefore, those who control what is said or written control the power over others. See also Lyon, *Postmodernity*.

34. Grenz, *Primer on Postmodernism*, 133. Foucault writes, "Power produces knowledge . . . [and they] directly imply one another . . . there is no power relation without the correlative constitution of a field of knowledge, nor any knowledge that does not presuppose and constitute at the same time power relations." For this and more see Foucault, *Discipline and Punish*, 27–28. Also Bouchard, "Nietzsche,

of deconstructing the words we use to disavow the power of established institutions such as church, government, schools, and parents.

Words were given different meanings from their traditional use. "Good" now meant "bad"; "cool" meant "hot"; and "hot" meant something different from the temperature of coffee. Today it is possible for people to have conversations and to use the same words but to have totally different understandings of those words. For some people, the word of God is the Bible; for many it is Jesus. They claim belief in Jesus, but mean only that he is an example of how they should live in love. Repentance, redemption, atonement, justification, and sanctification need not be involved. If everyone has his or her own meanings for words, how are we to understand one another?

Foucault's student Jacques Derrida argued that there is no inherent meaning to words. It is impossible to know what the writer intended. The meaning of a passage is now determined by the reader and contingent on the context he or she brings. We are already familiar with how "a phrase can mean one thing in one context and something different in another"[35] such as park, rock, or deck. A woman might park her car or take a stroll in the park. A man may deck someone or have dinner on a deck. Rock may be a large stone or what a mother does with her baby. But for Derrida, context alone now determines the meaning of everything.

Grenz understands this as an absence of meaning in written texts which leaves us only "with the repetition of the act of interpretation—and interpretation becomes unqualified free play divested of ontological anchors."[36] Therefore, our individualistic views of rights and freedoms lead many people to conclude that "we can just interpret things anyway we want . . . we can simply make up the meaning as we go . . . [and] you can make the Bible say anything you want."[37] This can be seen in the eyewitness accounts of a crime that produce as many different versions as there are witnesses. Our postmodern claim to the rights and freedoms of the autonomous self to make its own truth may have a lot to do with that.

Taking the deconstruction of language one step further, Richard Rorty divests truth from any one vocabulary. He writes, "It is useless to ask whether one vocabulary rather than another is closer to reality. For different vocabularies serve different purposes, and there is no such thing as a purpose that is closer to reality than

---

Genealogy, History," 163.

35. Smith, *Who's Afraid of Postmodernism*, 52. Derrida wrote, "Deconstruction [of language and knowledge (and hence, power?)] cannot limit itself or proceed immediately to a neutralization: it must, by means of a double gesture, a double science, a double writing, practice an overturning of the classical opposition and a general displacement of the system. It is only on this condition that deconstruction will provide itself the means with which to intervene in the field of oppositions that it criticizes . . . . Deconstruction does not consist in passing from one concept to another, but in overturning and displacing a conceptual order, as well as the nonconceptual order with which the conceptual order is articulated." From Derrida, "Signature, Event, Context," 329–30 See also Grenz, *Primer on Postmodernism*, 138–50.

36. Grenz, *Primer on Postmodernism*, 146.

37. Smith, *Who's Afraid of Postmodernism*, 53.

another purpose."[38] Erickson understands Rorty to mean that there is no "systematic philosophy" that "presuppose[s] a single unifying pattern to reality"; there is only an "edifying philosophy" that "seeks to continue a conversation rather than to discover truth."[39] So then, Foucault attacked the power of knowledge (always expressed in language) used by institutions to control people. Derrida deconstructed language by divorcing meaning from words and reduced understanding to context only—what it means to me. Rorty divested truth from the meaning of words, leaving us to discover our own truth. We are now empowered to reject outside authority. Almost all limitations are removed.

Deconstruction of the language separates us further from the truth of Scripture by making us "interested in interpretations that have been marginalized and sidelined, activating voices that have been silenced"[40] with no consideration that perhaps there had been good reasons they had been ignored. As a result, historical or moral documents, including the Bible, have come under attack as being simply the viewpoint of the people in power at the time in which they were written. Postmodernity suggests that the voices of minorities and oppressed peoples had been suppressed, and since we were only getting one side of the story it was impossible for us to have the full picture. This thinking rendered the context from which ancient documents were written unknowable; consequently postmodernists are now free to understand them in any way that suits them. Truth becomes only what the individual wants it to be. As a result, the individual is no longer obligated to follow any outside authoritative voice. The person is free to think and to act in ways that maximize his or her personalized satisfaction.

In this new paradigm of Postmodernity there are no longer common authority figures to wield legitimate power. The dangers of removing Christian thought as the moral norm of society that de Tocqueville foresaw had arrived. Writing at the end of the twentieth century, Stanley Grenz contends that "the loss of centeredness introduced by the postmodern ethos has become one of the chief characteristics of our contemporary situation."[41] The postmodern culture offers endless opportunities and "is rightly associated with a society where consumer lifestyles and mass consumption dominate the waking lives of its members."[42]

Robert Bellah and others assert that "the good life" in our culture means the "center is the autonomous individual, presumed able to choose the roles he will play and the commitments he will make, not on the basis of higher truths but according to the criterion of life effectiveness as the *individual judges* it" (italics are mine).[43] This life looks to the therapist (not to ministers of religion), who "enables the individual to think of

38. Rorty, "Introduction," 3.
39. Erickson, *Postmodernizing the Faith*, 87.
40. Smith, *Who's Afraid of Postmodernism*, 51.
41. Grenz, *Primer on Postmodernism*, 19–20.
42. Lyon, *Postmodernity*, 71.
43. Bellah et al., *Habits of the Heart*, 47.

commitments—from marriage and work to political and religious involvement—as enhancements of the sense of individual well-being rather than as moral imperatives."[44] The therapist's job is to affirm repeatedly that people are "worthy of acceptance" and to teach them "to be independent of anyone else's standards."[45] This self-fulfillment is best described as the "calculating managerial style" developed in industrial environments to bring about the highest profit for the company. Only now, individuals become the sole managers of their lives for the purpose of maximizing personal happiness. This personal management for maximum happiness dominates the areas of "intimacy, home, and community, areas formerly governed by the norms of a moral ecology."[46] The right act becomes nothing more than the one that will give the person "the most exciting challenge or the most good feeling about himself."[47]

There is no longer "any objectifiable criteria of right and wrong, good or evil; the self and its feelings become our only moral guide."[48] Individuals are now free to act one way in one situation and to say and to do something different in another depending on the circumstances. Each person is now free to say whatever he or she thinks other people want to hear regardless of the truth of the matter. The goal is twofold. It causes the other people to feel good about themselves, and it causes the person speaking to look good in the other's eyes. Hence, morality and truth have become relative to the circumstances and are determined only by what will portray the person in the best way possible and will give the person the most pleasure and happiness at that time. To fulfill the need for pleasure and happiness we now look to entertainment and not religion, reason, or the traditional rightness of a thing.

In spite of all of this, Providence and Modernity have not disappeared. Providence can be found in evangelist Billy Graham's twentieth-century success, the outpouring of the Holy Spirit in the Charismatic movement in the 1960s and 1970s, the Jesus Movement, and the Third Wave of the Spirit in the 1990s in which millions of people were called to faith in Jesus. Modernity can still be found in looking to science to solve health problems and produce more and better technology, or in looking to psychology to explain why someone is the way he or she is. When a tragedy happens we always want to know why.

The most powerful tool shaping this paradigm shift from reason to emotions, from absolute to relative truth, was television, which created "a film-like world—a realm in which truth and fiction merge."[49] Below we will examine how the computer figures into this scenario, but think about this: before the computer existed, the television did and still does exert tremendous influence over us. The vast majority of humans living in

44. Bellah et al., *Habits of the Heart*, 47.
45. Bellah et al., *Habits of the Heart*, 99.
46. Bellah et al., *Habits of the Heart*, 48.
47. Bellah et al., *Habits of the Heart*, 76.
48. Bellah et al., *Habits of the Heart*, 76.
49. Grenz, *Primer on Postmodernism*, 33.

our European and American culture have been raised in front of a television screen before they are able to operate a computer. Nothing has had the impact on our cultural language and practices more than television.

How Technology Has Changed Us

A quick survey of inventions over the last two thousand years will help us to understand what is happening in our age. Do not skip over this section thinking it will be boring. It may not be what interests you, but it is essential to understand the things that are happening now and what the church is up against when proclaiming the gospel in this culture. Postman claims that culture is a function of language, and with each new invention, language and the way of doing life changes. He points out how the clock taught the world to observe time differently and to regulate people's lives. The clock may have eroded God's sovereignty more than philosophy because "eternity ceased to serve as the measure and focus of human events."[50] The telescope reordered the world so that earth was no longer at the center of the universe. The printing press changed the way people communicated with each other and made ideas readily available to the average person. The telegraph brought communities news that was context-free from places far away and about people they never knew. The ability to report the news first (to scoop the other reporters) became power, and there was little anyone could do to check to see if it was accurate. The result was that "facts push[ed] other facts into and then out of consciousness at *speeds that neither permit[ted]t nor require[d] evaluation*" (italics are mine).[51] Additionally, photography brought folks images of people and things they had never seen.[52] The primary use of information was no longer to provide relevant facts for real situations people were facing or to solve problems they actually had. According to Postman, "the only use left for information with no genuine connection to our lives . . . [was] to amuse."[53] American culture was primed and ready for the next step in entertainment: television.

Bellah comments, "While television does not preach, it nevertheless presents a picture of reality that influences us more than an overt message could."[54] Postman labels television a "peek-a-boo world, where now this event, now that, pops into view for a moment, then vanishes again."[55] This world has little "coherence or sense" and "does not ask us, indeed, does not permit us to do anything; [it is] a world that is, like the child's game of peek-a-boo, entirely self-contained . . . it is also endlessly entertaining."[56]

50. Postman, *Amusing Ourselves*, 10–11.
51. Postman, *Amusing Ourselves*, 70.
52. Postman, *Amusing Ourselves*, 65–67.
53. Postman, *Amusing Ourselves*, 76.
54. Bellah et al., *Habits of the Heart*, 279.
55. Postman, *Amusing Ourselves*, 77.
56. Postman, *Amusing Ourselves*, 77.

Postman calls it a myth, by which he means "a way of understanding the world that is not problematic, that we are not fully conscious of, that seems, in a word, natural .... [It] is a way of thinking so deeply embedded in our consciousness that it is invisible."[57] Television has become the template to judge systems and institutions, and most people no longer think to question television's rendering but are inclined to doubt the institution or belief which does not fit into the mold television tells them is correct. This is especially evident in what we call the news.

The news comes to us in sound-bites as short as a few seconds. "No matter how grave any fragment of news may appear . . . it will shortly be followed by a series of commercials, that will, in an instant, defuse the import of the news . . . . This is a key element in the structure of a news program."[58] The news is introduced by upbeat music and given by smiling reporters. Humor is interjected to keep a positive note. "Complexity must be avoided . . . [and] visual stimulation is a substitute for thought."[59] "Variety, novelty, action, and movement" are the watchwords of the newscast. People are bombarded with so much information that it becomes impossible to think and to process it all. They end up with an "illusion of knowing something which in fact leads one away from knowing."[60] Information becomes fragmented, misleading, and superficial, geared to the emotions rather than to the intellect. This information produces our opinions, which become little more than our emotions, which can change week by week or even moment by moment.[61]

Another area of television's influence is found in the commercials. David Lyon points out that individual taste and style have become the central focus in todays "ideals, values and symbols of economic life," and consumers and consumerism hold the spotlight.[62] Accordingly, advertising has become focused on the character of consumers and not the quality of the product it promotes. It uses a therapeutic approach which appeals to the viewer's "psychological needs,"[63] implying that this product will make the person "feel valuable."[64] The commercial addresses itself to the immediately perceived need of the viewer and becomes not just therapy but instant therapy; problems can be solved quickly through technology, and lessons are taught through "vivid visual symbols."[65] From them consumers learn how they are to live their lives. The image is paramount and has little to do with reality. In similar ways, politicians do not need to have solutions to real problems; they need only to portray an "image of

57. Postman, *Amusing Ourselves*, 79.
58. Postman, *Amusing Ourselves*, 104.
59. Postman, *Amusing Ourselves*, 105.
60. Postman, *Amusing Ourselves*, 107.
61. Postman, *Amusing Ourselves*, 107.
62. Lyon, *Postmodernity*, 95.
63. Postman, *Amusing Ourselves*, 130.
64. Postman, *Technopoly*, 170.
65. Postman, *Amusing Ourselves*, 130–31.

church, family, and government with technology which further encourages individual truth and belief systems.

In this vein of making traditional and historical values obsolete, we see that technology has enabled us to find safety and solutions to life's problems apart from these traditional voices. Modern medicine replaces prayer; mobility replaces family roots; television or the internet substitutes for reading; immediate gratification overcomes restraint; psychotherapy displaces sin; and polling dictates politics.[30] Solutions to life's problems today are to consume more, to experience more pleasure, and to possess more things. In these Christians often look very much like everyone else. Gregory concludes that the interest in self, individual consumerism, and the privatization of religion and theology which began in the seventeenth century "is going stronger than ever today."[31]

There is one more thing Technopoly has taken from the church. It is not content simply to eradicate historical and traditional values; it aggressively evangelizes people to make converts, and it disciples them to grow and to advance in the technology which supports it in order to make more people dependent on it. It promises "heaven on earth" with no responsibilities or costs beyond faithfulness to the entertainment and pleasure it offers. The morality it promotes is subjective because there is no longer an objective source of authority. Everything the internet promotes is moral simply because it is practiced by a group of its followers. The exception is that those who try to say something is immoral are allowably considered to be immoral.

In spite of its advantages Technopoly is not without its problems. It affects our ability to learn and to remember and has raised our natural propensity for entertainment and enjoyment to addictive levels. Consequently we are easily bored and effectively isolated from those around us. Individual rights and freedom are claimed that result in privatized truth and moral conduct. From marriage, to schools, to work, or to recreation, the right behavior is what will maximize the individual's personal pleasure in the moment with little thought of the future. Gregory observes that the conflicting moral argument today of "whose morality" stems from the lack of agreement "about human nature . . . the human good, or indeed what ethics itself is or should be," and this

---

speak publicly of Jesus; even the generic use of "God" may bring law suits against schools that insist on prayer before athletic events. We have yet to see how recent laws promoting homosexuality will play out in our religious freedoms. This author does agree that Western culture has been set aside: surveys of young adults reveal that they know little history but massive amounts of pop culture. The traditional voices of reason and Providence have been made irrelevant and invisible.

30. This is *not* saying that we should not avail ourselves of modern medicine and therapy or that moving away from family in pursuit of a better life is wrong. It is pointing out that faith and trust in ourselves and what we can see and reason in the natural has replaced God. The authority of the individual self has co-opted the authority that had traditionally come from the church and family.

31. Gregory, *Unintended Reformation*, 364.

lack of agreement prevents people from reaching or even moving "toward consensus on the sorts of divisive issues characteristic of moral disputes in our era."[32]

Where We Are Headed

We have traced many changes since the first European settlers landed on this continent. Much has been written concerning where these changes are leading us. The tendency is to jump on the pendulum and to champion one idea over another. Instead we should see these seemingly conflicting ideas as pieces of a puzzle and discern how they fit together. Note that there may truly be pieces that do not belong to our puzzle and need to be set aside. We need discernment (which we will examine later in this book) to know which is which. For now, it is enough to realize that many pieces that may not look like they fit together may actually be the very parts we need.

God often works like this in the church, which is why she so often has conflicts. One person or group backs one thing and another supports something that seems incompatible. Rather than do the hard work of discernment, they argue and split. So let us try to make sense of the various ideas of where we are headed.

Postman likens today's culture to Aldous Huxley's *Brave New World*. There would be no "Big Brother" of George Orwell's *1984* to watch your every move, but people would love their oppression and the technologies that undo their ability to think. Books would not need to be banned for there would be no need to read them because of the television and the internet. Huxley feared not that information would be kept from people, but that they would be given so much that they would sink into "passivity and egoism" and that "truth would be drowned in a sea of irrelevance." He feared "we would become a trivial culture, preoccupied with some equivalent of the feelies." Everyone from civil rights activists to rationalists alike would fail "'to take into account man's almost infinite appetite for distractions'" which would result in their being ruined by what they love and "controlled by [those] inflicting pleasure" on them.[33] Nearly thirty years later, in hindsight, it would appear that Postman was correct. But this does not stop here. Change always happens. The voices of the past do not disappear so easily.

Already at the inception of Modernity in the mid-eighteenth century, de Tocqueville had warned what would happen if religion was ever replaced by materialism in America. Rather than tyrants taking the form of violence and cruelty, he predicted they would take the form of protectors and wrote, "I therefore believe that the kind of oppression that threatens democratic people is unlike any the world has seen before."[34] The new despotism would see each person "endlessly hastening after petty and vulgar pleasures . . . withdrawn into himself . . . virtually a stranger to the

---

32. Gregory, *Unintended Reformation*, 128.
33. Postman, *Amusing Ourselves*, xix–xx.
34. de Tocqueville, *Democracy in America*, 818.

the audience" so they can identify with him or her. Postmodern debates of today only allow time for the candidate to build an image of the self-interested voter.[66] Gone are the days of the Lincoln–Douglas debates, where lengthy and essential dialogue about the real issues of the day took place.[67]

Some scholars argue that the postmodern phenomenon was only an interim change leading us to another era as powerful as Modernity but not yet known. Millard Erickson writes, "Given the accelerating pace of change, culturally and intellectually, it is to be expected that the lifespan of postmodernism will be considerably shorter than that of modernism. Indeed, some of us think that we are already beginning to see the first glimmers of what will be the dawn of the next age, that of postpostmodernity."[68] Neil Postman has identified this next era as Technopoly.

In his book *Technopoly: The Surrender of Culture to Technology*, he warns that "new technologies alter the structure of our interests: things we think about . . . . the things we think with. And they alter the nature of community: the arena in which thoughts develop," and the strangest thing is that few people are even aware of this formation.[69] Instead of church, government, or communities, it is our technology that now structures our lives. Our tools have enabled us to work faster, to travel more quickly, and to accomplish more in less time, but ironically they have also raised our loneliness and boredom to levels previously unknown. This is fueled by the overload of information that distances us not only from the source of the event but from each other. Television (and radio) promoted the age of information, but this was just the beginning.

Summary

Just as Modernity broke the alleged shackles of traditional religion and Providence, so Postmodernity broke the perceived restraints of Modernity's reason and rationalism, and long suppressed emotions surfaced. Just as Modernity produced separate and specialized professions and jobs, so, too, Postmodernity produced isolated individualism in which truth became fragmented into as many views as there were people. Hence, because "the meaning of a text is dependent on the perspective of the one who enters into dialogue with it, it has as many meanings as it has readers."[70] The

---

66. Postman, *Amusing Ourselves*, 134–45.

67. In an election, a local station that could be in Anytown, U.S.A., covered a campaign in which it gave the Republican candidate about five to seven seconds to explain his plan. The Democratic candidate needed only two seconds. He simply said, "The Republicans are wrong!" That is a sound-bite and represents the way elections in this postmodern, high tech age are decided. There is no chance to ask the Democratic candidate what his position is. The fact that the Republicans are wrong is the only the argument the viewer needs. It is memorable and indefensible. The discussion is over.

68. Erickson, *Postmodernizing the Faith*, 23.

69. Postman, *Technopoly*, 20.

70. Grenz, *Primer on Postmodernism*, 6.

traditional sources of authority that used to decide the issues of right and wrong have been largely silenced. Consequently "there is no absolute truth; rather truth is relative to the community in which we participate."[71] Western culture is increasingly becoming a community of individuals obsessed with self who have been conditioned by the ever-changing media leading them into chaos. In the next chapter we will examine the effects the computer has had on the culture.

---

71. Grenz, *Primer on Postmodernism*, 8.

Chapter 2

The Computer Age and Where It Is Taking Us

> Technological progress has merely provided us
> with more efficient means for going backwards.
>
> —ALDOUS HUXLEY, *ENDS AND MEANS*

HUMAN PROGRESS HAS BECOME synonymous with the ever-improving superiority of technology that Neil Postman calls Technopoly, in which the computer reigns supreme.[1] Postman reports, "I am constantly amazed at how obediently people accept explanations that begin with the words . . . 'The computer has determined' . . . . It is Technopoly's equivalent of . . . 'It is God's will,' and the effect is roughly the same."[2]

Postman identifies three causes for this transformation. The first was the "American distrust of restraints . . . [which encouraged] radical and thoughtless technological intrusions." The second was "the genius and audacity of American capitalists . . . known as the Robber Barons [Rockefeller, Carnegie, Ford, Edison, Morse, and Bell that convinced Americans] . . . that the future need have no connection to the past." The third was the success of technology to provide "convenience, comfort, speed, hygiene, and abundance . . . [so that] there seemed little reason to look for other sources of fulfillment, creativity, or purpose."[3] Postman observes that "to every Old World belief, habit, or tradition, there was and still is a technological alternative."[4]

This technological alternative is not limited to the material things of this world, but extends to our worship as well. We are in awe of the computer and what it can do. When we are connected to the Web, we feel important and powerful. We can find answers to all of our questions there. Furthermore it trivializes the ancient ways, symbols, and beliefs. Postman claims that in this nation "the adoration of technology pre-empts the adoration of anything else." Furthermore, this "elevation of one god

---

1. Postman, *Technopoly*, 117.
2. Postman, *Technopoly*, 115.
3. Postman, *Technopoly*, 53–54.
4. Postman, *Technopoly*, 54.

requires the demotion of another. 'Thou shalt have no other gods before me' applies as well to a technological divinity as any other."[5]

He concludes that "the thrust of a century of scholarship had the effect of making us lose confidence in our belief systems and therefore in ourselves. Amid the conceptual debris, there remained one sure thing to believe in—technology . . . . it is clear that airplanes do fly, antibiotics do cure . . . computers do calculate and never make mistakes—only faulty humans do."[6] When an airplane crashes, the first reason given is pilot error. We see the doctor first and maybe pray later. Computers can only work with the information they are given as the saying goes, "garbage in, garbage out." It is always human error. But this technology is not without its downfalls. The detrimental effects that began with the television became epidemic in the computer age.

With the coming of personal computers and the internet in the last quarter of the twentieth century, information has become available at rates never before imagined. A "media revolution" has taken place in which information is digitalized and sent out "through our universal medium at the speed of light."[7] Newspapers have been particularly hard hit. Some of the oldest daily papers are going out of business, closing down the print components of their papers, or filing for bankruptcy.[8] News reporting has had to be condensed to "make the scanning of their contents easier" and contain more summaries in order to compete for people's time and attention spans. Nicholas Carr claims the internet creates "an environment that promotes cursory reading, hurried and distracted thinking, and superficial learning."[9]

Carr cites multiple university studies that have shown that the computer has not increased learning, but has actually attacked the brain's plasticity and "rewired our mental circuits" in a matter of days of using it so that people do not remember facts or reason well without the computer.[10] "The Web . . . places more pressure on our working memory, not only diverting resources from our higher reasoning faculties but obstructing the consolidation of long-term memories and the development of schemas . . . . The Web is a technology of forgetfulness."[11] He identifies the "key to memory" as "attentiveness . . . strong mental concentration, amplified by repetition

5. Postman, *Technopoly*, 165.
6. Postman, *Technopoly*, 55.
7. Carr, *The Shallows*, 88–89.
8. Carr, *The Shallows*, 93; some of these are *Christian Science Monitor*, *Rocky Mountain News*, *Seattle Post-Intelligencer*, *Washington Post*, *Los Angeles Times*, *Chicago Tribune*, *Philadelphia Inquirer*, and *Minneapolis Star Tribune*.
9. Carr, *The Shallows*, 116.
10. Carr, *The Shallows*, 116.
11. Carr, *The Shallows*, 193. For specific studies in this work, see Nancy Kanwisher of MIT's McGovern Institute for Brain Research (29); Eric Kandel, *In Search of Memory*; Georg Muller, Alfons Pilzecker, and Hermann Ebbinghaus, German psychologists; Louis Flexner, neurologist at the University of Pennsylvania; Kobi Rosenblum, head of the Department of Neurobiology and Ethology at the University of Haifa in Israel; and others (182–93).

or by intense intellectual or emotional engagement."[12] Unfortunately, by our current standards attentiveness is often considered optional; concentration requires too much effort, and repetition is seen as boring because it lacks the pleasure, excitement, and entertainment elements by which we judge the worth of all things.

By contrast, Carr describes the internet as "a concentration-fragmenting mishmash" and "an interruption system, a machine geared for dividing attention."[13] Think about how often a person will text or check emails or talk on the phone while having dinner with friends or family. We are constantly distracted by technology, whether it is computers, cell phones, television, or music. It becomes more difficult to focus on one thing; "our brains become adept at forgetting [and] inept at remembering.... As... the Web makes it harder for us to lock information into our biological memory, we're forced to rely more and more on the Net's capacious and easily searchable artificial memory, even if it makes us shallower thinkers."[14] Carr writes, "Research continues to show that people who read linear text comprehend more, remember more, and learn more than those who read text peppered with links."[15] Human memory is enhanced by the traditional ways of learning rather than with modern technology.

This does not deter us from our fascination with the Web. Although it is the antithesis of human memory, the internet delivers us from the drudgery and boredom of actual learning, does our remembering for us, and gives us unlimited entertainment and pleasure as it overloads us with information and distractions. The sheer volume of information it provides requires a computer to store and to recall it. Things once held in the human mind are now retained in computer memory. Every possible rabbit trail and advertisement, whether related or not to the current discussion, is offered (and often followed). "We are forever inundated by information of immediate interest to us—and in quantities well beyond what our brains can handle."[16] The effect in us is an addiction to constant change for the sake of change to keep us amused.

Current online games, movies, and TV shows are a few examples of how this distraction happens. The camera is constantly shifting so that the viewer receives a full 360° perception. Flashes of different angles of a scene or various scenes are displayed in rapid motion to give the sensation of a high intensity fight, a car speeding out of control, or a building exploding with people running. The mind cannot piece it together to tell what literally happened, but it is exciting. The observer has impressions, not facts. Now think about how often this technique is used, from advertising to teaching. What people "know" may not be anything more than images shot at them with increasing frequency creating impressions in order to satisfy perceived emotional

---

12. Carr, *The Shallows*, 193.
13. Carr, *The Shallows*, 131.
14. Carr, *The Shallows*, 194.
15. Carr, *The Shallows*, 127. For specific studies, see 120–43.
16. Carr, *The Shallows*, 170.

needs. Furthermore, each new generation is learning to process things entirely differently from the previous one.

Younger people are especially open to the influences of the internet because they have grown up with it, and in many cases have not been forced to digest things sequentially (linearly) as in pre-computer generations. The consequence is that they *feel* like the masters of information because of the constant bombardment of pictures, ideas, and news, but what they actually know may be quite different. This *sense* of empowerment brings about a further distrust of the wisdom of authority figures like parents, pastors, teachers, and government types, especially when these authorities must go to them for help in using the technology. Postmodernity has found its home in what Postman terms Technopoly, which is further eroding our connections with each other and our reception of traditional voices of external authority figures.

The internet has surpassed the television for de-contextualized information in both quantity and speed. The Net provides a "steady stream of inputs to our visual, somatosensory, and auditory cortices"; it is "a high-speed system for delivering responses and rewards," for its "interactivity gives us powerful new tools for finding information, expressing ourselves, and conversing with others. It also turns us into lab rats constantly pressing levers to get tiny pellets of social or intellectual nourishment."[17]

In addition to the conditioning, distractions, memory loss, and mistrust promoted by the internet, its speed-of-light delivery of all things has robbed us of another essential of cognitive thinking. Time, which has universally been the "filter of human thought," is no longer available, and we have no patience to wait through the process of reason, but instead are constantly being moved along by the newest, the latest, and the most recent "information of immediate interest."[18] The human brain is increasingly referred to as a computer. This should give us pause. We are becoming more like the machine which was intended to serve us.

We have the same independent spirit today as the founders of this nation. We are ready to protect our freedom against any threat, whether it is real or merely perceived, but our criteria have changed. David Lyon claims, "Consuming, not working, becomes the 'hub around which the life-world rotates.' Pleasure, once seen as the enemy of capitalist industriousness [of the Modern Age], now performs an indispensable role."[19] Perhaps we should understand Lyon's comment as pleasure being the logical outcome of work. Our technology and cultural systems have given us the "freedom" to indulge in entertainment and enjoyment to our hearts' content. "We want what we want when we want it" has become the motto of our independence and freedom.

It is probably correct to assume "that most people in the early twenty-first century will want more and better stuff whatever their beliefs about the Life Questions

---

17. Carr, *The Shallows*, 116–17.
18. Carr, *The Shallows*, 171.
19. Lyon, *Postmodernity*, 85.

or their income level."[20] Brad Gregory believes that the glue holding "Western hyper pluralism together" is a continued conforming to consumerism and writes, "No matter what, individuals must be left free to be selfish . . . . In a world pullulating with so many incompatible truth claims, values, priorities, and aspirations, what else could do the trick?"[21]

Where We Are and How We Got Here

Until the coming of the Enlightenment, Providence explained people's lives and dominated their cultures. Modernity desacralized the Western world by eliminating the need for truth from a higher source and putting faith in science and human reason to provide truth. For some, the Bible became no more important than any other ancient document. Modernity also proposed that God worked only through natural means, and therefore there were no miracles or prophecy. It further proposed that God was present in every person and in every aspect of creation with "no qualitative difference in the manner of his presence, not even in Christ."[22] There was no more of God in Jesus than in any other person or even in a tree.

Postmodernity placed the exclamation point by eliminating absolute truth altogether, thereby granting each person the right to make his or her own truth. Even at the height of the Industrial Age leading into Modernity, the pendulum had begun to swing from reason to emotions. Friedrich Schleiermacher (1768–1834) proposed that feelings were the basis of religion and not doctrine or ethics given by an external source of authority.[23] His ideas found a home in Postmodernity, which downplayed the influence of reason and elevated emotion to the level of ultimate authority, especially feelings of pleasure.

Television has led the way in our ultra-consumeristic lives. Families spend hours in front of a television, mindless of one another. Television fills the silence and makes bearable the anguish of isolation, of not having anything to say to one's own family, and of not understanding the very people with whom one lives. Radio and television fill the gap of silence; they provide the escapism we desperately want, and they dispense a narcotic of dreams. Unfortunately, they are instruments of human isolation, shutting people up in "an echoing mechanical universe," separating them farther from neighbors they do not know, and teaching them to listen to machines without dialogue or "face-to-face encounters."[24] There is an increasing trend toward interactive television where the viewer can register his or her opinion on a matter or vote for the contestants who will advance to the next round and hence determine

20. Gregory, *Unintended Reformation*, 236.
21. Gregory, *Unintended Reformation*, 296–97.
22. Erickson, *Christian Theology*, 333.
23. Schleiermacher, *The Christian Faith*, 10–11.
24. Ellul, *The Technological Society*, 378–79.

those who will not. However, responses are often based on what pleases the viewer rather than on any knowledge of the facts behind the subject or the concrete skills of the performer being judged.

The internet, iPads, and iPhones take what the radio and television do to people and raise it exponentially so that they are ever increasingly isolated from one another as can be witnessed by people texting each other when standing or sitting side-by-side. What is important is that they *feel* connected through their technology. The internet provides Facebook, Twitter, and texting, but while some discussion may occur in these venues it often boils down to nothing more than likes and dislikes. The internet makes it possible for a person to stay connected with events of a person's life on the other side of the world but not be able to communicate with those with whom he or she lives. Conversation often becomes superficial and may be downright hurtful as in cyber bullying.

What began in Postmodernity went viral in Technopoly. Postman describes this current stage as *"progress without limits, rights without responsibilities, and technology without cost . . . . [and] without a moral center"* (italics are mine).[25] In place of morality we emphasize "efficiency, interest, and economic advance" so we can consume more and experience more pleasure. Technopoly *"promises heaven on earth through . . . technological progress. It casts aside all traditional narrative and symbols that suggest stability and orderliness*, and tells, instead, of a life of skills, technical expertise, and ecstasy of consumption" (italics are mine).[26] Taking this one step further, Darrell Fasching has interpreted Jacques Ellul as saying, "Modern technology has become a total phenomenon for civilization, the defining force of a new social order in which efficiency is no longer an option but a necessity imposed on all human activity."[27] Postman believes its sole purpose *"is to produce functionaries for an ongoing Technopoly . . . . The story of Western civilization is irrelevant* . . . there is . . . a common culture whose name is Technopoly and whose key symbol is now the computer" (italics are mine).[28]

Furthermore, not only does Technopoly place itself at the center of culture, it "eliminates alternatives to itself . . . . It does not make them illegal . . . immoral . . . [or] unpopular. It makes them invisible and therefore irrelevant"; it does this "by redefining what we mean by religion, art, family, politics, history, truth, privacy, and intelligence so that our definitions fit its new requirements. Technopoly, in other words, is totalitarian technocracy."[29] This new paradigm has replaced the primary role of

25. Postman, *Technopoly*, 179.
26. Postman, *Technopoly*, 179.
27. Fasching, *Thought of Jacques Ellul*, 17.
28. Postman, *Technopoly*, 179.
29. Postman, *Technopoly*, 48. Since Postman wrote this, evidence suggests that Postmodernity and Technopoly have worked to make opposing voices unpopular, immoral, and illegal when they refuse to remain silent. One example is that the laws that were passed banning the Bible and the Lord's Prayer from our classrooms have resulted in the Ten Commandments being taken out of courtrooms. Political correctness has expanded the ban on the Bible and prayer so that Christians are not supposed to

fate of all the others.... He exists only in himself and for himself, and if he still has a family, he no longer has a country."[35]

This tyranny would assume the role of Providence. It would assume "sole responsibility for securing [people's] pleasure and watching over their fate. It is absolute, meticulous, regular, provident, and mild. It would resemble paternal authority ... [but] it seeks only to keep them in childhood irrevocably."[36] It wants to be the "sole agent and only arbiter" of people's happiness and wants them to rejoice incessantly (never taking time to think seriously). It provides for people's security, cares for their needs, "facilitates their pleasures, manages their most important affairs, directs their industry, regulates their successions, and divides their inheritances. Why not relieve them entirely of the trouble of thinking and the difficulty of living?"[37] This sounds similar to Huxley's brave new world, but de Tocqueville sees the consequences of a lifestyle of pleasure free from responsibility and making decisions.

As a result, free will becomes rare and futile. Increasingly individuals lose the use of their competencies. Society becomes enmeshed in "uniform, minute, and complex rules through which not even the most original minds and most vigorous souls can poke their heads above the crowd."[38] This form of tyranny "inhibits, represses, saps, stifles, and stultifies" until in the end the people become "nothing but a flock of timid and industrious animals, with the government as its shepherd."[39] De Tocqueville believed that the people would "console themselves for being treated as wards by imagining that they have chosen their own protectors.... [since they] emerge from dependence for a moment to indicate their master and then return to it.... [believing] that they have done enough to guarantee the liberty of individuals when in fact they have surrendered that liberty to the national government."[40]

Other observable characteristics of this tyranny are that the will of the people will be frustrated to the point that they will stop trying to express it. This tyranny "gradually smothers [their] spirit and saps their soul ... [until they] slowly [lose] the ability to think, feel, and act on their own."[41] Minor events would then need thousands of laws to tell people how to deal with them when at one time common sense would have handled it. On the other hand, major events would be open to individual prerogatives. De Tocqueville leaves the reader with two things to consider:

1. "It is indeed difficult to imagine how men who have entirely renounced the habit of managing their own affairs could be successful in choosing those who ought

---

35. de Tocqueville, *Democracy in America*, 818.
36. de Tocqueville, *Democracy in America*, 818.
37. de Tocqueville, *Democracy in America*, 818.
38. de Tocqueville, *Democracy in America*, 819.
39. de Tocqueville, *Democracy in America*, 819.
40. de Tocqueville, *Democracy in America*, 819.
41. de Tocqueville, *Democracy in America*, 820–21.

to lead them. It is impossible to believe that a liberal, energetic, and wise government can ever emerge from the ballots of a nation of servants."

2. "The vices of those who govern and the imbecility of the governed would quickly bring about its ruin, and the people, tired of their representatives and of themselves, would either create freer institutions or soon return to prostrating themselves at the feet of a single master."[42]

Miroslav Volf affirms that in the twenty-first century most of the West has reached this way of life. Volf points out that single-minded pursuit of pleasure and experience of satisfaction define happiness and have largely won the day. In the contemporary mind, personal satisfaction in the here and now is the sole determinant of what it means to flourish with little concern for how that satisfaction comes to be. Sources of this satisfaction may range from music, to dining, to sex, or to drugs and are usually based in the pursuit of pleasure for the individual. "What matters is not the source of satisfaction but the fact of it."[43] But the question that arises is "Can we sustain this?"[44] The pace we move, the mountains of information coming at us, and the consuming and discarding are getting faster every year. How long can we keep this up?

Robert Bellah anticipates two things will occur when a culture breaks down the traditional authority structures of family, church, and government and relegates all claims of external truth and authority to irrelevance. First, he believes the culmination of this euphoric pursuit of self-fulfillment will of necessity lead to anarchy. Second, he predicts that before complete chaos happens the government will step in to secure some semblance of order. Bellah calls this age of self-interest the "culture of separation." He writes, "If [the culture of separation] ever became completely dominant, [it] would collapse of its own incoherence. Or, even more likely, well before that happened, an authoritarian state would emerge to provide the coherence the culture no longer could."[45]

Summary

The more we rely on our technology to save us, the more incoherent we become—the less able we are to think for ourselves, to reason, and to make decisions based on facts and truth. The mob mentality is emerging.

Concerning this plunge into incoherence and anarchy, sixty years ago most families in many parts of the U.S. felt safe in their homes with no need to put locks on their doors. Today, we not only have locks on our doors but have installed total home-security systems. In Orwellian fashion, we see indicators of Bellah's authoritarian state

---

42. de Tocqueville, *Democracy in America*, 821.
43. See Volf, "Human Flourishing," 15.
44. Bellah et al., *Habits of the Heart*, 233.
45. Bellah et al., *Habits of the Heart*, 281.

happening with surveillance cameras on nearly every corner of major cities and in nearly every public gathering place, including schools, busses, classrooms, malls, and stores. We are watched everywhere we go. Additionally, the federal government and private organizations monitor our phones and electronic devices. Anyone with the right technology can track us by the chips in our phones, and they know our preferences and buying habits because these are recorded in data banks every time we use a plastic card. In the past we laughed and called people who talked about such things conspiracy theorists or just plain paranoid. Today we call it reality.

Perhaps Huxley's new world leads to Orwell's big brother when the traditional restraints of family, church, and government are removed. The warnings have been ignored and de Tocqueville's dissolving society, which brings about Orwell's big brother watching everything we do to prevent the chaos predicted by Bellah, has arrived. Can the authoritarian state be far behind?

America and Western society stands at a crossroads. God is asking us to choose the ancient path. It begins with the church. Unfortunately, the culture has seriously transformed the church in the past 150-plus years. This is like a cancer that must be accurately diagnosed and treated before the body can be restored to health. Next we will examine more closely how the culture has seduced the church in the twenty-first century, thereby preventing her from finding that Highway of Holiness and experiencing the revivals and reforms for which she longs.

Chapter 3

Contextualization or Capitulation: A Struggle Gone Awry

> In the past, happiness could appear as a very vague, very distant prospect for humanity, whereas now, people seemed to be within reach of the concrete, material possibility of attaining it . . . . This image of happiness brought us fully into the consumer society.
>
> —Jacques Ellul, *Perspectives on Our Age*

IN THIS CHAPTER AND the next two we will examine ways Western culture has influenced the church's mission and has turned it from the biblical mandate toward reflecting the culture's beliefs. My purpose in doing this is to help the church recognize and leave behind what is not of God and then replace those things with their biblical counterparts. Only then will she be equipped to tell the next generation the good news of Jesus.[1] This requires self-examination and repentance of those things not of God.[2] This is made more difficult because of the abundance of deceptions that Jesus warned would abound in the end times.

Christians take heart. Remember that the same prophet (Hosea) who wrote, "Sow the wind and reap the whirlwind" also wrote, "Sow righteousness and reap steadfast love." Just as cultural ways often produce a tsunami of turmoil, so too, God's people pursuing God's ways prepares the way for God to work love in the lives of Christians and to bring peace to the culture in which they live, work, and play. This is the goal, but the church struggles in communicating the gospel accurately without being indoctrinated by the culture to which she is ministering.

The challenge to the church in every age is to make disciples of Jesus Christ. Jesus commanded two ways for discipleship to be accomplished. The first is to baptize Jesus' followers in the name of the Father, the Son, and the Holy Spirit. The second is to

---

1. Scripture is filled with exhortations for God's people to turn from cultural ways and to seek God and his ways. Deut 4:29; 1 Chr 28:9; 2 Chr 14:4; 15:12; 30:9; 34:3; Neh 1:8–9; Pss 14:2; 53:2; 81:13–16; Isa 31:6–7; Jer 3:14–16; 4:1–2; Lam 3:40–42; Hos 14:1; Acts 26:20; 2 Tim 2:19; Heb 11:6; and 1 Pet 3:10–11.

2. Lam 3:40–42 and 2 Cor 13:5.

teach them to obey everything he commanded. This teaching goes beyond mere head knowledge because in Jesus' day a disciple learned *and lived* everything the master taught and did. In order to teach people, the church must communicate the gospel in ways they understand. As at Pentecost when the Holy Spirit enabled the apostles to speak the message in the different languages of the people who were present that day, so the church must make the gospel message clear to her listeners in this age as well. The first two chapters will help us recognize how this will look.

The culture determines the means she uses to connect with people. Speaking their language is a must. This goes beyond English or Spanish. If people have never seen or heard of snow, it is pointless to tell them that Jesus cleanses them of their sins and though they were blood red, they are now white as snow. It might be better to refer to white clouds or sand. The gospel message has not been changed, but the means to communicate it has changed from snow, which they cannot understand, to clouds or sand, which they can. This kind of communication is called "contextualization" because it changes the *way* the church communicates the gospel message without changing the *content* of the message.

When contextualizing, there is a real danger of overidentifying with the culture and changing the message to accommodate it. This happens especially when the church becomes too emotionally attached to the people to whom she ministers. Christians are commanded to love the people of the culture and to have compassion for them but must be careful not to adopt those behaviors that go against God's ways. When this happens, instead of presenting the gospel, which would necessitate some sort of change, they not only use the culture's language and means of communication but begin to embrace its habits, even those that contradict clear teaching in the Bible. When the church consents to and accepts practices that are contrary to the Bible's message, she has capitulated to the culture.

So then, contextualization is the necessary changing of the means of proclaiming the Christian faith to reach people of different cultures without changing the content. By contrast, capitulation is the changing of the message being communicated in order to accommodate the culture. Capitulation can be recognized in three ways. First, there is retreat from the purpose of making disciples for Jesus. Second, there is surrender to (stop resisting) the culture. Third, there is ultimately submission to (acceptance of and practicing) that way of thinking and acting.

Capitulation has progressively been happening in the churches in the second half of the twentieth century. She must identify the pitfalls, roadblocks, potholes, and ditches in the journey towards capitulation and avoid them. This chapter will describe some of the obstacles that have evolved throughout the modern and postmodern ages and beyond. Let us begin with a brief overview of the cultural effects that the paradigm shifts discussed in the first two chapters have had on the church.

An Aerial View of the Path to Capitulation

During the Age of Providence the church faced few challenges to its authority. Ignorance, superstition, and fear had to be overcome but did not seriously affect the church's guidance in people's lives. In fact, the mythical awe surrounding ignorance and superstition often connected with the mythical awe of God and strengthened the church's presence in culture. When an earthquake destroyed cities, people feared that God was angry with them and wanted to know what they needed to do to get right with him. During this time, the perceived needs of people were met by God and the church. Wherever the church went, she built schools to educate and hospitals to help the local population. Additionally, higher education aspired to understand the theological issues about the God of the Bible, so there was little challenge to the church's influence from this section of the culture either. Whenever the church slipped and became like the culture, God raised up reformers (like the judges of biblical times) to call the church back to its first-century roots. The Protestant Reformation began in earnest in the early sixteenth century.

The Reformation resulted in two major divisions of the church in the West: the Roman Catholic Church and the Protestant churches made up of Lutherans, Presbyterians, Anglicans, Anabaptists, and others. By the seventeenth century, new reformers were calling for a reformation of the Reformation churches. This brought new movements such as the Moravians and the Puritans and in the eighteenth century the Methodists. Religious persecution led many of these new reformers to the American continent to live out their beliefs. As the Puritans moved to settle the New England area, Governor Winthrop described their endeavor as being a city on a hill (Matt 5:14), the light of which would shine to all the world as they modeled community lived out according to God's ways. In this society, the church was inseparable from the culture, but change was on its way.

As the Reformation was ushering in new denominations, the Enlightenment was ushering in the Age of Reason and Modernity, in which human reason and science challenged mysticism and superstition. The church contextualized by developing strong propositions and systematic theologies to explain the faith. The propositions of righteousness, justice, judgment, sin, heaven, hell, and condemnation were easily communicated like the theorems and hypotheses of science. On the other hand it was nearly impossible to explain love, grace, and mercy in scientific terms, and they were often downplayed as emotionalism. Therefore, the church capitulated to the culture by severely limiting expressions of human emotions in its worship and practice. As time progressed, the church became more legalistic as she sacrificed these more emotive qualities to those more easily adaptable to the scientific way of thinking. Additionally, the scholarship that was to find truth began deconstructing the Bible by rejecting its claims of divine authorship, prophecy, and miracles.

Robert Bellah points out that already by the eighteenth century "it was possible for individuals to find the form of religion that best suited their inclinations."[3] At the inception of the United States some of its founders were saying, "I am a sect myself" (Thomas Jefferson) and "My mind is my church" (Thomas Paine).[4] During the eighteenth century the church maintained its influence in the culture through revivalists like Jonathan Edwards, George Whitefield, Charles and John Wesley, as well as the Moravians, and the many evangelists who traveled throughout the American colonies as well as England, Scotland, and Wales preaching the gospel of salvation in Christ alone.

In spite of the many revivals, as the nineteenth century advanced, churches had to compete for people's "individual religious tastes" that "operated with a new emphasis on the individual and . . . voluntary association" in which membership became fragmented, and sermons "became less doctrinal and more emotional and sentimental. . . . Religion . . . [became] a place of love and acceptance."[5] Evangelists continued to preach that apart from redemption in Jesus Christ there was no salvation and that hell was a just punishment for sin. They called people to repentance and to accept Jesus' death as atonement for their sins and the restoration of their souls.[6] However, they were unable to hold back the dramatic cultural change that was coming.

By the middle of the nineteenth century another split occurred among the churches of the Reformation between Conservatives (more legalistic in their communication of correct doctrine of the gospel) and Liberals (pursuing social justice in their attempt to keep the love of the faith). These churches were increasingly promoting right beliefs *or* social justice programs, thus separating what Holy Scripture never did. Jesus was never about either/or one of these but about both/and all of them. He is love and righteousness, mercy and justice (beyond social justice), grace and judgment (against sin of all sorts), peace and condemnation, and joy and self-denial.

Simply put, the Conservatives, led by the Fundamentalists, maintained the propositions; they wanted right doctrine. They boiled down right behavior to lists of dos and don'ts. Do pray, go to church, read your Bible, and give to charity. Don't play cards, smoke, dance, go to movies, or drink alcoholic beverages. As a result, people got the idea that Christianity was against everything that was fun. The Liberals wanted to show the love of God in which right behavior became social justice agendas, but they wavered on the major doctrines of the faith that they did not understand as loving. In their own way, both Fundamentalists and Liberals pursued a works-based faith.

Evangelicals emerged as a third group of Christians because they, like the evangelists, wanted to proclaim the gospel to bring about conversions and disciple new believers in the doctrines of the faith. They could be found in churches of both the conservative and liberal persuasions and at times became the dominant force in their

3. Bellah et al., *Habits of the Heart*, 233.
4. Bellah et al., *Habits of the Heart*, 233.
5. Bellah et al., *Habits of the Heart*, 222–23.
6. For more on this era see Hatch, *Democratization*.

own congregations. However, most evangelicals gradually contextualized their message to portray primarily God's love. Bit by bit they dropped the ancient doctrines of holiness, judgment, condemnation, God's wrath, and his sovereignty and downplayed righteous living. They still agreed with these doctrines but neglected to talk about them in a significant way. They continued to preach the gospel of salvation through Jesus, but were perhaps overly cautious in how they presented the message by promoting God's love, grace, and mercy to the neglect of doctrines that could be perceived as negative. This left new Christians in local congregations where they were rarely challenged to grow in the entirety of their faith.

These changes came slowly. At first the influence of the Enlightenment's elevation of human reason and science infiltrated colleges, universities, and seminaries. Then through the media it filtered into the streets and homes of everyday people. Perceptions changed and produced cultural change. Gradually the very doctrines of the faith that had united the church up through the mid-nineteenth century became the very source of division. Increasingly, the doctrines of holiness, righteousness, justice (beyond social justice), judgment, God's wrath, sin, and the need for atonement were abandoned in order to attract the changing public as well as to maintain a fragile unity among Christian brothers and sisters. If you doubt this, ask the average church attender and many pastors to explain what these doctrines mean. Many would not have a clue or would say they are unimportant to us today.

Avoidance of these major doctrines signaled the arrival of Postmodernity in the mid-twentieth century and the acceptance of almost every behavior and activity that enabled people to do what is right in their own eyes. The church (Liberals and Conservatives alike as well as Evangelicals, though usually to a lesser extent) has not only contextualized the message of God's love through Jesus Christ but has capitulated in varying degrees by changing God's love to look exactly like the self-serving love demanded by the current Western culture.[7] Additionally, piety has become internalized and much privatized so that it is politically incorrect to speak of a personal faith in Jesus in public because someone might be offended. Increasingly, a personal faith in Jesus and repentance for sin was replaced by a faith that encouraged everyone to be themselves because they were good and deserved good things. With the Liberals leading the way, the church's focus of doing good works as the expression of godly love easily connected with the Postmodern Age of "what is in it for me?" And this was often limited to earthly goods and services.

Now that we have travelled the road of the general effects of Western culture on the church, let us examine more closely the cost of losing this struggle of contextualizing vs. capitulating to Modernity, Postmodernity, and Technopoly.

---

7. How this is happening will be explored in more detail in chapters 7, 11, 12, and appendix 3.

Specific Cultural Dangers to the Twenty-First Century Church

The Dangers of Contextualizing Christianity with Psychology

One of Postmodernity's destructive influences on the church is the rise of a therapeutic model of psychology which promotes the innate goodness of a person (first proposed by the Enlightenment) and encourages an "I'm okay; you're okay" attitude. This new belief system emboldens people to be true to themselves regardless of what consequences it may have. This new paradigm assumes that no one has the right or the authority to judge the individual or his or her perception of truth. Personal happiness becomes the goal to which people aspire, and there is no outside authority to limit or to direct the way that happiness is implemented. Now when Christians ask why something has happened, they look for scientific or psychological reasons, not spiritual ones. Robbed of its ability to influence public or private lives, the church has been reduced to the social services she can provide to the community and the personal good feelings she can generate in individuals.

Closely related to these characteristics of a therapeutic model at work in most churches is listening without judging and telling people they are accepted by God just as they are. The church invites people to come "Just as I am" with no need to change. This approach among church people is often encouraged from the pulpit. Millard Erickson writes, "Preaching, even in evangelical pulpits, tends to be therapeutic, and the pastor is seen as the CEO of a corporation, responsible for its efficiency and growth."[8] He or she will give entertaining speeches which provide laughter and will rarely require anything of the people that does not fit *comfortably* with their cultural views or will apologize profusely if he or she does.

Expanding on the comfortableness promoted by the therapeutic model in this postmodern culture, Scot McKnight observes how most people, including Christians, read the Bible only for God's comfort in his blessings and promises. While there is nothing wrong with looking for comfort and affirmation in the Bible, it becomes a problem when people ignore or reject those things that cause them to be uncomfortable. McKnight calls this a distortion of what the Bible truly is and writes, "Calendar companies may provide us with a blessing a day, but Jeremiah's calendar may have offered a warning of God's wrath each day."[9] Jeremiah does not make people feel good about themselves. He does not fit the therapeutic worldview held in this postmodern culture, and, therefore, he must go. The church of the twenty-first century is very comfortable with ignoring large portions of the Bible. In this aspect, the church looks and acts very much like the therapeutic model of the culture. Christians must abandon the goal of making themselves and others comfortable according to the standards of the culture and recover the willingness to suffer for their faith in order to communicate God's truth accurately.

---

8. Erickson, *Postmodernizing the Faith*, 34–35.
9. McKnight, "Scripture in the Emerging Movement," 108.

The Sinkhole of Spiritualism

Since the 1960s, this nation has been "attracted to a vague pantheistic mysticism that tended to identify the divine with a higher self" that included harmony with the earth and feelings of wanting to be pure.[10] Of course this purity was self-defined purity and not from any outside authority. "Mysticism is found most often among prosperous, well-educated people," which is most likely why it has been so well received in this country; it "lacks any effective social discipline . . . [and] is probably the commonest form of religion among those we interviewed, *and many who sit in the pews of the churches*" (italics are mine).[11] It allows people to do what seems right *to them*.

Bellah describes events of the 1960s in part as "an upwelling of mystical religious feeling . . . which . . . made us sensitive . . . [to] ecology, peace, opposition to nuclear weapons, internationalism, [and] feminism." It also came with its distortions of "inner volatility and incoherence, its extreme weakness in social and political organization, and above all, its particular form of compromise with the world—namely, its closeness to the therapeutic model in its pursuit of self-centered experiences and its difficulty with social loyalty and commitment."[12] With its inconsistencies of thought, rejection of logic, denial of absolute truth, disavowal of well-rounded doctrine, rise of therapy, and self-centered consumerism, Postmodernity has left the church wide open to spiritualism, which makes people feel close to God when in reality that may be a god of their own making and not the one, true God. This has also left the church susceptible to propaganda that previous generations would have easily spotted.

The Pitfall of Propaganda

Writing in the 1960s Jacques Ellul claims that inconsistencies and lack of logic are the primary foundation on which propaganda thrives. Providence with its focus on absolute truth and Modernity with its focus on human reason and logic enabled people to discern and to resist propaganda. Postmodernity, which rejects absolute truth, reason, and logic, leaves people wide open to the influences of propaganda. This set the stage for technopoly, which functions best in an environment of propaganda. The propagandist "can lead a man where he does not want to go, without his being aware of it, over paths that he will not notice."[13] Much of media does this expertly with its information overload, news, commercials, and non-stop entertainment showing us how to live, and few people realize it.

---

10. Bellah et al., *Habits of the Heart*, 233.
11. Bellah et al., *Habits of the Heart*, 246.
12. Bellah et al., *Habits of the Heart*, 246.
13. Ellul, *Propaganda*, 35. Interestingly, sin has been described by some in similar terminology, "Sin will take you farther than you want to go, keep you longer than you want to stay and cost you more than you want to pay." —Unknown

The church needs to consider seriously the effects propaganda has on people in order to reach those outside her walls. Ellul can help in this area. He identifies the emerging culture as being made up of people who are empty and "devoid of meaning.... very busy, but... emotionally empty, open to all entreaties and in search of only one thing—something to fill his inner void."[14] He believes America is a culture in search of myths to replace the beliefs on which this nation was founded and thinks that movies and entertainment have readily supplied them. The propaganda of pleasure-filled consumerism is trying to fill this deepest emotional void by providing people with reasons behind the unfolding situations facing them. Furthermore, it promises solutions for the seemingly unsolvable problems that arise.[15] There will always be a new product or a new adventure for people to pursue that is guaranteed to distract them from the void that keeps rising up within them. If they keep watching and listening to television or surfing the Web, they will not notice their emptiness.

This propaganda of a self-centered, consumer-oriented approach to happiness makes the church's call to disciple people more difficult than it has ever been. Ellul notices that "a propaganda that stresses virtue over happiness and presents man's future as one dominated by austerity and contemplation would have no audience at all."[16] Thus, Ellul shows us how the propositions of holy living, sin, condemnation, judgment, righteousness, and hell that connected with the culture in the ages of Providence and Modernity are now seen by the children of Postmodernity and Technopoly as absurd. He warns that "people manipulated by propaganda become increasingly impervious to spiritual realities, [and] less and less suited for the autonomy of a Christian life." He asserts that church members have relinquished their true autonomy and have reacted "pretty much like everyone else. As a result, an almost complete dissociation takes place between their Christianity and their behavior."[17]

Many Congregations no longer talk about holiness or any of the great doctrines in church history such as sin, judgment, righteousness, and repentance but replace them with the propaganda of a kind of worldly love, mercy, grace, and peace that is acceptable to the culture and that will always make people feel good about themselves. The result is that Christians seldom "see what they might do that would be effective and at the same time be an expression of their Christianity."[18] The church capitulates to culture and is unable to effect the much needed change for which she hopes. She must begin to recognize the propaganda prevalent in this culture and then recover the doctrines lost to that propaganda.

---

14. Ellul, *Propaganda*, 147.
15. Ellul, *Propaganda*, 147–48.
16. Ellul, *Propaganda*, 40.
17. Ellul, *Propaganda*, 228–29.
18. Ellul, *Propaganda*, 228.

The Chasm of Consumerism

Consumerism and its cousin, materialism, propelled by the doctrines of marketing and evangelized through the medium of technology, are the new religion of the twenty-first century. They offer the people in this Western culture purpose, faith by which to live, rituals, and transcendence. They even provide salvation. Jason Clark describes the consumer culture this way. The question "What is the good life?" is answered by "living somewhere nice, living to a ripe old age, having certain life experiences before we die. And it offers to save us from the worst fate of all human fates: *boredom*" (italics are mine).[19] The Church of Consumerism demands total commitment to buy more continually. This materialism becomes the salvation of and transformation for life in America with little or no care for eternal things.

Consumers also have beliefs. Unfortunately, the "consumer culture relates to beliefs as commodities to be used and marketed" and therefore perceives no need to defend its beliefs.[20] They become just another commodity to be acquired and discarded as they bring happiness, enjoyment, and pleasure to the person holding them, much like clothing styles that come and go. Furthermore, this belief in the consumeristic life that gratifies our innate desire for enjoyment also makes change nearly impossible. The more people criticize consumerism, the greater the edge it gives marketing and publicity that "uses any critique as raw materials for new consumer products."[21]

According to James K. Smith, marketing and not religion determines the meaning to life. It accomplishes this by creating in us the need to buy "the latest thing to come along simply to satisfy the desire that has been formed and implanted in us" through advertising that offers transcendence "through the powerful instruments of imagination and ritual."[22] Transcendence, desire, satisfaction, and need used to belong to the church and used to refer to God. Additionally, those who try to resist this cultural flow often come across as angry and are promptly dismissed. There is, however, a downside to consumerism.

Although consumerism and its handmaiden, advertising, offer the promise of "experiences and ways of life, security and transformation to the congregation of consumer culture,"[23] they deliver instead isolation, "driving us deeper into our fallen human condition of separation from God and one another . . . . [it] demands . . . our time, energy, and money."[24] Alexis de Tocqueville warned of this already in the mid-nineteenth century.

---

19. Clark, "Consumer Liturgies," 43.
20. Clark, "Consumer Liturgies," 42.
21. Clark, "Consumer Liturgies," 42.
22. Smith, *Who's Afraid of Postmodernism*, 104–5.
23. Clark, "Consumer Liturgies," 42.
24. Clark, "Consumer Liturgies," 56.

De Tocqueville calls materialists proud and pernicious and warns that materialism is particularly dangerous in a democracy because it naturally "encourages the taste for material gratifications," which then "weds with marvelous ease the defect of the heart." Soon people come "to believe that everything is mere matter," which ends in a "fatal circle" of materialism, pursuit of gratification, and shortsightedness.[25] The church must overcome the propaganda of consumerism and materialism. *Things* should not be so important to Christians, who should have an eternal perspective.

The Chasm of Consumerism in the Church

How does this consumeristic maximization of pleasure affect the church? For starters, people feel free to pick and to choose which church they will attend based on the entertainment value of music, preaching, coffee bars, and socialization. No one would ever tell them they are wrong or need to change their behaviors or attitudes. Additionally, their *perceived* needs would be met. They would be told how good they are and how valuable they are to God much like the therapeutic model prevalent in the culture.

This consumer-oriented church encourages Christians to separate their beliefs from their daily life practices. Clark observes that as church members become more conformed to consumerism, the church is "in danger of continuing to produce new ways of doing church that support those perverted forms of identity rather than creating ones that lead to Christian identity."[26]

Some of these new ways of doing church include making God over into the individual's image, looking to consumerism for health and meaning in life, and giving people something to which they can be deeply committed without being religious (or so they think). Clark discerns that "many ways of doing and being church seem to be about giving people the resources to continue making meaning of God on their own terms, isolated from others," and "where once community and religious groups were a means to psychological health and human well-being, today consuming has replaced them."[27] He goes a step further to "wonder if, in a secular and consumer society where people think of themselves as nonreligious, they are in fact deeply religious," and asks, "What if the people we interact with are so deeply embedded in a religious system that they are unable and unwilling to convert to Christianity as an alternative reality? Is there something about this alternative religious reality that co-opts and undermines our best missional interactions, rendering them powerless?"[28]

Erickson supports Clark and writes, "Some of the traditional ways of presenting the Christian message are not only not being accepted, but are not even understood

---

25. de Tocqueville, *Democracy in America*, 635.
26. Clark, "Consumer Liturgies," 56.
27. Clark, "Consumer Liturgies," 44–45.
28. Clark, "Consumer Liturgies," 41.

or heard by contemporary persons."[29] The idea of denying the self sounds strange to twenty-first-century ears and must be outrageously wrong in the age of "I want what I want, and nobody is going to tell me I cannot have it!" Christians dare not let themselves get discouraged at this point. According to Mark Shaw, "the seed of revival is sown in . . . discontent, uncertainty and volatility," which abound in our culture and "arise from a widespread sense of fear and uncertainty about the future."[30] The church must understand consumerism as an alternate religion and must examine her own practices to see to what extent she has been converted.

The Chasm of Consumerism in Evangelicalism

If the church wants to recover its identity she must pursue change based on Scripture, which has historically been called revival and reformation. In this high-speed, technological, and consumeristic age of information glut with relative truth claims all aimed at self-approval, it is imperative that Christians understand what has been lost and recover it. Evangelicalism, that commonly leads revival and reformation movements, is becoming one of the casualties of this revolution of self-aggrandizement by becoming what Richard Lints calls "a democratized coalition of diverse religious traditions" that are "built around a *fragile* consensus of the authority of Scripture, the personal nature of salvation, the unique work of Jesus Christ, and the manifest importance of the Christian life" (italics are mine).[31] Like our multicultural community asking, "Whose morality?" the church is asking, "Whose evangelicalism and which renewal?"[32]

Peter Gillquist attempts to answer that question and asserts that evangelism as it has been conducted has brought many decisions, but "has not even begun to slow the world down on its godless rush to inevitable self-destruction."[33] He assigns this failure to the American independent spirit that dominates Christian attitudes and organizations in Western culture and writes, "We have been taught to make it on our own with God, and such individualism has not won the day."[34] The church has lost her saltiness, and the two primary qualities that she has lost according to Gillquist are holiness and righteousness.

These are not the only things missing, but he assures us that "if we can mend [these two], we will be well on the way to having the impact we must have in the world" and proposes that "religious action . . . apart from holiness and righteousness, is futile in effecting change in the world in which we live."[35] Bible study, cru-

29. Erickson, *Postmodernizing the Faith*, 144.
30. Shaw, *Global Awakening*, 23.
31. Lints, "Introduction," 1–2.
32. Lints, "Introduction," 2.
33. Gillquist, *Why We Haven't Changed*, 17.
34. Gillquist, *Why We Haven't Changed*, 18.
35. Gillquist, *Why We Haven't Changed*, 20.

sades, personal witnessing, and working for social reform will not bring the change for which the church longs unless they come from hearts made soft and pure in holiness and righteousness. Gillquist warns that "social reform in and of itself does not equal change," which can only come from a changed heart of a person or group.[36] Decades of social reform projects have not brought about less oppression of the poor and helpless because they have not dealt with the heart of the problem, which is the brokenness and sin at work in each human. He writes, "Holiness is not some 'extra accessory,' added on to the Gospel. It is part and parcel of our salvation, not something separate from it."[37]

Ronald Sider agrees with Gillquist about the loss of holiness and righteousness in the church and takes it a step further to claim that the church has reduced salvation to a "no-lose proposition" in which a person only needs to say the magical words and he or she has purchased "a no-cost fire insurance policy."[38] Increasingly the message becomes, "believe in Jesus and your sins, past, present, and future, are forgiven," with no suggestion of repentance and turning away from that sin or of the transformation that must take place as believers in Christ. Jesus becomes Savior, but making him Lord is optional; "responsibility and accountability in the body of Christ has largely been lost. The gospel of individual self-fulfillment now reigns."[39]

Evangelicals are following suit, giving in to political correctness and promoting love above everything else, allowing the secular definition of love to rule the day. However, Jesus calls his people to radical obedience. In times of revival and reform, it was this astonishing quality of Christians' lives that attracted people to Jesus.

The gap between what Christians say they believe and what they do further drives a wedge between the culture and the church. Sider charges, "Today, our hypocrisy often drives unbelievers away."[40] The church must remind herself that the greatest witness to the unsaved world is the life lived according to biblical truths in both word and deed. Jesus warned that this could be downright uncomfortable and might involve persecution and suffering. Christians must rethink their consumer oriented priorities as it relates to salvation in Jesus Christ and especially the pursuit of "what is in it for me?" when that means material goods, entertainment, constantly padding the ego, and being told how valuable you are to God.

---

36. Gillquist, *Why We Haven't Changed*, 20. I have often heard it said that it is the systems that are oppressive. Popular thinking says change the system and oppression will end. I would say that every system that does not follow the truth set forth in Scripture will be/become oppressive. It is a matter of the hearts of the people running them.

37. Gillquist, *Why We Haven't Changed*, 71.

38. Sider, *Evangelical Conscience*, 56, 58.

39. Sider, *Evangelical Conscience*, 85.

40. Sider, *Evangelical Conscience*, 31–2.

The Dead-End Effects of Entertainment, Television, and Psychology in Preaching

With the advent of television, the church's message became dramatically altered to fit the new preference for entertainment and the therapeutic expectation for everyone to be made to feel good about himself or herself.[41] Like everything else in the media, the message becomes entertaining, stripped of its historicity, its sacredness, and its profound human activity. Neil Postman calls television preachers "the enemy of religious experience . . . not so much [because of] their weaknesses but [because of] the weaknesses of the medium in which they work."[42] He argues that the medium determines the message; therefore the message that was originally given in one medium (the church gathered together) cannot "be expressed in another [to individuals alone in their homes] without significantly changing its meaning, texture or value."[43] For one thing, the activities in the home that are going on while people take in the message will most likely be no different than for other programs. People may be cooking, eating, making coffee, or reading a newspaper at the same time, which would keep them from entering into an otherworldly "state of mind required for a nontrivial religious experience."[44]

Furthermore, there would be a "strong bias toward a psychology of secularism" for always being upbeat, having quick solutions, and containing sound-bite–length statements in messages that entertain. Postman reminds us that the "unwritten law of all television preachers" is high ratings which come only if the preacher gives the people what they want. He supports his view noting that "what is preached on television is not anything like the Sermon on the Mount. Religious programs are filled with good cheer. They celebrate affluence. Their featured players become celebrities . . . . [and] because their messages are trivial, the shows have high ratings."[45] He maintains that "Christianity is a demanding and serious religion. When it is delivered as easy and amusing, it is another kind of religion altogether."[46] Additionally, he asserts that "entertainment is the means through which we distance ourselves" from something, and, in this case, it is God who becomes a "vague and subordinate character."[47]

What has happened on television has become the norm in most churches. Christians must stop basing their approval (their attendance, giving of their time and money, and the renewal of the pastor's terms of call) on the entertainment value and feel-good therapy of the messages. Christians must stop their consumer approach

---

41. For a discussion of how specific televangelists have done and are doing this today see Steven P. Miller, *The Age of Evangelicalism*.

42. Postman, *Amusing Ourselves*, 116–17.

43. Postman, *Amusing Ourselves*, 117.

44. Postman, *Amusing Ourselves*, 121.

45. Postman, *Amusing Ourselves*, 121.

46. Postman, *Amusing Ourselves*, 121.

47. Postman, *Amusing Ourselves*, 122.

about what they will and will not believe or allow based on the entertainment attraction and therapeutic way of life. They must require themselves to be challenged biblically to be holy because God is holy.

Caught in the Quicksand of Morality and Goodness

In our culture, the goodness of each person is a given (in spite of all the news we see to the contrary), and the church has capitulated. Reflecting on much of today's preaching, John Eldredge observes, "Nowadays most Christian leaders bend over backward to come across as very cool and hip and in no way whatsoever judgmental or condemning. It's the new PR campaign for Jesus."[48] This public relations campaign has led Christians to adopt some really abnormal behaviors and beliefs that have blurred the moral differences between the church and the culture to which she ministers and has cast doubt over a faith intended to be sure and certain.

Cultural views of morality and goodness have influenced the way the church views sin and goodness. She has confused the need for redemption from sin with the weight of different sins. It is true that any sin will separate people from God so that they need Jesus' atoning work on the cross to save them, to redeem them, and to restore them in a right relationship with God, but this has come to mean that all sins are equally devastating. That is not the case. Littering may be a sin because the person is contributing to the pollution of the earth, but adultery, greed, and murder (especially as defined in the Sermon on the Mount) are destructive of the very foundational relationships a person needs to be whole. Stealing a loaf of bread in order to stave off hunger is not on par with preventing food from being delivered to starving people.

Eldredge believes that blurring the moral differences and "confusing the weight of sins actually hurts our ability to resist temptation," and people in general and Christians in particular "can't pursue genuine holiness if [they] are walking around under the crushing weight that tossing a wrapper on the sidewalk is just as bad as harboring resentment toward [their] parents. It's crippling; it also keeps [them] from focusing on what Jesus called 'the weightier matters.'"[49] Yes, sin is sin in that any sin requires redemption through the blood of Jesus (more about this in the next chapter). Some sins are "weightier" because they are more destructive in the lives of the person, the family, and the community in which they live (see Col 3).

When the lines of morality are blurred, confusion in people's understanding of goodness quickly follows. The new morality has more to do with recycling: how your food is grown, eco-friendly energy, cars, and fair-trade products. This criteria of goodness is based on convenience and selective morality. Such things may make people feel good and moral while they fume in their bitterness towards others, beat the dog (or a spouse), and leave their children unsupervised or unfed.

48. Eldredge, *Utter Relief of Holiness*, 49.
49. Eldredge, *Utter Relief of Holiness*, 76–77.

Eldredge calls this "popular goodness" that makes people seem wonderful on the outside but does nothing to transform the inside. "I think the culture of popular goodness has confused a lot of young people who are sincere about pursuing holiness.... [These things] are important, but a Christian has a lot more things that are far more important."[50] By society's standards a person or group concerned about the environment or civil causes is considered to be good and moral, and God is not needed or desired in order to do them. A strong dose of doubt is needed to maintain these beliefs of morality and goodness. Not only has the church not challenged them in any noticeable way, but many of the people sitting in the pews are their staunch followers.

Danger: Doubt Ahead

All people doubt; that is human, but society was never intended to make doubt a way of life. Eldredge agrees that "dogmatic people ... have done a lot of damage.... Good people don't want anything to do with that, and so—by a leap of logic—they don't want to be seen as having strong convictions"; so they go with their feelings instead of their reason and "end up embracing doubt because it feels authentic."[51] Doubt is seen as a virtue. This plays out in things as simple as a group of friends trying to decide where to go for lunch. No one wants to make the decision. Eldredge counters that while this culture sees doubt as "a prerequisite for respect.... conviction is not the enemy. Pride is. Arrogance is. But not conviction."[52]

The casualty of doubt is certainty which brings conviction. Lack of conviction opens another sinkhole into which many Christians have fallen. It excuses them from acting on their beliefs. If they are never sure of anything, then they are never convicted to do anything. Eldredge challenges the church to "take notice just how convenient doubt is for you. Motives are at play here.... so ... remember this truth: Doubt is not a virtue. Doubt is not humility. Doubt is doubt. It is unbelief. Jesus ... wants us to get past it, not embrace it."[53]

De Tocqueville also wrote about the toxic effects that doubt has on a culture. He believed that doubt inevitably takes hold of "the highest regions of the intellect" and when "a people's religion is destroyed" it "half paralyzes all the others [regions of the intellect]."[54] When this happens people become confused and fluctuate in matters of great importance to society. People either give up their opinions or defend them poorly. They despair of resolving their own problems and eventually stop thinking about them altogether. Materialism becomes the great escape. Doubt places things in a "perpetual state of agitation" until people "become anxious and fatigued. With

---

50. Eldredge, *Utter Relief of Holiness*, 79.
51. Eldredge, *Utter Relief of Holiness*, 81.
52. Eldredge, *Utter Relief of Holiness*, 83.
53. Eldredge, *Utter Relief of Holiness*, 85.
54. de Tocqueville, *Democracy in America*, 502.

the world of the intellect in universal flux, they want everything in the material realm, at least, to be firm and stable, and, unable to resume their former beliefs, they subject themselves to a master."[55]

When religion no longer has strong influence over people, doubt will arise and will weaken the human will. This prepares people for servitude and deprives them of true liberty. It also disables them from making commitments. This leads quickly to following the path of least resistance. American culture has proven de Tocqueville correct. American Christianity has capitulated by refusing to deal with the difficult issues that would make her unpopular with the media and by adopting behaviors clearly forbidden in Scripture. Although there is still a right and a wrong way to do moral things, we are drowning in a sea of doubt. Christians must recognize along with Eldredge that most people are not objecting to certainty as much as the arrogance with which certainty is often expounded. They must find their conviction and commitment to Jesus Christ of Scripture if they are to make a difference in this world.

The Path of Least Resistance: Plurality, Offenses, and Ignorance

Tolerance, diversity, and inclusiveness can be expressed by one word: plurality. Plurality has also caused people to back away from strong convictions for fear of offending someone. In order not to have strong convictions, it is easier not to know more than a minimum of what you believe. Thus, plurality has encouraged obliviousness and has altered what people actually know about Christianity. Philip Jenkins writes, "A generation ago . . . students could be expected to absorb information about the faith from churches, families, or from society at large. Today, though, that is often not a realistic expectation, and one encounters dazzling levels of ignorance about the basic facts of the religion."[56] Never assume people understand what was once considered common knowledge of the basics of Christianity—this is true even of people sitting in church week after week. This ignorance has caused many battles in both society and the church with people claiming to know what the Bible says when they have never read it outside of a few passages that make them feel safe and warm. Sacrificing biblical truth to political correctness and culture's interpretation of tolerance, diversity, and inclusiveness will never win the world for Christ.

Misdirection from Media

The media often paints the picture of the glaring failures of Christianity such as the Crusades, imperialism, wars fought in Europe, and "outmoded supernatural doctrines and moral assumptions."[57] It began when Modernity affirmed that God works only through

---

55. de Tocqueville, *Democracy in America*, 502–3.
56. Jenkins, *Next Christendom*, 270.
57. Jenkins, *Next Christendom*, 11.

natural means; therefore, the church was not needed to find God or his truth. Today, the media continues to report "that Christianity has failed and is collapsing and will continue to do so unless and until the religion [comes] to terms with liberal orthodoxies on matters of sex and gender. The need to rationalize seems all the more urgent in the face of the attacks."[58] Many Christians have bought into this misdirection of the media and have given up on the longstanding historical testimony.

One area where the media has made major inroads in the church as well as the culture is to make sin look very attractive and appealing. Sex is promoted everywhere and all the time, from shaving cream to comedies. Pornography is easily accessible at the push of a button through the internet. Sexual activity outside of marriage is portrayed as commonplace and right. Nancy DeMoss observes that Christians, some Evangelicals included, have "managed to redefine sin; we have come to view it as normal, acceptable behavior—something perhaps to be tamed or controlled, but not to be eradicated and put to death." She continues, "We have sunk to such lows that we can not only sin thoughtlessly, but astonishingly, we can even laugh at sin and be entertained by it."[59] She warns that "sin will disappoint you"; "sin will deceive you"; "sin will dominate you"; "sin lures us with the illusion that it is the doorway to freedom"; and "sin will destroy you."[60] The church has become so comfortable with sin that she "no longer sees it as a deadly monster. Sin is more dangerous than wild bears, more deadly than blazing forest fires."[61]

As a result of this misdirection, the media now determines right and wrong, and the Bible has come to be judged by what the media portrays rather than the other way around. Christians must read Scripture more and follow the media less until Scripture once again sounds like the norm. Then they will be able to discern the propaganda and lies portrayed by the media. It is imperative to find a reliable source for news and to learn to think independently of what the media portrays.

Christians, take heart! In this atmosphere the church must remember that since its inception, every time it has looked like Christianity was about to collapse and disappear, God has raised up evangelists and pastors like Jonathan Edwards, George Whitefield, Charles Finney, Billy Sunday, R. A. Torrey, Dwight L. Moody, and Billy Graham. He has sent countless moves of the Spirit as in Azusa Street, the Charismatic movement, the Jesus Movement, and innumerable no-named evangelists who called people back to faith in God through Jesus Christ. God will not let his church disappear, but she must recover what has been surrendered to culture if she is to tell people about Jesus. She must sow holy righteousness, and see what God will do!

---

58. Jenkins, *Next Christendom*, 11.
59. DeMoss, *Holiness*, 71.
60. DeMoss, *Holiness*, 72–74.
61. DeMoss, *Holiness*, 75.

CONTEXTUALIZATION OR CAPITULATION: A STRUGGLE GONE AWRY

The Quicksand of Self-Help Christianity

One sin becoming more prevalent in the church through the media is the belief that individuals and/or groups can make themselves into the people they should be. This is the natural outcome of the free and independent spirit when Christ is limited or removed. There are thousands of books, videos, and web pages devoted to helping people in their self-improvement quest. Sometimes they hire coaches in their self-help journey. Christians used to call this operating in your own strength. Michael Horton describes much of what happens in churches as a "Christless Christianity," by which he means that the same names and correct titles are spoken, but they are removed from the "unfolding historical plot of human rebellion and divine rescue . . . Jesus [becomes a] life coach, therapist, buddy, significant other, founder of Western civilizations, political messiah, example of radical living, and countless other images."[62] As a result, people are diverted from "Christ as Redeemer from God's wrath."[63]

He warns against reducing "Christianity to good advice . . . [that] blends in perfectly with the culture of *life coaching*," and reminds us that Christianity is not merely a moral code but the true story of a loving God who was rejected by the very people he created in his image.[64] Instead of rejecting them, he sent his Son to redeem them and to reconcile them to himself. Christianity is not about people making themselves good enough for God to accept them. It is about the "historical events of God's incarnation, atonement, resurrection, ascension, and return and the exploration of their rich significance. At its heart, this story is a gospel: The Good News that God has reconciled us to himself in Christ."[65] This is something we can never do for ourselves. The danger of self-help Christianity is that it completely goes off the road. Instead of us becoming who Jesus calls us to be, he becomes what we want him to be. "What would Jesus do?" becomes nothing more than what I think a good person would do. Salvation becomes "not a matter of divine rescue from the judgment that is coming on the world but rather a matter of self-improvement in order to have your best life now."[66]

Horton has a good handle on what has come to pass in many churches. A coach can be ignored. People can still call their own plays when they want, and if things get too bad, they can always get a different coach who will tell them what they want to hear. When Jesus becomes the coach, the church loses sight of life as submitted to God in humble obedience to his commands. The church needs the Lord, not a coach, therapist, or buddy.

---

62. Horton, *Christless Christianity*, 144.
63. Horton, *Christless Christianity*, 144.
64. Horton, *Christless Christianity*, 102.
65. Horton, *Christless Christianity*, 102.
66. Horton, *Christless Christianity*, 74.

Summary

Already in the eighteenth century "leading thinkers began to argue that the ever more successful scientific project would make the 'hypothesis' of God unnecessary. Nothing exists except the material world described with ever-greater scientific precision."[67] However, reason and the science project based on the powers of the human intellect that was going to solve all of our problems and to save the world gave us instead two world wars with nerve gas and atomic bombs, economic recessions and depression, and multiple localized wars that produced agent orange and DDT. It is reasonable to conclude that it has failed, but instead of returning to God, our culture turned elsewhere. God, reason, and science have been replaced with a different center of the ever important self, which is based on personal happiness defined most often as pleasure in the here and now. Unfortunately, to a large extent, the church has capitulated by living the good life of consumerism and entertainment instead of being content to live a good life in God's holiness, righteousness, and truth with an eye to eternity.

It is obvious that in the twenty-first century the church has not transformed the culture but the culture has transformed the church. She has capitulated to the demand for self-improvement which usually means more material goods, more entertainment, more pleasure, more independence, and more rationalization. Spiritually, the church often tries to fulfill her mission to make disciples through her own human powered programs and ingenuity and often conforms to the new morality that is freed from the idea of absolute truth, where the Ten Commandments become the ten suggestions. She has largely surrendered ministry and preaching to the therapeutic model, which always entertains and tells people they are good just the way they are; consequently there is no need for change, but there has been change.

In varying degrees all Christians and churches have been evangelized by the culture and have been transformed into the culture's image. It is essential that they recognize the ways that media, politicians, corporations, and individuals influence them so that they are not controlled by the culture but can minister effectively to the people around them. This influence becomes deception, which includes self-deception, for people (including Christians) may not even know they are being misled since this is just the way things are done today. The things addressed here are not intended to make Christians feel bad or to lay a guilt trip on them, but to help them to reorient the compass, to get off the broad road, and to return to biblical thinking. In the next two chapters we will examine how cultural beliefs and actions have changed the church's interpretation of her biblical doctrines and theology.

---

67. Sider, *Evangelical Conscience*, 86.

Chapter 4

The Compromise of Theology with Culture

If you just set out to be liked, you would be prepared to compromise on anything at any time, and you would achieve nothing.

—Margaret Thatcher, Press Interview May 3, 1989[1]

In this chapter and the next we will examine ways cultural beliefs have influenced the great doctrines and theology of the Christian faith. The biblical mandate to do this is given by Jesus in Matthew 24 where his disciples ask for the sign of his coming and the end of age. Most people focus on the disasters and miraculous signs, but Jesus' warning heavily emphasizes the need for the church to be vigilant against deception. He frames his answer with it and brings it up again in the middle. Jesus knew that the world system would become adept at distorting God's truth so that even the elect could be deceived, if that were possible. The prevalence of propaganda, spiritualism, materialism, consumerism, independence, and pleasure are all evidences that this deception is happening.

Deception poses great danger to the witness of the church because by its very nature it is so difficult to discern. The good and faithful servant will be found doing *God's work in God's way*. As others have said, today American Christianity looks far too much like the culture. In this chapter we will evaluate how extensively cultural deceptions have influenced the core beliefs concerning Scripture, love, unity, godliness, judgement, and discipline. In chapter 5 we will examine additional changes that have influenced the church's understanding of sin, evil, conviction, repentance, forgiveness, justice, justification, sanctification, law, morals, prayer, and faith.

It is human nature to miss the mark. In varying degrees and in various ways every person has missed God's wonderful ways. This is not new. What is different is the pervasiveness of the media and the deception it promotes. The church must not perpetuate cultural error but be free to be transformed in mind, body, spirit, and soul to love God and to be like Jesus. But it is impossible to change behaviors and beliefs if people are not even aware of the need for change. If the church wants revival and reformation, she must return to the ancient, godly path.

1. Moncrieff, "Interview for Press Association."

You may find that some things will convict you and others may trouble you. Hopefully you will find yourself in agreement with most of what is recorded here. Peter Gillquist has challenged the church that all of her good works, evangelism, and programs have not slowed this country's headlong rush to self-destruction. The church can no longer afford to indulge in the twenty-first-century mindset that everything is okay and all people deserve to be comfortable and worry free. The place to begin is with Holy Scripture since it lays the foundation of all Christian belief.

Some Twenty-First-Century Cultural Influences on Christian Theology

Remove the Guardrail of Holy Scripture and Go off the Cliff

A guardrail is placed along the side of roads in areas where there is potential for great danger. Scripture is God's guardrail to keep his people from great harm. If it is jettisoned, there is no end to the perils into which they can fall. In the age of Providence, God's word, the Holy Scripture, reigned supreme with little to challenge it except the human condition and the hardness of a person's heart. In the Reformation era, Protestant churches wrote several confessions to describe what they believed about Scripture. From them we can tell that the guardrail was firmly in place. The Scots Confession of 1560 affirmed both the Old and New Testaments as the written word of God whose author was the Holy Spirit. These Scriptures contained everything necessary for the salvation and perfecting of the people of God. These Scriptures were not open to any public or private interpretation but had to be interpreted by other passages of Scripture which were clear (2 Pet 1:20–21). This confession stated that "we dare not receive or admit any interpretation which is contrary to any principal point of our faith, or to any other plain text of Scripture, or to the rule of love," and "we believe and confess the Scriptures of God sufficient to instruct and make perfect the man of God, so do we affirm and avow their authority to be from God, and not to depend on men or angels."[2]

The Belgic Confession of 1561 (written for Belgium and the Netherlands) declared that "this word of God was not sent nor delivered by the will of men, but that holy men of God spoke, being moved by the Holy Spirit, as Peter says." Furthermore, they distinguished between the things men wrote and the Scriptures, which they considered divine. It did not matter how great a name they had or what position they held or that it was a well-known council. Everything was to be compared to the truth found in Scripture, and if the two did not agree, it was the ideas of men and not Scripture that was to be rejected.

Their stand was, "Therefore we reject with all our hearts everything that does not agree with this infallible rule, as we are taught to do by the apostles when they say, 'Test the spirits to see if they are of God;' and also, 'If anyone comes to you and does

---

2. Knox et al., Articles 18, 19, and 20, in "The Scots Confession, 398–99.

not bring this teaching, do not receive him into your house."³ If the teachings and doctrines of people did not conform to the clear teaching of Scripture, they were to be rejected by the church. These are important concepts that would come to play a large role as the Enlightenment engulfed the culture.

The Second Helvetic Confession of 1561 (German-speaking Swiss) affirmed, "We believe and confess the canonical Scriptures of the holy prophets and apostles of both Testaments [the Old and New] to be the true word of God, and to have sufficient authority of themselves, not of men. For God himself spoke to the fathers, prophets, apostles, and still speaks to us through the Holy Scriptures." Additionally they believed that "Scripture Teaches Fully All Godliness. We judge, therefore, that from these Scriptures are to be derived true wisdom and godliness, the reformation and government of churches; as also instruction in all duties of piety; and, to be short, the confirmation of doctrines, and the rejection of all errors, with all exhortations." They took seriously the command to test the spirits to see of what sort they are, and they rejected what did not conform to Scripture. "We therefore detest all the heresies of Artemon, the Manichaeans, the Valentinians, of Cerdon, and the Marcionites, who denied that the Scriptures proceeded from the Holy Spirit; or did not accept some parts of them, or interpolated and corrupted them."⁴ Today, there is a move in the church to recover these voices that were discarded with little discussion about reasons why the early Christians rejected them.⁵ The recovery of these long forgotten voices has more to do with the victim mentality than with knowing God's truth.

Nearly a century later the Westminster Confession of Faith (1643–1649) was written to call the church back to the Reformation principles. It begins with a discussion of Scripture, for if the church's view of Scripture is accurate, she will function with greater truth and clarity. The following are some of its declarations. The sixty-six books of the Old and New Testaments are "given by inspiration of God, to be the rule of faith and life." "The authority of the Holy Scripture, for which it ought to be believed, and obeyed, dependeth not upon the testimony of any man, or church; but wholly upon God (who is truth itself) the author thereof: and therefore it is to be received, because it is the word of God." "Our full persuasion and assurance of the infallible truth and divine authority thereof, is from the inward work of the Holy Spirit bearing witness by and with the word in our hearts." Additionally, they proclaimed that the infallible rule of interpretation was other Scripture where the meaning was clearer, and Scripture may not be taken to mean

---

3. de Brès, Articles 3, 5, and 7, in "The Belgic Confession," 408–9.

4. Bullinger, Chapters 1.1, 2, 3, and 8, in "The Second Helvetic Confessions," 460–61. They cite 2 Tim 3:16–17, 1 Tim 3:14–15, and 1 Thess 2:13. Some of these theories said Jesus was only a man; others said Jesus was God and no man at all—he was only a spirit. Some claimed to have higher knowledge than what was in Scripture. A contemporary example can be found in Dan Brown's *The Da Vinci Code* on alleged departures from the scriptural presentation of Jesus. This is a complete work of fiction, but many were fascinated with the possibilities of an alternative interpretation of Jesus as can be seen in the popularity of the book and the movie of the same name.

5. Two of these are the Gospel of Thomas and the Gospel of Philip.

conflicting things because *the author is the Holy Spirit*, who does not contradict himself. Therefore, "all controversies of religion are to be determined, and all decrees of councils, opinions of ancient writers, doctrines of men, and private spirits, are to be examined, and in whose sentence we are to rest, can be no other but the Holy Spirit speaking in the Scripture."[6] The common thread among all reformers was belief that God through the Holy Spirit wrote the Holy Bible and that it was not simply the writings of men. Therefore, every teaching and proclamation or belief must be tested against the infallible word of God, which meant to them the written word.

Although the Enlightenment began to chip away at the traditional view of Scripture through intellectual endeavors discussed in chapter 1, the prominence of the Providential view could be seen in Modernity as late as 1934 in Nazi Germany when a group of pastors led by Karl Barth and calling themselves the Confessional Synod of the German Evangelical Church gathered to write The Theological Declaration of Barmen. Their purpose for writing this declaration was to appeal to the churches that had joined Hitler's national church to return to their roots. This state-controlled church combined Christianity with patriotism, purity of the Aryan race, and persecution of Jews.

The Barmen was a call to remain loyal to the Scriptures and the Confessions. It also challenged all who called themselves Christians to "try the spirits whether they are of God!" They urged the German state churches to "prove also the words of the Confessional Synod of the German Evangelical Church to see whether they agree with Holy Scripture and with the confessions of the fathers." The criteria to be used to determine truth is Scripture, and if anyone is promoting ideas contrary to the totality of Scripture you are not to listen to him or her. They pleaded with the churches following Hitler, "But if you find that we are taking our stand upon Scripture, then let no fear or temptation keep you from treading with us the path of faith and obedience to the word of God [Scripture], in order that God's people be of one mind upon earth." They took their stand on Scripture, "I will never leave you, nor forsake you," and "Fear not, little flock for it is your Father's good pleasure to give you the kingdom."[7]

Although they did not specifically describe what they meant by Holy Scripture, it is clear that they stood with the interpretation put forth by the Reformers. For them, faith and obedience to Scripture was the paramount principle for unity and the experience of God's promises. This is crucial for what would happen in many American churches in the late twentieth and early twenty-first centuries.

The reasoned thinking of Modernity left us empty and fearful of nuclear weapons and chemical pollution. Postmodernity entered with its emphasis on the autonomous self and pursuit of pleasure and provided the way for many churches and church goers to break away from their sacred bond with the Holy Scriptures. The popularity of Foucault

---

6. Chapter 1.2, 4, 5, and 8, in "The Westminster Confession," 606–7.

7. Barth et al., Chapter 1, in "The Theological Declaration of Barmen," 505. These can be found in 1 John 4:1, Heb 13:5, and Luke 12:32.

and Derrida in the 1950s brought the deconstruction of the language and left us with only context for determining the meaning of words, which, of course, was impossible to know with certainty for the ancient writings. The ever-present media brought the new ideas rapidly into the homes and daily lives of everyday people much more quickly and more effectively than the scholastic ideas of Modernity in the nineteenth century. People were primed and ready for pursuit of self-made happiness.

A major shift occurred among many leaders in mainline churches. This shift can be seen in the PCUSA's addition of the Confession of 1967 to its "Book of Confessions." Of the Bible it records the new thinking, "The Scriptures, given under the guidance of the Holy Spirit, are nevertheless the words of men, conditioned by the language, thought forms, and literary fashions of the places and times at which they were written. They reflect the views of life, history, and the cosmos which were then current."[8] God, the Holy Spirit, was no longer the author but a guide only. The writings were those of men and reflected only their interpretation of events surrounding them. This left the door wide open for new interpretations of Scripture which included the freedom to ignore or to reinterpret those passages that seemed to restrict the pursuit of self-independence and pleasure of this age.

This new idea of men as the authors of the Bible has led to all manner of divisions and has set many churches loose on the sea of cultural capitulation to drift aimlessly without a rudder to steer them or without a sail by which the Holy Spirit can move them (Eph 4:11–16). Among a growing number of churches Jesus is no longer the anchor that keeps them from drifting from the God of the Bible and the Great Commission of making disciples. The engine, which powered great historical and traditional mission work to make disciples, has all but been dismantled so that much of the emphasis today is only on those areas of reconciliation recognized and approved by popular culture, such as social justice, rights of individuals, feeding and clothing the poor, and ecological issues.

There were congregations and individual Christians who sought to be faithful to the traditional view of Scripture, but they often rejected the scholarship needed to know accurately what that was. Where this has happened the church tends to go with what she feels or thinks she knows about the faith without seriously studying the Scriptures, all the while claiming the leading of the Holy Spirit. However, how is she to test the spirits (1 John 4:1) if she has not diligently studied the Scripture against which she is to judge them?

Contrary to what it may seem, the church does not need to fear scholarship. It is not the tools as much as it is the preconceptions behind the use of the tools which determine the results. The tools used in belief that God wrote the Bible and that miracles and prophecy are possible will produce very different results than those same tools used in the belief that it is only men's writings and nothing supernatural ever happened or could happen.

8. "The Confession of 1967," 9.29, in "Book of Confessions," 257.

Consider these words which Kirsopp Lake wrote in the first half of the twentieth century. Although he contributed to the debunking of Scripture, Lake warned the "educated persons" that the fundamentalists[9] had it right when it came to "the Bible and the corpus theologicum of the Church."[10] However, he considered fundamentalists to be uneducated and to hold only partially to the "theology which was once universally held by all Christians," and asked, "How many were there, for instance, in Christian churches in the eighteenth century who doubted the infallible inspiration of all Scripture?" He answered, "A few perhaps, but very few. No, the fundamentalist may be wrong; I think that he is. But it is we [the new intellectuals] who have departed from the tradition, not he."[11]

In his statements, Lake revealed two things. He viewed fundamentalists as uneducated, and hence they represented less than the universal beliefs held by Christians throughout history. Additionally he admitted that it boiled down to what a person chose to believe. It was not the fundamentalist, however incomplete his or her knowledge might have been, who departed the faith but the scholar who arrived at different understandings due to his or her unbelief. History stands with the fundamentalist and the evangelical.

Throughout Christian history the Bible has been considered reliable and accurate. It is only when people refuse to believe what it affirms that inconsistencies arise. The church need not be afraid to take scholarship seriously as Os Guinness challenges Evangelicals in his book *Fit Bodies Fat Minds*. The solution is not to reject all scholarship and the tools it has given us but to use them to challenge the scholars on the presumptions they bring to their work and which lead them to all sorts of errors. When faith-based communities use these same tools, they have a better understanding of their Bible and are empowered with Holy Spirit-given knowledge to live holy and blameless lives (Eph 1:4) and to answer the questions of the culture surrounding them (1 Pet 3:15). This knowledge can only be found in Scripture whose author is God.[12]

Where Holy Scripture is considered to be only the writings of men that reflect the thoughts and beliefs of a previous age, the church becomes free to design for herself what she will think and believe in this age. Christians must take seriously the study of the Scriptures like the Bereans of Acts 17. When they do not, they are open to being deceived by what *sounds* right. Increasingly, in this age, due to

---

9. Fundamentalists with a capital "F" refers to an ultra-conservative group of Christians who believed in the literal interpretation of the Bible. Christians who are conservative in their beliefs and evangelicals may also be called fundamentalists with a lower case "f" because they believe in the fundamentals of the faith.

10. Lake, *Religion of Yesterday and Tomorrow*, 62.

11. Lake, *Religion of Yesterday and Tomorrow*, 61.

12. Christians must be careful here not to assign special powers to the words themselves. That would be tantamount to casting spells and incantations where the person only has to say the right words and a thing happens. The power is not in the words but in the author of those words as he sees fit to answer them which will always be according to his good purpose and for his glory.

the pervasive influence of the media, the beliefs of Christians are being shaped to reflect beliefs of the world around them much more quickly and thoroughly than Christians of previous eras. This results in their faith being reduced to the lowest common denominator upon which all can agree.

Most are in agreement that Scripture points people to Christ. However, they cannot agree on what that means. Jesus may be a good man, a teacher, a prophet, or the Son of God. Furthermore, what he requires is often left open to private interpretation, which usually conforms to the culture's belief in relative truth. First John 4:1 fades from the Bibles they use. Christians no longer test the spirits because they have nothing by which they can test them except the culture's standards and personal beliefs. Below we will examine the effects of how such interpretations and handling of Scripture have set the church adrift on the sea of public opinion.

The Sinkhole of Victims' Rights

A phenomenon has swept this culture that makes everyone a victim of some kind of oppression whether it is parents, governments, schools, or businesses to name a few. Although it is not directly what we think of as a theological issue, it has had a devastating impact on the church's theology and great doctrines and especially her understanding of love. Morality and victim's rights are inversely linked. The decline in morality gives people more reasons to feel like victims: first, because greater immorality produces greater woundedness in more people, and second, people perceive themselves as victims when anyone tries to speak out against the degeneration. N. T. Wright notes that as the culture's moral literacy drops it accepts and promotes things not allowed by this culture even thirty to fifty years ago, let alone allowed by the Bible.

Often the church has not taken a stand against such changes, and many churchgoers have agreed with the culture. The church is being changed by the very culture it is trying to transform. Wright believes "the only moral high ground we now recognize is that occupied by the victim, or someone who claims to be a victim." He explains, "We instinctively feel sorry for someone who's left out of the party, someone who doesn't yet seem persuaded that there's an answer to their problems, someone who has not managed yet to abandon their pride and accept the free forgiveness offered in the gospel." He concludes, "Grand-sounding statements of universalism are offered on this basis; it cannot be right, we are told, for the redeemed to enjoy their heaven as long as one soul is left in hell."[13]

C. S. Lewis also identifies this victim mentality in *The Great Divorce* when he describes people who want to make themselves victims and who refuse God's grace, mercy, and love offered through Jesus and the cross. Concerning the doctrine of eternity, these folks object to the belief that some people will spend eternity in heaven

---

13. Wright, *Justice of God*, 140.

while others will be in hell. Instead of grace, they claim their rights, which include the right to accuse anyone and everything that does not happily admit everyone to God's new world.[14] Increasingly, in the name of love and compassion, the church has capitulated. Even if Christians say they agree with the biblical view of hell and salvation, their actions and words often betray them.

The emphasis today of not offending anyone (and hence making them a victim) overrides the commitment to make disciples for Jesus. Wright observes, "Of course, by thus appealing to our sense of feeling sorry for the one left outside the party, we put that person in a position of peculiar power, able to exercise in *perpetuity a veto on the triumph of grace*" (italics are mine).[15] Contemporary thinking is that any doctrine, indeed, any Scripture that puts people outside the kingdom of God must be restrained or abandoned altogether in order to make people feel good about themselves. The church has acquiesced to this way of thinking and feeling by dropping the doctrines of evil, sin, hell, judgment, the wrath of God, and to a large extent the doctrines of holiness, righteousness, and the need for Jesus to be the only way to God.

The Roadblock of the World's Love Confused with God's Command to Love

The culture of victimization asks for a God of love, but this love is merely human love that is increasingly self-gratifying, and the church has largely complied. When was the last time you heard a sermon preached on the wrath of God, judgment and hell, the reprobate mind, or the need for discipline? Many churchgoers today want a "God of love" who never disciplines and rarely declares anything approved by culture to be wrong, and the church has gladly given them one, but scholars warn us of this danger.

Michael Horton cautions that where God is portrayed as the "extravagant lover . . . . love overwhelms law." Law has fallen from favor with twenty-first-century Americans and has been replaced with a new form of grace (to be discussed below), which says that God would do nothing to offend anyone because he sets aside requirements and duty, and simply welcomes the prodigal child home. In varying degrees, God becomes predictable, and predictably "everything is okay—with little or no mention of Christ's self-sacrifice as the only way of reconciliation."[16] In this view, God's love does not need God's holiness, righteousness, and justice, and if it can so easily ignore them, "then Christ's death on the cross seems like a cruel waste."[17] Horton calls this a "human-centered approach" in which God and creation exist "for us to consume for our happiness" and which leads to anything and everything

---

14. Lewis, "The Great Divorce", 320–25.
15. Wright, *Justice of God*, 140.
16. Horton, *Christless Christianity*, 56.
17. Horton, *Christless Christianity*, 56.

that feels good in the moment, without any thought that it might offend God or be harmful to us in the long run.[18]

Lewis warns us of another danger of this false love and reminds us of the need to replace it with holy love in this dialogue taken from *The Great Divorce*:

> "But someone must say in general what's been unsaid among you this many a year: that love, as mortals understand the word, isn't enough . . ."
>
> "The saying is almost too hard for us."
>
> "Ah, but it's cruel not to say it. They that know have grown afraid to speak. That is why sorrows that used to purify now only fester."
>
> "Keats was wrong, then, when he said he was certain of the holiness of the heart's affections."
>
> "I doubt he knew exactly what he meant. But you and I must be clear. There is but one good; that is God. Everything else is good when it looks to Him and bad when it turns from Him. And the higher and mightier it is in the natural order, the more demoniac it will be if it rebels . . . . The false religion of lust is baser than the false religion of mother-love or patriotism or art, but lust is less likely to be made into a religion."[19]

Lewis wrote this before the unleashed age of television where sex is used to sell everything from aftershave to cars. Today he might modify that last sentence. Lewis is telling us that human love falls far short of God's love. Love as humanity understands it, apart from God, cannot purify or heal. It can only put a Band-Aid on a wound without cleaning it out, leaving it to fester and to infect the entire body. The more powerful the source of the distortion of love is, the greater the influence it will have for destruction. The media-led culture, and not God, has become the most powerful determiner of the perception of right and wrong in this world of love. This has happened not simply because the pleasure the world offers is so powerful, but because the church has often changed her message to accommodate what the culture wants.

Lewis reminds the church that an incomplete view of God's love is just that—incomplete. While no one this side of heaven will ever have the complete view, the church has succumbed to the victim mentality of no one left behind. It has acquiesced to nearly every behavior that used to be called sin, and has *rushed* to comfort people in their distress that sin causes before the Holy Spirit can bring about the good for which God planned to use that suffering (2 Cor 7:9–10; 1 Pet 1:6–7).

The prophet Hosea warned that sowing the wind (living for self-pleasure and parties) will reap a whirlwind of problems. But he also promised that when God's people sow God's righteousness they will reap his unfailing love, his genuine, holy love, and not the world's cheap imitation. The church must remember that the psalmist (Ps 89) assures God's people that his steadfast love goes forth for his people out of

---

18. Horton, *Christless Christianity*, 56.
19. Lewis, "The Great Divorce," 349–50.

the foundation of his righteousness and justice (beyond social justice). Remove the foundation of any building and the structure collapses. Love without God's righteous standard and justice is collapsing all around us.[20]

The Missing Guardrails of Holy Unity and Godliness

In the Psalms, God says, "How good and pleasant it is when brothers live together in unity" (133:1, NIV). This unity is more than simply keeping the peace. It comes about by agreement on God's truth as found in the Scriptures. Such unity elicits God's blessing, "even life forevermore" (133:3b, NIV). Even the best folks of culture and the church have missed it due in large part to the staunch American independent spirit that encourages people to make their own truth.

Peter Gillquist identifies two ways God's people have missed it. First, there is a lack of unity. Second, holiness or godliness is thought of only as a matter of correct behavior which is often defined by the media through its technological tools.[21] Today many people, including Christians, call for unity but have no standard on which to base it. They mean only that everything must be accepted, or that they simply (and always) agree to disagree. There is little reference to anything beyond what seems right in their own eyes. The Bible usually gets relegated to an ancient myth that can easily be ignored when what it affirms becomes inconvenient. The result is that only independent human thinking is left to unite us, and with each person making his or her own truth, the church or the culture should not be surprised when unity breaks down.

Similarly, the guardrail of godliness disappears when the church confuses "goodness" with godliness or holy living. In a desire for a loving God, Christians often choose a "gentle Jesus meek and mild" over the Jesus who drove the money changers out of the temple and went toe-to-toe with the Pharisees, calling them white-washed-sepulchers. Today, goodness is connected with the new morals and may mean recycling, driving an electric car, shoveling the neighbor's driveway, feeding the poor, fighting for the rights of the oppressed, or remembering someone's birthday. None of these require a transformation of the inner life which results when a person comes to God through faith in Jesus Christ. Good deeds always seem to conform to what the media tells us is correct, and anyone can do them apart from God. Neither God nor his word is needed in the current understanding of goodness. Sadly, this has been carried into the church. How often do you hear "but she is a good person" spoken in the church to defend the wrong actions of believers and non-believers, as if being a good person is enough to get them to heaven?

Closely related to goodness is morality. Like goodness, the church must be careful not to confuse morality with godliness. Morality is determined culturally by what seems right in people's eyes and according to their way of thinking. Morality changes in every

---

20. For a more in-depth discussion of God's love see chapters 10 and 11 and appendix 3.
21. Gillquist, *Why We Haven't Changed*, 32.

age and almost weekly in this culture. These changes rapidly become accepted as the new morality even without an act of Congress or a ruling by the Supreme Court.

On the other hand, godliness remains constant because God is unchanging. Godliness is the fruits of the spirit: love, joy, peace, kindness, gentleness, faithfulness, longsuffering, and self-control. It seeks first the kingdom of God and his righteousness. It is holy, compassionate, and humble, and places others first. It does not harbor bitterness or anger. It forgives. Godliness is not anxious or worried. It seeks true peace, not merely an absence of conflict which can only lead to bullies controlling the circumstances. Godliness is committed to God's truth. It is faithful to God, spouse, and children. It honors parents, respects people and their property, and is honest. Godliness reflects the consistently Holy God.

There is one more distinction between morality and godliness. Morality is taught; godliness is caught. Morality is a function of pleasing people; godliness lives to please God. A person can be raised to know the difference between right and wrong, but never have a relationship with God. It is all head knowledge. In the end it profits him or her nothing, but to others, the person looks really good. On the other hand, godliness can only be caught through a relationship with Jesus Christ. It results in death being swallowed up in life, but in the here and now, the world may not think this looks good at all. The goodness and morality of the world wants the blessings of God without the commitment to serve God. It wants God to give them good things but on its terms. Holy living often goes against what many people think they want, and their response may not always be pretty.

In trying to work through the problems that arise in pursuing unity and holy living, the church tends to swing on a pendulum between two extremes. The first is legalism, which imposes man-made rules for righteousness. The second is licentiousness, which leads to immorality and rebelliousness that adopts an "I'm okay; you're okay" mentality that either denies or dismisses sin. According to Gillquist, both legalism and licentiousness promote a growing tendency to focus on "a purely individual walk with Christ, with little or no attention to the role of the Church in firm support and *gracious* discipline" (italics are mine), which produces "homeless Christians."[22] Whatever justification Christians give, their staunch independence is destroying unity and holiness in their churches.

The Missing Guardrail of Judgment

There are two kinds of judgment that are largely ignored or misunderstood by today's church. The first is God's judgment of sin. This doctrine has fallen from favor in this postmodern age. Gillquist explains that the church has made "living the good life" synonymous with the Christian life and victory over darkness and writes, "The smell

---

22. Gillquist, *Why We Haven't Changed*, 32–33, 53–54.

of smoke and fire that adorned the robes of the ancients has all but disappeared from our vestments. We have been tamed."[23] Most churchgoers, including pastors, would think this is a good thing, but this attitude has stripped the church of her unity and authority and hence, her ability to bring about change in the people inside her own walls, let alone the people outside totally immersed in the culture.

The second kind of judgment is human judgment of other humans. In the Postmodern age of Technopoly, judging others has become taboo. Like the culture, the church has decided that God alone (if he or she exists) should judge people's lives (if he or she chooses to do so, but it is doubtful). After all, Jesus said (Matt 7:1), "Do not judge." Robert Jeffress observes that this interpretation of judgment usually results in churchgoers and church leaders who pride themselves "that everyone is welcome in our congregation," meaning that morality is not addressed in any significant way that differs from the culture at large.[24]

In the Sermon on the Mount, when taken in context, Jesus' charge not to judge does not mean God's people are not to judge people's words and actions. Preceding this part of the sermon, Jesus commands his people not to try to serve two masters but to seek first the kingdom of God and his righteousness. Both of these require judgment. In the verses that follow, he instructs his disciples to identify the dogs and the pigs and the narrow road and gate as opposed to the broad road and the wide gate. Additionally, they must recognize the false prophets by the fruit they bear. All of this requires judgment. What Jesus did say was that "those offering correction must already have dealt with sin in their own lives."[25] Remove that log from your eye so you can see clearly to remove the splinter from your neighbor's eye.

The apostle John helps to clarify how proper judgment works. In John 5:25 (NIV) Jesus says, "By myself, I can do nothing; I judge only as I hear, and my judgment is just, for I seek not to please myself but him who sent me." Perhaps John 7:24 (NIV) sheds the most light on this seemingly absolute command not to judge, "Stop judging by mere appearances, and make a right judgment." "Do not judge" refers to the condemnation of people and to judging according to your own personal standards. It does not restrict judging according to what God says in Scripture, and all of it must be considered, not just the parts that support what you want to say, do, or believe. Picking and choosing which parts you will follow is like the pharisaical practice of judging by the clothes people wear, the power positions they hold, and the liturgical practices they follow. Jesus did only what he heard the Father telling him. The church must recover the practice of holy judgment, which is not done according to what *seems* right to a person or group but is practiced according to God's holy standard. Judgment must begin in the house of God and among his own

---

23. Gillquist, *Why We Haven't Changed*, 52.
24. Jeffress, *Grace Gone Wild*, 181.
25. Jeffress, *Grace Gone Wild*, 194.

people before it can venture outside the church.[26] The Bible and the Holy Spirit are her guides, and they will not contradict each other.

The Missing Guardrail of Discipline

Since discipline requires judgment, where judgment is disallowed, discipline declines. The two exist or decline together. A major blow to discipline occurred in the early years of postmodernity with the publishing of the 1957 edition of Dr. Spock's *Baby and Child Care*.[27] Many have interpreted his work to mean that children should be allowed to choose nearly everything for themselves. Discipline underwent a dramatic change, the effects of which are increasing with the passing of time. These changes have not been limited to the discipline of children, but have invaded every facet of culture, including the church. One reason the church has opted not to discipline is that past models were punitive, unnecessarily harsh, and lacked redemption, reconciliation, and restoration as their goal. However, the answer to overly harsh discipline is not no discipline at all.

In reaction to the harshness, the church has swung to the opposite extreme of accepting everything, which becomes a license to do whatever the person wants regardless of the cost. Ronald Sider thinks that the church must recover holy discipline in order "to end the scandal of cheap grace and gross disobedience"[28] that can be found in the twenty-first-century church. In the past fifty years, the church has succumbed to the culture's understanding of love, forgiveness, and mercy. This mentality often declines to discipline. It justifies this choice with the argument, "If Jesus died to forgive people their sins, then they are forgiven. Who am I to tell them what is right and wrong? After all, I sin too, and I am not to judge."

The heart of the issue is this, "If I call out other's sins, then they might do the same against me and that would make me uncomfortable, or they might react negatively by calling me names and stop being my friend, which would also make me uncomfortable." In a subtle way churchgoers have agreed to forego discipline and to ignore each other's sins and have rationalized this by calling them a person's failings or disorders. Who can fault someone for these? But Jeffress insists that "discipline is necessary to maintain the witness of the church" and asks, "When a non-Christian sees little difference in the morality, business ethics, response to tragedy, or attitudes

---

26. In addition to the passages mentioned above, see Matt 7:2–5; 1 Pet 4:17; and 1 Cor 2:15–16.

27. Spock, *Baby and Child Care*. Initially Spock was concerned with the practice of strict regimens for feeding and caring for infants. Wisdom at that time said to feed an infant only every four hours and not to hold the child when he or she cries. Spock argued that infants cry when they need something and should be fed and nurtured whenever they cry. This was subsequently expanded to say that children should not be spanked or in some cases they should not be disciplined in any way. It is easy to see the trend that has developed since Spock wrote his book.

28. Sider, *Evangelical Conscience*, 109.

of Christians compared to non-Christians, what motivation does that person have to take up his or her cross and follow Christ?"[29]

Ironically, contrary to this new, no-discipline ethic, the culture has been disciplining Christians to privatize their faith and to change their doctrines to accommodate the culture.[30] This has crept into every facet of life from our homes to the public square and from our workplaces to the church. Today's discipline rejects the old forms and endorses a kinder and gentler way that allegedly builds self-esteem. All the while, there is a not so subtle and not so gentle disciplinary effect of the Information Age that Christians must recognize. The culture's discipline trains people not to question anything or anyone except those who claim to know the truth. This discipline creates in people the desire to consume more and more and elevates the self as the source of truth and knowledge and as the object of worship. Anyone who goes against this way of thinking will be disciplined by mocking, name-calling, ostracism by friends and family, loss of job, and increasingly by institutional and governmental action.

The result of this new understanding of discipline is that the church has largely forgotten that love, forgiveness, grace, and mercy are not unqualified get-out-of-jail-free cards automatically applied to all. The Christian life requires repentance, confession, commitment, and change that come from self-discipline and corporate discipline under the direction of the Holy Bible and the Holy Spirit. Godly discipline is made enormously more difficult by the deception to which the heart is vulnerable, but discipline is needed to maintain God's holy love as well as his holy justice so that God's people can learn to be like Jesus—holy. But instead of disciplining her people, the church has been disciplined by the culture to keep her faith private and not to act differently from the culture around her lest she be called a fanatic or an extremist. Instead of seeking God's approval, she seeks the approval of the culture.

Where discipline has been practiced, it is often done poorly. Roger Olsen identifies two major areas of faulty discipline within the church. The first problem is that many have given up on discipline and holiness as discussed above. The second area of flawed discipline is that churches swing on the pendulum to land at the other extreme from judging nothing to judging everyone and everything. They "shore up the boundaries and denounce the flagrant sinners outside the church, on its margins, and inside the fellowship."[31] This group clearly identifies and can judge right from wrong, but rather than using discipline to bring the person to repentance in order to restore him or her to God and the church, they condemn him or her. Olsen recommends a third way to discipline, which is to accept people into fellowship "who admit their sins and

---

29. Jeffress, *Grace Gone Wild*, 180.

30. For more on the culture disciplining the church see "The Missing Guardrails of Sanctification and Law" below.

31. Olsen, *How to Be Evangelical*, 174.

seek God's help to overcome them *without affirming their sins*" (italics are mine).[32] This becomes complicated.

Two difficulties can occur when people in the congregation come to know people living outside of the normally accepted boundaries of Christianity. The first struggle is with the temptation to overlook their sins because they are "good" people, and discipline makes everyone uncomfortable, so why do it? This argument appeals to the current thinking on Christian love and compassion for support. It is reinforced by our victim mentality and the culture's interpretation of love that rarely disciplines unless it is to discipline those who think differently than it does. So it has the feel of being the right thing to do. The church must always remember that at the human level, being nice or being good does not remove the need for repentance of sin, for salvation, and for sanctification which involves godly discipline. That goes for all people whether inside, on the margins, or outside of the church.

The second struggle that may occur when the church welcomes people from all sorts of lifestyles is that she may actually then begin to affirm there is nothing wrong with the sin of these folks. Olsen reminds us that "the problem is not being a sinner, which we all are; the problem is calling evil good."[33] In varying degrees Christians do this when they judge their own shortcomings to be the "lesser" sins such as anxiety, worry, fear, unthankfulness, gossip, slander, and pride, to name only a few.[34] It is human nature to overlook personal sins while noticing the sins of others. Hence, Jesus admonishes people to remove the log from their own eyes before they try to remove the splinter from another's eye.

We must remember that affirmation leads to acceptance and approval. In this age, broken human nature, spurred on by the "I'm okay; you're okay" culture, has elevated to new levels the acceptance and approval of sin as normal. It is no wonder that the list which now calls evil good grows exponentially every year to include practically everything under the sun. Without the guardrail of godly discipline, the church is in grave danger of going off the road and plunging down a steep cliff. The results will be disastrous.

Summary

In our culture, the individual person has become compartmentalized into mind, emotion, and will using whichever paradigm works for a given situation. This change has been reflected in the truth, traditions, and doctrines of the Christian faith, but what began as a slow trickle in the seventeenth and eighteenth centuries has reached flood level in the twenty-first century. Richard Lovelace asserts that evangelicalism became

32. Olsen, *How to Be Evangelical*, 182.
33. Olsen, *How to Be Evangelical*, 182.
34. For more information on sins acceptable to Christians, read Bridges, *Respectable Sins*; Stanley, *Landmines in the Path of the Believer*; and Cook, *Seven: The Deadly Sins and the Beatitudes*.

one of the casualties when it lost its focus on the changed heart "for three different false pieties . . . emotional tastes . . . will power and works . . . [and] notional orthodoxy."[35] The deterioration can only be prevented by the Spirit's penetration of the heart and the transformation of the entire person "by balancing affective, intellectual and volitional parameters. . . . thus any movement of awakening which does not aim steadily at a comprehensive renewal of the heart registering at all these levels of the personality is bound to miscarry."[36] But the church has grown accustomed to the division and has become far too comfortable with sin.

While revival and reformation are high on the priorities list of churches seeking to maintain themselves in this time of seeming religious downturn, it remains God's work. Christians seeking to be obedient to the Great Commission (to take the gospel into all the world, making disciples, baptizing them, and teaching them to obey everything Jesus has commanded) must remember that revival and reformation are products of the Holy Spirit working in the hearts of God's people to make them holy. As time has passed, the church, including evangelicalism (although usually to a lesser extent), has capitulated to the culture's demand for entertainment, self-help, and a god who reflects identically whoever or whatever the individual says he or she is. We have examined how this looks in the rejection of the divine authority of Scripture and in the way the church understands love, unity, judgment, and discipline, but it does not stop with these. In the next chapter we will examine additional compromises of the great doctrines of the faith, such as conviction and repentance of sins, justification, and sanctification.

---

35. Lovelace, *Dynamics of Spiritual Life*, 250–51.
36. Lovelace, *Dynamics of Spiritual Life*, 251.

Chapter 5

More Consequences of Compromising with Culture

Be careful not to compromise what you want most for what you want now.

—Zig Ziglar[1]

Several paradigm shifts in the way humans think and process information have occurred since the inception of this nation. The Enlightenment's proposal that says all people are good and not sinful as Scripture tells us has taken root. Modernity has elevated the human mind and has provided the rationale used by many to reject the supernatural, prophesy, and much of Scripture. Darwin has given us an alternative to creation, and modern medicine has enabled us to forego prayer when sick. Postmodernity has placed the autonomous self at the center of life, free to choose its own truth, which has further removed us from God's truth, salvation through Jesus, and the Christian doctrines of hell, judgment, and condemnation. And technology has turned these innovative ways of thinking into a new religion.

Technology along with consumerism has promised the good life here and now and has turned our focus away from eternity. Technology promises transformation as it makes us gods in our own right through our access to endless information and limitless possibilities, causing us to feel powerful. Added to that, it saves us from boredom by the never ending stream of entertainment and the new things it creates to make our lives easier. Corporations and governments hire evangelists whose job it is to get us to buy their product and to bring us on board with their cause. Forbes posted, "An evangelist is a person who builds up support for a given technology, and then establishes it as a standard in the given industry."[2] This article further describes the position as a lifestyle in which the person makes history, converts people, and exposes them to new things. They work anywhere and at any time to change the world for which they receive a tithe. They do this by creating stories that are real, transparent, and stir passion. They adapt quickly to new situations, are opinionated, and connect the dots for others to see.[3] A new religion has been born using Christian terminology and practice

---

1. Quoted in Edwards, "Fighting, Family and Finding Peace," para. 9.
2. Priestley, "Every Tech Company," para. 2.
3. Priestley, "Every Tech Company" paras. 6–11.

but without God, and few are aware that it has happened—especially not the church when she apologizes for her beliefs and practices.

With the split of the church in nineteenth-century Modernity, the doctrines that united the church came under scrutiny and became the source of divisions. This continues to this day. We have already explored how she has been influenced by cultural beliefs and how this has changed the core beliefs about Scripture, God's love, unity, judgment, and discipline. In this chapter we will look at additional beliefs she has conceded to the culture.

More Casualties in the Compromise with Cultural Beliefs

The Lost Perspective of Sin and Evil

Christians who buy into the no-person-left-behind mentality have pushed aside the seriousness of sin. Unlike Paul in Romans 6, they tend to revel in the fact that all people are sinners. In fact, this brand of Christianity usually allows a person to continue in his or her personal sin preferences after believing in Jesus.[4] The church must recover the doctrine of evil in order to bring back the concept of God's righteous wrath against people's sin. The church must understand that God's wrath is never "reckless and irrational passion" but is "a consistent opposition to sin and evil." God's "wrath is a necessary reaction of a loving and Holy God, a good and beautiful God, to evil. God's wrath is *a temporary and just verdict on sin and evil*" (italics are mine).[5]

In order to recover the doctrine of evil the church must first understand what it is. N. T. Wright describes evil as "the force of anti-creation [and] anti-life, the force which opposes and seeks to deface and destroy God's good world of space, time, and matter, and above all God's image-bearing human creatures."[6] Evil is already at work in the human heart and manifests itself in people's attitudes and actions. James Bryant Smith explains why God is adamantly opposed to evil and sin: "God cares deeply about sin because it destroys his precious children. And God longs for holiness in us because it is the way to wholeness."[7] Because holiness leads to wholeness, and sin destroys wholeness, he also claims, "Being soft on sin is not loving because sin destroys. I want a God who hates anything that hurts me."[8]

Nancy Leigh DeMoss looks at sin from the perspective of what our sin does to God. She describes sin as "intensely personal," having "profound relational implications," but what makes it "so heinous and grievous is that it is against God" because "it violates His

---

4. For a more theological discussion of sin see chapter 7.
5. Smith, *Good and Beautiful God*, 120–21.
6. Wright, *Justice of God*, 89.
7. Smith, *Good and Beautiful God*, 125.
8. Smith, *Good and Beautiful God*, 125.

holy Law and character."[9] She continues, "When we tolerate our sin and refuse to be parted from it, we spurn the love and the grace of Christ; we trample His cross and count His sacrificial death of no value."[10] In the Sermon on the Mount Jesus was adamant about "cutting off every avenue and enticement to sin" when he instructed people to cut off the hand or to pluck out the eye that caused them to sin.[11]

In this same vein, DeMoss shares how she had to commit to watching no television when she was alone because her viewing time "had become a weed that was choking out holiness in my life. It was dulling my spiritual sensitivity and diminishing my love and longing for God. Slowly, subtly, the world was stealing my affection, altering my appetites, and seeping into the pores of my being." She found that she was "being entertained by behavior, speech, attitudes, and philosophies that the world (and many Christians) would consider acceptable, but that I knew were unholy."[12]

Additionally, she found that the longer she justified her actions the less motivated she was to change. She made the commitment to stop watching television and found almost immediate results: "My love for God was rekindled, my desire for holiness was renewed, and my spirit began to flourish once again."[13] She allows exceptions for news coverage of major disasters, but has never regretted the decision. To the charge of legalism, she responds, "We do need to guard against making absolutes out of personal standards that are not specified in Scripture, or assuming that others are sinning if they don't adopt our standards about issues that may not be traps for them."[14] Then she asks, "Why are we so prone to defend our choices that take us right to the edge of sin, and so reluctant to make radical choices to protect our hearts and minds from sin?"[15] The short answer is that in varying degrees, churchgoers have made the autonomous self their authority. We want what we want when we want it.

No matter how hard people work to carve out a new world, ultimately God's view of sin and evil will prevail. The church and eventually the culture will find that God cannot be held hostage to selfish, evil desires because his holiness prevents it. Wright insists "that in the new world God himself will be beyond the reach of the moral blackmail of unresolved evil" such as "the gnawing resentment, the unscratchable itch of jealousy or anger, which are the moral and spiritual equivalents of physical decay and disease."[16] God's new world is not like the utopian dream world where human kindness and progress will bring about a better place built "on the bones of those who have suffered in the

---

9. DeMoss, *Holiness*, 67.
10. DeMoss, *Holiness*, 50.
11. DeMoss, *Holiness*, 107.
12. DeMoss, *Holiness*, 105–6.
13. DeMoss, *Holiness*, 106.
14. DeMoss, *Holiness*, 106.
15. DeMoss, *Holiness*, 106–7.
16. Wright, *Justice of God*, 143.

past."[17] To the contrary, this new world is built on the blood of God's Son where "not only the physical pain but also the mental anguish of unresolved anger and bitterness will be done away with, as we are enabled fully and finally to forgive as we have been forgiven."[18] The church must recover a holy responsiveness to sin. The proper dealing with sin requires appropriate conviction, repentance, and forgiveness.

The Warning Signs of Conviction and Repentance

In their compassion, contemporary Christians are often too quick to comfort people in their struggles with personal sin.[19] Second Corinthians 7 explains that the purpose for godly sorrow is to bring people to the genuinely loving and Holy God and to his holy grace, holy mercy, and holy goodness in order to worship and to enjoy him, increasingly now and completely when they get to heaven. However, many in today's churches feel it is inhumane to let people suffer in this way and rush to give them the solution—Jesus has already forgiven them. What this does though is stop the Holy Spirit from taking them through the godly process of conviction, repentance, and sorrow for sin.

This premature offer of Jesus' forgiveness requires no commitment on the part of the people on whom the Spirit is working. There is little need for them to confess and to repent of their sins and to get right with God. The result is that people receive the assurance of heaven without the necessity of commitment on their part to be purified and to be made holy. They may actually miss regeneration and salvation. They may not have had time to meet the Holy God, to understand the seriousness of their sin, and what it cost God to redeem them. Consequently they begin the Christian life out of their *human* compassion asking the right question, "What would Jesus do?" but often without the regenerated relationship or the biblical knowledge to answer that question correctly.

As a result, conviction and repentance of sin have also become casualties to the victim mentality and misguided love. Christians have been trained to feel sorry for folks who are struggling with problems, which is good. But they have also been disciplined simply to try to help the person out of their pain as quickly as possible with no consideration that there might be sin that needs to be faced (conviction) and of which they need to repent. I believe this comes from the opposite swing of the pendulum where bad theology taught people to live in constant guilt because of their sin and ignored the meaning of forgiveness and the true freedom it brings. The irony is that just as constant guilt without the freedom forgiveness brings misses the mark, Christians

---

17. Wright, *Justice of God*, 144.
18. Wright, *Justice of God*, 145.
19. This is does not include bullying or sexual, physical, or emotional abuse. These are sins committed against a person which are doing him or her real harm. In such cases, the church should be the person's advocate for immediate help.

may be leaving the person in his or her guilt and everlasting judgment when they cut short the working of the Holy Spirit and try too quickly to make the person feel better about himself or herself.

The church must discern the difference between perpetual guilt and conviction. To leave a person without true repentance is to leave them in their guilt. It is more loving to work with them through God's conviction to genuine repentance and a relationship with Jesus Christ, which brings freedom. However, as Bellah, Ellul, Postman, and others have noted, Christians are mostly unaware of how Modernity, Postmodernity, and Technopoly have disciplined them.

Erroneous Signs of Forgiveness

Forgiveness is another area where the church has been disciplined by culture to downplay, if not outright reject, the biblical understanding. The danger this creates is like a serpentine road sign that shows inaccurate turns that lead people off a cliff to certain destruction. The need for forgiveness of sins comes from the poor choices people make. Choices have consequences that this age of seemingly endless choices tries to ignore. A man may choose to rob a bank and land in jail. A woman may choose to gossip or live in anger and end up alone and without friends. A CEO may sleep around and be infected with an STD. God is not obligated to keep people from the consequences of their poor choices. Neither is God obligated to forgive the sins resulting from those poor choices. God's forgiveness is not automatic but is contingent on another choice each person must make.

That choice centers on what people decide to do about Jesus and the forgiveness that is offered by God through him alone. Wright reminds us that it is "those who accept God's invitation to God's party on God's terms [who] will indeed celebrate the feast of deliverance from evil."[20] They will know God's forgiveness. However, he warns that a person's choices will determine whom he or she will become and that God will honor those choices. Therefore, God's forgiveness hinges on the person's decision about Jesus. Like the prodigal son's older brother, people have the right to sit out the party, "but [they] do not have the choice to sulk in such a way as to prevent God's party going ahead without [them]."[21]

The culture and many churchgoers connect forgiveness with the victim mentality that means no one can be left out. The thinking goes something like this. People point to passages like Psalm 103:3a and 12 that tell God's people that he forgives all their sins and removes their transgressions from them as far as the east is from the west. Another favorite passage is Jeremiah 31:34, which informs the people of the new covenant that God will not remember their sins. This cannot be a literal promise because God knows everything. There are no holes in his memory. It is a hyperbole, an exaggeration, to

20. Wright, *Justice of God*, 147.
21. Wright, *Justice of God*, 147.

show how completely he no longer holds anything against those who have made Jesus their Lord and Savior. Just as he remembers, God may have Christians remember past offenses in order to deal with issues that affect their character and prevent their sanctification (becoming like Jesus) in the present. However, those issues will no longer separate them from him and should not be used to create guilt, shame, pain, or blame. By making Jesus Lord and Savior of their lives they are justified.[22] These people alone have immediate access to God and heaven.

However, the secular world and many in today's churches reason that since Jesus died to forgive the sins of the world then everyone is automatically forgiven and going to heaven, "for God so loved the world that He gave his only begotten son" (John 3:16a). Nevertheless, this thinking ignores the conditions God places on the *effectiveness* of his forgiveness through Jesus. God forgives those who believe in Jesus (John 3:16b). Additionally, Scripture says that the only work a person must do or can do to be saved is to believe on Jesus (John 6:29).

The righteousness that is needed for heaven comes from God to the person who has faith in Jesus Christ and believes on him (Rom 3:22). John states very clearly in 1 John 3:23 that anyone who denies Jesus, the Son, does not have the Father. To have the Father means that the person's sins are forgiven, thereby giving him or her direct access to the thrice-Holy God and eternity in heaven. Later John writes in 1 John 5:5 and 12 that the person who has Jesus has life and the person who does not have Jesus does not have life. It is only through faith in Jesus that Christians overcome the world. It is little wonder, then, that Satan and the world work so hard to destroy the faith of the church and to beguile her to work in her own strength and on the world's terms. What is often ignored by many churchgoers is that faith in Jesus and forgiveness of sin go hand in hand. This is truly a case where you cannot have one without the other.

With a misappropriation of God's forgiveness to people, it is not surprising that the horizontal act of forgiveness of person to person also becomes messed up. Any action that is the result of the condition of the human heart without the correction of God's word (Scripture) and Spirit will be flawed. Replicating the error of God's forgiveness mentioned above, the church tells people "just forgive and forget." The implication may be that personal justice must be ignored; just forgive! In contrast, holy forgiveness is not simply a matter of an attitude adjustment and does not require selective amnesia pretending an offense did not happen.

Another distinction between holy forgiveness and the world's forgiveness can be seen when individuals claim forgiveness of sin for themselves but refuse to grant it to people who have hurt them. In the Sermon on the Mount (Matt 6:12–15, NIV), Jesus teaches that forgiveness from God is dependent on the person's willingness to forgive others: "Forgive us our debts as we forgive our debtors." In case the people missed it,

---

22. If terms like justification and sanctification are not part of your vocabulary please see chapter 7 for a more thorough discussion of them. Belief in Jesus means to make him Lord as well as Savior. It means to be committed to him and surrendered in all areas of life.

he repeats it in the negative, "If you do not forgive men their sins, your Father will not forgive your sins." Jesus knows that harboring unforgiveness prevents the healing of the injuries caused by the ones he or she is expected to forgive.

Abuse is one area where forgetting is outright harmful. One reason to remember a hurtful event is so individuals do not keep putting themselves in harm's way, thereby repeatedly subjecting themselves to evil. Their healing occurs not because the victim forgets the offense but when he or she no longer feels the pain it caused and when it no longer controls him or her. God is really good at making that happen. Real offenses require people being brought to justice by governments or others in authority whom God has ordained in Scripture to protect their people.

Forgiveness does not negate God's charge to governments to keep their people safe. "Sin must have its punishment or the very structure of life disintegrates. And God alone can pay the terrible price that is necessary before men can be forgiven. Forgiveness is never a case of saying: 'It's all right; it doesn't matter.' Forgiveness is the most costly thing in the world."[23] Forgiveness does not always negate the consequences of an action while on this earth. Those who violate the law, human decency, or respect may still be required to make retribution or to serve jail time or worse.

Why, then, is the proper understanding of forgiveness crucial to the church? First of all, it is crucial for salvation. False promises could lead to people missing God's forgiveness entirely. Additionally, with regard to life in the here and now, unforgiveness breeds grudges, anger, bitterness, and resentment, which result in fighting and division among people and also cut the person off from knowing God's joy and peace. Furthermore, the one who inflicted the pain continues to hold the injured person captive as long as he or she refuses to forgive. Moreover, as long as a person refuses to forgive, he or she is exercising his or her desire for revenge instead of leaving it in God's hands for him to repay the offender as he sees fit (Rom 12:19 and Heb 10:30). Clarissa Pinkola Estes observes, "How does one know if she has forgiven? You tend to feel sorrow over the circumstance instead of rage; you tend to feel sorry for the person rather than angry with him. You tend to have nothing left to say about it all."[24]

Additionally, Lewis Smedes states, "When we feel the slightest urge to wish that life would go well for them, we have begun to forgive."[25] When you reach this stage you have truly forgiven, but it may take years of repeatedly and intentionally forgiving until you arrive at that point. The goal according to Smedes is "to set a prisoner free and discover that the prisoner was you."[26] Forgiveness brings freedom, healing, and peace with God, with self, and with others for the one doing the forgiving. It sets the forgiver free from the pain and the control of the one who wronged him or her. To forgive is difficult; its costs are high, but the cost of unforgiveness is greater. Forgiveness is both

23. Barclay, *Letter to the Hebrews*, 129.
24. Estes, *Women Who Run with the Wolves*, 403.
25. Smedes, *Forgive and Forget*, 29.
26. Smedes, *Forgive and Forget*, 133.

required and offered on the basis of the choices we make. People choose who they will become, and God honors their choice. It is imperative that the church recover and maintain a biblical understanding of forgiveness.

The Broad Versus the Narrow Road of God's Justice and the Need for Justification

Similar to the issues of forgiveness, the church has also been culturally disciplined to misunderstand God's justice. Justice is the working out of God's truth, which can be found in his law. Timothy Keller reminds the church that God's law "is so magnificent, just, and demanding that [people] could never fulfill it . . . the Lord takes his law so seriously that he could not shrug off [their] disobedience to it . . . [but] that he *had* to become human, come to earth, and die a terrible death . . . [therefore, the church] must take that law very seriously too. The law of God demands justice and equity and love of one's neighbor."[27]

Justice entails not only working for social justice, but involves the honesty, integrity, and rightness according to God's Word in everything the Christian does. It also demands fair and respectful treatment of all people because they are made in God's image. This is what makes people inherently worthy of respect and fair treatment regardless of their position in life. This is justice based on God's Word (Scripture). God's Word is truth.

Therefore people's understanding of truth determines their view of justice. A woman may march for minority rights, but if she cheats on her husband or beats her kids, she may seem just in her own eyes because of the good things she has done, but she has not fulfilled God's call for justice. Similarly, if the chair of the board gives generously to hospitals, schools, and human rights organizations, but swindles money from the retirement fund of his employees, he has missed God's meaning of justice. A woman may be on every auxiliary board and raise millions of dollars for research to find a cure for cancer and for funding the hospital, but if she gossips and lies about people, she has failed to meet God's standard of justice. In this current age, justice is often limited to social justice, which is a necessary part of God's holy justice because all people are made in the image of God. However, social justice alone does not encompass the full extent of holy justice that calls sin, sin and that will one day judge the world.

Holy justice requires God's truth, honesty, humility, and meekness in every aspect of life. However, in the absence of absolute truth in today's culture, often "what *justifies* an activity or a given life-style or activity is [reduced to] the satisfaction it generates—the pleasure [it gives]."[28] That leaves justice wide open to personal interpretation. Many people rely on their good works and social activities to save them, but if works could in

27. Keller, *Generous Justice*, 100–101.
28. See Volf, "Human Flourishing," 15.

any way contribute to people's fulfillment of God's holy justice, it would provide people with a reason to boast in themselves, and that is not scriptural.

By contrast Paul's powerful discussion in Ephesians 2:8–10 states that individuals are saved *by* God's grace *through* faith in Jesus (and that is not of themselves but is a gift from God) *for* good works so that no one can boast. Martyn Lloyd-Jones points out that boasting in good works and religious living was typical of the Pharisees. Paul mentions his own boasting before Jesus appeared to him on the road to Damascus (Phil 3). Lloyd-Jones remarks, "The saints have always suffered most acutely at the hands of good, moral, religious people."[29] He reminds us that "it is not a question of good works leading to Christianity, but Christianity leading to good works."[30] Ephesians 2 opens with the statement that people are dead in their sins and proceeds to tell us God made Christians alive and raised them up with Christ (Eph 2:1, 4–7). Lloyd-Jones interprets it this way: "I am dead, and I am an enemy, and I am opposed to God, I do not understand, and I hate. But God gives me life. He has quickened me together with Christ. Therefore, boasting is entirely excluded, boasting of works, boasting even of faith . . . . Salvation is altogether of God."[31] But the church has all but lost sight of justification (see chapters 6 and 7) or has treated it far too glibly. Salvation, God's justification of individuals, is God's work alone so that no one can have any reason to boast. Quite the reverse of boasting, God actually calls his people to be poor in spirit, but this goes contrary to the culturally driven self-focused desires, which connect with the self-centeredness of the human heart.

Many Western Christians struggle with what it means to be poor in spirit. Their understanding may range from denying that God commands it in the first place to limiting it to the materially poor. Poor in spirit "means to see that you are deeply in debt before God, and you have no ability whatsoever to redeem yourself. God's free generosity to you, at infinite cost to him, was the only thing that saved you."[32] People whom Keller identifies as "middle-class in spirit" tend to think that they have worked hard for what they have and that somehow God "owes them" something and tend to be indifferent to the poor. He asserts that the "spiritually poor find their hearts gravitating toward the materially poor. To the degree that the gospel shapes your self-image, you will identify with those in need."[33]

Keller agrees that God commands Christians to care for the orphans and widows, to protect and to provide for those too weak or too marginalized to protect themselves, but he also cautions the church that "to consider deeds of mercy and justice to be identical to gospel proclamation is a fatal confusion . . . evangelism and social justice . . . .

---

29. Lloyd-Jones, *God's Way of Reconciliation*, 134.
30. Lloyd-Jones, *God's Way of Reconciliation*, 135.
31. Lloyd-Jones, *God's Way of Reconciliation*, 136–37.
32. Keller, *Generous Justice*, 101–2.
33. Keller, *Generous Justice*, 102.

should exist in an . . . inseparable relationship."[34] His bottom line is "justification by faith leads to doing justice, and doing justice [beyond social justice] can make many seek to be justified by faith."[35] If you struggle imagining what that could be, you may need to narrow your road and rethink your concept of God's holy justice.

The Missing Guardrails of Sanctification and Law

Scripture calls the church to sanctification, to act according to what she claims to believe based on God's law and precepts and to become holy and blameless. Sanctification involves law and discipline of self and community. As we have seen above neither is popular today. Often churches drop sanctification from their requirements and allow people to continue in their sin for fear their attendance might drop. Most people in the pews have only a vague understanding at best of what justification and sanctification mean. Like the culture around them, they see the Old Testament Law as outdated and cumbersome. After all, as the argument goes, Jesus fulfilled the law, and the church is free from it. Yes, Christians are free, but free to become like Jesus.

The law reveals to us who God is and what he expects of his people. Robert Jeffress compares the law to an x-ray and explains, "The x-ray itself is not your problem; it only reveals your problem. Similarly, the law is a spiritual x-ray that diagnoses the sin problem residing within each of us."[36] Michael Horton reminds people that the law was given for their happiness because they "were created in God's image and therefore were designed to find [their] deepest fulfillment in glorifying and enjoying God."[37] To enjoy God people must understand who he is and what he wants of them. Where there are commands, or laws, there is discipline. Without discipline there can be no sanctification.

However, Christians have capitulated to the culture with silence and actions that look virtually the same as everyone else. Horton's concern "is not that God is treated so lightly in American culture but that he is not taken seriously in our own faith and practice."[38] The evidence that this is true is how much like the culture the people in the churches are and how little like Christ they are. The church has removed the guardrails of sanctification and rarely calls for the transformation of her people to become holy like God is holy. Where judgment and discipline are weakened or missing, sanctification will be sacrificed on the altar of public opinion. The church must recover these if she is to become God's instrument of change.

---

34. Keller, *Generous Justice*, 138–39.
35. Keller, *Generous Justice*, 140.
36. Jeffress, *Grace Gone Wild*, 45.
37. Horton, *Christless Christianity*, 136.
38. Horton, *Christless Christianity*, 23.

MORE CONSEQUENCES OF COMPROMISING WITH CULTURE

Lost between Law and Moralism

Too often our approach to obedience to God's commandments is to turn something given by God for life into an opportunity for death. The biblical view of the law "is to keep us spiritually perceptive, open to God, [and] attentive to his voice,"[39] but we have confused God's law with moralism, legalism, and manmade rules of dos and don'ts. Roger Olsen writes, "We have specialized in moralism toward society outside the church while neglecting church discipline. The thrust of the New Testament is the other way around." He continues, "We fail to be authentically evangelical insofar as we rely on an outward code of conduct and threats of punishment to reform people's lives. Our message is rather the good news that people can't reform their lives apart from an inward change called conversion."[40] He describes the moralism too often practiced by the church as "making people behave using rules and shame; [but] evangelical morality is about fostering an environment where God's Spirit can inculcate the desire to please God through a life of obedience. Moralism is outward and focused on judgment; evangelical morality is inward and focuses on transformation of persons."[41]

Jesus tells his disciples that they must remove the log from their own eyes before they can see clearly enough to remove the splinter from another person's life. Olsen counsels Christians that "before trying to change society, evangelicals must reform themselves and their congregations and institutions away from individualism, consumerism, and therapeutic Christianity ('your best life now')" and become "radical Christian communities that serve as beacons of faith, hope, and love to the dying world around them."[42] Olsen agrees that "unfortunately, too many evangelical churches and organizations have taken on the values and behaviors of the secular world while casting aspersions at it."[43]

In this same vein, John Piper admonishes preachers to be the person they want to see in their parishioners. He believes this will only happen through a biblical understanding of sin, conviction, and repentance and writes, "The spirit we long to see in our people must be in ourselves first. But that will never happen until . . . we know our own emptiness and helplessness and terrible sinfulness."[44] The only way to understand sin and its seriousness is to understand the Law. Christians must recover discernment of the difference between law and morality if they are to see change in the culture. Recovering a healthy respect for God's holy law is a good place to begin this change.

---

39. Frost and Hirsch, *Shaping of Things to Come*, 177.
40. Olsen, *How to Be Evangelical*, 49–50.
41. Olsen, *How to Be Evangelical*, 57.
42. Olsen, *How to Be Evangelical*, 126.
43. Olsen, *How to Be Evangelical*, 126.
44. Piper, *Supremacy of God*, 101–2.

EQUIPPED TO TELL THE NEXT GENERATION

The Roadblock of Hell and the Canyons of Tolerance, Diversity, and Inclusiveness

To the secular twenty-first-century American culture, hell is seen as a roadblock to Christianity, and a loving God would never send anyone there (the victim mentality). This God would tolerate every diverse act and belief and include every person in his heaven, and frequently the church capitulates to the culture's message of tolerance, diversity, and inclusiveness. However, the tolerance, diversity, and inclusiveness promoted by this culture become the very roadblocks which keep Christians from dynamic Christianity.[45]

Nevertheless, Christians continue to conform to the culture in this way, and pastors are often as compliant as their parishioners. Piper has identified a "casual cleverness" that has crept into sermons that downplays the gravity of sin and hence justice and judgment leading to hell, so that "people will unconsciously learn that the realities of heaven and hell are not serious."[46] Instead of heaven and hell, the preacher focuses on messages that make people feel good about themselves (no matter what their thoughts and actions may be), provoke laughter, and cause them to like the preacher. It has all the marks of successful preaching because it is entertaining, but it cultivates acceptance of everything and creates "an atmosphere in which [revival] could never come."[47] Without the reality of hell, all people find themselves laughing their way to a guaranteed heaven because this humorous approach promotes a tolerant and inclusive view of everything except God's wrath and judgment against sin. Furthermore, it bestows God's grace and forgiveness on everyone regardless of lifestyle or commitments.

In this false religion, the church has lost holy justice, holy judgment, holy forgiveness, and hence, the biblical view of hell. Inclusivity renounces God's justice because it does not distinguish between good and evil. Diversity eliminates judgment because in order for everything to become acceptable you must be forbidden to judge. Tolerance negates holy forgiveness because when all people are good, forgiveness is automatic without the need for a changed heart, confession, or repentance, but God's truth will prevail. In the in-between-time, Christians must pursue holy forgiveness because of God's holy justice and holy judgment and the reality of hell. This means they must be competent "to name evil and to shame it . . . to do everything in [their] power to resume an *appropriate* relationship with the offender after the evil has been dealt with . . . [and] not allow this evil to determine the sort of people [they] shall then become . . . unlike a soggy tolerance which merely takes the line of least resistance" (italics are mine).[48]

---

45. This is not saying that the church should be intolerant or that there is no room for diversity. God creates great diversity within his parameters of holiness, which include righteousness and love, justice and mercy, judgment against sin and grace through repentance and faith in Jesus Christ. See the section on love and chapters 11 and 12.

46. Piper, *Supremacy of God*, 59.

47. Piper, *Supremacy of God*, 59.

48. Wright, *Justice of God*, 152.

Today, the guardrails that warn people of evil, sin, hell, judgment, and God's wrath have been removed, and the deadly canyons of tolerance, diversity, and inclusion of everything but an external source of eternal and divine authority are being experienced. Christians must realize that what seems like a roadblock to the culture is often the way for the church and the culture to thrive. The church must recover a biblical understanding of hell, tolerance, diversity, and inclusivity if she is to be God's instrument of change in this world.

The Dead End of the Absence of Revival Prayer

Another area missing in most church settings today is concerted prayer for changed hearts. Most prayer in today's churches focuses on personal and congregational health and financial problems. While Christians should pray for these things, prayer should not be limited to these alone. Perhaps the best way to illustrate this lack of understanding of prayer is to review what Scripture reveals about the way Jesus and the Apostles prayed. This kind of prayer:

- Seeks God to send workers to bring in the harvest (Matt 9:38).
- Seeks God to save people and to transform their daily lives by the gospel of Jesus Christ and the Holy Spirit (Rom 12:1–2).
- Asks that Christians would be active in sharing their faith (Phlm 1:6).
- Asks that the gospel would spread quickly and be honored (2 Thess 3:1).
- Asks that Christians would live lives worthy of Jesus, growing in knowledge of God, and having great endurance and patience, and bearing the fruit God considers good (Col 1:10–12).
- Prays that Christians' love would grow in knowledge and depth of insight of God's ways so that they can discern the best from the better way, be filled with the fruit of righteousness that comes through Jesus, and be kept pure and blameless throughout their lives until they are with Jesus, and all of this is for the praise and glory of God and not their own personal glory and praise (Phil 1:9–11).
- Asks that the God of Jesus would give the saints wisdom and revelation to know him better and to know the riches of their inheritance and the power that is available to them (Eph 1:17–19). These riches and this power have little to do with the riches and power of twenty-first-century Western civilization but are primarily spiritual.
- Asks that prayer be made for powerful, accurate, and fearless preaching of the gospel (Eph 6:18–19).

Scripture also commands that Christians "pray continually" (1 Thess 5:17). How does your personal prayer life and the prayer life of your church compare?

Walter Kaiser Jr. sees prayer as the "universal testimony of all the revivals in the Bible and in history," and declares, "revivals are dead before they get started" without these kinds of prayers, which he calls intercession.[49] He warns, "If this [intercession] is not the very atmosphere in which God's work goes forward, then we must count on being soundly thrashed by the present world system . . . . Mark it well: where intercession goes thin or ceases altogether, there the saints and the churches drift into spiritual lethargy, and the forces of evil have a field day in the culture."[50] Look around you and consider this warning, whether it is true. The church may take the command to pray lightly, but it leads to a dead end instead of the end of death promised in the Bible.

Another Dead End: Growing Independence and Personalized Faith

God has no homeless children. Unfortunately, a growing number of Christians believe they can ignore Hebrews 10:25 and think they can live a holy life independent of others, which also precludes corporate worship and prayer. There are many excuses. Many have been wounded by people in their churches or disillusioned with what they see and hear. With increasingly independent spirits, consumer attitudes, and the information conditioning of the Net and television, many people think their "spiritual needs can be met simply by plugging into the Internet," but DeMoss cautions, "Being disconnected from the local church, for whatever reason, is a dangerous way to live . . . . [Christians] are vulnerable to predators of every sort."[51] She calls for a restoration of accountability to a body of believers as the means to protect individual followers against sin.

In addition to being hurt by churchgoers, some reasons people resist being connected to a church come down to pride, lack of humility, and trust issues, but God calls Christians to be held accountable. Accountability can only occur when other people are involved. James connects confessing sin to the elders with healing prayer. It is difficult to confess to another when self is the only member of the group. With deception so prevalent in the heart, accountability is usually effective only with the help of others. As the Bible says, "Iron sharpens iron." Have you ever sharpened a knife without a whet stone or something similar? Trying to live the Christian life independent of the church is a deception that leads to nowhere and opens the person up to worshiping a god created in his or her own image. The church must become a vital part of the Christian life.

A Christian Response to Sin and the Evil It Unleashes

Sadly the church has grown so accustomed to the divisions and rejections of Scripture that have come upon her that she barely notices, and she has become far too

---

49. Kaiser, *Revive Us Again*, 69.
50. Kaiser, *Revive Us Again*, 235.
51. DeMoss, *Holiness*, 128.

comfortable with sin. Sometimes it seems that churchgoers actually revel in their sin when they should be devastated that they are spurning the God who loves them so much that he sacrificed his only son. DeMoss calls these divisions and acceptance of sin a kind of heartbreak and compares them to a sewer line break. If that were to happen in the natural world people would report it and call for immediate action. Public works officials would respond quickly to fix it because of the potential health hazards of sickness and disease. DeMoss identifies sin as raw sewage that is running through lives of professing Christians, including evangelicals, that is going unnoticed by most. "The floodgates of unholiness . . . have opened within the church. Adultery, drunkenness, abuse, profanity, outbursts of temper, divorce, pornography, immodest dress" are as commonly found in the church as are "overspending, unpaid debts, gluttony, gossip, greed, covetousness, bitterness, pride, critical spirits, backbiting, temporal values, self-centeredness, and broken relationships."[52] This has happened because the spirit of tolerance and pleasure has crept into the church's thinking, and she has willingly capitulated to the culture. In identifying ways in which this has happened in the church, DeMoss has recognized the essence of these first five chapters:

- "The church—the place that is intended to showcase the glory and holiness of God—has become a safe place to sin."

- "The evangelical church, by and large, has abandoned preaching on sin and holiness."

- "Many have rewritten the law of God and have prostituted the grace of God, turning it into a license to sin."

- Most have "accepted the philosophy that it's OK for Christians to look, think, act, and talk like the world."

- Countless churches have "made it an offense to admonish people about their sin, either privately or, when necessary, publicly. (If only Christians were as loath to commit sin as they are to confront it!)"

- "The spirit of tolerance has triumphed over the spirit of truth."

- "There is little conviction of sin, little life transformation, and little manifestation of the presence of God, who simply won't make Himself at home in an unholy place."[53]

I believe she has described the heart of most twenty-first-century American churches.

---

52. DeMoss, *Holiness*, 164.
53. DeMoss, *Holiness*, 164–65, 174–75.

Summary

DeMoss challenges Christians, "The church has been waiting for the world to get right with God. When will [she] realize that the world is waiting for the church to get right with God?" She asks, "Where are the believers whose eyes are filled with tears, whose hearts ache when they see an unholy church partying and entertaining herself to death, and whose knees are sore from pleading with God to grant the gift of repentance?"[54] They have surrendered to the culture. Perhaps Lloyd-Jones identifies why and writes, "The real trouble with many of us [contemporary Christians] is that our conception of what it is that makes us Christian is so low, is so poor; it is our failure to realise the greatness of what it means to be a Christian . . . . It is God who has done something, it is God who is working; we are His workmanship."[55]

How are we to be faithful Christians who promote revival and prayer in our individualistic, pluralistic, materialistic, relativistic, and consumeristic culture that is constantly bombarded by the internet and television with information flowing at the speed of light? We begin with recovering the holiness of God in our churches and living holy lives personally and corporately. In the next chapter, we will examine holiness and how that informs the great doctrines of the church in chapter 7. The remaining chapters will be devoted to uncovering the light that has been hidden in our day but that Christians have always had that will bring solutions to our situation today.

---

54. DeMoss, *Holiness*, 175–76.
55. Lloyd-Jones, *God's Way of Reconciliation*, 137.

Chapter 6

Understanding Holiness

> I might have chosen a subject more popular and pleasant. I am sure I might have found one more easy to handle. But I feel deeply I could not have chosen one more seasonable and more profitable to our souls.
>
> —J. C. Ryle, *Holiness*

Few doctrines of the church have come under such intense attack as holiness. It has become synonymous with legalism and mostly rejected by culture and often among churchgoers as well. At the very least today it ranks as one of the most misunderstood and ignored ideas in the Bible in spite of how often it occurs. When we think of holiness, words like righteousness, purity, justice, and godliness come to mind, and sometimes judgment and wrath. "Holy" is usually defined as set apart. Sometimes we hear the word consecrated. What does that mean in today's world?

We value our uniqueness, but we balk at being set apart from others. To postmodern ears that sounds elitist or even racist. Holiness requires commitment, but we struggle with commitment as evidenced by high divorce rates and unwillingness to marry in the first place. Commitment to something sacred or holy sounds positively dull, downright scary, or even offensive. The ordinary person in the pew and many of those preaching do not understand holiness. Therefore, before we can examine how holiness can help us to reach the people in our day for Jesus Christ, we must develop a working description for it.

God Is Holy

Let's begin with a pastoral/evangelical look at holiness. Jerry Bridges understands the holiness of God simply as "the absolute absence of any evil in Him.... He is Himself the essence of moral purity," and "all of His thoughts and actions are consistent with His holy character."[1] A. W. Tozer points out "the immutability" of God's holiness. "God cannot change for the better. Since He is perfectly holy, He has never been less holy than He is now and can never be holier than He is and has always been. Neither

---

1. Bridges, *Pursuit of Holiness*, 22–23.

can God change for the worse. Any deterioration within the unspeakably holy nature of God is impossible."[2] Tozer explains that to think along the lines of God's changing for the better or for the worse relegates God to nothing more than "an object" which is "something else and someone less than He. The one of whom we are thinking may be a great and awesome creature, but because he is a creature he cannot be the self-existent Creator."[3] Johnathan Edwards makes a key point, "'Tis the glory of God's immutability, that it is a holy immutability, and not an inflexible obstinacy in wickedness."[4] If you or I were to be inflexible and never change, it would be out of our hard-heartedness and would result in much evil and pain for those around us, but for the Holy God who is perfect in every way, it would mean becoming imperfect. John Owen describes holiness as "the infinite, absolute perfection and rectitude of his nature, as the eternal original cause and pattern of truth, uprightness, and rectitude in all."[5] Holiness, which is immutably true and upright, is what makes God different or set apart from what we experience in this world.

Theologians describe holiness by relating it to the people and things of this world. Millard Erickson points out two fundamental aspects in God's holiness: his "uniqueness" and "his absolute purity or goodness." "Uniqueness" he describes as being "totally separate from all of creation," and "absolute purity or goodness" as being "untouched and unstained by the evil in the world."[6] Wayne Grudem believes "*God's holiness means that he is separated from sin and devoted to seeking his own honor . . . . both a relational quality (separation from) and a moral quality (the separation is from sin or evil, and the devotion is to the good of God's own honor or glory).*"[7] "God himself is the Most Holy One" and "provides the pattern for his people to imitate"; this holiness calls for separation "from evil and sin . . . and . . . devotion to God" and calls the church as well as individuals to "grow in holiness!"[8]

Thomas E. McComiskey understands that "the biblical viewpoint would refer the holiness of God not only to the mystery of his power, but also to his character as totally good and entirely without evil."[9] Additionally, he connects cultic and moral practices with holiness and insists that the objects belonging to God must also be without "cultic pollution," which he recognizes as "moral pollution." These objects are not just set apart from ordinary use but must be "dedicated to what is good and kept

---

2. Tozer, *Knowledge of the Holy*, 49.
3. Tozer, *Knowledge of the Holy*, 49.
4. Edwards, "Religious Affections," 257.
5. Owen, *Holy Spirit*, 427.
6. Erickson, *Christian Theology*, 311.
7. Grudem, *Systematic Theology*, 202.
8. Grudem, *Systematic Theology*, 202–3.
9. McComiskey, "קדש," 787.

from what is evil. The separation of men from what defiles ceremonially is but typical of the holiness that is spiritual and ethical."[10]

Holiness and the People Who Serve God

Thus, there is a connection of holiness with all people, places, and things who serve God. John Calvin declares "that the only legitimate service to him is the practice of justice, purity, and holiness," and we are totally indebted to God for all good things because "he ever remains . . . himself, the friend of righteousness, the enemy of unrighteousness, and whatever his demands from us may be, as he can only require what is right, we are necessarily under a natural obligation to obey. Our inability to do so is our own fault."[11] Later he urges us to remember, "When mention is made of our union with God . . . holiness must be the bond; not that by the merit of holiness we come into communion with him . . . but because it greatly concerns his glory not to have any fellowship with wickedness and impurity."[12]

This brings us to the most commonly held understanding of "holy" which is "absolute moral perfection." Wrapped in this we find purity, righteousness, and sanctification. We see this in the Psalms. "Who may live on your holy hill? He whose walk is blameless and who does what is righteous" (15:1b–2a, NIV). In response to this passage Calvin warns us not to be indifferent to purity but urges all who call themselves Christians to "lead a holy and unspotted life." In this psalm, Calvin understands "that those only have access to God who are his genuine servants, and who live a holy life."[13] Calvin combines "holy" with an "unspotted life."[14] "Holy" and "blameless" are taken from Paul in Ephesians 1:4 (KJV), "According as he hath chosen us in him before the foundation of the world, that we should be holy and without blame before him in love."

Martyn Lloyd-Jones believes these words, "holy" and "without blame," "describe the same thing but do so from different aspects. They both refer to sanctification."[15] He sees holiness as "a state of . . . internal purity" while blameless or "without blame" is an "external purity." Holiness is positive, while "without blame" is negative. He declares that "positively . . . holiness is light, and negatively . . . there is no darkness."[16] "You are positively holy, but that means negatively that there is the absence of pollution."[17] This "absence of pollution" signifies that God "is absolutely pure without any suspicion of

10. McComiskey, "שקד," 787.
11. Calvin, *Institutes*, 2.8.2 (p. 234).
12. Calvin, *Institutes*, 3.6.2 (p. 446).
13. Calvin, *Book of Psalms*, 205.
14. Also found in Eph 1:4; Col 1:22; and 1 Thess 2:10.
15. Lloyd-Jones, *God's Ultimate Purpose*, 96.
16. Lloyd-Jones, *God's Ultimate Purpose*, 97.
17. Lloyd-Jones, *God's Ultimate Purpose*, 96.

alloy or any admixture," and taken together the two terms "mean an essential purity or state of health, or wholeness. They mean a true and real life and being . . . a perfect harmony with every part fulfilling the function for which it was designed . . . . Holiness is ultimately an essential attribute of God."[18] Holiness is "internal purity," "positive," "light," "no darkness," "absence of pollution," "essential purity," "state of health," "wholeness," and "real life and being." Lloyd-Jones claims not only that holiness is "ultimately *an* essential characteristic," but holiness is "a *perfect harmony with every part fulfilling the function for which it was designed*" (italics are mine).[19] Edwards also sees harmony and proportion in the beauty of God's holiness.[20]

Holiness is what keeps righteousness and love in perfect balance and harmony. The same is true for justice and mercy, judgment and grace, and every characteristic of God mentioned in Scripture. We can carry this one step further to include the fruits and the gifts of the Spirit. If these are the result of the work of the Spirit of God in his people, then these characteristics and actions must be the outcome of holiness since they are produced and given by God's Spirit who is *holy*.

Returning to the Psalms, in 24:3–4 (ESV) we read, "Who shall ascend the hill of the LORD? And who shall stand in his holy place? He who has clean hands and a pure heart, who does not lift up his soul to what is false and does not swear deceitfully." Calvin reminds us "how vain a thing it is to make an external profession unless there be, at the same time, truth in the inward man," and "it will not suffice to frame the hands, feet, and eyes, according to the rule of righteousness, unless purity of heart precede outward continence."[21] Calvin is saying it gains us nothing before God to do what is "good" and "right" outwardly if we do not have purity of thought and mind on the inside first. We will see more of this later in the Sermon on the Mount. Moreover, Calvin declares, according to this psalm, no one has the right to enter (or to access) God's sanctuary "unless he sanctify himself in order to serve God in purity."[22] Additionally, "What he [the psalmist] says concerning the tabernacle of the covenant must be applied to the continual government of the church."[23] The church must consider God's holiness and live in the tension of love, grace, and mercy along with his righteousness, justice, and judgment.

Congregations must take seriously Scripture passages like Psalm 85:10–11 (NIV), "Love and faithfulness meet together; righteousness and peace kiss each other. Faithfulness springs forth from the earth, and righteousness looks down from heaven." We

---

18. Lloyd-Jones, *God's Ultimate Purpose*, 97.
19. Lloyd-Jones, *God's Ultimate Purpose*, 97.
20. Edwards, "Ethical Writings," 562. His editor, Ramsey, observes that "agreement, harmony, consent, concord, symmetry, uniformity, union, answerableness, fitness, meetness, adaptedness, correspondence" are characteristic of Edwards's view of holiness; Edwards saw the beauty of holiness reflected in the harmony of music and the complement of colors in a painting.
21. Calvin, *Book of Psalms*, 405.
22. Calvin, *Book of Psalms*, 404.
23. Calvin, *Book of Psalms*, 405.

easily accept "love and faithfulness" meeting, but some today would separate righteousness and peace as being at odds with one another. The question of whose morals we should adopt is just one example. The Bible tells us that "righteousness and peace kiss each other." Have you ever tried to kiss your husband or wife, girlfriend, boyfriend, or child when the other is not present? It is impossible. This is how a Holy God sees righteousness and peace. God brings them together to work as he designed them.

Another key Old Testament passage is Isaiah 32:15–17 (NIV) where God promises Israel that the land will become a wasteland "until the Spirit is poured upon us from on high, and the desert becomes a fertile field, and the fertile field seems like a forest. Justice will dwell in the desert and righteousness live in the fertile field. The fruit of righteousness will be peace; the effect of righteousness will be quietness and confidence forever." A Holy God has righteousness producing peace, not conflict. Disharmony enters not because of righteousness, but because of the willful self-centeredness of people wanting to please themselves.

In the New Testament, Paul writes to the Romans (14:17–18, NIV), "For the kingdom of God is not a matter of eating and drinking, but of righteousness, peace and joy in the Holy Spirit, because anyone who serves Christ in this way is pleasing to God and approved by men." In God's holy kingdom "righteousness," "peace," and "joy" exist harmoniously together. Paul reminds Timothy,

> Everyone who confesses the name of the Lord must turn away from wickedness. In a large house there are articles not only of gold and silver, but also of wood and clay; some are for noble purposes and some for ignoble. If a man cleanses himself from the latter, he will be an instrument for noble purposes, made holy, useful to the Master and prepared to do any good work. Flee the evil desires of youth, and pursue righteousness, faith, love and peace, along with those who call on the Lord out of a pure heart. (2 Tim 2:19b–22, NIV)

God's people are to "turn away from wickedness" and to "pursue righteousness" as well as "faith, love and peace," for it is by all of these the servant of God is "made holy." This is no easy thing to do.

Righteousness is holy, but it is not synonymous with holiness. Lloyd-Jones explains the difference. "Righteousness gives the impression of . . . right ordering, right understanding, and therefore right living . . . . Holiness suggests something which is entirely separate from evil . . . . It not only separates itself from evil, but it hates evil! It means essential purity of nature and of being."[24] We will consider this in greater detail as we progress through this work. For now we will investigate what God's righteousness entails.

---

24. Lloyd-Jones, *Darkness and Light*, 180.

Holiness and the Law

As you might expect, the path of righteousness is revealed in the law. What you may not know is the law is holy (Rom 7:12). Edwards refers to God's law as "the holiness of God in writing" and describes "the commands and precepts" of God as "all pure, perfect, and holy." Edwards also connects the Sermon on the Mount with God's laws which must be "engraven on the fleshly tables of your hearts" in order for you to be "truly sanctified."[25]

Calvin asserts, "There cannot be a doubt that the claim of absolute perfection which God made for his Law is perpetually in force . . . . the Law was given from heaven to teach us a perfect righteousness"; the only way to gain favor with God is through "obedience alone." Furthermore, "to go wandering after good works which are not prescribed by the law of God, is an intolerable violation of true and divine righteousness."[26] For Calvin, human requirements that are added to Scripture do not impress God. For Owen, God "exerts" holiness "in all he doth, naturally and necessarily, so particularly in his law; which is therefore good, holy, and perfect, because it represents the holiness of God, which is impressed on it." He goes so far as to say, "Whatever is contrary unto or different from the law of God is so unto and from the holiness of God himself."[27] Since the law of God represents his holiness, then to do anything "contrary" or "different" from God's law is to depart from God's holiness, which is a serious problem.

The confessions of the church reveal a collective belief that the Law is holy. Question ninety-five of the Westminster Larger Catechism (1648) tells us that "the moral law is of use to all men, to inform them of the holy nature and will of God."[28] The Second Helvetic Confession (1566) declares, "1. We teach that the will of God is set down unto us in the law of God; to wit . . . what is good and just, or what is evil and unjust. We therefore confess that 'the law is holy,'" and "2. We believe that the whole will of God, and all necessary precepts, for every part of this life, are fully delivered in this law."[29] It is apparent that the concept of the law representing God's holiness was at one time commonly accepted in the church.

Today many believe we are free from all Old Testament laws. "Not so!" according to Calvin. "We must not imagine that the coming of Christ has freed us from the authority of the law; for it is the eternal rule of a devout and holy life, and must, therefore, be as unchangeable as the justice of God, which it embraced, is constant and uniform."[30] In direct reference to the law in the Sermon on the Mount (Matt 5:17,

---

25. Edwards, "Way of Holiness," 473.
26. Calvin, *Institutes*, 2.8.5 (p. 236).
27. Owen, *Holy Spirit*, 427.
28. Beeke and Ferguson, "Westminster Larger Catechism," 131.
29. Beeke and Ferguson, "Second Helvetic Confession," 130.
30. Calvin, *Harmony of the Evangelists*, 277.

NIV) Jesus announces that he has "not come to abolish the Law and the Prophets . . . but to fulfill them." The thrust of the Sermon on the Mount is to take the law which could only be measured by outward appearances, of which the Scribes and Pharisees were expert examples, and make it internal, written on the heart.

For Charles Quarles, the Sermon on the Mount reflects the righteous life of the Old Testament prediction in Jeremiah 31:33–34, "God would change His people from the inside out so that their character resembled His own holy character and their lives would be pleasing to Him."[31] The Beatitudes in Matthew 5 describe this holy life. When Jesus calls his disciples to obey God or to "desire holiness . . . such language simply was not powerful enough. The true disciple hungers and thirsts for righteousness. He yearns to live a godly life as much as a starving man longs for his next piece of bread or a parched tongue yearns for a drop of water."[32] "The pure in heart" reminds us of Psalm 24. "Holiness is a prerequisite for entering God's presence. The pure in heart pass this test, so they will see God and experience intimate fellowship with him,"[33] writes Craig Blomberg. Craig Keener understands the "'pure' heart before God" as meaning "a heart of unmixed emotion to God."[34] Christians are not divided in their devotion to God. They cannot serve two masters.

In the middle of the Sermon on the Mount we find direct references to the law. Not only is murder wrong, but the anger inside a person that leads to murder is judged just as guilty. The act of adultery is condemned and so is the lust in a person's heart that leads to the act. J. C. Ryle draws heavily on the Sermon on the Mount when he describes a holy life: "True holiness is a great reality. It is something in a man that can be seen, and known, and marked, and felt by all around him. It is light: if it exists, it will show itself. It is salt: if it exists, its savour will be perceived. It is a precious ointment: if it exists, its presence cannot be hid."[35] To be a faithful child of God means to be holy because God is holy, and it will be visible to others.

The law reveals the holy righteousness of God, but it also implies justice and judgment, which some today seriously misunderstand. The curses contained in the law are particularly difficult. Speaking of these, Calvin notices that "the threatenings attest the spotless purity of God which cannot bear iniquity, while the promises attest at once his infinite *love of righteousness* . . . and his wondrous kindness" (italics are mine).[36] God's holiness is both love and righteousness. Notice how he does not simply use "love" but "love of righteousness" and combines this with "wondrous kindness."

---

31. Quarles, *Sermon on the Mount*, 32–33.
32. Quarles, *Sermon on the Mount*, 59.
33. Blomberg, *Matthew*, 100.
34. Keener, *Gospel of Matthew*, 170.
35. Ryle, *Holiness*, 47.
36. Calvin, *Institutes*, 2.8.4 (p. 235).

Holiness and Love

Today many people discount the righteousness component of holiness because they equate this along with God's justice, judgment, and wrath as a contradiction of God's love. Certainly God's wrath can be seen in the Old Testament and in Revelation. In contrast, the churchgoers of today delight to point out how Jesus' gospel is different. To prove this they quickly quote John 3:16a, "For God so loved the world that He gave his one and only son." God's love does trump his wrath but does not do away with it. Love does not negate God's righteousness because God is holy. In the Gospels, we see God's righteousness, justice, judgment, wrath, and love at the cross. What are often ignored are verses 3:16b and 18 where Jesus makes it clear that only those who believe in God's one and only son "will not perish but have everlasting life" and that those who believe will not be condemned, but those who do not believe are already condemned (judgment). Jesus' coming did not automatically do away with condemnation which is closely associated with God's wrath (and will be discussed in the next chapter). Many in our churches today cannot understand how a loving God can condemn anyone and want to eliminate the holy righteousness of God in favor of love only.

Perhaps the problem lies in the understanding of love we investigated in chapter 4. Owen reminds us of the connection of holiness with God the Father's "electing love . . . His aim and design in choosing of us was that we should be holy and unblamable before him in love." This is also "the exceeding love of the Son" as seen in Ephesians 5:25–27 (NIV), "Christ loved the church and gave himself up for her to make her holy, cleansing her by the washing with water through the word, and to present her to himself as a radiant church, without stain or wrinkle or any other blemish, but holy and blameless." To be made holy is "the very work of the love of the Holy Ghost. His whole work upon us, in us, for us, consists in preparing us for obedience."[37] Holiness is imparted through faith in Jesus by the Holy Spirit working in Christians individually and in the church corporately. If individuals are living holy lives, they should be producing a body of believers which is also holy.

It is certain that God loves his people because he gave the life of his Son to redeem them. In both the Old Testament and the New Testament God refers to his people as his bride or the bride of Christ. Lloyd-Jones points out that "this love, this God-like love, is altogether above the erotic and philanthropic" love of this world. The essential difference is it desires to "give for the benefit of the other."[38] In Ephesians 2:4–8 (NIV) we learn that "because of his great love for us, God, who is rich in mercy, made us alive with Christ even when we were dead in transgressions . . . it is by grace you have been saved . . . . through faith . . . and this not from yourselves, it is the gift of God." Today it is easy for us to accept that God can be loving, merciful, and gracious. The church must remind herself that these come from God's holy nature for his glory and are not simply

37. Owen, *Communion with God*, 182–83.
38. Lloyd-Jones, *Life in the Spirit*, 140–41.

in and of themselves somehow separated from all of what some might perceive as the negative attributes of righteousness, justice, judgment and wrath. Scripture connects many of these qualities of holiness we would divide.

Psalm 89 tells us that righteousness and justice are the foundation of God's throne and his steadfast love and faithfulness go before him. Psalm 33:5 (NIV) says, "The LORD loves righteousness and justice; the earth is full of his unfailing love." We have already looked at Psalm 85:10. Contrary to popular thinking, righteousness produces peace, not conflict. Whether it is the Old or New Testament there exists an unbreakable positive bond between righteousness, love, and peace.

Holiness and Discipline

Closely connected with righteousness and justice is discipline. Many of us remember the unjust discipline of our parents and wince. One or both may have been abusive. For certain there were times when they punished us wrongly or too harshly out of their frustration and anger. We tend to attribute this kind of discipline to God, but not so says Peter T. O'Brien. God is not arbitrary in his judgments but always acts with "infinite love and wisdom" for the purpose "that we may share in his holiness." Reflecting on Hebrews 12:10 (NIV), "but God disciplines us for our good that we may share in his holiness," O'Brien sees holiness as "an essential attribute of God himself," and since discipline has our ultimate good as its purpose, it is to be seen as "loving correction" without which it is impossible "to share in it [God's holiness] at all."[39] Holiness is "the crown toward which God's discipline directs his people (12:10),"[40] says Robert Hodgson Jr. who also believes Paul understands holiness as "ethically and theologically" grounded in righteousness. This, then, becomes "a preeminent quality of day-to-day Christian life."[41] Righteousness combined with loving discipline brings God's people to holiness. Holiness is the goal; discipline, righteousness, and love are the means.

Holiness and Peace

Hebrews 12 develops the theme of godly discipline further in verses 12–14 and shows that its outcome leads to peace and holiness that is corporate as well as individual. Owen writes that God keeps peace with himself through holiness and adds, "It is holiness that keeps up a sense of peace with God . . . . Hence, God as the author of our peace, is the author of our holiness."[42] Holiness must be developed in us in order to know God's peace. Gareth Lee Cockerill sees "the pursuit of the God-given,

39. O'Brien, *Hebrews*, 468.
40. Hodgson, "Holiness (NT)," 252.
41. Hodgson, "Holiness (NT)," 251, 254.
42. Owen, *Holy Spirit*, 369.

Christ-provided 'holiness'" as the only means to peace.[43] All agree we must "pursue peace with everyone." However, there is little or no talk about "the holiness without which no one will see the Lord," but to pursue holiness is to pursue and to find peace. In order to pursue peace, one must pursue God's holiness.

Peace and holiness are not for individuals alone but also for the church as a whole. For Cockerill "the 'peace,' harmony, and wholeness of their common life" is a result of holiness.[44] Owen and Cockerill view the passage positively and focus on what we gain—peace, harmony, and wholeness. Calvin, however, looks at the flip side. Never one to think about people's feelings, he reminds us how difficult it is to live in peace in a pluralistic society bent on accommodating everything. Calling on Hebrews 12:14, he finds one exemption when pursuing peace is not possible. The exclusion is when peace requires *approving* the "vices and wickedness" of the ungodly. He writes, "The friendship of the wicked is not to be allowed to defile or pollute us, for holiness has an especial regard to God."[45] How often has it been flaunted to Christians by people regarding their sin, "Are you worried we might pollute you?" as a way to shut them down?

Herein lies a major problem. We cannot think of ourselves or anyone else as "defiled" or "polluted"; it is not politically correct and goes against our humanistic worldview of the goodness of people, but holiness reveals just those things about us which is why it has been ignored. Think about this: if the humanist view of people is correct, then why is the therapeutic model identified by Bellah (chapter 1) needed? No one has been telling people they are inherently bad for generations. Why do we continue to need to be told how good we are? Why do we medicate ourselves with antidepressants, antianxiety medications, and pain killers of all sorts including prescription and non-prescription opioids and alcohol? Kathlyn Stone reports that in the top classes of drugs prescribed in the U.S., "antihypertensives and pain medications were among the most prescribed medications of 2018." She reports that antidepressants are one of the fastest growing classes of drugs.[46] Additionally, why must we be told repeatedly that we deserve only good things and that it is somehow wrong when we do not get them unless deep down we really do know that the humanists are wrong? Calvin warns us that holiness is not to be relinquished. Scripture tells us why: without holiness no one will see the Lord.

Yes, Christians must work hard at living peacefully with all people, but Calvin puts one restriction on this pursuit: "Though then the whole world were roused to a blazing war, yet holiness is not to be forsaken, for it is the bond of our union with God."[47] Christians are to seek peace, but not peace at any price and especially not at the cost of holiness. Calvin is saying to pursue peace without compromising holiness.

43. Cockerill, *Hebrews*, 634.
44. Cockerill, *Hebrews*, 633.
45. Calvin, "Epistle to the Hebrews," 324.
46. Stone, "The Most Prescribed Medications," paras. 3 and 12.
47. Calvin, *Hebrews*, 324.

Scripture is clear about this as seen in Isaiah (32:17, NIV), "The fruit of righteousness will be peace, the effect of righteousness will be quietness and confidence." In both the Psalms and James (3:18, NIV) we read, "The fruit of righteousness is sown in peace by those who make peace." Peace can never be achieved by ignoring what is right and true. Many struggle with this because we associate holiness with legalism, but there is more we need to understand about holiness.

Two Kinds of Holiness

O'Brien identifies two kinds of holiness in Hebrews 12:14, "perfected holiness . . . is indispensable for seeing God." He draws on the holiness of Hebrews 10 and the "pure in heart" in the Sermon on the Mount, which he sees as "integrally related."[48] The first kind of holiness was "procured for believers by the sacrifice of Christ . . . which enables them to approach God (10:10, 14)"; this he calls the "initial gift of holiness."[49] Hebrews 10:10, 14 (NIV) says, "And by that will, we have *been made holy* through the sacrifice of the body of Jesus Christ once for all. . . . because by one sacrifice *he has made perfect* forever *those who are being made holy*" (italics are mine). The first holiness we commonly call justification and can only be acquired through Jesus' sacrifice. The second, "being made holy," deals with the process of sanctification. This cannot happen unless the first kind of holiness is a reality in a person's life. "Entire sanctification" is "the goal for which God is preparing his people"[50] as described in Hebrews 12:14 (NIV), "Make every effort to live in peace with all men and to be holy; without holiness no one will see the Lord."

Christians frequently confuse justification and sanctification (we will cover these in more detail in the next chapter). Ryle explains the differences for us. Justification declares us righteous not on our own merits but by applying the "everlasting perfect righteousness" of Jesus Christ. His righteousness is imputed to us at the time of our faith in him, and we are justified. Justification is "finished and complete" and "perfect . . . the moment [a person] believes." There is no possibility of "growth or increase." When we are justified, we are delivered from guilt and given "our title to heaven, and boldness to enter it."[51] Justification declares us holy. Sanctification comes from the root word holy. Sanctification means "the process or *result of being made holy*" (italics are mine).[52]

Therefore, sanctification "is the process of actually making a man inwardly righteous," and this righteousness "is our own . . . wrought in us by the Holy Spirit" with hard work, prayer, great struggling and striving, imperfect though it may be.

48. O'Brien, *Hebrews*, 473.
49. O'Brien, *Hebrews*, 468.
50. O'Brien, *Hebrews*, 468.
51. Ryle, *Holiness*, 37.
52. Douglas and Tenney, "Sanctification," 894.

Perfection will only be reached in heaven.[53] Sanctification is a "progressive work" of the Holy Spirit with the person's cooperation, which produces "continual growth . . . as long as a man lives." It is what prepares us for heaven in order to enjoy it when we arrive. "Sanctification is the work of God *within* us, and cannot be hid in its outward manifestation from the eyes of men."[54] Bridges also sees these two kinds of holiness and writes, "Scripture speaks of both a holiness which we have in Christ before God, and a holiness which we are to strive after. These two aspects of holiness complement one another, for our salvation is a salvation to holiness."[55]

The Sermon on the Mount helps us to understand this sanctification. There we see additional characteristics stemming from God's holy righteousness. "Acts of mercy, of reconciliation and peacemaking, of seeking justice were in accord with the intent of God and with the true nature of the human person created by God and redeemed by Jesus."[56] Not only are God's people blessed because they are "pure in heart" and "hunger and thirst for righteousness," but also because they are merciful, peacemakers, and mourn for their sins. Matthew's beatitudes talk about the "poor in spirit" as "the acknowledgement of one's spiritual powerlessness and bankruptcy apart from Christ."[57] Those who mourn do so for their situation, which covers a whole array of things from personal loss to sin. All of these reflect the holiness of God and prepare us for his glory.

Holiness outside the Box of Reason

We have seen that love, peace, mercy, grace, and all the fruits of the Spirit must be added to the more commonly held understanding of holy as absolute moral perfection, but there is still more to holiness. Rudolf Otto calls this "numen" or "numinous," and describes it as "*mysterium tremendum*" and "mystical awe." The former he describes as a feeling that "may at times come sweeping like a gentle tide, pervading the mind with a tranquil mood of deepest worship. It may pass over into a more set and lasting attitude of the soul, continuing, as it were, thrillingly vibrant and resonant, until at last it dies away and the soul resumes its 'profane', non-religious mood of everyday experience."[58] He also connects strong emotions with holiness: "It may burst in sudden eruption up from the depths of the soul with spasms and convulsions, or lead to strangest excitements, to intoxicated frenzy, to transport, and to ecstasy. It has its wild and demonic forms and can sink to an almost grisly horror

---

53. For a different view on sanctification and "Christian Perfection," see Collins, *John Wesley: A Theological Journey*; Wesley, *A Plain Account*; Baker, *Letters*; and Outler, *Sermons I, II, III, IV*.

54. Ryle, *Holiness*, 37–38.

55. Bridges, *Pursuit of Holiness*, 32.

56. Senior, *Gospel of Matthew*, 104.

57. Blomberg, *Matthew*, 98.

58. Otto, *Idea of the Holy*, 12.

and shuddering."[59] Holiness cannot be pigeonholed into one kind of manifestation; "it has its crude, barbaric antecedents and early manifestations, and again it may be developed into something beautiful and pure and glorious. It may become hushed, trembling, and speechless humility of the creature in the presence of . . . . that which is a mystery inexpressible and above all creatures."[60]

This concept of holiness is strongly emotional. Holiness is no longer relegated to the sphere of reason, right living, morals, ethics, justice, and love. Otto thinks all these commonly held views are present in holiness, but they are not sufficient to describe it completely. We need to expand our understanding to include the emotions. It may manifest itself from a "tranquil mood of deepest worship," to "sudden eruption up from the depths of the soul with spasms and convulsions." It may be experienced as "intoxicated frenzy" or "transport and ecstasy." It can "sink into grisly horror and shuddering" or may rise to "something beautiful and pure and glorious." "Mystical awe" he explains as, "the 'shudder' reappears in a form ennobled beyond measure where the soul, held speechless, trembles inwardly to the farthest fibre of its being. It invades the mind mightily in Christian worship with the words: 'Holy, holy, holy' . . . . It has become a mystical awe."[61] We need to expand our understanding of holiness to include the full range of emotions. The numinous, our concept of holy, must be felt deep in the soul. It touches the person's innermost being and causes him or her to tremble. The numinous is God, and the single word that most connects with the numinous is the tripartite "holy."

Other aspects of holiness grow out of Otto's understanding of the numinous. The moving effect that music has on us is one example. This could be considered an intangible component of holiness. Another such aspect of holiness is beauty. Jonathan Edwards has much to say about this, and we will explore his thinking in chapter 8. The King James Version of the Holy Bible talks about "the beauty of holiness."[62] This is a literal translation of the original Hebrew. Unfortunately many modern translations use "the splendor of holiness" or "holy splendor," taking their cue from the Greek that uses "the court of holiness" which may reflect the reaction of Isaiah in his heavenly vision. In two of the passages on the "beauty of holiness," the people "tremble before him." In another, a great battle was won as Jehoshaphat "appointed singers unto the LORD, and that should praise the beauty of holiness, as they went out before the army, and to say, 'Praise the LORD; for his mercy endureth for ever'" (2 Chr 20:21, KJV). The fourth talks about the voice of the Lord, "the God of glory," as powerful, thundering, striking like lightning and shaking the desert and concludes with God on his throne. We should not be surprised that beauty is part of God's holiness, for Revelation describes heaven in terms of gold and the most beautiful gems that we can imagine. The beauty of heaven would surpass this because John was limited to earthly language and concepts we can understand.

59. Otto, *Idea of the Holy*, 12–13.
60. Otto, *Idea of the Holy*, 13.
61. Otto, *Idea of the Holy*, 17.
62. 1 Chr 16:29; 2 Chr 20:21; Pss 29:2; 96:9, KJV.

Two other intangibles we encounter in heaven are light and hope. There is no longer any need for the sun or the moon because "the glory of God gives it light, and the Lamb is its lamp" (Rev 21:23, NIV). John tells us that "God is light; in him there is no darkness at all" (1 John 1:5, NIV). There is hope (Rom 5:5, NIV) "because God has poured out his love into our hearts by the Holy Spirit."

How Holiness Relates to God's Other Attributes

Is holiness just one among the many of God's attributes, or does it have a unique position among the others? R. C. Sproul argues for the second option and explains why holiness encompasses so many aspects of God: "When the word *holy* is applied to God, it does not signify one single attribute. On the contrary, God is called holy in a general sense. The word is used as a synonym for his deity. That is, the word *holy* calls attention to all that God is."[63] Because it is the general term for God, "it reminds us that His love is holy love, his justice is holy justice, his mercy is holy mercy, his knowledge is holy knowledge, his spirit is holy spirit."[64]

The holiness of God is not just one among the many of his attributes. It is a "synonym for his deity" and brings to mind "all that God is" so that every characteristic of God known to humanity is to be thought of as holy. We may not just think of righteousness, judgment, and grace as separate terms but as holy righteousness, holy judgment, and holy grace coming from the Holy God in order to lead his people back to holiness and fellowship with him.

Bridges thinks along these same lines. He claims, "Holiness is God's crown . . . . Holiness is the perfection of all His other attributes; His power is holy power; His mercy is holy mercy; His wisdom is holy wisdom."[65] Correspondingly, Emmett Russell sees love as just one aspect of God's holiness and also connects holiness with worship of God. Because of this, he believes God's people must also embody holiness and declares that "holiness means the pure, loving nature of God, separate from evil, aggressively seeking to universalize itself."[66] Therefore, "this character is inherent in places, times, and institutions intimately associated with worship; and that holiness is to characterize human beings who have entered into personal relationship with God."[67]

Summary

We have examined holiness from the perspectives of God and his people. Hopefully this has caused us to think more deeply about this subject. We can accept we are moral

63. Sproul, *The Holiness of God*, 60.
64. Sproul, *The Holiness of God*, 60.
65. Bridges, *Pursuit of Holiness*, 25.
66. Russell, "Holiness, Holy," 445.
67. Russell, "Holiness, Holy," 445.

agents by virtue of the discussions about how to teach our children, but there is so much more to holiness. At all times we must remember that the difference between us and God is that we are accustomed to change as we mature. The danger is that we project our human capacity for growth and change on God. This results in a god of our own making who can and does modify his requirements of us. I will now summarize the things discussed so far.

God, through Scripture, talks a lot about holiness. Holiness is what is pronounced in the throne room scenes in both the Old Testament and the New Testament and is the only godly characteristic raised to "the third power" in all of Scripture. This holiness is seen as the whole earth being filled with the glory of God. The working knowledge by which we are to understand God's holiness in the rest of this book is: God's holiness means "set apart," "unique," "totally separate from all creation," "untouched, unstained by evil in the world," the "absolute absence of any evil," "the essence of moral purity," "infinite, absolute perfection," and "absolute purity or goodness" which is "immutable for it cannot become better or worse." Holiness is a "synonym for God's deity." God's holiness brings "perfect harmony" with "every part fulfilling its function for which it was designed." God's holiness gives us truth and uprightness. God's law is holy because it informs us of the "holy nature of God" and distinguishes for us what is good and just from what is evil and unjust. Holiness is righteousness, justice, discipline, and judgment, which includes wrath, but it goes beyond the legal disciplines to include love, joy, peace, grace, mercy, faithfulness, quietness, confidence, hope, and the full range of emotions. Holiness is God's "innermost essence," his essential character which informs everything he does and brings the greatest glory to him.

People might experience holiness in their emotions like "a gentle tide," "a tranquil mood of deepest worship, a "thrillingly vibrant and resonant" attitude of the soul, or a "sudden eruption from the depths of the soul with spasms and convulsions," "intoxicated frenzy," "transport," or "ecstasy." It may be understood as "wild and demonic," "pure and glorious," or as the soul trembling and speechless in every fiber of its existence. It is beauty and light and brings hope. There is no darkness.

God also calls his people to holiness that comes from a pure heart to live inwardly and outwardly the qualities of God in beauty and light and in an absence of pollution and darkness. It is to be thought of as positive, a "state of health," "wholeness," and "real life and being." The fruits and the gifts of the Spirit must be thought of as holy. Hence, love must be "holy love," grace must be "holy grace," and so on. God's people are justified and sanctified to serve God in love but also in righteousness, justice, and purity. They are light and salt to the people of their age and the bearers of hope. They have no merit of their own but they are called into communion with a Holy God in which holiness must be the bond of their union with God. They are called to be holy because he is holy and without holiness no one will see God.

Chapter 7

Is It Reasonable to Expect Holiness in People?

> Man is not God, he has been made in the likeness, in the image of God; he is a created copy of something that is essential in God.
>
> —D. MARTYN LLOYD-JONES, *DARKNESS AND LIGHT*

BEFORE WE CONSIDER HOW holiness would look in the lives of Christians and address the problems we face, we must consider whether such an examination is feasible. We have seen that Christians are commanded to be holy because God is Holy, and that holiness is the highest ideal. By the vast extent of what holiness entails, a person might feel overwhelmed and conclude it is unreasonable to hold people to such a high standard. He or she would be correct except for two things: people were initially created in the image of God (Gen 1:26–27), and God himself works in Christians to will and to do his good pleasure through the Holy Spirit, who is given to everyone who believes on his Son (Phil 2:12–13 and Eph 1:13).

The Image of God in People

First, all people are made in the image of God. Many argue this refers to our reasoning and intellect. Some think it refers to our ability to rule or to stand upright. All of this may be true, but clearly we know that God is holy, and being "created in his likeness" Adam and Eve were holy at their creation. This implies that "image" or "likeness" conveys much more than intellect, reason, or power. John Calvin writes, "It is important to know that we are endued with reason and intelligence, *in order that* we *might cultivate a holy and honorable life*, and regard a blessed immortality as our destined aim" (italics are mine).[1] Likeness must reflect the totality of holiness we described above. Writing about the image of God in humans, John Owen claims, "This [holiness] was our honour at our creation, this exalted us above all our fellow . . . creatures here below . . . we were made in the image of God."[2] Martyn Lloyd-Jones includes in this image "self-consciousness," "the power to reason and to think," "self-contemplation,"

---

1. Calvin, *Institutes*, 2.1.1 (p. 147).
2. Owen, *Communion with God*, 184.

and even "the uprightness of a man's body," but more importantly "God made man, originally . . . . righteous and holy and true . . . . fit for communion with God and one who enjoyed communion with God" and who had "moral and intellectual integrity."[3] Jonathan Edwards saw two attributes in the image of God, his holiness and those things we might call natural attributes of intellect, reason, strength, and dominion over the things of this planet. Based on this, he believes "there is a twofold image of God in man, his moral or spiritual image, which is his holiness, that is the image of God's moral excellency (which image was lost by the fall); and God's natural image, consisting in men's reason and understanding, his natural ability, and dominion over the creatures, which is the image of God's natural attributes."[4] If we were created to be holy, righteous and true, and "fit for communion with God," what happened?

The Image Lost

Christianity calls it "the fall" to which Edwards alluded above. God created the entire universe and pronounced it "good." God created Adam and Eve in "their [God's] image and likeness" and pronounced them "very good." They enjoyed communion with God and had everything they needed. God gave them one restriction only: do not eat from the tree of knowledge of good and evil. It seems so simple to do when they had it all in a perfect world, but it did not work out that way. Eve succumbed to temptation and ate the forbidden fruit, and Adam joined her.[5] The result as Edwards observes is that "Adam's posterity come into the world without original righteousness, as that Adam continued without it, after he had once lost it."[6] Furthermore, "Adam continued destitute of holiness" once he lost it, and never would have regained it "had it not been restored by a Redeemer."[7] This was both the natural and penal consequence of his sin. "God, as the Author of nature . . . in righteous judgment, continued to absent himself from Adam, after he became a rebel; and withheld from him now those influences of the Holy Spirit, which he before had."[8]

Many have called this "original sin" that is passed on to every human.[9] Their fellowship with God was forever altered. Gone were the long walks in the beauty of the evening sunset with the cool breezes. They would have to work hard for minimal results compared to what they had. There were also spiritual effects of the fall on the image of

---

3. Lloyd-Jones, *Darkness and Light*, 176–77.
4. Edwards, "Religious Affections," 256.
5. For other views on Adam and Eve, see Canedy et al., *Four Views on the Historical Adam*, and Shuster, *The Fall and Sin*.
6. Edwards, "Original Sin," 386. (Hereafter cited as WJE 3:page number).
7. WJE 3:386.
8. WJE 3:386.
9. For more information on "original sin," see Edwards, "Treatise on Original Sin"; Shuster, "Mystery of Original Sin."

God in humanity. John Wesley describes original sin as "all men are conceived in sin, and 'shapen in wickedness;' . . . that hence there is in every man a 'carnal mind, which is enmity against God, which is not, cannot be, subject to' his 'law.'"[10] Wesley understood this to be so complete that it "infects the whole soul, that 'there dwelleth in' him, 'in his flesh,' in his natural state, 'no good thing;' but 'every imagination of the thoughts of his heart is evil,' only evil, and that 'continually.'"[11] Furthermore, he agrees with Scripture that in Adam all died meaning that all "spiritually died [and] lost the life and the image of God," because it was not possible for Adam to bear children in anything but his own likeness of spiritual death and separation from God.[12] Wesley understands Romans 3:23, "for all have sinned and fall short of the glory of God," as pertaining to falling short of "that glorious image of God wherein man was originally created."[13]

For Calvin "original sin" meant "the deprivation of a nature formerly good and pure." He describes this depravity as the withdrawal of "wisdom, virtue, justice, truth, and holiness" which were replaced with "blindness, impotence, vanity, impurity, and unrighteousness."[14] Furthermore, he sees "original sin" as "a hereditary corruption . . . extending to all parts of the soul." This makes us "obnoxious to the wrath of God" because we are "perverted and corrupted in all parts of our nature, we are . . . deservedly condemned by God, to whom nothing is acceptable, but righteousness, innocence, and purity."[15] This total depravity does not mean that in human terms people cannot do good or even moral things, for people can still function intellectually with reason, understanding, and knowledge. However, these actions are darkened by incomplete knowledge, faulty logic, and abuse of power brought about by our self-absorbed lives as a result of the Fall and sin. Sin infects every aspect of our lives and erects a barrier between us and God because God is Holy, and we are not. Total depravity refers to the fact that while people can do good deeds in human terms, there is nothing within any person to qualify him or her for fellowship with the perfect goodness of God.

Sin is like leaven or yeast; if a little gets mixed in with the other ingredients, the entire lump is altered. No part is spared. Only people and things that are holy can survive in God's presence. Owen declares, "This [holiness] we lost by sin, and became like the beasts that perish."[16] Lloyd-Jones describes it as, "when man fell the image of God in man was defaced." He calls this "the tragedy of man," because "he still bears some of the marks of the image of God. He can still think; he can still reason; he still stands erect . . . he can reason about himself and contemplate himself . . . . But what was really the crowning gift of the image . . . the righteousness, the

---

10. Wesley, "Original Sin," III.1.
11. Wesley, "Original Sin," III.1.
12. Wesley, "Original Sin," para. 4.
13. Wesley, "Original Sin," para. 4.
14. Calvin, *Institutes*, 2.1.5 (p. 150).
15. Calvin, *Institutes*, 2.1.8 (p. 152).
16. Owen, *Communion with God*, 184.

uprightness, the holiness, the truth . . . was lost, and man was driven out from the presence of God and became a stranger to Him."[17]

Calvin reminds us "that without holiness *no man shall see the Lord*; for with no other eyes shall we see God than those which have been renewed after his image."[18] In more practical terms Sproul explains that "the smallest sin involves a sin against the whole law. The law is the standard of holiness for us. In our slightest transgression we sin against that standard; we violate the call to holiness."[19] The image of God in us is damaged. Owen asks an important question, "When we were in our best condition by nature, in the state of original holiness, vested with the image of God, we preserved it not; and is it likely that now, in the state of lapsed and depraved nature, it is in our own power to restore ourselves, to re-introduce the image of God into our souls?"[20] What hope then is there for us?

The New Creation: The Image Restored

Calvin sees a solution. Remembering from what we have fallen can be a catalyst to seek restoration with God. He observes that "it is impossible to think of our primeval dignity without being immediately reminded of the sad spectacle of our ignominy and corruption, ever since we fell from our original."[21] He sees in this a catalyst for change; "we feel dissatisfied with ourselves, and become truly humble, while we are inflamed with new desires to seek after God, in whom each may regain those good qualities of which all are found to be utterly destitute."[22]

This is supported in Scripture where it talks about a "new person." In the Old Testament, Jeremiah declared that there would come a time when God would write his law on the hearts of his people (Jeremiah 31:33–34). Calvin believes this to be the Old Testament law that will be written on human hearts and "will be confirmed and ratified, when it shall be succeeded by the new."[23] The New Testament is the fulfillment of this Jeremiah passage. We find references to this new person in Ephesians 2:15. The King James Version uses "new man" but more modern translations use "new self." Paul commands the Ephesians (4:24, NIV), "Put on the new self, created to be like God in true righteousness and holiness." To the Colossians, he writes (3:10, NIV), "Put on the new self, which is being renewed in knowledge in the image of its Creator." What does this new person look like? What is restored, and what is the purpose?

---

17. Lloyd-Jones, *Darkness and Light*, 177.
18. Calvin, "Epistle to the Hebrews," 324.
19. Sproul, *The Holiness of God*, 257.
20. Owen, *Holy Spirit*, 382.
21. Calvin, *Institutes*, 2.1.1 (p. 147).
22. Calvin, *Institutes*, 2.1.1 (p. 147).
23. Calvin, *Harmony of the Evangelists*, 277.

For Lloyd-Jones the new person is something created brand new in the old person. It is entirely different than self-help or self-improvement books we read today. He writes that this new person is not merely a "renovation" or an "improvement" on the old person but is altogether "a creation, a new work."[24] He describes it as God putting into a person "something that was not there at all before. That is what it means to become a Christian." This is not dependent on human self-help and effort. "Something absolutely new is put in at the centre . . . 'created'! That is the whole meaning of regeneration, of being born again. . . . the Christian is entirely different! Absolutely new!"[25] The new creation is not simply human striving to be better. There is literally a new creation within the person in which the Holy Spirit now resides working in the person to restore God's image. This new thing restored to Christians (only) is "that they receive back the righteousness, holiness and truth which were lost through sin and the Fall."[26]

Owen agrees and writes, "It is by holiness" that God's "image is renewed in us again," and elaborates, "To this honour, of conformity to God, of bearing his image, are we exalted again by holiness alone . . . . This . . . is still all that is beautiful or comely in the world."[27] The holiness aspect of the image of God is restored to us in order that we may be restored to our former glory and have fellowship with God again to the glory and honor of God. Personal holiness, obedience, and righteousness "is one eminent and especial end of the peculiar dispensation of Father, Son and Spirit, in the business of exalting the glory of God in our salvation."[28] The renewed image of God in us is "our holiness" which "consists in a holy obedience unto God by Jesus Christ, according to the terms of the covenant of grace, from the principle of a renewed nature."[29] Out of this holiness, "the fruits of his love, of his grace, of his kindness, are seen upon us; and God is glorified in our behalf."[30] The glory always goes to God.

Lloyd-Jones picks up on Otto's *numinous* and *mysteruim tremendum* (chapter 6) and argues that this new person must also reflect the mystery of God's holiness. This new person "is a reflection of this essential characteristic or attribute of God . . . holiness! Purity! Something ineffable! Something which we cannot describe because of the inadequacy of our language, but something which is eternally different from sin and evil in its essence and in all its manifestations. The Holiness of God! God is holy!"[31]

---

24. Lloyd-Jones, *Darkness and Light*, 173.
25. Lloyd-Jones, *Darkness and Light*, 173.
26. Lloyd-Jones, *Darkness and Light*, 177.
27. Owen, *Communion with God*, 184.
28. Owen, *Communion with God*, 182.
29. Owen, *Holy Spirit*, 386.
30. Owen, *Communion with God*, 183.
31. Lloyd-Jones, *Darkness and Light*, 180.

About this new creation, he continues, "Man again becomes as he was at the beginning, with everything in the right position in his make-up . . . . the new man loves that which is right, and therefore does that which is right in all his relationships in life."[32] He continues with "the man has been created anew in righteousness and holiness of the truth!" to which he adds, "Truth takes up the whole man, and moves the entire being."[33] He identifies this truth as "the great message of the Bible from beginning to end."[34] When a person becomes a Christian, the complete image of God is restored in him or her, which must then reflect God's truth and righteousness as found in the totality of Scripture.

What This New Creation Will Look Like

Scripture calls God's people to holiness in various places and ways. Paul urges (Rom 12:1–2a, NIV), "in view of God's mercy, to offer your bodies as living sacrifices, holy and pleasing to God . . . this is your spiritual act of worship. Do not conform any longer to the pattern of this world, but be transformed by the renewing of your mind." We are to honor God with our bodies as well as our minds or inner piety.[35] O'Brien takes Hebrews 12:14 as a command to make "every effort to be holy . . . . not falling short of the grace of God" and cautions us to watch out that "no one falls short," "no bitter root grows up," and "no one is apostate or irreligious" (sexually immoral and godless).[36] Owen believes God does not only require "holiness indispensably in all believers," but this is *all* that he requires because holiness "compriseth the whole duty of man."[37]

The most concise passage of Scripture to portray this new creation is the Sermon on the Mount. Donald Senior believes it describes "the heart of what it means to be a faithful child of God in the world."[38] M. Eugene Boring adds, "In the Sermon on the Mount, Jesus will present the nature of the life of the kingdom he proclaims and represents. He has reversed the idea of human kingship."[39] People no longer rule in their own name and own will, but will submit to God's name and God's will. Boring also sees the nature of the "true people" of God's kingdom as those who "know their lives are not in their own control and that they are dependent on God . . . . Persons who are pronounced blessed are not those who claim a robust ego and strong sense of self-worth, but those whose only identity and security is in God."[40] Senior reminds us the "acts of mercy, of

---

32. Lloyd-Jones, *Darkness and Light*, 180.
33. Lloyd-Jones, *Darkness and Light*, 184.
34. Lloyd-Jones, *Darkness and Light*, 184.
35. See 1 Cor 6:19–20; 2 Cor 7:1; Phil 2:12–13; and Heb 12:14.
36. O'Brien, *Hebrews*, 472.
37. Owen, *Holy Spirit*, 376.
38. Senior, *Gospel of Matthew*, 102.
39. Boring, *Gospel of Matthew*, 178.
40. Boring, *Gospel of Matthew*, 178.

reconciliation and peacemaking, [and] of seeking justice were in accord with the intent of God and with the true nature of the human person created by God and redeemed by Jesus."[41] We know this true nature to be holiness.

Pursuit of God's holiness by the new creation was a given for Edwards. He believed that once a person has received the initial gift of holiness through faith in Jesus and has the Holy Spirit dwelling in him or her, he or she will affirm what God has said in Scripture as the truth and the will of God. He writes that holiness requires God's people to conform to him not only in eternity or because of his infinite power, but "to his will [now], whereby he wills things that are just, right, and truly excellent and lovely . . . real perfection . . . and perfectly abhors everything that is really evil, unjust, and unreasonable." Wanting to do what is right is not enough; they must also be doing those things God would do "in acting holily and justly and wisely and mercifully, like him. It must become natural . . . it must be the constant inclination of the new nature of the soul, and then the man is holy, and not before."[42] The new creation is evidenced in a person by his or her affirmation that what God says is truth that must be followed and which becomes "the *constant* inclination of the new nature of the soul" (italics are mine).

This new creation will exhibit certain identifiable behaviors. Ryle discerns twelve marks of a holy man. The first is that the person will have "the habit of being of one mind with God. . . . measuring everything in this world by the standard of His Word. He who most entirely agrees with God, he is the most holy man."[43] Additionally a holy man will: "*endeavor to shun every known sin, and to keep every known commandment*," "*strive to be like our Lord Jesus Christ* bold and uncompromising in denouncing sin," and "follow after *meekness . . . . temperance and self-denial . . . . charity and brotherly kindness . . . . mercy and benevolence towards others . . . . purity of heart . . . . the fear of God . . . . humility . . . . faithfulness in all the duties and relations in life . . . .* [and] *spiritual-mindedness.*"[44] Furthermore the Christian, the saint, God's holy one, will control his or her tongue, pursue the fruits of the Spirit, crucify lusts, curb passions, and will keep clear of temptation. Additionally, the new creation will hold the things of this world very lightly and value them only as they lead him or her closer to God.[45] No wonder Scripture calls them saints.

For Wesley, this new creation that we call a Christian will at all times and in everything have his or her thoughts on God continually and seek to do his will. All Christians have "the loving eye of their minds still fixed upon him [God], and ever [see] him that is invisible."[46] Not only will this new creation in Christ have their

41. Senior, *Gospel of Matthew*, 104.
42. Edwards, "Way of Holiness," 472.
43. Ryle, *Holiness*, 42.
44. Ryle, *Holiness*, 42–46.
45. Ryle, *Holiness*, 42–46.
46. Wesley, *Longing for Holiness*, 41.

minds set on Christ, but they will "now have *clothed themselves with compassion, kindness, humility, meekness, and patience* so that they *bear with and forgive each other, just as the Lord has forgiven them.*"[47] Additionally, they will know they belong to God through the witness of the Holy Spirit residing in them. They will bless God and praise him in all circumstances, good and bad. They will learn to be content in every situation of life. They will pray without ceasing and continually give God thanks for all the good things he bestows.[48]

Christians must remember that goodness to this extent is what the Bible requires to be called good. For sure, every person has sinned and falls short of God's holy standard. Additionally, there is no spiritual eraser that can remove past sins. Is it any wonder Calvin called our natural state *total* depravity? However, Scripture talks about the saints, the people who pursue God's holiness. Let's hear Owen again. He sees the Christian walk "in the light of new obedience" as the basis for "communion with God, and in his presence is fullness of joy for ever; without it, there is nothing but darkness and wandering, and confusion."[49] He even goes so far as to say, "A man without holiness is good for nothing."[50] These are strong words and distressing to our ears. There is nothing anyone can do in their own power to recover this holiness. The new creation, new birth, is the only thing that can make a person holy as God is holy.

A person wanting to acquire holiness is like a space ship reentering the atmosphere. If the angle is not accurate, it will either skip off out into space or burn up in the atmosphere. Either one brings death to the astronauts. There is only one way that will get them safely home. Similarly, without holiness no one will see God, and this holiness can only be restored in one way. Lloyd-Jones reminds Christians that they are created anew when they come to faith in Jesus. God's divine nature has been restored in them, manifesting in holiness, righteousness, and truth. Furthermore, the Christian "is a created copy of something that is essential in God."[51] At best, the new creation is a created copy. Jesus is the only one born of God. The rest of us are created by him. This is why only Jesus can save anyone.

Lloyd-Jones claims, "If only every true Christian in the world today realized that this new creation, this new man, this new being, was within him, the whole Church would be revolutionized."[52] He also laments, "All our failures, all our sins, are ultimately to be traced to the fact that we do not realise as we should what God has done to us, and the character and the nature of the new man, the new life, that He has put within us."[53] That nature can only come from Jesus.

47. Wesley, *Longing for Holiness*, 41–42.
48. Wesley, *Longing for Holiness*, 40.
49. Owen, *Communion with God*, 185.
50. Owen, *Communion with God*, 185.
51. Lloyd-Jones, *Darkness and Light*, 177.
52. Lloyd-Jones, *Darkness and Light*, 177–78.
53. Lloyd-Jones, *Darkness and Light*, 178.

Why Jesus Is Needed to Recover Holiness

If holiness is the criteria for seeing God, and we have none, then there must be something to restore the totality of God's image in broken and sinful people if anyone is going to see God. That something is redemption given by the life, death, and resurrection of Jesus to all who believe on him. Edwards explains that "Christ, by the great things which he did and suffered in the world, has purchased grace and holiness for the elect. John 17:19."[54] He was the only one who could acquire this "grace for them to that end that they might walk in holy practice. He has reconciled them to God by his death to redeem them from wicked works, that they might be holy and unblamable in their lives."[55] Edwards then directs us to Colossians 1:21–22, "And you, that were sometimes alienated and enemies in your mind by wicked works, yet now hath he reconciled in the body of his flesh through death, to present you holy and unblamable and unreprovable in his sight."

The price to recover holiness is the death of a perfect (literally) person. Jesus was that person. Being fully God and fully human he was born like Adam was created with the ability not to sin. Unlike Adam, Jesus lived without rebelling against God. Therefore, his death was the perfect sacrifice, the Lamb without blemish provided by God himself. That is why Jesus, and only Jesus, is the way of salvation. He alone is the spiritual eraser that can remove our sins. No one else can do what he did, for we all die in our own sins. Only Jesus died in yours.

The act of believing in Jesus (more than mere intellectual assent or acknowledgment) is the moment we are justified and declared holy before God; Jesus' righteousness is applied to us. It happens instantly at what many call our conversion and is what Paul calls being made "alive with Christ." This is what we have noted previously as justification and is only the first step of our salvation, which is "by grace through faith . . . it is the gift of God . . . and not by works lest any man should boast" (Eph 2:8–9, NIV). People are called to faith in Jesus Christ as the means to God's grace. Owen points out that Jesus confines sanctifying, holy faith to be in him alone (John 14:6) and declares, "There is no other way to attain that holiness which may bring them unto the heavenly inheritance, or make them meet for it, Col. i. 12 . . . . And, indeed there can be no greater contempt cast on the Lord Jesus, and on the duty of believing in him . . . than to imagine that without faith in him anyone can be made holy."[56]

Because he was perfect (without sin), Jesus, in shedding his blood, has paid "a ransom for us" and has born our iniquities and in so doing has "answered the law, removed the curse, and reconciled us to God, pacified his anger, satisfied justice, procured for us eternal redemption" so that now we have access to God through him.[57]

---

54. Edwards, "Ethical Writings," 295. (Hereafter cited as WJE 8:page number.)
55. WJE 8:295.
56. Owen, *Holy Spirit*, 414.
57. Owen, *Nature and Beauty of Gospel Worship*, 61.

Scripture tells us that "without holiness no one will see the Lord." Scripture also makes clear that God provides the way for this to happen through faith in his one and only son, Christ Jesus. This faith calls us to a commitment to our Holy God and to his commands, but we are not left to our own devices to accomplish it, for that would be impossible for the new creation let alone fallen human nature to do.

The Role of the Holy Spirit

The work of restoring the image of God in a Christian is done by the Holy Spirit. In the Old Testament God promised to place his Spirit in each of his people (Ezek 36:26–27). Owen reminds us of the role of the Holy Spirit in justification and sanctification and writes, "The work of regeneration is *instantaneous*, consisting in one single creating act. Hence it is not capable of degrees in any subject. No one is more or less regenerate than another; every one in the world is absolutely so, or not so, and that equally.... But this work of sanctification is *progressive*, and admits of degrees."[58] Furthermore, "*the universal renovation of our natures . . . into the image of God,* [takes place] *by the Holy Spirit . . . through Jesus Christ.*" Owen also acknowledges that God "dwells in us, as in his temple; which is not to be defiled. Holiness becometh his habitation for ever."[59]

Therefore, since God's Holy Spirit dwells in all who have been regenerated through the reconciling work of Jesus by faith in him, "all our corruptions [must be] thoroughly subdued, and our souls thoroughly sanctified"; "the work of sanctification [is] gradually carried on, and holiness increased. And this addition of one grace unto another, with the progress of holiness thereby, is also from the Holy Ghost."[60] Therefore the Holy Spirit "is the immediate peculiar sanctifier of all believers, and the author of all holiness in them."[61] No one can achieve holiness in status or actual behavior apart from God's work of the Holy Spirit in them.

Lloyd-Jones agrees, "This is the essential New Testament teaching on holiness and sanctification; it is something which is done in us by the Holy Spirit using the Word [Scripture].... It is a progressive cleansing until we shall be free from every spot, or wrinkle... free from every blemish we shall be entirely holy."[62] For Owen, "In respect of sanctification.... This new creature is fed, cherished, nourished, kept alive, by the fruits of holiness."[63] The new self is sustained by the Holy Spirit who produces these fruits, all of which are holy because God is holy.

In cooperating with the Holy Spirit we must examine ourselves. Calvin describes it as the search for truth and knowledge that leaves us with no "confidence in our own

58. Owen, *Holy Spirit*, 387.
59. Owen, *Communion with God*, 184.
60. Owen, *Holy Spirit*, 392.
61. Owen, *Holy Spirit*, 385.
62. Lloyd-Jones, *Life in the Spirit*, 160.
63. Owen, *Communion with God*, 186.

powers, [which] leaves us devoid of all means of boasting, and so inclines us to submission. This is the course which we must follow, if we would attain to the true goal, both in speculation and practice."[64] Owen also included self-examination in the Christian life. In meditation, "the heart goes over . . . . its own sinfulness, and filling itself with shame and self-abhorrency of that account"; at other times "when grieved and burdened by negligence, or eruption of corruption, then the soul goes over the whole work, and so drives things to an issue with God, and takes up the peace that Christ hath wrought out for him."[65] This is so unlike the current practice of ignoring wrongs and focusing only on anything positive we can find to prove the person is good.

Edwards was known for his self-examination as can be seen in his "Resolutions." In resolutions 24, 25, 37, and 56 he resolved to examine himself every night and to "fight and pray with all my might" against any sin he found, tracing it back to the origin. Sin included whatever was in him "which causes me in the least to doubt of the love of God."[66] He had overarching examinations weekly and monthly. Each year he would reassess his resolutions to see if they needed to be revised. Edwards took his directions from Scripture (2 Cor 13:5, NIV) which says, "Examine yourselves to see whether you are in the faith; test yourselves. Do you not realize that Christ Jesus is in you . . . unless, of course, you fail the test?"

The Role of Grace

"But," you may be thinking, "What about grace? Where does God's grace come in? Does not grace trump holiness?" After all, James writes (2:13, NIV) that "mercy triumphs over judgment." Again, Owen helps us here. Because we "have no sufficiency of ourselves" to "comply with the command" of God in a single instance, we must rely on the promise of God's grace, something *we in no way ever deserve*, in order to attain "the least part or degree of holiness." We must rely on faith in the promise of grace that the Holy Spirit "who is *the immediate, peculiar sanctifier* of all believers," is also the "immediate dispenser of all divine grace" and "operator of all divine gracious effects in us."[67] Owen identifies two kinds of grace. The first he calls the "habit of grace," which is "a created quality" given to the new creation, and although he does not specifically mention justification, it corresponds to that work of Christ applied to the disciple's life at the moment of his entry into the life of faith in Jesus as his Lord and Savior. The person with the "habit of grace" is changed inwardly in his or her ability to understand and to agree with God. This person is enabled to obey all that God commands.[68]

---

64. Calvin, *Institutes*, 2.1.1 (p. 147).
65. Owen, *Communion with God*, 197.
66. Edwards, "Resolutions," 754–57. (Hereafter cited as WJE 16:page number.)
67. Owen, *Holy Spirit*, 385.
68. Owen, *Communion with God*, 200.

The second grace he calls "actual grace," which "is an illapse of divine influence and assistance, working in and by the soul any spiritual act or duty whatsoever."[69] He compares this to Philippians 2:13 (NIV), "for it is God who works in you to will and to act according to his good purpose." "Habitual grace" is always present in the soul of the believer and is the cause/enablement or "meet principle for all those holy and spiritual operations which by actual grace are to be performed."[70] This saving grace is realized only in the one who believes in Jesus as Lord and Savior.[71] While "habitual grace" is constant, "actual grace" may fluctuate. There may be more in some than in others, and within the same person there may be "more at one time than another. Hence are those dyings, decays, ruins, recoveries, complaints, and rejoicings, where of so frequent mention is made in the Scripture."[72] God's grace is given to restore a person to holiness and is not to be abused or presumed (Rom 6).

Ryle has also considered grace in his quest for understanding God's holiness in people. God's grace administered through faith in Jesus does triumph over God's judgment and eternal condemnation. However, there is another aspect of grace that he calls "growth in grace," which corresponds with Owen's "actual grace." By this he means that a person's "sense of sin is becoming deeper, his faith stronger, his hope brighter, his love more extensive, his spiritual-mindedness more marked. He feels more of the power of godliness in his own heart. He manifests more of it in his life. He is going on from strength to strength, from faith to faith, and from grace to grace."[73] For him, grace is never a get-out-of-jail-free card that empowers and excuses sin. He identifies several marks of growing in grace which are similar to the marks of holiness: increased humility, faith and love towards Jesus, holiness of life and conversations, charity, and concern for the salvation of souls.[74] So then, according to Ryle the person growing in grace is keenly aware of his or her sins, increasingly recognizes his or her need of the Savior, and is more grateful to Jesus as time passes, becomes more holy with the passing of time, progressively demonstrates the fruit of the Spirit especially toward those of the faith, and will more and more be concerned about bringing others to faith in Jesus Christ.[75]

Ryle also discusses the means of growing in grace and admonishes Christians to be diligent "in the use of private means of grace . . . private prayer, private reading of the Scriptures, and private meditation and self-examination . . . [and] carefulness in the use of public means of grace . . . uniting with God's people in common prayer and

---

69. Owen, *Communion with God*, 200.

70. Owen, *Communion with God*, 200–201.

71. Saving grace is not to be confused with general grace, which God shows on all of his creatures by sending the sun and the rain on all to provide for their life on earth.

72. Owen, *Communion with God*, 200.

73. Ryle, *Holiness*, 101.

74. Ryle, *Holiness*, 105–8.

75. Ryle, *Holiness*, 105–8.

praise, the preaching of the Word, and the sacrament of the Lord's Supper."[76] In fact he is so certain of the corporate means of grace that he goes so far as to say, "I firmly believe that the manner in which these public means of grace are used has much to say to the prosperity of a believer's soul . . . . It is a sign of bad health when a person loses relish for his food; and it is a sign of spiritual decline when we lose our appetite for means of grace."[77] Ralph Martin agrees, "To rest content and self-satisfied with an unholy life is to receive the grace of God in vain ([2 Cor] 6:1, 2)."[78] Additionally, means of grace could be thought of as warnings to watch "over our conduct in the little matters of everyday life" and to be cautious "about the company we keep and the friendships we form."[79] This is quite different from today where increasingly in both the culture and the church grace is used to excuse everything.

Summary

In our age of "if it feels good, do it"; "you *deserve* a break today"; "we make our own truth"; and "we want what we want, when we want it," it is easy to fall into a consumer approach to Scripture and how we live the life of faith and how we view holiness and grace. I will conclude this chapter with a few statements of encouragement and caution. Lloyd-Jones charges Christians to keep "intact the relationship between a saint and being faithful, the relationship between holiness and being a believer in the Lord Jesus Christ. These things should never be separated."[80]

Owen cautions the church to distinguish moral virtue from holiness. He writes, "I concern not myself much how *moral virtue* . . . is preserved and sustained in the minds and lives of men"; there are people who can discern the proper way to behave in specific circumstances, but that does not make them holy or the recipients of God's grace "for *grace* and *holiness* . . . depend merely and only upon their relation unto that spring and fountain of all grace which is in Christ, and the continual supplies of it by the Holy Spirit, whose work it is to communicate them, Col. iii. 3; John xv. 5; Col. ii. 19."[81] Additionally he cautions those who would separate grace from holiness or sanctification, "our duty and God's grace are nowhere opposed in the matter of sanctification, yea, the one doth absolutely suppose the other."[82] If you have received God's grace, you will work to please him according to the totality of Scripture.

---

76. Ryle, *Holiness*, 110–11.
77. Ryle, *Holiness*, 111.
78. Martin, *2 Corinthians*, 210.
79. Ryle, *Holiness*, 111–12.
80. Lloyd-Jones, *God's Ultimate Purpose*, 33.
81. Owen, Holy *Spirit*, 393.
82. Owen, Holy *Spirit*, 384.

Sproul draws our attention to one more thing. "It's dangerous to assume that because a person is drawn to holiness in his study that he is thereby a holy man."[83] Like the person who may be drawn to study Scripture, but remain unaffected by its contents, so too, a person may be drawn to learn about holiness, but remain in his profaneness. Sproul admits he is a "profane man . . . who spends more time out of the temple than in it. But . . . [and this is what makes the difference] I have had just enough of a taste of the majesty of God to want more. I know what it means to be a forgiven man and what it means to be sent on a mission. My soul cries for more. My soul needs more."[84]

Grace does not do away with holiness as some might interpret it today. Instead, it proceeds from God, who is holy and works to draw us *back from* our fallen nature in order to restore the image of God in us; that image is holiness. Those who acknowledge their desperate need for God will inherit the kingdom of heaven; those who mourn their sin and sinfulness will be comforted; those who are humble will inherit the earth, those who hunger and thirst for righteousness will be filled; the merciful will receive mercy; the pure in heart will see God, and the peacemakers will be called the children of God. God's love, faithfulness, mercy, grace and peace, beauty, and light come forth from the foundation of his righteousness and justice. They all come from holiness because they come from God, and they are sent to restore the image of God in broken human beings, to return them to the holiness they lost in the fall. We have looked at what holiness is and what it looks like in the new creation restored to the image of God through Jesus by the power of the Holy Spirit. Next we will look at how holiness informs the solutions to many of the problems the church faces in the twenty-first century.

---

83. Sproul, *The Holiness of God*, 51.
84. Sproul, *The Holiness of God*, 51.

Chapter 8

The Beauty of Holiness

> Holiness is a most beautiful and lovely thing . . . . There is nothing in it but what is sweet and ravishingly lovely.
>
> —Jonathan Edwards, "The Miscellanies"

I BEGAN THIS BOOK with a quote from Kenneth Scott Latourette stating that when God entrusted people with more knowledge and mastery of the environment, he took a risk knowing that some would debase that gift and use it for evil. We live in an age with unprecedented knowledge and ability to master our environment. Just one example is the air conditioning we have in our homes, cars, boats, planes, and farm equipment cabins. To see the abuse we have made of the gifts of knowledge and technology that have been given us, you need only watch the nightly news. Cyber-bullying and predators luring unsuspecting teens into molestation or human trafficking only scratch the surface. We have also seen how the church has gone well past contextualizing the gospel message and has capitulated to much of American culture.

The church has compromised her major teachings of love, grace, and mercy and has all but jettisoned the doctrines of holiness, righteousness, and judgment. The wrath of God has become politically incorrect as is the need for a crucified Savior among many professing Christians today. Justice has been collapsed to a singularity of social justice. Culture has taken our words such as belief, faith, freedom, grace, peace, and unity and changed them to mean things never intended in Scripture. Corporations use evangelism as the way to promote their product while the church shies away from the "E" word. Additionally, within the walls of churches, the "word of God" has been obfuscated so that to some it can only refer to Jesus, thereby separating him from Scripture. This separation has brought confusion instead of unity.

However, Latourette does not leave us in the gloom and doom but encourages us by assuring the church that God was "confident that others will be so gripped by the Gospel that they will be stirred and empowered not only to counteract the evil but also to produce fruits far greater than if the possibilities for the abuse of God's gifts had not been present."[1] Latourette reassures Christians that God's purpose was

---

1. Latourette, *History of Christianity*, 968.

to "produce men of character, not automatons" and "that He is sovereign and will not permit evil to get completely out of hand, but will overrule it for His own purposes of love."[2] One way Christians can work with God to accomplish this is to be aware of the influences that media and technology have had on the way they communicate the gospel and to be sure it is the Christian gospel that is being communicated and not some cultural capitulation. But this is only the beginning. God has also endowed the church with some awe-inspiring tools to communicate his gospel. One of them is beauty and the pleasure it gives.

I have been claiming that holiness is the key to revival and reform in this age. This is why: Our culture seeks pleasure like no generation before us. I say this because while hedonism was common to all ages, our technology makes pleasure infinitely more available to everyone, including children. Rather than condemn the pursuit of pleasure, enjoyment, and happiness, the church must come to understand that pleasure, happiness, and enjoyment are the very things for which people were created. Scripture commands us to delight in God (Ps 37), and tells us that the typical state of believers in Christ is to be rejoicing in a glorious and inexpressible joy (1 Pet 1:8). Paul commands (Phil 4:4), "Rejoice in the Lord always, and I will say it again, rejoice!" Nehemiah writes (8:10), "The joy of the Lord is your strength." The Psalms are full of references to the joy of the Lord. We were created to have joy and pleasure.

Jonathan Edwards points out that God is glorified by being received by the entire soul: by both knowledge (intellect) and desire of the will (heart). He writes, "God is glorified not only by his glory's being seen, but by its being rejoiced in, when those that see it delight in it: God is more glorified than if they only see it; his glory is then received by the whole soul, both by the understanding and by the heart."[3] He further reminds us that "God made the world that he might communicate, and the creature receive, his glory, but that it might [be] received both by the mind and heart. He that testifies his having an idea of God's glory don't glorify God so much as he that testifies also his approbation of it and his delight in it."[4] God wants the delight of him to be not just in the minds of the Christians, but in their hearts and in their lives as well. However, this truth is often betrayed by the stoic faces of most Christians and the seeming lack of delight and joy in most Christian worship services. How has this happened?

Lewis links this stoicism with the Age of Reason's understanding of self-denial and writes, "The notion that to desire our own good and earnestly to hope for the enjoyment of it is a bad thing, I submit . . . has crept in from Kant and the Stoics and is no part of the Christian faith. Indeed, if we consider the unblushing promises of reward and the staggering nature of the rewards promised in the Gospels, it would

---

2. Latourette, *History of Christianity*, 968–69.
3. Edwards, "The Miscellanies," 495. (Hereafter cited as WJE 13:page number.)
4. WJE 13:495.

seem that Our Lord finds our desires not too strong, but too weak."[5] He concludes, "We are half-hearted creatures fooling about with drink and sex and ambition when infinite joy is offered us.... We are far too easily pleased."[6]

Yes, Jesus calls Christians to deny themselves, to take up their cross, and to follow him, but to deny self is to say no to those things and temptations that take us away from a holy life of service to God and obedience to God's will as laid out in Scripture. This does not do away with what Lewis calls "pleasure of the inferior," which he defines as "the pleasure of a beast before men, a child before its father, a pupil before his teacher, a creature before its Creator"; it is the moment when "the satisfaction of having pleased those whom I rightly loved and rightly feared was pure."[7] It is like the sheer delight of a child opening a present on Christmas morning to find it is exactly what she wanted. It is the feeling Christians will have when God looks at them and says (Matt 25:21, 23), "Well done, good and faithful servant." The problem the people of this world face is seeking their joy and pleasure in the wrong places and making good things the ultimate things.

Again, Lewis helps us to understand pleasure as it was intended by God in contrast with the disappointment so often felt in the pleasures of this world. Pointing to the very real desire found on earth in which food fulfills a baby's hunger, sex satisfies a person's longings, and water enables a duck to swim, Lewis claims, "If I find in myself a desire which no experience in this world can satisfy, the most probable explanation is that I was made for another world.... earthly pleasures were never meant to satisfy it, but only to arouse it, to suggest the real thing."[8] We see in this two sources of pleasure. The first is godly; the second is natural (earthly). Natural pleasures are intended only to reflect God and to point people to him and the true pleasures for which they were created.

Ted Dekker expands on this idea and compares earthly pleasures to a banquet of foretastes which decay over time and must be replenished. They are delightful, but never last. He identifies a second banquet of everlasting bliss which "may be seen through the windows but not eaten until the master returns to throw open the door for his banquet, which promises to make all other banquets pale in comparison."[9] The first banquet is open now for all humanity. It is like the *hors d'oeuvres* offered before the main event. Dekker claims that "God *has* bottled some of heaven for us to engage with our five physical senses. He has given us a physical representation of the bliss that awaits us. It is another one of his great gifts to us now, while we live on earth. We call this gift *pleasure*."[10] However, we all abuse this gift in one form or another.

5. Lewis, *The Weight of Glory*, 26.
6. Lewis, *The Weight of Glory*, 26.
7. Lewis, *The Weight of Glory*, 37.
8. Lewis, "Mere Christianity," 76.
9. Dekker, *Slumber of Christianity*, 164.
10. Dekker, *Slumber of Christianity*, 162.

Contemporary culture tries to tell the church that there is nothing beyond earth's pleasures and that looking for heavenly pleasure is wishful thinking without merit and without practical application. If heaven is considered at all, our only thoughts of it are as a place to reunite with loved ones. Dekker counters that "true happiness on earth is the figment of our imaginations. Heaven, on the other hand, not only exists, but it's our only true source of happiness."[11] He encourages Christians to "embrace . . . [earthly] pleasure as a gift from God and direct your thoughts to heaven as you do. But above all, do not expect from that pleasure anything it can't deliver"; what it cannot deliver is heaven *on* earth.[12] The church must remember and communicate that heaven is real; it is wonderful, exciting, and full of joy, happiness, and pleasure. She must also remember and communicate that heaven is not here. We are still on the outside of that perfect world and all of our best efforts will not change that fact. Until God renews the created order at the end of time (Rom 8 and Rev 21–22), the food still spoils and becomes rancid. This is why so many people judge God. They want heaven on earth, and when suffering comes, it must be God's fault and therefore he is not worthy of our worship and trust. We shall examine this further in chapters 10 and 11.

Pleasure is God-given, but like every gift God gives, on earth it usually falls short of what God intended. The joy and pleasure I am recommending to the church is what Lewis calls self-interest. This is different from the selfishness found in this Postmodern era typified by the world's self-interest as explained in chapters 1 and 2. John Piper uses the love between a husband and a wife to illustrate the difference between the two and explains, "Selfishness seeks its own private happiness at the expense of others. Love [holy love which enables Lewis's self-interest] seeks its happiness in the happiness of the beloved. It will even suffer and die for the beloved in order that its joy might be full in the life and purity of the beloved."[13] How different from most marriages today (if couples can even make that commitment) in which individuals seek to satisfy themselves and expect or even demand that their partner make them happy or they will leave. The church must be able to communicate this self-interest that is positive in contrast to the world's self-interest, which is really self-centeredness. By combining righteousness and love, holiness provides the means to determine which is which and lifts our sights outside of this world to genuine reality and real pleasure.

As mentioned above, we often feel like there is more or something better than what we see, feel, touch, taste, smell, and hear on this earth. The church can meet people at this level of their self-interest to lead them out of selfishness to the genuine self-interest of Scripture in the delight of God and the beauty of his holiness. In spite of the constant bombardment by the media, technology, and our educational systems, if we take time to truly look inside ourselves all of us find an emptiness that has not been filled. In this technological age, this rarely happens until people are challenged,

---

11. Dekker, *Slumber of Christianity*, 172.
12. Dekker, *Slumber of Christianity*, 174.
13. Piper, *Dangerous Duty of Delight*, 63.

or forced, to go without their smart phones, iPads, twitter, tweets, and internet instant everything. Parents, supervise your children.[14] Church, challenge people to find out who they really are by turning off their devices.

Only Christianity can tell them what the emptiness is they experience and how to fill it. Lewis claims that "most people, if they had really learned to look into their own hearts, would know that they do want, and want acutely something that cannot be had in this world . . . . Things in this world . . . never quite keep their promise."[15] We most often sense this acute longing as the light fades after a beautiful sunset or the last notes of music fade. Sadly, we realize that "we have been mere spectators. Beauty has smiled, but not to welcome us; her face was turned in our direction, but not to see us. We have not been accepted, welcomed, or taken into the dance . . . . we pine. The sense that in this universe we are treated as strangers . . . longing to be acknowledged, to meet with some response, to bridge some chasm that yawns, between us and reality, is part of our inconsolable secret."[16]

Lewis asserts that "apparently, then, our lifelong nostalgia, our longing to be reunited with something in the universe from which we now feel cut off, to be on the inside of some door, which we have always seen from the outside, is no mere neurotic fancy, but the truest index of our real situation."[17] He further observes that simply seeing beauty and experiencing pleasure as we do now is not enough. We want to be joined with it. He writes, "Ah, but we want so much more . . . . We do not want merely to see beauty . . . . We want something else which can hardly be put into words—to be united with the beauty we see, to pass into it, to receive it into ourselves, to bathe in it, to become part of it."[18] What Lewis is describing is our longing to have the image of God restored in us, to be united with God in our original state of being, and to be in relationship with him. We desire to become one with the beauty of holiness that can be found only in the thrice-Holy God of Scripture.

The joy of beholding God is the highest pleasure a human can experience. God is "holy, holy, holy," and to look on God is to feast your eyes on the beauty of holiness. Therefore, this beauty is the ultimate source of pleasure, happiness, and enjoyment. Recall that God's holiness is not only pure and righteous but emotionally satisfies us to our core. Roland Delattre asserts, "Beauty is not the only important ingredient in a morally and spiritually fulfilling life, but its absence in people's lives is powerfully destructive and the unfulfilled hunger for beauty tends to be so enervating it makes everything else of value seem less important. It will no longer do for religious ethics to leave beauty and aesthetics to the philosophers, art historians, art critics, and the

---

14. For more on how to guide children and families through this age of technology see Andy Crouch, *The Tech-Wise Family*
15. Lewis, "Mere Christianity," 75.
16. Lewis, *The Weight of Glory*, 40.
17. Lewis, *The Weight of Glory*, 42.
18. Lewis, *The Weight of Glory*, 42.

fashion industry."[19] The church must be careful at this point not to mistake love for the totality of beauty. Love is only one aspect of the beauty of holiness. In the next several chapters we will look at how righteousness, discipline, and law are also part of the delight of the beauty of holiness we are examining here.

The great minds from Calvin to Edwards and Lewis to Eldredge remind us of this delight. Lewis tells us that the problem with people is not that they seek pleasure; it is that they are far too easily pleased. We are too easily satisfied with making mud pies in the backyard when we could be making castles at the beach.[20] This is an approach that the church can "sell" to a consumeristic, pleasure driven culture, but she must embrace it and model it first. However, she must be careful not to separate pleasure and beauty from righteousness and purity and make them the ultimate goal of the Christian life. The church must present the beauty of holiness and the pleasure it gives to the people of this culture as a means to give them the gospel while at the same time being careful not to capitulate as she has done with God's love.

If pleasure is separated from the beauty of holiness, people will be left exactly as they are, missing the mark. To miss the mark is the meaning of sin. It must be holy pleasure which is different from the excesses in which our culture indulges. The church must recover the beauty of holiness and reflect the pleasure it brings in order to evangelize the people of this age. I often wonder why, since the Westminster Catechism informs us that the chief end for which people exist is to worship God and enjoy him forever, that people are so bored in worship services? Enjoyment and worship of God is solid ground from which to do mission and outreach in this culture when it reflects the beauty of holiness and the delight and joy it brings.

Enjoyment and pleasure define the relationship Adam and Eve had with God before the fall and original sin. John Eldredge calls this relationship a "Sacred Romance" that includes "intimacy, beauty, and adventure." He admonishes us that "the heart does not respond to principles and programs; it seeks not efficiency, but passion. Art, poetry, beauty, mystery, ecstasy: These are what rouse the heart."[21] He shows us how a "Sacred Romance" summons our hearts every day of our lives through friends, loved ones, the birth of a baby, music, or sunsets. He challenges us to see that "the Romance is even present in times of great personal suffering: the illness of a child, the loss of a marriage, the death of a friend. Something calls to us through experiences like these and rouses an inconsolable longing deep within our heart, wakening in us a yearning for intimacy, beauty, and adventure."[22]

Furthermore, Eldredge claims these are the most powerful motivators of all people in all areas of life and writes, "This longing is the most powerful part of any

---

19. Delattre, "Aesthetics and Ethics," 277–97. For suggestions on how to do this see Crouch, *Culture Making*.
20. Lewis, *The Weight of Glory*, 26.
21. Eldredge, *The Sacred Romance*, 6.
22. Eldredge, *The Sacred Romance*, 6–7.

human personality. It fuels our search for meaning, for wholeness, for a sense of being truly alive. . . . it is the most important thing about us, our heart of hearts, the passion of our life. And the voice that calls to us in this place is none other than the voice of God."[23] You may be wondering how holiness connects with this. Recall Otto's *"mysterium tremendum."* Holiness moves us to our deepest core. It is utter and complete satisfaction, love, and a shudder. Eldredge's "inconsolable longing" for meaning, wholeness, and desire connects with Otto's *"nuamin"* or the *"numinous."* Perhaps Edwards can help us the most.

Edwards spent most of his life pursuing God's holiness. He began his "Miscellanies" with an entry on holiness, even ahead of "Christ's Mediation." Michael J. McClymond and Gerald R. McDermott see here the beginning of Edwards's "emphasis on beauty that evolved into the most developed aesthetic theology in the history of western Christian thought."[24] I began this chapter with the opening lines from Edwards's powerful thoughts. Read now the rest of his introduction to holiness in which he writes,

> We drink in strange notions of holiness from our childhood, as if it were a melancholy, morose, sour and unpleasant thing [but]. . . . 'Tis the highest beauty and amiableness, vastly above all other beauties. 'Tis a divine beauty, makes the soul heavenly and far purer than anything here on earth; this world is like mire and filth and defilement to that soul which is sanctified. 'Tis of a sweet, pleasant, charming, lovely, amiable, delightful, serene, calm and still nature. 'Tis almost too high a beauty for any creatures to be adorned with; it makes the soul a little, sweet and delightful image of the blessed Jehovah.[25]

He maintains that holiness makes all things "peaceful and loving of all things but sin." It makes the soul "more excellent than other beings," and he asks, "How is it possible that such a divine thing should be on earth?"[26] For Edwards holiness is to the soul "like a delightful field or garden planted by God . . . that is all pleasant and delightful, undisturbed, free from all the noise of man and beast, enjoying a sweet calm . . . where the sun is Jesus Christ; the blessed beams and calm breeze, the Holy Spirit; the sweet and delightful flowers, and the pleasant shrill music of the little birds, are the Christian graces."[27] For Edwards the beauty of holiness is above any and all beauty this

---

23. Eldredge, *The Sacred Romance*, 7.
24. McClymond and McDermott, *Theology of Jonathan Edwards*, 25.
25. WJE 13:163–64.
26. WJE 13:163–64.
27. WJE 13:164. He continues rather poetically, "Or like the little white flower: pure, unspotted and undefined, low and humble, pleasing and harmless; receiving the beams, the pleasant beams of the serene sun, gently moved and a little shaken by a sweet breeze, rejoicing as it were in a calm rapture, diffusing around most delightful fragrancy, standing most peacefully and lovingly in the midst of the other like flowers round about. How calm and serene is the heaven overhead! How free is the world from noise and disturbance! How, if one were but holy enough, would they of themselves as it were naturally ascend from the earth in delight, to enjoy God as Enoch did!"

world can produce. It is like a delicate white flower in a peaceful garden with Jesus as the sun and the Holy Spirit the breeze.

He has much to say to the modern church that analyzes and critiques everything and exegetes every nuance until the life is departed from it. Today's church knows a lot about a lot of things, but does she really *know* them? Edwards warns, "There is a difference between having an opinion that God is holy and gracious, and having a sense of the loveliness and beauty of the holiness and grace. There is a difference between having a rational judgment that honey is sweet, and having a sense of its sweetness."[28] Edwards expands this idea of intellectual (rational) knowledge of holiness versus the experiential (relational) knowing to our concept of beauty and writes, "So there is a difference between believing that a person is beautiful, and having a sense of his beauty. The former may be obtained by hearsay, but the latter only by seeing the countenance. There is a wide difference between mere speculative, rational judging anything to be excellent, and having a sense of its sweetness, and beauty. The former rests only in the head, speculation only is concerned in it; but the heart is concerned in the latter."[29] When beauty penetrates the heart it will feel pleasure in it; "the idea of it is sweet and pleasant to his soul; which is a far different thing from having a rational opinion that it is excellent."[30]

The Christian life is not simply a matter of knowing something to be true; it must be taken into the heart where it has sway with the person's will and desires. The remainder of this chapter is devoted to helping us experience this sense of the beauty of holiness and not simply knowing about it. Holiness is not just an emotionless, rational, and dutiful obedience to a set of laws as it became known in the Modern Age. It is relational. God is holy, and his people must be holy.

How Holiness Satisfies Our Deepest Desires

As we have seen, Edwards understood holiness as the highest beauty of every beauty and far above any beauty in the created universe. He experienced God as the most satisfying encounter here on earth. Recall Lewis's words, "We do not want merely to see beauty . . . . We want something else which can hardly be put into words—to be united with the beauty we see, to pass into it, to receive it into ourselves, to bathe in it, to become part of it."[31] This is the picture of what happens when we come to salvation through Christ. The beauty of God's holiness is restored in us at the moment of our salvation (justification) by faith in Jesus the Christ, and we are given more access to that beauty as we surrender and commit to following his ways (sanctification), thereby living a holy lifestyle. Remember Delattre's assessment that beauty is needed

---

28. Edwards, "Divine and Supernatural Light," 414. (Hereafter cited as WJE 17:page number.)
29. WJE 17:414.
30. WJE 17:414.
31. Lewis, *The Weight of Glory*, 42.

for a morally and spiritually satisfying life. The absence of this beauty is destructive and leaves a person unfulfilled, depleting his or her ability to recognize what is truly important.[32] This explains much of what we see in our twenty-first-century culture. The church must present the beauty of her Holy God to our culture. Therefore let us examine Edwards's view of holiness and beauty as a means of reaching twenty-first-century Americans for Christ.

Edwards defines beauty as consent to being and the greatest beauty as the consent to being in general, which is God. For Edwards, that which is excellent "is that which is beautiful and lovely. That which is beautiful . . . only with respect to itself and a few other things, and not as a part of that which contains all things—the universe—is false beauty . . . . that which is beautiful with respect to the university of things has a generally extended excellence and a true beauty."[33] We must realize that Edwards uses universal and university to mean God's ways, plans, and purposes for which he created the universe. He does not mean universal or majority agreement among people. When a person consents to only those things that are important to him or her or group of likeminded people, he or she is beholding false (or lesser) beauty. The more generalized (consent to the being in general) or universal consent (to God), the greater the beauty will be.

We must be clear that for Edwards, this extended or general excellence is God and specifically God's holiness. Edwards explains further that "excellence in and among spirits is, in its prime and proper sense, *being's consent to being*. There is no other proper consent but that of minds" (italics are mine).[34] While all excellence and true beauty must be experienced in the affections, the mind can consent or dissent to what the will wants. The mind gives consent to a person (being) or object as something beautiful. Furthermore, since "God has so plainly revealed himself to us, and [since] other minds are made in his image and are emanations from him, we may judge what is the excellence of other minds by what is his."[35] God is the original mind, if you will, and people made in his image are extensions or reflections of his. God has communicated his mind to us in Scripture. Therefore, what is truly excellent and beautiful in the minds of people must conform to the mind of God (as known in Scripture) since he is the primary or highest beauty. "Now God is the prime and original being, the first and last, and the pattern of all, and has the sum of all perfection. We may therefore doubtless conclude that all that is the perfection of spirits may be resolved into that which is God's perfection, which is love."[36]

We must realize that for Edwards love is always holy love and is to be viewed the same as holiness. Without holiness, this love of self would constitute narcissism.

32. Delattre, "Aesthetics and Ethics," 277–97.
33. Edwards, "Scientific and Philosophical Writings," 344. (Hereafter cited as WJE 6:page number.)
34. WJE 6:362.
35. WJE 6:362–63.
36. WJE 6:363.

Edwards explains elsewhere that "'tis peculiar to God [because of the Trinity] that he has beauty within himself, consisting in being's consenting with his own being, or the love of himself in his own Holy Spirit; whereas the excellence of others is in loving others, in loving God, and in the communications of his Spirit."[37] Only the Triune God is capable of knowing beauty in and by himself.[38] People must consent to others or at least to other things to perceive beauty.

Furthermore, Edwards identifies a primary and a secondary excellence or beauty. All excellence and beauty consist in a being's consent to being or in one person (being) agreeing with (consenting to) another person (being) or thing, but not all consent is equal. A person's consent to God "may be called the highest, and first, or primary beauty that is to be found among things that exist . . . which are the highest and first part of the universal system for whose sake all the rest has existence."[39] This is holiness and is completely set apart from profane or common beauty, which we see and experience in this world. Edwards describes this world as an "inferior, secondary beauty, which is some image of this [God's original or primary beauty], and which is not peculiar to spiritual beings, but is found even in inanimate things."[40] This secondary beauty "consists in a mutual consent and agreement of different things in form, manner, quantity, and visible end or design; called by the various names of regularity, order, uniformity, symmetry, proportion, harmony, etc."[41] Examples of this secondary beauty would be the way things like music, art, a sunset, order and symmetry, or the love of person to person move us at the core of our being.

The primary beauty is God's because he created the universe and defines perfection. When humans consent to other humans it is similar to God's consent between himself and is higher by degree than when a person consents to an animal or object. Nevertheless, it is still a secondary beauty because neither of the beings in this consent is God and therefore lacks perfection. Similarly, consent to animals, music, art, and things would be secondary beauty.

A being's consent to being may be thought of as liking music. Some (human *beings*) think country is best (what they consent to) while others prefer rock or classical. Consent to being is when some find beauty in gardens or others see it at the ocean. For some it is sports; for others it is found in ballet. Even within sports, some consent to being in football while others prefer soccer. Perhaps the highest known consent to being in this world can be seen when a man and woman consent to commit their lives together in mutual love. To others in the world, they may appear average, but to each other they are beautiful, wonderful, and magnificent. However, at its best it is still a secondary or natural consent to being meant to point us to God's primary beauty.

37. WJE 6:365.
38. For more in-depth discussion on this see Donald Fairbairn, *Life in the Trinity*.
39. WJE 6:365.
40. WJE 6:365.
41. WJE 6:365.

God is the primary beauty because he is the "true, highest, moral, spiritual, divine, or original beauty." Nature is the secondary beauty that is inferior to the primary beauty because it "consists in a very different sort of agreement or consent—although it may be an image or shadow of primary beauty."[42] Since secondary beauty is natural, it may be perceived internally by any individual. On the other hand, primary beauty requires a relationship between beings and specifically a relationship with God. Since God is three Persons—Father, Son, and Holy Spirit—he is the only Being who can contain ultimate or absolute beauty within himself. For Edwards, this makes God "being in general . . . the divine Being, for he is an infinite being. Therefore all others must necessarily be considered as nothing . . . . in metaphysical strictness and propriety, he is, as there is none else. He is likewise infinitely excellent, and all excellence and beauty is derived from him . . . all being and all other excellence is, in strictness, only a shadow of his."[43] Primary beauty always refers to God, the divine being who is the only being complete in himself. Secondary beauty always refers to any other being (person) or object. This implies a degradation of beauty outside of primary beauty.

This degradation of being and beauty from the primary to the secondary results in deformity and nothingness. Secondary beauty is only a shadow of God's beauty. Furthermore, as people dis-consent (dissent) to being in general (God) it becomes deformed digressing to nothing (Edwards does not use "ugly" to describe it). Edwards's premise is "what disagrees with being must necessarily be disagreeable to being in general. Agreeableness of perceiving being is pleasure, arid disagreeableness is pain. Disagreement or contrariety to being is evidently an approach to nothing, or a degree of nothing, which is . . . the greatest and only evil."[44] God is the being in general and the source of beauty. The more a person dissents or disagrees with him (being in general), the more digression from true beauty he or she will see and experience and eventually results in nothingness but with pain. This nothingness is what the Bible calls darkness. Jesus warned (Matt 6:23, NIV), "If then the light within you is darkness, how great is that darkness!" If a person consents to those things (calling them beautiful) that disagree with being in general (God), he or she has rejected the light (beauty) and is in deep darkness. It is like a building designed to be rectangular that is not symmetrical. One corner is not square and one wall is of different height. The framing is different everywhere. It disagrees with its blueprint and is deformed. When it is finished, it will be condemned as being unsafe because it was not built to code. For Edwards, the greatest deformity is a being's dissent from a being that consents to him or her, which is God. He calls this odious and unnatural and it produces "jarring and horror in perceiving being."[45]

---

42. Delattre, *Beauty and Sensibility*, 17.
43. WJE 6:363–64.
44. WJE 6:335.
45. WJE 6:363.

Delattre helps us to understand Edwards's distinction between primary and secondary beauty as, "beauty is to being as deformity is to nothing. Good and evil are measured on this same scale running from the fullness of being and beauty toward nothing."[46] True beauty is determined by how close it is to God on a descending scale. The closer it is to God, the more beautiful it is. That is why the beauty of loving relationships is more beautiful than music. Within music or art there is more beauty where there is harmony and proportion. Edwards sees the order of "harmony and proportion" in the arts, architecture, and mathematics as being placed in such exact order, having such mutual respect one to another, that they carry with them into the mind of him that sees or hears the conception of an understanding and will exerting itself in these appearances."[47] This beauty, like holiness, extends beyond the emotions to engage the intellect and reason, "We, by reflection and reasoning, are *led to an extrinsic intelligence and will* that was the cause" (italics are mine).[48] For Edwards, it is the order, harmony, and proportion of the notes or art that lead us to the author (creator, if you will) and his intent. Chaos, disproportion, and discord fail to do that. In such cases, the meaning "would seem to be in the notes and strokes themselves.... I can conceive of no other reason why equality and proportion should be pleasing to him that perceives, but only that it has an appearance of consent."[49]

Since harmony and proportion reveal a will and an intellect behind the music or art and are designed to lead a person to the original intent of that will and intellect, we should not be surprised that as Modernity waned, free form and total randomness became the norm. Modernity had already removed the supernatural from the Bible; Postmodernity now works to remove every trace of a Grand Designer. The effect of this is to bring further degradation of God's beauty and to keep people from perceiving an ultimate creator. I find it interesting that Foucault and company at the outset of Postmodernity declared we could not know what was intended by an author, composer, or artist. Only the person perceiving it could declare what it meant to them. Perhaps this inability to know the intended meaning is the result of the collapsing harmonies and proportions witnessed in the arts during Modernity (see below). This would also explain the success of "Cats," the longest running musical on Broadway. Each person could decide for himself or herself what it meant. There was no metanarrative. This is the dissent to being that Edwards describes as leading to degeneration and nothing. He asserts that "one alone, without any reference to any more, cannot be excellent; for in such case there can be no manner of relation ... no such thing as consent."[50] Our current culture with emphasis on individual freedom and relative truth is the model of dis-consent. We are finding that true harmony and proportion which are pleasing

46. Delattre, *Beauty and Sensibility*, 44–45.
47. WJE 6:382.
48. WJE 6:382.
49. WJE 6:382.
50. WJE 6:337.

and give beauty to secondary things because of their agreement with and consent to others are fading from the public mind.[51]

The arts are often early harbingers of the culture in which they exist. It is interesting to note that as Modernity was finding major inroads into the doctrine and actions of the church and society at large, the impressionists of the second half of the nineteenth century were already breaking with tradition's "linear perspective and avoided the clarity of form" to adopt a more relaxed style which would "capture the momentary, sensory effect of a scene."[52] The art world surmises that "the Impressionists conveyed the new sense of alienation experienced by the inhabitants of the first modern metropolis [Paris]," and Claude Monet is quoted as saying, "Impressionism is only direct sensation . . . . It is mainly a question of instinct."[53] At the height of Modernity's reason, instinct was making itself felt first in the arts; a rebellion of sorts was occurring. Impressionism was followed by pointillism, cubism, and surrealism by Picasso, to pure abstract art just prior to and contemporary with the influences of Rorty, Derrida, and Foucault, whose ideas we considered above as instrumental to Postmodernity. In Edwards's day, music and art represented the highest level of human accomplishment of harmony and proportion because they displayed consent to being. "The more the consent is, and the more extensive, the greater is the excellency" and beauty.[54] However, harmony did not last. The movement went from Baroque, to Classical, to Romantic, to a realism where instruments clashed to imitate the noise of cars in rush hour with their horns blaring, to serial music, to rock and roll, and finally to simply noise, as some describe it. What are the arts and philosophers telling us about who we are and what we have become?

As dis-consent to God's being increases it breeds conflict, discord, and distortion. Beauty becomes deformed. The less consent to being there is, the more deformity there will be in its beauty until there is nothing left of beauty and nothing to point us to God. It is utterly and completely gone. Please note that Edwards compares the spiritual with the natural world and not with material things per se.

This great beauty for which we long can be found only in a person's consent to a relationship with God in which God's image is restored in us. Surprisingly, this is more objective than subjective. Delattre understands this consent to being as "objective relations of consent and dissent among beings," and the participation in the highest beauty "is defined by conformity to God . . . rather than by degree of subjective pleasure."[55] Beauty is to be understood as objective and relational. (We will examine this more in detail in later chapters.) Edwards writes, "It is by a sensible participation in the divine beauty . . . his holiness . . . that we are most immediately

---

51. WJE 6:382.
52. Wolf, "Impressionism," para. 1.
53. Wolf, "Impressionism," para. 6.
54. WJE 6:336.
55. Delattre, *Beauty and Sensibility*, 22.

related to the Divine Being and are transformed into the spiritual likeness or image of God."[56] This is the only thing that will fill that longing we discussed above. To Edwards, "beauty—even the beauty of holiness—is given in and through experience of an encounter with definite, concrete, substantial being and not in and through the abstract ethereal, incommunicable, or untouchable."[57] Beauty is consent to being and therefore is connected with a real objectifiable person or thing. It is not nebulous, and although the experience may be difficult to put into words, the being in the encounter is real and objectifiable.

Therefore, true beauty is God's holiness, which is an actual experience given to people who are related to him through a relationship with Jesus Christ and who are being transformed into God's holy image according to objectifiable and certifiable principles. This is the highest pleasure possible to people. Reflecting on Edwards, Belden C. Lane describes this concrete and objective beauty and pleasure as "more full of infinite delights, more prone to the endless expansion of relationships, more astonishingly beautiful . . . than anything we can imagine in this stunningly sensuous world around us."[58] He elaborates, "In effect, he [Edwards] said, if you think this world is sensual and beautiful, you haven't seen anything yet! All this is but a dim, quasi-sensual reflection of God's still greater glory, overflowing spontaneously from the mystery of God's inner-trinitarian life. That is where all desire and all connectedness find their birth."[59]

In a very Edwardsian style, Lane continues, "Our senses open us to harmonies of sound and delicacies of scent, as they teach us to delight in the play of light in a bubbling fountain of water; they offer a spiritual training in the knowledge of God."[60] Our sense of pleasure in the secondary beauty leads us to God's primary beauty and God's holy truth.

Therefore, it follows that beauty reveals what is real and good to us. Delattre summarizes Edwards's view of how this works: "It is the primary beauty of being's cordial consent to being and the shadow or image of such beauty in the secondary beauty of harmony and proportion that provides them [people] with their surest clue to the deepest penetration of the mystery of the things that are and the things that are good."[61] Beauty leads us to reality and goodness. It is primary beauty found in the Holy God and the secondary beauty that is proportional and harmonic and not the intellect (alone) that enables us to discern amidst the ambiguities around us what is good, right, and true. Perhaps this is why children and mentally challenged people can see what is good even when those with superior intellect cannot. Often, the more intelligent we are; the

56. Delattre, *Beauty and Sensibility*, 50.
57. Delattre, *Beauty and Sensibility*, 50.
58. Lane, "Jonathan Edwards," 53.
59. Lane, "Jonathan Edwards," 53.
60. Lane, "Jonathan Edwards," 53.
61. Delattre, *Beauty and Sensibility*, 99.

more disjointed and disproportional we become, and the more we lose sight of what is genuinely real, beautiful, and good and what brings true peace.

The role of the intellect in the perception of beauty is to devise objective, definite, and concrete means to communicate its being's consent to being (what the individual consents to/recognizes as beautiful and worthwhile). The intellect is amoral. It can rationalize anything from love to abortion and from racism to freedom of sexuality. It can declare the Bible is the writings of men only and full of errors or the inerrant word of God. Yes, the human mind can rationalize almost anything. Hence, Edwards states that it is in the being's consent to being in general, which is the beauty of holiness, that we find what is real and good. Furthermore, the higher the beauty to which the person consents, the greater the goodness will be to which he or she can aspire, and the greater the reality in which he or she lives. So then, the intellect is necessary for consent to being, but something else must be at work.

Edwards has also considered from where this consent to being comes. What causes a person to choose one being over another is the person's affections, which he describes as "the more vigorous and sensible exercises of the inclination and will of the soul," which view, judge, and discern things whenever they consider or regard something.[62] Affections are the "inclination and will of the soul" that determine what pleases or displeases us and those things to which we are inclined and disinclined.[63] They are the strong inclinations that determine in what we delight and have joy or find grief and sorrow. These strong inclinations drive us to like or to dislike things, and to select them or to reject them. Affections are sometimes thought of as passions, but they are "more extensive . . . used for all vigorous lively actings of the will or inclination."[64] Passions are "more sudden . . . more violent, and the mind more overpowered, and less in its own command."[65]

Having described affections as the strongest inclinations of the will of the soul, Edwards now asserts that "true religion, in great part, consists in holy affections."[66] Reason alone is a servant and not the totality of true religion. Affections are the great part of it. In fact, Edwards's premise is "true religion, in great part, consists in holy affections" which are not only true, but pure, excellent, beautiful, loving, and joyful, in short, what we have come to understand as marks of holiness. As Edwards understands them, religious affections integrate the cognitive and the emotive aspects of the person.

Consequently, we find that pleasure is perceived in the affections and may come from both the primary and secondary sources of beauty. Therefore, pleasure in something is an unreliable basis to decide what is truly beautiful and spiritual. The highest

---

62 Edwards, "Religious Affections," 96. (Hereafter cited as WJE 2:page number.)

63. WJE 2:97.

64. WJE 2:98.

65. WJE 2:98.

66. WJE 2:95.

beauty is found in conformity to God and is objective and not subjective, "for primary beauty is defined objectively by conformity to God rather than subjectively by the degree of pleasure in finite perceiving being."[67] Subjectivity implies dissent from something else, making it one alone from the many and therefore less beautiful.

When we dis-consent to God's holy beauty, we are taking pleasure in lesser beauty. The more discordant and distorted secondary beauty becomes, the less likely we are to find true beauty and genuine pleasure. Eventually, in this dissent, beauty dissolves and beings de-evolve into deformity and nothingness. It is like we have become little green Gumby people who actually have little to contribute and who are easily stretched out of proportion.[68] We think we are playing in the crystal-clear water having a great time when all the while we are becoming distorted and deformed and sinking into nothingness.

We see this discord and de-evolution in our culture as we push God out of the public consciousness and as each person seeks his or her own truth and right to live and to do anything he or she wants. For example, about the time the Bible and prayer were removed from public schools, I was a student in an inner-city high school. My classmates knew better than to try to fight anywhere on school grounds. Shootings and knifings were nonexistent unlike today. I never feared for my safety either at school or walking through some of the worst neighborhoods to and from school. Six years later my sister attended the same school and the violence had already begun. She feared walking the same streets I had walked only six years earlier. By the end of the twentieth century the first school shooting occurred in Columbine. The rest is history.

There are many economic, environmental, and social aspects to what is happening in America since the Bible and prayer were removed from our schools, but the church, because of the Holy God of the Bible, is the only entity that can resist the allure of the false beauty that calls us. Only the church can offer true repentance, regeneration, and reconciliation with him and the genuine beauty he is. It is critical for her to be about the business of revival and reformation, which she can do by offering true beauty and pleasure.

Another way to think of the beauty of holiness is as light. The further we dissent from God, the less light we have; and the less light we have, the more difficult it is to see things as they really are. Things become distorted and deformed, but because of our assent to them we still call it beauty. We have deceived ourselves, consented to darkness, and call it light. It is no wonder Jesus said in the Sermon on the Mount (Matt 6:22–23, NIV), "The eye is the lamp of the body. If your eyes are good, your whole body will be full of light. But if your eyes are bad, your whole body will be full of darkness. If

---

67. Delattre, *Beauty and Sensibility*, 61.

68. Gumby was an early claymation figure that was flat, nearly two-dimensional, green to represent growing things, and had a high voice. He had a small vocabulary, was never confrontational, was extremely loveable, and always pliable. This was especially true of the rubber figures marketed to the public after the show's success.

then the light within you is darkness, how great is that darkness!" Many in this country are walking in darkness and calling it light, thinking it is beautiful. It is the church's responsibility to take the light of the beauty of holiness to them so the Holy Spirit can work his saving grace in them. Beauty and the pleasure it brings are powerful ways to connect with the people of the twenty-first century.

Summary

In the opening quote of this book, Latourette points out how people have used knowledge God has released into the world to do evil. It is time for the church to use this knowledge to stand against evil and to bring about the greater fruits of which he also speaks. God's beauty counteracts evil in all but the hard-hearted. God still uses the secondary beauty (of this world) to point us to his primary beauty of holiness. Beautiful sunsets or a beautiful garden or a bird in flight or the majestic power of the ocean will always point people to something greater than themselves. It is the church's mission to show this culture who and what that is.

Lewis, Piper, and Dekker remind us that we were created to have enjoyment and pleasure in God, but since the fall, we try to find that in created things rather than in the Creator. This never satisfies us for long and always leaves us empty and broken. In linking beauty with what we consent to, Edwards has given Christians the means to connect with this culture in a way that they can understand without talking overtly about sin and does not change the message of the gospel. Beauty is the deep pleasure and enjoyment we are seeking to be part of. The beauty of holiness, God's beauty, is the highest (primary) beauty we can experience that also brings the greatest pleasure and enjoyment. And it never ends! The things in this world (secondary beauty) are only a reflection of God's beauty and are meant to direct our attention to him. When we focus only on this secondary beauty is when we feel the emptiness.

Furthermore, the greater our dis-consent (dissent) is to those things that belong to God's (primary) beauty, the more profound the degradation of it will be along with the enjoyment and pleasure we used to find there until we are left with nothing, empty, and in pain. Like an addiction, we crave more and more of what we think will fill that void, but always end up feeling hollow and hopeless. We have become blind and are living in darkness. Delattre surmises, "If men's ideas of beauty ascend no higher than what Edwards regards as merely secondary beauty, they will be blind to primary beauty [God], and their vision can be restored only by *providing a new foundation* for their apprehension of being and beauty. Edwards is confident that God can be relied upon to do so" (italics are mine).[69]

A Holy God has chosen to provide this new foundation through Christ's crucifixion, which "represents the conjunction of God's infinite justice and mercy." But people

---

69. Delattre, *Beauty and Sensibility*, 113.

must receive God's gift of grace, which "depends not only on recognizing that God is the ultimate source of our perceptions of beauty but also on recognizing the particular beauty of Christ as well as the beauty of Christ's particular love for human beings."[70] It is only in God's beautiful holiness that we can understand why our sin necessitated the cross and the reason for God's justice, judgment, wrath, mercy, grace, and love.

God is holy, and his people are called to be holy, but today most people live in a world of their own creation, making their own truth because they are unable to face the truth they find in the real one—a sinner in need of *repentance* and *forgiveness* and not simply excused to continue sinning. Unfortunately, the church often tells people only to believe in Jesus, meaning they need only an intellectual belief which leaves the affections of their hearts unchanged so they can continue to do what they want. These folks are usually encouraged to do good works: provide food for the hungry, protect the environment, and work for forms of social justice. What is often ignored is the regenerated heart, the new creation that comes from perceiving and objectively conforming to God's ways (Eph 4:24; 2 Cor 5:17). Rather than dull or boring, this regeneration becomes a way of life that comprises the highest beauty and greatest pleasure that can be found on earth and in heaven.

These pleasures and this beauty can only be found in God through Jesus and, by reflection, in the saints, his redeemed children. The beauty of holiness makes all pain and suffering worthwhile. Whatever the world may perceive as sacrifice is nothing compared to God's holiness and beauty, and the pleasure it brings. As Edwards reminds us, we may know honey is sweet, but until we have tasted it, we do not have the experience or true sense of its sweetness. To understand the beauty of God is to understand "something about God himself, to be instructed about the being of God in such a fashion as to not only open up and unfold to view a whole new dimension of the divine being but also open up to view a whole new world."[71] This is God's world which for Edwards is the universal world, the only real one in contrast to the fabricated world in which we live, and it is *beautiful*!

Furthermore, the beauty of holiness is the overarching quality of God's glory and is greater than his power and authority. The beauty of holiness enables us to come to God through Jesus with joy instead of despair, with pleasure instead of stoicism, with happiness instead of sadness, and with love instead of fear that the unbelieving world expects. This is the beauty of the gospel. It is the unexpected delight uncovered when a person faces his or her depravity and repents. Christians, show the world this is true!

Only the church can lay this foundation in any culture. In our culture, so caught up in materialism, consumerism, and pleasure, she must do this by engaging it right where it thrives—its quest for the beauty and pleasure that satisfy their senses. Only she can show them and tell them that there is a higher, more satisfying beauty for which they were created that will make everything that seems exciting to them now

---

70. Danaher, "Beauty, Benevolence, and Virtue," 404.
71. Delattre, *Beauty and Sensibility*, 125.

fade away in comparison, but instead, she often looks, acts, and speaks just like the culture. So then, beauty is one way the church can engage our culture to lead them to our Holy God. We will now turn our attention to how the beauty of holiness addresses another great concern to everyone today: wholeness and wellness.

Chapter 9

Holiness Brings Wholeness

> I believe that divine love, incarnate and indwelling in the world, summons the world always toward wholeness, which ultimately is reconciliation and atonement with God.
>
> —WENDELL BERRY, THE ART OF THE COMMONPLACE

CREATION, AS GOD DESIGNED it, is whole. When it breaks relationship with him, it becomes broken. Interestingly, it has only been since the 1960s when we formally removed God from our public life that people began to seek wholeness instead of seeking God. Unfortunately, they sought it in all the wrong places. Some pursued Eastern religions, while others looked for it in various New Age movements. Increasingly, we have medicated ourselves and devoted ourselves to endless distractions to avoid noticing just how broken we have become.[1] This chapter will examine how this brokenness worked itself out in the church and what she must do to recover God's wholeness in order to tell the next generation about Jesus.

God's holiness holds in perfect balance every characteristic and makes all parts work together as they should. Therefore, we might expect God to embody the quintessential wholeness for which we long.[2] When wholeness is applied to people and this world, it is often interpreted as completeness, entirety, or maturity. Jesus does this when he asks (Matt 16:26, ESV), "What will it profit a man if he gains the whole world and forfeits his soul?" Frederic R. Howe identifies two kinds of completeness corresponding to justification and sanctification. The completeness found in justification he calls "evangelical perfection [which] is applicable to every Christian, regardless of the degree of growth in sanctification. Through evangelical perfection

---

1. For an in-depth look at how Americans have become broken see Toffler's *Future Shock*. Also see Guinness, *The Dust of Death*.

2. However, wholeness is not directly taught in the Bible. Erickson and Gruden do not deal with it directly in their anthologies (it does not appear in the index). Many Bible dictionaries do not list it. *The Wycliffe Bible Dictionary* directs you to their entry on "Perfect, Perfection," 1307–8. There you find that it "usually connote[s] that which is complete, conformed to a standard or pattern . . . . in an absolute theological sense, perfection can be seen in the Triune God alone. Often his attributes are called perfections, for they are aspects of His very Being." They cite no Scripture. The Old Testament word, *shalom*, that best corresponds to this wholeness will be discussed in the next chapter.

the believer is viewed as complete or perfect in Christ, and accepted by God in this positional sense."[3] The completeness associated with sanctification he calls a "comparative perfection [that] applies to the Christian who is advanced in progressive sanctification." Howe supports this by using the Sermon on the Mount (Matt 5:48), "Be perfect, even as your Father in heaven is perfect." Whether we realize it or not, when people seek wholeness they are responding to this "appeal to excellence in Christian growth, [which is] greater and greater conformity on a finite level to the biblical standard of completeness in Jesus Christ."[4]

John Wesley understands Christian perfection as "loving God with all our heart, mind, soul, and strength. This implies that no wrong temper, none contrary to love, remains in the soul; and that all the thoughts, words, and actions are governed by pure love."[5] Perfection means to have the mind of Christ and to walk as Christ walked, or "in other words, to be inwardly and outwardly devoted to God; all devoted in heart and life."[6] He also affirms "that there is no such perfection in this life as implies an entire deliverance, either from ignorance, or mistake, in things not essential to salvation, or from manifold temptations, or from numberless infirmities, wherewith the corruptible body more or less presses down the soul."[7] Perfection of all attitudes, thoughts, actions, and speech is the goal to which every Christian must aspire (Phil 2:12–13 and 3:12–13), understanding that he or she will only fully realize it in heaven. Only perfection can bring wholeness. Anything less is incomplete; consequently it is not whole.

William D. Mounce also limits his discussion of wholeness to the idea of completeness or entirety connected with people finding God when they seek him with their whole heart.[8] Concerning James 2:10, Mounce writes, "If we keep 'the whole law' but stumble in just one commandment, we are guilty of being lawbreakers, for the *law is an undivided unity*."[9] Perhaps this is why we struggle so much with the law because it "is an undivided unity," but we are compartmentalized with different words, actions, and truth for every area of life: work, family, friends, church, and so on. We will examine below how the law leads to unity and why it is essential for wholeness.

How We Find Wholeness

The beauty of God's holiness brings harmony, determines what is good, maintains the order needed to escape anarchy, and always results in wholeness. According to Roland

---

3. Howe, "Perfect, Perfection," 1308.
4. Howe, "Perfect, Perfection," 1308.
5. Wesley, *A Plain Account*, 53.
6. Wesley, *A Plain Account*, 36.
7. Wesley, *A Plain Account*, 34.
8. Deut 4:29; 2 Chr 15:12; Ps 119:2, 10; Jer 29:13; Matt 22:37; and Luke 10:27.
9. Mounce, "Whole," 785.

A. Delattre, beauty "is a model of order" because it brings harmony and proportion as it holds together objectivity and subjectivity, the intellect and the affections. The beauty of holiness results in wholeness because it insists "upon the importance of the passions, emotions, and affections in the moral life without surrendering the vision of structured order in the moral and natural world."[10] The beauty of holiness unites all the different aspects of life, thereby bringing wholeness.

To have wholeness there must be order, harmony, and proportion. We cannot deny emotions, but neither can they be allowed to trump reason, truth, and order. Delattre reminds us that holiness must determine goodness, and the value of a thing must be determined by its validity and not the other way around. Just as in the natural world order is understood in terms of "harmony and discord, of proportion and deformity," in the "moral world [order and disorder] are seen in terms of consent to being and dissent from being rather than primarily in terms of obedience and disobedience."[11] For Delattre, "*the difference between obedience to command and consent to being and beauty defines the difference between legal and evangelical faith and morality*" (italics are mine).[12] Sheer obedience becomes legalistic morality; consent to being and beauty functions in the realm of faithful devotion to God's holy ways.

These ideas are incredibly important. First, we must understand that holiness and primary beauty cannot be judged by cultural standards of goodness and values. Just because something is valued by people in our culture or church, that does not make it valid. Christians must learn to value the things Scripture declares are valid. The beauty of holiness is what determines the validity of the goodness and the value of people, actions, speech, and things. Our culture has this reversed.

Second, the church needs to rethink obedience to God, which is not optional but integral to the journey of faith. Instead of presenting it as a duty or as love *owed* to God, it would be given as a person's consent to God's being, to his beauty of holiness which gives the highest pleasure and delight the person can have. God says that we will find him when we seek him with all our heart and all our soul. This is a description of our personal consent to God's being, which implies time willingly spent with God.

Relegating our time spent with God to a short daily devotional and an hour or two for worship on Sunday with maybe a Bible study once a week only scratches the surface. Christians should not be surprised that this great pleasure and delight of God experienced by our ancestors is only glimpsed by relatively few in this culture. It is a matter of priority (our choices) that makes our lack of time spent with God a kind of dissent from God, which is sin. This dissent from God's being becomes less beautiful and more destructive the further it diverges from God's holiness. This leads us to the third point Delattre would have us understand, which is that the genuine beauty we see and experience in this world is expressed in harmony and proportion. The more distorted

---

10. Delattre, "Aesthetics and Ethics," 112.
11. Delattre, *Beauty and Sensibility*, 112.
12. Delattre, *Beauty and Sensibility*, 112–13.

this beauty becomes, the more distorted and deformed its expression becomes, the less whole people become. Look around you. What do you see?

Sin Robs Us of Wholeness

The beauty of holiness brings harmony and order and leads to wholeness. When human beings consent to God's being there is "genuine community among men."[13] It is the natural consequence of consent to being in general since his ways are universal, designed so that all may experience the community of the Trinity within itself. This is what we witness in Acts right after Pentecost. Many have tried to model these natural values that resemble the primary beauty and true virtue of God in utopian societies, but human effort alone can never provide the wholeness and community for which we seek. These efforts *may* align with the higher law of God on the one hand in which case they will lead to God and his wholeness and will produce "gratitude, love of justice, sense of desert, conscience, and bonds of affection for members of one's family . . . community . . . or nation."[14] On the other hand, human effort based on secondary beauty alone often influences people to "set up their private kingdoms against each other and against the universal system and against God, its one head."[15]

This second possibility is a fair description of our American culture. Each person building his or her own kingdom always leads to sin and brokenness because it breaks relationship with the universal design of God and with each other. DeMoss reminds us that "sooner or later, sin will strip and rob you of everything that is truly beautiful and desirable."[16] It is only in consent to being in general and participation in primary beauty, which is holiness, that "the fullness of freedom is to be found," and without it "there will be disharmony, discord, and deformity."[17] William J. Danaher Jr. advances this idea and writes, "The beauty of an object, idea, or relation depends on the harmony achieved from its constituent parts, so that the greater the harmony achieved, the more beautiful something is."[18] As we lose beauty, harmony, and order, we lose wholeness. As our culture crumbles around us, this is a valid starting place for Christians to engage it with the gospel.

Sin that brought brokenness has also brought deception into the hearts of people so that they cannot perceive the ultimate beauty or be transformed without a supernatural working of the Holy Spirit. Lane writes, "Sin has distorted the full sensory apparatus of the human person. Responding to God's self-communication in nature . . . requires the exercise of a particular sense of the heart, something received in the

13. Delattre, *Beauty and Sensibility*, 185.
14. Dellatre, *Beauty and Sensibility*, 195.
15. Delattre, *Beauty and Sensibility*, 195.
16. DeMoss, *Holiness*, 39.
17. Delattre, *Beauty and Sensibility*, 201.
18. Danaher, "Beauty, Benevolence, and Virtue," 386–410.

regenerative work of the Holy Spirit."[19] What the church must understand and communicate is that no matter how beautiful or wonderful something is here, it is only a mere shadow of God's beauty and completeness that is offered through Jesus. He alone can bring regeneration and the work of the Holy Spirit, which will ever and only lead to holiness and acceptance of Scripture and God's ways and to the truth and wholeness found there.[20] If people reject Scripture and God's ways, they cannot perceive primary beauty but secondary beauty only, which is never sufficient in itself to cause rebirth. At best, it can point us to what is good or bad. Secondary beauty cannot save us. At worse, it misdirects us from God, from salvation, and from wholeness.

Secondary beauty deceives us if it does not point us to primary beauty, who is God. One way it deceives is to convince people that sin does not really matter. As long as the church looks the other way regarding sin, there will be brokenness, pain, shame, and immense suffering. Edwards reminds us that "sin is the most cruel tyrant that ever ruled, [it] seeks nothing but the misery of his subjects; as in the very keeping [of] God's commands there is great reward, so in the very breaking of them there is great punishment."[21] Like a cruel tyrant, sin brings "a woeful confusion and dreadful disorder in the soul, whereby everything is put out of place, reason trampled under foot and passion advanced in the room of it, conscience dethroned and abominable lusts reigning."[22] As long as sin reigns there will "be a dreadful confusion and perturbation in the mind; the soul will be full of worry, perplexities, uneasinesses, storms and frights, and thus it must necessarily be to all eternity, except the Spirit of God puts all to rights."[23] This state of sin in the person prevents God from making him truly "happy while he is wicked, the nature of the thing would not allow of it, but it would be simply and absolutely impossible."[24]

Holiness is not the cause of brokenness, pain, and suffering. No, it is quite the opposite. It is every person doing what is right in his or her own eyes that brings it about. Unfortunately, this is the stuff on which the American dream is founded today with our endless search for individual pleasure. We have forgotten de Tocqueville's warnings and have become a post-Christian nation.[25] We have sown the wind and are reaping the

---

19. Lane, "Jonathan Edwards," 58.

20. Collectively, the church must hold to this truth. Individuals will be at various levels of maturity, growth, and acceptance of some things at any given time. There should be a visible move towards these truths taught in Scripture.

21. Edwards, "Way of Holiness," 475. (Hereafter cited as WJE 10:page number.)

22. WJE 10:475.

23. WJE 10:475–76.

24. WJE 10:476.

25. Shortly after de Tocqueville's visit, Christians in antebellum America began to bifurcate the gospel over the issue of slavery, some using it to advance their own personal economic kingdoms, wants, and desires. Others were not able to counteract this in a convincing way beyond appealing to the Bible's general teaching on sin and morality. (The tools of scholastic criticism were only in their infancy at this time and often misunderstood or abused.) This using the Bible to make it support what you want instead of being transformed by the word was one component that led to the Civil War and

whirlwind of chaos and anarchy, but thank God that the prophet who wrote those words also wrote that if God's people sow righteousness they will reap love. It will not be easy to convince people of the error of their tenuous philosophies of self-truth, self-goodness, and self-help which they are being fed, but the beauty of holiness and the wholeness it brings are powerful places to begin because you are giving them what they are seeking deep down, the true God and Jesus of Scripture.

The Great Divide

In every age there are people who have promoted love over holiness and righteousness or the other way around, thereby breaking what God intended to work together. This is not new. What has changed in twenty-first-century America is that with the advent of never-before-seen advances in knowledge and technology, these two doctrines have become separate branches of Christianity that have been developed into full-scale theologies nearly independent of each other. The two major paradigm shifts in American thinking discussed in chapter 1 have promoted this bifurcated gospel. The first was the Age of Reason, which became known as Modernity. It demanded natural explanations for everything (usually based on the scientific method of being able to be reproduced) and relegated the supernatural to the realm of superstition. The role of the Holy Spirit was downplayed in the church, and miracles were explained away by giving everyday physical and psychological explanations of how they happened: it was medicine that healed the person, not God; you were just lucky that the parking space opened when and where you needed it; visions were dismissed as hysteria; the person was not really sick in the first place, or it was just in the mind. Righteousness and truth fit in well with this paradigm. This focus on righteousness and justice accompanied by the downplay of love and emotions gradually led folks to trust in what seemed reasonable to the human mind or could be proved scientifically.

The middle of the twentieth century saw another paradigm shift that threw off the shackles of reason and brought the emotions to the forefront. We still wanted to know why about everything and demanded the benefits that technology, medicine, and science could give us, but we rejected the belief in one overarching truth. After all, it had brought us two world wars, the Great Depression, the atomic bomb, and agent orange. We decided there was no truth except what made sense to each individual person. Right and wrong became whatever we wanted them to be. Advertising and social media pioneered the way; politicians were not far behind.

In this new paradigm, politicians, corporations, and social media have become the new pastors and prophets, telling people how they should live their lives by giving them what they want. It has become okay to spin anything to get everything you want. Lies and half-truths are given and accepted as whole truth, and there are no criteria by which

---

a subsequent mistrust of Scripture that we are still living out to this day. For an in-depth discussion of what happened, see Noll's *The Civil War as a Theological Crisis*.

to judge whether a thing is good or bad, helpful or hurtful. This nation, once known as the melting pot of the world in pursuit of Truth, has become splintered into increasingly smaller units of those who like or agree with each other. These units have become the new social classes which dominate this nation. Each group or individual claims its own truth, and no one has the right to challenge it. This is the antithesis of wholeness.

Since God created us, he knows how we are to function. His way is the universal path to health, wholeness, happiness, peace, fulfillment, pleasure, and unity both within ourselves and with our fellow human beings. People doing their own thing will always destroy wholeness and lead to discord, disparity, imbalance, and inequality. Self-centeredness leads to chaos and anarchy, or as Edwards puts it, it leads to nothingness. The misuse of our bodies and the good things God has given us brings decay like the spoilage that would occur if we were to buy a microwave and a refrigerator but then store the food in the microwave and cook it in the fridge. We would quickly become ill, and maybe die. Biblically, the human way of doing things (no matter how good it seems) is just as destructive and always misses the mark. It is called sin.

Sin has created incredible brokenness in our individual lives and in our culture.[26] Lying has become commonplace, as has parents walking out on their children, and addicts killing or stealing to get their next fix; but sin is not limited to the things we can easily identify. Timothy Keller describes sin as "not just the doing of bad things, but the making of good things into ultimate things. It is seeking to establish a sense of self by making something else more central to your significance, purpose, and happiness than your relationship to God."[27] This could be family, work, sports, games, and endless entertainment. This also contributes to why we have so little time to spend with God. When we add these potential things to the obvious ones, sin becomes the Mount Everest of brokenness in this nation.

John Eldredge challenges us to "think of the devastation caused by sin on this bleeding planet" and to "think of the rescues that could have happened if people had chosen holiness."[28] He asserts that "holiness rescues us from sin and its repercussions."[29] He clarifies for us that we "can't repent [our] way out of brokenness . . . . We repent our sins; brokenness must be healed."[30] He concludes that holiness is worth whatever it may cost you in worldly terms "because holiness is an utter relief. It is a joy and a healing of your creation. It will make you powerful in the Spirit, it will rescue you again and again, it will fortress you to the enemy's attacks, it will make your life a

---

26. Suicide could be one measure of brokenness. While there was a decline in suicide rates just before the new millennium (perhaps optimism in a new beginning?), they have been on the rise since then. See Asrar, "Suicide Rate on the Rise in U.S."; Lubell, "Suicide Trends among Youths"; and Bichell, "Suicide Rates Climb in U.S."

27. Keller, *Reason for God*, 168–69.

28. Eldredge, *Utter Relief of Holiness*, 160.

29. Eldredge, *Utter Relief of Holiness*, 161.

30. Eldredge, *Utter Relief of Holiness*, 150.

compelling argument for Jesus because it is of the same quality as his."[31] Finally, he reminds Christians that "in these last days, the saints are being sorely tested. Holiness is your strength and your safe passage through the trial. It is worth it."[32] Holiness is our path to wholeness. Let us examine how this works.

Divergent Paths of Love and Righteousness Must Merge

The greatest polarization that has taken place in the past 150 years from which we must recover is the bifurcation of the gospel into love or righteousness (and their related characteristics of mercy or justice, grace or judgment, and wrath or forgiveness). Figure 9-1 illustrates what we have been doing to these doctrines.

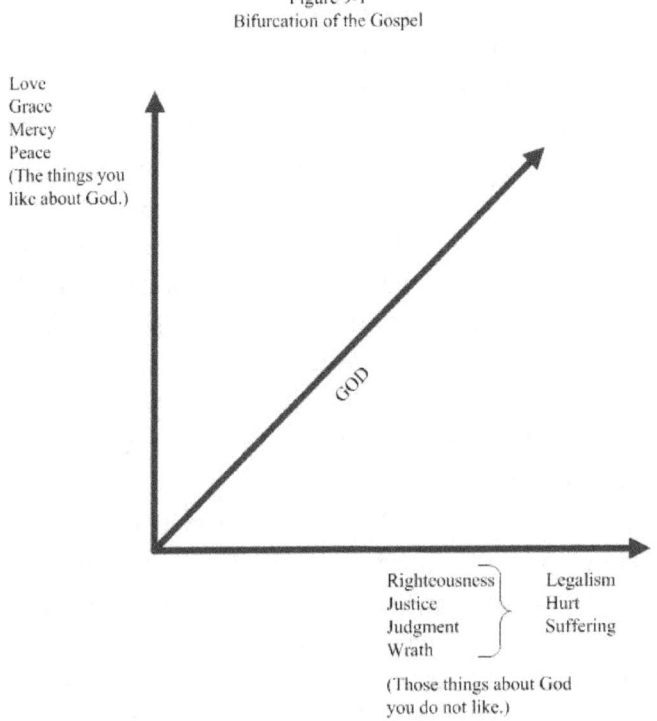

Figure 9-1
Bifurcation of the Gospel

In Fundamentalism (Modernity), Christianity was frequently reduced to righteousness and living according to a list of dos and don'ts. Often these were man-made: don't smoke, drink, dance, play cards, go to movies, and the like. This always becomes legalistic because of its focus on less significant things and its neglect of the weightier matters of true holiness that deal with anger, bitterness, and hatred that are the precursors of adultery, murder, unforgiveness, slander, gossip, and bearing

---

31. Eldredge, *Utter Relief of Holiness*, 168.
32. Eldredge, *Utter Relief of Holiness*, 168.

grudges which destroy community. Adulterous thoughts and pornography destroy the most basic community of all—the family.

What we do not recognize is that we have often done the same thing with love. We have separated it from righteousness and holiness because of the alleged damage they have done. In our minds we may think of love, grace, mercy, and peace as the vertical axis which is subtly pointing up towards heaven and, hence, only good. An intellectual agreement that the Bible describes God as love and righteousness, mercy and justice, grace and judgment would then place God on the diagonal line where all of these characteristics meet equally.

When we operate out of human reason (righteousness) or human emotions (love) instead of God's holy righteousness and holy love as described in the totality of Scripture, we will not find the peace, happiness, unity, beauty, and wholeness promised there. When we leave out or misinterpret holiness and emphasize love over everything else or righteousness over everything else, we miss the mark (the definition of sin). The church of the twenty-first century tries to separate love and righteousness, but rather than illustrate this with love being the vertical axis (notice there are no negatives associated with the love axis in figure 9-1), let us reorient the graph by extending the horizontal line to the left where love, grace, and mercy now go. Figure 9-2 would be a more biblical representation.

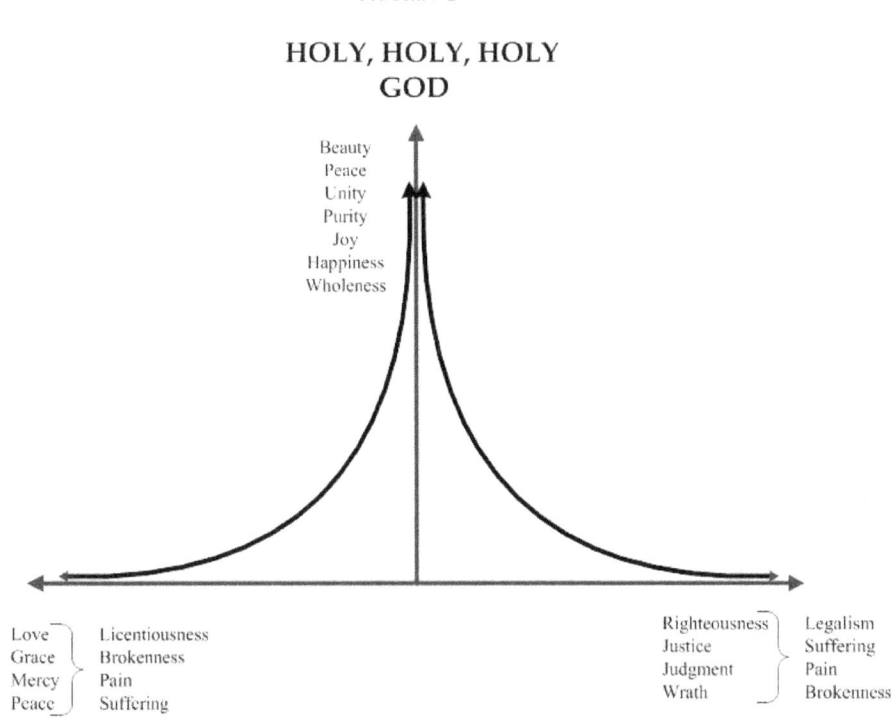

FIGURE 9-2

In this scenario God is at the top of the vertical axis pointing up towards heaven where he belongs. Our human understanding of love so often expounded today is separated from God's holiness and righteousness and leads to licentiousness. Wholeness then vanishes as everything under the sun becomes legal (ignoring Rom 6), and pain, shame, blame, and suffering replace it. Keller writes, "The belief in a God of pure love—who accepts everyone and judges no one—is a powerful act of faith. Not only is there no evidence for it in the natural order, but there is almost no historical, religious textual support for it . . . . The more one looks at it, the less justified it appears."[33] So whether we follow the human interpretation of love or righteousness, we end up with a works-based religion trying to save ourselves by our good deeds.

When people separate what God intended to function together, it will always result in brokenness, and suffering. The solution is not either/or, but both/and. It is not to choose righteousness *or* love, but to remember that righteousness and justice are the foundation of God's throne, and faith and love proceed out from them. Keller explains it in the context of the cross, which gained a result and set a pattern for us. He writes, "To understand why Jesus had to die it is important to remember both the result of the Cross (costly forgiveness of sins) and the pattern of the cross (reversal of the world's values). On the cross neither justice nor mercy loses out—both are fulfilled at once."[34] Holiness holds all of God's qualities in perfect balance, which brings wholeness. "Jesus's death was necessary if God was going to take justice seriously and still love us. This same concern for both love and justice [personal, spiritual, moral, and social] should mark all our relationships."[35]

Instead of the two groups arguing which is better and rushing away from each other, they need to turn towards God in whom both exist and are held in perfect balance by his holiness. Our journey calls for those on the "love" side to become more righteous, and those on the "righteousness" side to become more loving. Then, although we may find ourselves on the curve on either side of the vertical line, we will be moving closer to the thrice-Holy God and to each other. The more we can embrace all the characteristics of God and do the difficult work of keeping them in balance under God's direction and power given through the Holy Spirit and Scripture, the more we will experience beauty, wholeness, peace, unity, happiness, joy, and all the promises of Scripture. Brokenness always arises when we separate what God holds together. Holiness only becomes problematic when people separate its beauty from its righteous requirements. As in the Sermon on the Mount, finding the balance requires a change of motive or, according to Edwards, a change of heart. It requires loving God for who he is and not for what we can get from him. It requires staying focused on what he wants instead of what we want. It requires being holy because he is holy. How might this look?

33. Keller, *Reason for God*, 86.
34. Keller, *Reason for God*, 204–5.
35. Keller, *Reason for God*, 205.

Sin and the Role of the Law in Christian Wholeness

Loving a Holy God means we will change our behavior and thinking to conform to his. The clearest place to understand what God thinks about perfect and pure, whole and complete human behavior and thought can be found in his moral law. God's law shows us how to be whole by avoiding the things that cause brokenness. This is not to say that Christians are "under the law" and must keep it to have salvation. No, salvation is and always has been by grace through faith in Jesus.[36] To be under the law means to go it on your own without God's provision for salvation.

There is no middle ground. You will be in one camp or the other. If you choose to live life without Jesus, then you must be perfect to be accepted by God into heaven. One slip makes you a sinner and leaves you without the holiness that is needed to see God. The law cannot help you because it is powerless to restore the human soul once it has sinned (Rom 8:3a). The law can only tell you the right and wrong way to live. No one can live up to the standards of the law (if we are honest, we never even live up to our own standards of goodness), which is why everyone needs God's Savior, Jesus (Rom 8:3–4).

However, today many people take the Christian belief of salvation by grace alone to mean that that they can ignore the law. "After all," the thinking goes, "Paul said that where sin abounds, grace abounds even more." Paul did write that, meaning that there is no sin that God's grace in Jesus cannot cover, but Paul makes it clear that he did not mean it as a license to sin by asking and answering his own question (Rom 6:1–2, NIV), "What shall we say, then? Shall we go on sinning so that grace may increase? By no means! We died to sin; how can we live in it any longer?" Later he asks (6:15, NIV), "What then? Shall we sin because we are not under law but under grace? By no means!" We may not use grace as an excuse to sin. In fact, in the Sermon on the Mount and throughout Scripture, God's people are called to be perfect or holy as he is perfect. Christians are called to put to death the deeds of the flesh. Therefore, since the law exposes sin, it provides the map for Christians to follow Jesus more obediently. Not surprisingly then, we discover that Paul affirms that the law is holy, righteous, and good (7:12, 16) and spiritual (7:14). Furthermore, it is only by knowing what the law says that we know how to love others and to fulfill God's commandments and become whole. It is in obeying Christ's commands that we become whole.

The psalmist describes how the Law of God is beautiful. David, in Psalm 19, writes that the Law of God is "perfect, reviving the soul" (v. 7); it makes people wise and gives light for them to see clearly. The law is perfect, trustworthy, right, pure, and sweet. The law endures forever and is sure. The law warns people of sin, and those who obey it are

---

36. Paul makes it clear (Rom 6–8) that Christians are not under the law but under grace. To be under grace means that the person accepts Jesus' work on the cross, believes in him, and has become the new creation discussed above. Because of Jesus' life, death, and resurrection, anyone who believes in him has, by grace, overcome the death penalty that sin requires.

blessed and find great reward.³⁷ This is the language we have come to understand as God's holiness. The psalmist summarizes the role of the law of the Spirit under grace in 119:11 (NIV), "I have hidden your word in my heart that I might not sin against you [God]." A large part of God's word is the law, which tells us how life is to be lived in order to be whole as it brings unity and peace.

Today Christians live under grace and are informed by the holy actions of the law that bring wholeness when followed. God always had this plan, even in the Old Testament. In Jeremiah 31:31–34 God promised a new covenant in which he would write his law on his people's hearts and put it in their minds. This is the covenant that Jesus instituted with his own blood shed for the forgiveness of sins. This prophecy has been and is still being fulfilled today by the gift of the Holy Spirit who was breathed out by Jesus to the disciples in the upper room on resurrection Sunday and poured out on Pentecost to every person who believes in Jesus. Edwards reminds us that "the commands and precepts which God has given us are all pure, perfect, and holy. They are the holiness of God in writing, and, when the soul is conformed to them, they have holiness of God upon their hearts."³⁸ In the law, we see into God's holiness and how we can begin to participate in it even now, but it can never be done by human effort alone. Participation has always and only been given by the Holy Spirit to the people who seek God with all their heart and soul. They will find Jesus, and it is wonderful.

The law of God shows us how to participate in God's completeness and peace. It enables us to flow together because of the unity and wholeness it brings. When each person decides to follow his or her own truth, it is inevitable that we will end up bumping into one another with each of our conflicting interpretations of how to live. We become like water molecules heating up until we boil from the disappointment and anger at not getting what we want as we bump against others wanting different things. We see this happening in the increase of domestic violence, terrorism, and violence in schools, malls, and even churches. The law shows us how to live together peacefully and brings wholeness. The two commandments given by Jesus, to love God with all your heart, mind, soul, and strength and to love others as yourself, are a summary of the law, not its replacement.

Paul continues his discourse (Rom 8:15–26) on the law and the Spirit by comparing the lives of natural people (not yet redeemed to God by virtue of their lack of relationship with Jesus) with the lives of those redeemed by Jesus (redeemed by virtue of their personal relationship with him). The natural person wants what he or she wants

---

37. Ps 119 (number in parentheses are verses) asserts that the law is righteous (75, 106, 128, 142, 144, and 164). The law is true (30, 43, 142, 151, and 160). It is eternal (89, 91, 152, and 160), fully trustworthy (138), thoroughly tested (140), wonderful (18 and 129), sweet (39), good (39), and gracious (29). The law gives light (105 and 130), understanding (34, 99, 100, and 130), and wisdom (98). The law brings peace (165), delight (24, 35, 77, 92, and 143), joy (111), hope (43, 49, and 74), comfort (50 and 52), and freedom (32, 44, and 45). The law preserves life (50, 93, and 149) and makes people blessed in purity (9) as it makes them blameless (1–3) (when they follow it).

38. WJE 10:473.

according to personal desires; they cannot please God, for their minds are hostile to God. They do not submit to his law, and this brings physical and spiritual death. Those in whom the Spirit resides, because of their relationship with Jesus, have their minds set on what God wants and find peace and life; their spirits are alive because of righteousness. They will be given life even in their mortal bodies (to some extent while on earth, but most definitely in heaven). So then, to live according to the sinful nature brings death, but to live according to the Spirit (God's way in Jesus, the Way of Holiness) brings life. If you live in the Spirit you have an obligation to put to death the misdeeds of the body. This is the way to wholeness.

Earlier in Romans Paul informs us that we are all slaves (6:15–23), and there are only two camps. Either you will be a slave to sin and death or a slave to God and life. It is determined by to what or to whom you offer yourself; even offering part of yourself to sin leads to ever increasing wickedness and makes you a slave to sin and brokenness. This is talking about a willful and habitual state of sinning and not the "Oh my gosh! I can't believe I did that!" sin. Dane C. Ortlund, reflecting on Edwards, writes, "Sin is false beauty. It is ugliness masquerading as loveliness" like the sirens of Greek mythology who lured men to their deaths with their beautiful songs. Only Jason was able to resist them because he was captivated by a superior beauty.[39] Only offering yourself as a slave to God's righteousness through Jesus Christ leads to wholeness and makes you free because it makes you holy.

Choosing whom you serve extends to your thought life and to all your senses. Leonard Sweet warns that "either we subjugate our thoughts to Christ or be subjugated by them. Part of the 'whatsoever things' [Phil 4:8] that must be brought under subjugation to Christ are not just visual: they are smells, tastes, touches, and sounds"; then he adds, "Music theorist and critic Wilfrid Mellers doesn't listen to heavy metal because for him it is 'propaganda for death.' Every sense has its own poison."[40]

Jesus said (John 8:34–36) that everyone who sins is a slave to sin and has no permanent place in the family, but that he, the Son, can set you free. The Synoptic Gospels record Jesus telling his disciples that they must deny their natural inclinations, put them to death, and follow his ways.[41] People who try to hold on to their lives and try to save themselves by following what seems right in their own eyes will end up losing their lives. Jesus is talking about obedience, but not simply a gut-it-out, painful, and sorrowful determination to do what is right. He is talking about the effects of holiness on the new creation resulting from being born into God's kingdom.

Ortlund helps us to understand this obedience better when he writes, "Holiness [is] a matter of the soul. This is critical to understand about authentic obedience: it is centrally about what is happening in our souls, not by our hands. To be sure, if beauty is alive in our souls, our hands will work. But hands can work apart from anything

---

39. Ortlund, *Edwards on the Christian Life*, 144.
40. Sweet, *Post-modern Pilgrims*, 100.
41. See Matt 16:24–26, Mark 8:34–37, and Luke 9:23–25.

beautiful taking place inside us."⁴² Of these works by our hands only, Jesus asks (Matt 16:26, NIV), "What good will it be for a man if he gains the whole world, yet forfeits his soul? Or what can a man give in exchange for his soul?" The good works that count in heaven are only those done by people who let go of their right to fulfill their natural desires, deny themselves the world's perceived pleasures that are contrary to God's way that their natural self demands, and follow Jesus, the Holy One, who will save their lives. Amazingly, as this becomes delightful and satisfying, it makes us whole. The emptiness is gone and is replaced with contentment, belonging, and indescribable joy.

Summary

Always remember that our culture is constantly trying to create in its brokenness the heavenly party that it can only see from the outside looking in through a window. We all want to be "accepted, welcomed, [and] taken into the dance," but we have not been.⁴³ Lewis, Edwards, Eldredge, Piper, and Keller remind us that cultural things are only meant to direct us to the ultimate joy, pleasure, and acceptance for which we were created, but we forget and, too often, they distract us and lead us into brokenness instead. Christians must stop making the pleasures of this world their ultimate pleasure and begin modeling the pleasure of God and the wholeness that brings. Remember, according to Keller, that the making of good things into the ultimate thing is sin.

Sin always results when the church bifurcates God's word (Scripture) to elevate one of his characteristics above another (or ignores them completely) when they were meant to be lived together, such as love and righteousness, grace and judgment, or God's righteous wrath and peace. Sin always brings shame, blame, and pain. Eldredge challenges us to think of the pain and suffering that could have been avoided if people had chosen holiness through faith in Jesus.

Edwards reminds us that the law of God is his holiness in written form. It shows us how to live a holy life, a whole life. Christians are not under the law but under grace, but this does not mean they can do whatever they want. The Holy Spirit is their teacher; the law and the totality of Scripture is the textbook he uses to teach them how to become like Jesus. Next we will look at the very complex and often emotional connection between wholeness and healing.

---

42. Ortlund, *Edwards on the Christian Life*, 145.
43. Lewis, *The Weight of Glory*, 42.

Chapter 10

Wholeness and Healing

> Something ancient in us bends us toward the origins of the whole thing. We either drown in the splits and confusions of our lives, or we surrender to something greater than ourselves.... In surrender, we descend down... into what is divided in order to get back to the wholeness before the split.... To heal is to make whole again; wholeness is what all healing seeks and what alone can truly unify our spirit.
>
> —MICHAEL MEADE, *THE GENIUS MYTH*

WHEN WE THINK OF wholeness, we always think of healing, and specifically physical healing. Now that we have laid the foundation for wholeness, we are ready to look at this deeply emotional and sometimes controversial aspect of wholeness. The Old Testament word שָׁלוֹם, *shalom*, appears about 250 times and is frequently translated as peace. However, the word means much more than simply an absence of conflict. It may be the result of an agreement between business partners, warring enemies, or between God and humanity. G. Lloyd Carr describes *shalom* as "completeness, wholeness, harmony, fulfillment .... [and it implies] the idea of unimpaired relationships with others and fulfillment in one's undertakings."[1] We see *shalom* being expressed in terms of holiness. It is often used as a blessing in a greeting or parting expression. When it is withheld, it could be considered a curse.[2] Today it is often used much like hello or goodbye.

Biblically, *shalom* is also connected with God's covenant people. It is the result of God's activity and righteousness. Two-thirds of the occurrences describe "the state of fulfillment which is the result of God's presence."[3] Specifically, *shalom* describes the Messiah who is "identified as the Prince of Peace (*sar shalom*—the one who brings fulfillment and righteousness to the earth)."[4] In Ephesians 2:14–15 (NLT) Paul attributes these things to Jesus: "For Christ himself has brought peace to us. He united

---

1. Carr, "שָׁלֹם," 931.
2. Carr, "שָׁלֹם," 931.
3. Carr, "שָׁלֹם," 931.
4. Carr, "שָׁלֹם," 931.

Jews and Gentiles into one people when, in his own body on the cross, he broke down the wall of hostility that separated us. He did this by ending the system of law with its commandments and regulations. He made peace between Jews and Gentiles by creating in himself one new people from the two groups." Thus Paul applied the Old Testament idea of God's presence bringing covenant righteousness and peace found in *shalom* to the New Testament in Jesus' covenant established by his own blood shed for the redemption of any who would believe in him. This, *shalom*, total well-being, wholeness is a work of God alone, resulting from his presence, which can be found most directly in Jesus alone. Total well-being is the goal; healing of the body, mind, emotions, and relationships is the by-product of God's presence.

What about Healing?

Certainly, total well-being includes physical healing. Jesus healed many people while he was on earth. He passed that ministry on to his disciples (Matt 10:1; John 12:12–14). Zeb Bradford Long has identified four dimensions of healing in people: spiritual healing, inner healing, physical healing, and relational healing. Spiritual healing is the most basic one because it "is the restoration of our fundamental relationship with God the Father."[5] This is the basis for all wholeness and healing as it is given through a personal relationship with God's Son. In this relationship the person becomes the new creation in which the image of God is restored as discussed in earlier chapters. Everyone needs this healing in order to have the holiness restored that is needed to see God.

The second kind of healing Long describes as inner healing, which is "the process of undoing the hurtful effects of sin."[6] Again, everyone needs this, because all have sinned and fall short of God's standard. All have been broken, hurt, and wounded not just from their own sin but by sins committed against them by others. Long connects this kind of healing with sanctification as Christians increasingly yield to the Holy Spirit, become conformed to Christ, and display the fruits of the Spirit. He writes, "Inner healing is that transformation of our heart through the Holy Spirit that overcomes the hurt of sin and enables us to reflect the character of Jesus."[7]

The third kind of healing Long identifies is physical healing. This he recognizes as God's restoration of people to their "originally intended health and immortality," which will not be complete until Christ's return and the resurrection. He writes, "Through Jesus we are brought into the river of life now. The physical healings that we may experience now, through natural and supernatural means, are signs of God's original design for human life, and harbingers of the abundant life . . . fulfilled in the New Heaven and New Earth."[8]

---

5. Long et al., *Healing Ministry of Jesus*, 21–22.
6. Long et al., *Healing Ministry of Jesus*, 21.
7. Long et al., *Healing Ministry of Jesus*, 22.
8. Long et al., *Healing Ministry of Jesus*, 22.

The fourth kind of healing Long classifies is relational healing. This "takes place as Jesus heals our web of fallen relationships. This starts with the most basic relationship between male and female. It then extends . . . to include the healing of injustice between social classes and the healing of the nations."[9] The healing of race relations and racism would fall here.

The Source of Sickness and the Goal of Healing

God created all things good and whole, but Adam and Eve's rebellion broke that wholeness. As sin entered the world, sickness and brokenness of all sorts became a fact of life. Long writes, "As a result of being out of harmony with God, the true center and source of all life, everything was thrown into chaos. (Dis-ease literally means to be out of harmony with God, self and others.)"[10] Additionally, the Tree of Life, which could be used for healing of all sorts, including the differences between nations, was taken out of this world. Nevertheless, God acted to counter this brokenness and to restore healing and wholeness.

In the Old Testament God made a covenant with Abraham whom he blessed to be a blessing to the nations. In the exodus we see God's healing concern for his people at the bitter water at Marah and later in the healing of poisonous snake bites. In both cases God used herbs and a natural image of a snake, respectively, through which he brought the healing, indicating that medicine and healing by natural means is one way God chooses to work. The law includes dietary rules possibly to prevent disease and to control contagion.[11] Additionally, Isaiah wrote that the One whom God would send would not only save people from their sin but heal their bodies as well.[12]

In the New Testament, we encounter Jesus healing one person after another and sometimes whole groups of people, such as the ten lepers and those who came to Peter's mother-in-law's house that first evening. Jesus also connects faith with healing. In his hometown of Nazareth he could not heal many folks because of their lack of faith. However, lack of faith was not always on the part of the one receiving prayer. When the disciples were unable to heal the boy brought to them by the father while Jesus was on the Mount of Transfiguration, he rebuked the disciples for having so little faith, not the father or the boy.

While Jesus often healed many people and could heal every kind of disease, his primary goal was preaching and teaching that the kingdom of God was present in him. His first concern was for the spiritual healing that would reconcile people to God

---

9. Long et al., *Healing Ministry of Jesus*, 22.
10. Long et al., *Healing Ministry of Jesus*, 30.
11. Christensen, *Deuteronomy 1:1—21:9*, Deuteronomy 14:3–21. See also Albright, *Yahweh and the Gods of Canaan*, 154–55.
12. See Isa 35:5–6; 53:4–5; 61:1; and Mal 4:2.

from whom wholeness and all other healings flow. Again, we see this most clearly in the story of the healing of Peter's mother-in-law.

When folks heard that Jesus had healed her, they brought others to him for healing, and out of his godly compassion and love, he obliged them. However, he spent much, if not all, of the night in prayer, and when the disciples found him and told him about the crowds that had gathered to be healed, he left *without healing them*. He told the disciples that he must move on to proclaim the good news of the kingdom of God. Another time, Jesus went to one lame man among the many who lay by the pool of Bethesda and asked him if he would like to get well. Only that one person was healed at that time. How are we to understand this? Around that time Jesus began to tell his disciples that he can only do what he sees his Father doing and can only say what he hears him say.

Certainly God loves everyone. He sent his son, Jesus, to satisfy his righteous justice and judgment on our behalf, and there lies the focus that the church must not forget. Ministering to physical needs is important but not the ultimate goal. To paraphrase Jesus, "what if you gain perfect health on earth, but lose your soul?" Remember that at all times God is sovereign and will do what is best and what will bring the most glory to both himself and the person (Matt 18–20). His is an eternal perspective that sees what will maximize his kingdom and will bring ultimate good for everyone, including those left in affliction (we will examine such a life below). The church must recover the same eternal perspective and trust her Holy God always to do what is best, right, and good, and yes, loving even if it means temporary suffering on earth.

In the Sermon on the Mount Jesus told the crowd (Matt 6:19–21, NLT) not to store up treasures on earth where they can be consumed, rusted, destroyed, stolen, and otherwise lost. His disciples are to store up treasure in heaven where it will always be safe, for "wherever your treasure is, there the desires of your heart will also be." The wealth of this world and all the entertainment, pleasure, and comfort it provides are secondary and pale in light of the godly, primary (genuine) treasures of eternity. The sovereignty of God and the eternal perspective often get lost in this postmodern, post-Christian age of human love that ignores God's truth, righteousness, and holiness and seeks ultimate pleasure and comfort now.

Sin and Healing

Scripture often connects sin with the need for healing. In 2 Chronicles 7:14, God tells Israel that when plagues or drought or sickness hit, if they will humble themselves, turn from their wicked ways, and pray, he would hear and forgive their sin and heal their land. James picks up on this theme and writes (5:16, NIV), "Therefore confess your sins to each other and pray for each other so that you may be healed." David calls on the Lord to have mercy on him and to heal him, for he had sinned against God (Ps 41:4). Psalm 103:1–5 (NIV) opens with praise to God's holy name, "who forgives all your sins and heals all your diseases, who redeems your life from the pit and crowns you with love and compassion, who satisfies your desires with good things so that your youth is renewed like the eagle's."

We find Jesus forgiving the sins of a paralytic who had been let down through the roof by his friends when they could not get him through the crowd.[13] When the Pharisees objected, Jesus healed the man of his paralysis, asking them which was harder: to forgive sin or to heal? Obviously Jesus did both, and they were somehow connected. At another time we see Jesus connecting sin and the need for healing with the paralyzed man at the Pool of Bethesda (John 5:14).

So then, in some cases sin, disease, and suffering are connected, as in the case of a man who sleeps around and contracts an STD, a drug addict who uses dirty needles and is infected with HIV, or a woman who eats only fatty red meat (no vegetables or fruit of any kind) and has a stroke. In some cases there is a direct correlation between a sinful action and an illness. However, much sickness and suffering is not caused directly by the sin of the one who is suffering, as in the case of a victim of rape or of a car accident when the other person was driving under the influence of drugs or alcohol. Additionally, we live in a fallen world where the use of pesticides, herbicides, and genetic engineering contaminate our food and water. Chemicals that were never intended to be consumed are added to most of what we eat. Added to that, the air we breathe is often polluted. Then we wonder why we are sick. God never intended us to live this way. It is no one's individual sin, but the collective sin of living in a broken world that greatly contributes to many of our diseases. So then, what is the response of the church to be?

Matthew records in 4:23 and again in 9:35 that Jesus went around the country preaching and teaching, healing all their diseases, and casting out demons. In 10:1 he delegates that ministry to the disciples. Later (Luke 10), he sends out seventy disciples to do the same. Their message would introduce people to the one who could forgive their sins as they taught and preached the kingdom of God was at hand. John records Jesus telling the disciples that they will do everything that he has done and more. They need only to ask in his name (more about this in chapters 15 and 16). Some argue that this ended with the last apostle's death. I would respond that we do still see healings today. The fact that Jesus sent out the seventy and his high priestly prayer for those that would follow the apostles bear this out.

Healing is a ministry of God's church. Long helps us here also. Jesus bore our pain and suffering on the cross, and we are to bear one another's burdens and be like him. He writes, "To live and work lovingly with difficult persons, to be faithful in an unsatisfying covenant relationship, to give sacrificially, to witness heroically, to do good to those who hurt us, to forgive the despicable deed—this is the call of suffering love which we are to accept."[14] But beyond this he urges Christians not to "passively

---

13. See Matt 9:2–7; Mark 2:1–12; Luke 5:17–26.
14. Long et al., *Healing Ministry of Jesus*, 35.

accept sickness" but to ask for whatever we need in Jesus' name.[15] Still, not everyone receives physical healing in this life.

The church must always keep the ultimate goal of healing in mind. Picking up on Isaiah 53, Peter writes (1 Pet 2:24, NIV) that Jesus bore our sins in his body on the cross "so that we might die to sins and live for righteousness; by his wounds you have been healed." Christians have been healed by Christ's wounds and have been given the ministry of reconciliation, which by the very nature of God in Christ includes healing and wholeness. Long explains, "While Jesus came to make us well, in every sense of the word, His priority was to save us from sin and reconcile us to God eternally."[16] He reminds us that "we still live in a world where there is sin and death. The result is that while spiritual healing of restoring our relationship with God is completed by the sacrifice of Jesus on the cross, the rest of our healing is in process."[17]

First and foremost, this healing brings redemption, regeneration, and reconciliation to God (then to others). When a person is born again and becomes the new creation through faith in Jesus, there is a spiritual awakening that now finds God and his ways attractive. This is what Dane C. Ortlund calls "regenerating grace," which "changes us by getting down underneath even the very level of our desires and changing *what we want* . . . . regenerating grace does not enable us to do what we don't want to do. More deeply, it brings us to want to do what we should want to do. Regenerating grace is grace that softens us way down deep at the core of who we are."[18] He describes this as a "taste-bud transformation" in which "in a miracle that can never be humanly manufactured, we find ourselves, strangely, delighting to love God. We are changed. The will itself is renovated. We see things as they really are. True beauty is now seen to be beautiful."[19]

This miracle cannot be manufactured by human effort because it is the gift of the Holy Spirit given to each one who believes in Jesus as Lord and Savior. When this happens, instead of dreading things God calls good (holiness) there is an honest desire and joy to do them, and the joy of the Lord is your strength (Neh 8:10). This transformational healing (regeneration) begins at the moment of our redemption, continues to grow throughout life, and is complete only when we arrive in heaven, either at our death or the Lord's return.

Do not be deceived; God takes sin seriously because he knows it destroys his children. The church must regain God's perspective on sin and holy living because it is the only way to find healing and wholeness. Holy living brings peace, unity, joy, and hope because people are living the way God created them to live. It brings respect for others because they are made in the image of God. It brings harmony and order

---

15. Long et al., *Healing Ministry of Jesus*, 35.
16. Long et al., *Healing Ministry of Jesus*, 32.
17. Long et al., *Healing Ministry of Jesus*, 24.
18. Ortlund, *Edwards on the Christian Life*, 43.
19. Ortlund, *Edwards on the Christian Life*, 43.

out of chaos because it is beautiful. Holy living heals the brokenness that Eldredge describes above and brings wholeness to the person, to the church, and to every group that would be surrendered to it. The fighting, bickering, and wounding often found in churches is the result of people wanting their own way and not because of holy living. Let us unpack this further.

The Role of the Church in Restoring Wholeness

The greatest thing Christians can offer that will bring wholeness to a dark and chaotic world is forgiveness and redemption for repentance (not absolution to continue living the same way). This goes beyond working for social justice, as important as that is. It includes proclamation of the good news of Jesus and prayer for healing of the mind, body, emotions, and soul. The last is the only one guaranteed to be completed while here on earth thanks to Jesus and the cross.

Later, I will discuss prayer in more detail, but for now I will tell you that the church must intentionally be praying for the salvation of souls. Additionally, she should be praying for physical and relational healing. It is best to do this in teams of two or more.[20] Nearly twenty years ago I was part of a group that prayed for a young mother of two boys for healing of a cancerous brain tumor. To my knowledge she is still living and healthy today. About the same time, I prayed for a man for healing of cancer, but God answered in a different way. Instead of bringing physical healing in this world, he gave the man and his wife such a strong sense of his presence that the remaining six months of his life were so joyous that he could not stop telling people how wonderful God is. I seldom feel directed to pray for a specific kind of healing as in the case of the young mother, but I can always pray with certainty of faith for God to touch them in a special way that only he can.

One time I prayed this way with a man dying of cancer of the mouth who had little use for the church or Jesus. That Sunday he startled his wife, who was still in their bedroom, by talking to someone in the living room when she thought they were alone. She went to investigate. Every time she tried to ask who he was talking to, he shushed her. All she could hear were her husband's responses of "Yes, Lord." He was moved to tears. Later he explained that Jesus had presented himself to him that morning telling him that he is real and exists just as he had been taught. The man came to faith that morning in his living room and was changed. He maintained the faith right up to the end. When God shows up—*wow*!

The world will see it when Christians model Christ's beauty and the wholeness life in him brings. According to John Piper, Christians must show the world that "Christ is the all-satisfying treasure that we embrace whether we live or die; Christ is praised by being prized. He is magnified as a glorious treasure when He becomes

---

20. Whenever possible, I prefer to pray with at least one or two other Christians, but I have prayed solo when the circumstances require it.

our unrivaled pleasure. So if we are going to praise Him and magnify Him, we dare not be indifferent as to whether we prize Him and find pleasure in Him."[21] Piper concludes, "If Christ's honor is our passion, the pursuit of pleasure in Him is our duty."[22] The world will notice this.

Piper captures the essence of Christian living when he writes, "Nothing makes God more supreme and more central than when people are utterly persuaded that nothing—not money or prestige or leisure or family or job or health or sports or toys or friends—is going to bring satisfaction to their aching hearts besides God."[23] Furthermore, "this conviction breeds people who go hard after God on Sunday morning."[24] When those around you see how God brings beauty, pleasure, and wholeness to your life, they will be open to hearing how that could happen for them. It is not "to demonstrate the strength of our devotion to duty, nor to reveal the vigor of our moral resolve, nor to prove the heights of our tolerance for pain; but rather to manifest, in childlike faith, the infinite preciousness of his all-satisfying promises."[25] Piper closes with this gem, "The pursuit of joy in Christ, whatever the pain, is a powerful testimony to Christ's supreme and all-satisfying worth. And so may it come to pass that all the peoples of the world will see the beauty of Christ, the image of God, and magnify His grace in the gladness of saving faith."[26]

It would be easy to jump on the pendulum and to seek beauty, pleasure, and wholeness without holiness. It's simply human nature. Dekker has identified some potholes into which the church might fall: be careful of turning something good into something offensive to God; be careful not to over-indulge in earthly pleasures; and be careful not to swing on the pendulum of extremes using things God intended for our good for either legalism or licentiousness.[27] To this I would add: be careful not to make the good things of earth like physical healing the ultimate thing. The church recovers wholeness as she engages in pleasures as God intended his people to do: to see them as a foretaste of heaven, "as limited samples of far greater pleasures to come—seeing him face to face in glory."[28] We are to enjoy what God has given us, but any abuse of the way he intended these things to be used will corrupt (is sin) and should be off limits to the believer. Sin always destroys wholeness and brings woundedness, suffering, shame, pain, and blame. Let go of the pursuit of this world's ideas of money, entertainment, power, and satisfaction and model for your neighbors the wholeness that biblical Christianity brings.

21. Piper, *Dangerous Duty of Delight*, 27.
22. Piper, *Dangerous Duty of Delight*, 27.
23. Piper, *Dangerous Duty of Delight*, 57.
24. Piper, *Dangerous Duty of Delight*, 57.
25. Piper, *Dangerous Duty of Delight*, 83–84.
26. Piper, *Dangerous Duty of Delight*, 84.
27. Dekker, *Slumber of Christianity*, 176–78.
28. Dekker, *Slumber of Christianity*, 178.

Healing, Wholeness, and Real-Life Experiences

We often see so much suffering and pain and ask how a loving God could allow it. The short answer is that God allows you and everyone on this planet to have free will. Since the fall (discussed in chapter 7) this world is under a curse due to the sins we all commit. The purpose of pain and suffering is to get us to see that we need God (2 Cor 7:9–10 and 1 Pet 1:3–9). Our wisdom, strength, knowledge, and abilities are woefully inadequate to address all of life's challenges. Suffering drives us to seek God, but some choose to get angry and to blame God, and they miss the wholeness that could be theirs. As I close this chapter, I want to introduce you to one woman who chooses to keep the faith through her suffering and has discovered the healing which brought wholeness.

Joni Eareckson Tada was an active teen until a diving accident left her paralyzed. "Quadriplegic" is never a diagnosis anyone would choose, let alone a teenager. She could have become bitter and blamed God for ruining her life, but she chose to delight in him instead, and it has made all the difference in her life and in the lives of hundreds of thousands of hurting people around the world. Today she is founder and CEO of Joni and Friends, an organization that ministers to handicapped folks everywhere. She is a painter, author, and public speaker.[29]

God has been glorified in her life. He has used her to expand his kingdom on earth and to tell the gospel message to the next generation. She admits it would never have happened had she not had that accident. The story does not end there, but after four decades of faithful service of radiating the beauty of God's holiness, she began to experience excruciating pain that nothing could stop. Below is some of the wisdom she found by seeking God, who did not heal her physical body but did restore her to wholeness. She views physical healing as an acorn that will one day become a tree with many uses. In the same way God's salvation in Jesus is complete but not yet finished. In the meantime it is not the disease and wounds that "rob us of the freshness of Christ's beauty" but the possessions and attachments to this world and our pride that keep us from seeing it. She differentiates between giving thanks (a choice) and being thankful (an emotion). Give thanks because you trust God, and he is in control. "Distressing medical reports" are "meant to awaken us to the reality of God, His nearness, His care, His presence, and His ever-present help." She writes, "Whatever it is I have lost, it will all be regained in heaven" and so much more that even the best things here will pale in comparison. She describes how every good thing and treasured memory such as running through a field, swimming, and peeling an orange are only hints of better things to come when she sees Jesus.[30]

Does this sound familiar? She has not read this book, but she has read The Book. It is all there. She has learned the beauty of holiness and has been made whole. Her

---

29. Eareckson Tada and Musser, *Joni*.
30. Eareckson Tada, *Place of Healing*, 64–65, 86, 140, 142, 167–68.

physical healing may not yet have happened, but it will: if not on earth, then in heaven. She has also learned to examine herself to see if she is acting like she believes God is all she needs. I urge you to use her questions as your criteria to examine yourself when life throws problems at you, and you find it difficult to see God's beauty and wholeness: "What do I have?" "Am I using what I have?" "Am I prepared to lose what I have?" "Am I ready to receive what I don't have?" The key to enjoying Christ's beauty is to be content with what I have and to use all I have for God's kingdom. The real test is question three. "If I lose possessions, health, power, recognition, family, or life itself, will I continue to serve God or rail against him like those who do not know him?" Joni asks one more question that I want to pass along to you: "How long has it been since you've done a thoughtful inventory of your possessions?"[31]

In our culture, that is what it usually comes down to: possessions and pleasure. Too often, we want God to bring wholeness to our lives through the things of this world: money and the things it can buy, such as a Mercedes, endless entertainment and diversion, a five-bedroom, five-and-a-half-bath, six-thousand-square-foot home on a hundred acres, invitations to radically great parties, and endless pleasure as we identify it, but these things cannot bring you lasting peace, lasting joy and happiness, or contentment. Ironically, this week as I have been writing this chapter, I got news of a young man who pursued the world's pleasures with abandon. He left his wife and child to go after endless parties and fun wherever that would lead him. He just committed suicide. Obviously, not everyone goes to that extreme, but for every one of us, when the thrill of something new wears off, the emptiness will still be there. Too often we look for the next new thing to distract us. That has become the American way. God wants more and better for everyone and especially for his people.

Joni is a wonderful example of the wholeness God brings, but perhaps you cannot identify with her story. Allow me to describe my encounter with a pastor whom I have met recently who told me about his young married daughter, with a three-year-old son, who had a brain aneurism that Thanksgiving. God miraculously spared her life, and she is back home and resuming her life's daily activities. In this past year, he has had surgery for a brain aneurism, and his wife has developed a painful condition. During this same week that I received news of the young man committing suicide, I received news that this pastor's mother-in-law is near death and her sister had passed just the day before. Overwhelming, you say? Yes, it is, but this man is keeping his focus on Jesus and keeps on going with strength that is not his own. Countless stories like his exist. The church must be careful not to fall into the trap of looking for beauty, pleasure, happiness, joy, delight, and satisfaction in the same places the culture does. Worse still, she must not make secondary beauty and worldly pleasure the ultimate things by demanding that God provide beauty, delight, healing, and satisfaction in the same way the culture demands them. God's

---

31. Eareckson Tada, *Place of Healing*, 202–4. For more details see appendix 2. I highly recommend this book to everyone who is looking for a practical application to the material found in this book.

way restores the wholeness that was broken in the fall and continues to be shattered the further we drift from the beauty of God's holiness.

Summary

Eldredge observes that Christians are under great trials today and reminds them that holiness is their strength and safe passage through the testing. He also observes that "for many of us, the waves of first love [for God] ebbed away in the whirlwind of Christian service and activity, and we began to lose the Romance. Our faith began to feel more like a series of problems that needed to be solved or principles that had to be mastered before we could finally enter into the abundant life promised by Christ."[32] The solution is to seek God with your whole heart, mind, strength, and soul for who he is—holy—and not for what he can give you. Christians must once again develop an eternal perspective and realize that the pleasures and the good things in this world are temporary, only secondary, and only a glimpse of greater pleasure and rewards to come that will last forever.

To help us reach this goal, Thomas Merton reminds us that "there is something in the depths of our being that hungers for wholeness and finality. Because we are made for eternal life, we are made for an act that gathers up all the powers and capacities of our being and offers them simultaneously and forever to God."[33] Scripture informs us that the purpose of sorrow and suffering is to bring us to this point of refocusing our attention from the secondary beauty and pleasures this world offers to the primary beauty and ultimate pleasure and good of the God who is holy, holy, holy, where we find wholeness.

In that vein, Jesus commands that we ask, seek, and knock, which to me tells us to pray for God's intervention and healing, to go after all that modern medicine has to offer us, and to keep both up until we get an answer. Always remember not to be attached to the things in this world, which, according to Lewis, are "only the image, the symbol . . . [and that] Scripture invites me . . . .to pass in through Nature, beyond her, into that splendor which she fitfully reflects." He asks us to imagine, "What would it be like to taste at the fountainhead that stream of which even these lower reaches prove so intoxicating? Yet, that, I believe, is what lies before us. The whole man is to drink joy from the fountain of joy."[34] This is wholeness. Eternity with God in heaven for those who believe in Jesus is where physical healing will be permanent and complete. This is ultimate healing, but wholeness begins now. Lewis adds, "When human souls have become as perfect in voluntary obedience as the inanimate creation is in its

---

32. Eldredge, *The Sacred Romance*, 6–7.
33. Merton, *No Man Is an Island*, 147.
34. Lewis, *The Weight of Glory*, 44.

lifeless obedience, then they will put on its glory, or rather that greater glory of which Nature is only the first sketch."[35]

We can see this in a woman called Joni and in multitudes of people like her. God's stream is intoxicating and brings wholeness; he may or may not heal the physical body at this time, but the emptiness is filled and truth reigns. God is sovereign and sufficient. He warrants our trust and always brings wholeness to those who seek him with their whole being. They who truly find Jesus also find all the wonderful things the Bible talks about concerning him. They find confidence instead of insecurity, desire to give and to help others instead of greed to get all that they can for themselves, and respect for people and things that builds them and ourselves up instead of bullying, racism, and hatred that steal, kill, and destroy. Christians can love others because they are loved by a trustworthy God based on righteousness because he is holy. This is wholeness. Healing will come, if not on earth, then in heaven. In the next chapter we will look at this holy love that makes the way for this to happen.

---

35. Lewis, *The Weight of Glory*, 43.

Chapter 11

Biblical Love Is Holy Love

> Whoever does not love does not know God, for God is love.
>
> —1 John 4:8, NRSV

THERE HAVE BEEN THOUSANDS of songs written about love during my lifetime. Hundreds of them were written and never heard. Some of the well-known songs include: "Love Is a Many Splendored Thing" (Four Aces, 1955). "Love Makes the World Go Round" (Carnival, 1961). "She Loves You"; "Love Me Do"; "Can't Buy Me Love" (The Beatles, 1964). "What the World Needs Now Is Love, Sweet Love" (Jackie DeShannon, 1965). "You've Lost that Lovin' Feeling" (Righteous Brothers, 1965). "All You Need Is Love" (The Beatles, 1967). "Love Story" (Andy Williams, 1971). Add the thousands of poems, romance novels, and romantic comedies and you get the idea that we are more than just a little preoccupied with love. You might say we are obsessed with love. There is a logical and spiritual reason for this—God is love.

Background

First John 4:8 and 16 inform us that God is love. Therefore, since God created people in his image it stands to reason that we were designed to be loved and to give love, which explains our fascination with love. However, since the time of Adam and Eve every human has chosen to rebel against God. As a result, our human understanding of his love has become distorted. This should not surprise us since humanity's rebellion against God has always been based on lies (and partial truths that contain lies), which are designed to mislead. Now, as in the garden of Eden, Satan, the father of lies, whispers in your mind, "Did God really say, 'You will die if you eat from the tree of knowledge of good and evil?'" He might suggest that God is keeping something good from you when he forbids you to do something or that God did not really say or mean what is in the Bible. Satan wants you to question God's motives, asking, "Would a loving God keep you from doing something you like?"; "Would God not want you to be rich and make millions?"; or "Would he allow suffering?"[1]

---

1. Lewis provides an unusual take on how the demonic realms does this in *The Screwtape Letters*.

It works like this. Our Enemy plants doubt and suggests that God is being unfair or preventing your freedom and fun. When you and I fail to discern the lies, no matter how small, we open ourselves up to untold evil. It may not seem like much at first, but as time progresses, so does the error. It is like the construction of the first transcontinental railroad. If the construction crews on each side of the country had been off by even a degree or two (one to the north and the other to the south), they never would have met in the middle. Similarly, the seemingly insignificant rebellious mindset that leads to seemingly insignificant rebellious acts opens the door for greater rebellion that will lead the church, God's people, further from the narrow path, the ancient road, which God calls the Highway of Holiness.

Regarding evil today, Christians often want God to change the world, but God may want to change his people first. The church is his chosen instrument of change in the world; so if she is not up to the task, God may need to work in her before he can work to restrain evil in the world. The essence of this battle of good and evil begins in the mind. Paul tells us (2 Cor 10:3–5, ESV), "For though we walk in the flesh, we are not waging war according to the flesh. For the weapons of our warfare are not of the flesh but have divine power to destroy strongholds. *We destroy arguments and every lofty opinion raised against the knowledge of God, and take every thought captive to obey Christ*" (italics are mine).

Evil begins in the mind in the form of arguments and lofty opinions people imagine against God's truth. It is crucial for the church to understand two things: *that* evil happens (a real evil attacks God's truth) and *how* evil happens (the tactics it uses such as lies, unforgiveness, slander, and anger to name only a few). God's love has been especially targeted.

God Is Love

Because the popular interpretation of God's love looks strangely like the world's view of love, M. M. Thompson cautions Christians to be careful how they read, "God is love." In logic and mathematics there are four symbols that can be used to represent the verb "is." These indicate the direction of the primary influence of one thing over another or whether they are identical. They are =, ↔, →, and ←. See figure 11-1.

	Mathematical Symbol	"is" replaced by = or ↔	"is" replaced by →	"is" replaced by ←
	"God is love"	God = love or God ↔ love	God → love	God ← love could be written as Love → God
	Meaning of "is"	Exactly equal, e.g., 7 + 3 = 7 + 3. There is no difference between God and love.	God is greater than love	Love is greater than God and could be written: Love → God
	Interpretation	God and love are completely synonymous. Whatever the one is, the other is also.	God is the source of love and defines the characteristics of love. God's standards determine what love is.	Love is the source of God and defines the characteristics of God. Since there are no standards beyond human thought and what seems right to the individual, each person determines who or what his or her god is.

Figure 11-1. Possible meanings of God is love (1 John 4:8 and 16)

The first column makes God and love equal, identically the same with no differences whatsoever. However, God is more than love. He is truth, mercy, righteousness, and holiness to name only a few of his qualities. Since the totality of God is more than love, what John wrote, "God is love," must be interpreted in one of the next two ways.[2] The *Bible portrays* "God is love" (1 John 4:8 and 16) as the meaning found in the second column in which God is the source of love. His standards define love. However, the *culture interprets* 1 John 4:8 and 16 using the third column, "Love is God," making the human understanding of love the source of God, thereby constructing him or her in the person's own image.

---

2. • The explanation of column 1: "is" can be replaced with "=" or "↔." God = love is the same as God ↔ love and means that God and love are identically equal, like 7 + 3 = 7 + 3. Therefore it would be absolutely true to say that God is love and love is God with the = and the ↔ representing "is" and meaning there is unconditionally no difference between God and love.
   • The explanation of column 2: "is" can be replaced with "→." Then God → love would mean that God is the source of love and is not limited to it or by it. In fact, in this scenario God determines what love is. The implication according to Thompson and others is that "if we want to know what love is, then we must let God define it. . . . Love does not describe the fullness of God, but God defines the fullness of love" (Thompson, *1–3 John*, np).
   • The explanation of column 3: "is" would be replaced by the final symbol "←" and would be understood as "Love is God." This option means that love is the source of God. There would no longer be any absolute standards of love. Therefore, human love that puts self first in order to maximize personal pleasure would provide the only standards that determine who god is. Hence, an individual's personal wants, desires, and beliefs would define God and what he, she, or it is like. God would be different for each person.

Unfortunately, today, the church has progressively been interpreting John as saying, "Love is God," thereby mirroring the culture's belief that the individual is free to define god as whomever or whatever pleases him or her. This leads to two major errors in our thinking about love. The first is that love means you can do anything you want. For example, if the belief that God loves you just as you are leads you to believe that you never need to change anything, that you are free to keep on willfully sinning because God will always automatically forgive you, then you have bought into the "Love is God" way of thinking.

William Klassen has identified a second error commonly held today. He cautions Christians not to fall into the converse of God is love "as if wherever there is love, there is also God."[3] Just because a person says or does something we associate with love does not automatically mean God is in that person or in the event. All people are made in God's image and will naturally have some of God's characteristics. Like Edwards's idea of secondary beauty, this could be called secondary love, which is meant to give us only a glimpse of the glory that is God and to point us toward the fullness of love found in God alone. Therefore, the display of these characteristics, including love, without the confession of faith in and obedience to Jesus, should not be interpreted as salvation for that person. Sadly, the church is becoming more comfortable with our cultural spin on love and God, and less comfortable with what the Bible teaches. The solution is for Christians to saturate themselves in the word of God, but that may not be easy to do. In addition to the struggle of finding the time to do so, they may have accepted some flawed assumptions about biblical Christianity that keep them from seeing the truth.

Some Wrong Turns of False Assumptions

Knowing that God's truth, and especially the truth about God's love, can be distorted, John commands God's people to test the spirits to discern whether they are from an evil spirit, the human spirit, or God's Spirit (1 John 4:1). The first wrong turn Christians take (false assumption #1) is to assume Scripture is full of errors and outdated or only contains suggestions of how to live. However, God's Spirit will never contradict the Scriptures, for God is their author. A second wrong turn (false assumption #2) is to believe that love is a feeling, and if I feel warm and positive towards a person, place, or thing, I love them. The corollary to this assumption is that if I love them, I will not tell them they are wrong or point out their errors.

One way to test whether you are in agreement with Scripture or the culture is to examine the lyrics of popular songs and the messages pervading our media and the sampling of Christian songs and Scriptures included in appendix 3. In our culture's songs you will find all of the world's criteria for love. Love is often reduced to what

---

3. Klassen, "Love (NT and Early Jewish)," 391.

it can do for me. These popular sentiments about love of touching, feeling, and sex saturate our subconscious and seep into our thoughts like propaganda, *conditioning us* to think of love as a means to maximize personal pleasure. It may actually encourage people to use love to manipulate others in order to gain for themselves the freedom to be and to do whatever they want.

The repetition is what drives it into our long term memory (like learning your addition facts or multiplication tables). Now, consider the thousands of movies, commercials, and internet images that teach us to see "fifty shades of gray" in everything. It is no wonder that when people read Scripture they think it sounds harsh and the God they find there to be some strange fiend, especially in the Old Testament and Revelation. How comfortable are you with this God who is jealous and can despise people?

A third wrong turn (false assumption #3) is that the God of the Bible is not the God of Jesus, whom we know is loving, gentle, and mild. In the Song of Solomon, the Bible reveals that God is not willing to share his people with other gods or with the world system. His love is strong and powerful, and he knows that people cannot divide their love between the world (and its idols) and him (1 John 2:15–17). They will always end up serving one and hating the other (Jesus in the Sermon on the Mount, Matthew 6). In this culture, we are used to thinking of a loving God as someone who will only and always do nice things *for us*. He is a teddy bear bringing us comfort, as our culture has conditioned us to interpret that, and not a lion who rips and tears (Hosea 5:14–15) what is evil and rebellious. But sin destroys God's creation. Is it not more loving to stop that which destroys than to allow it to continue masquerading for a time as good? See appendix 3 for some images of God usually rejected or ignored today.

A fourth wrong turn (false assumption #4) is to believe the person must be good enough before God will accept them. A close corollary is that a person can earn his or her salvation. It is precisely because none of us is ever good enough that Jesus had to come and die in our place. What Jesus did for us on the cross cannot be bought. Salvation cannot be earned or paid for by anyone other than Jesus. God scorns those who would try. How would you feel if you were to throw a huge party for your son who just won the Nobel Peace Prize, but guests insist on paying you for the privilege of attending and then bash his work in front of the other guests? You would probably be insulted and tell them to leave or not let them in.

Holy Love Examined

Scripture tells us that God is love, but we must be clear in our understanding of how he loves. Key New Testament passages (Heb 12; John 1:12–14; 3:16–18, 14–15; 1 John; and the epistles) clearly indicate a special relationship God has with those who are in a personal relationship with Jesus. "But," you may think, "doesn't God love everyone the same?" These passages and others would answer that in the negative.

It is true that God made every person and loves them equally in that he provides everything they need to sustain life. It is also true that God desires that all would "be saved and come to knowledge of the truth [that] there is one God and one mediator between God and men, the man Christ Jesus, who gave himself as a ransom for all men" (1 Tim 2:4–6a, NIV). In this sense, God does love everyone and wants all to be saved and live with him for eternity. However, salvation must be applied on his terms, and people are free to reject them and him.

From John we know that the apostles taught that people who rejected Jesus did not belong to God; only those who believed, who devoted themselves to following Jesus' commands (all of them) have entered into that covenant relationship with God through Jesus and have become his adopted children.[4] These are the ones to whom the many precious promises of Scripture are made. This is a specific love not generally given. It is offered to everyone, but only those who receive Jesus receive this love. It is similar to the general revelation in nature that God exists versus the specific revelation of him in Scripture. There is a general love that God has for all people, and there is a specific love that he has for his adopted children. This is nothing new. What is new is the thinking that God loves everyone identically.

In the Old Testament we encounter two Hebrew words with respect to love. The verb is ’*ahab*. The word occurs 220 times in the Old Testament but with the primary use of a person's love of another or an object.[5] It can mean anything from sexual relations with a prostitute, to love of things, to human love towards God. "The word carries the connotation of setting one's heart and mind upon the object mentioned, giving it special attention or dedicating oneself to pursuing it."[6] It does not normally include an intimate relationship. In Deuteronomy 6:5, it is used to call people to love God with all their heart, soul, and strength, which is to be expressed "by obedience to God's commandments, serving God, showing reverence for God, and being loyal to God alone"; it is "not primarily a matter of intimate affection."[7] It is also the word used in Leviticus 19:18 in the command to the Israelites to love their neighbor.

When used of God's love in the Old Testament, it occurs "less than 25 times. Nevertheless, the concept of God's love is an important aspect of OT thought (especially when *ḥesed* is also considered)."[8] The Bible tells us that God loves people (specifically Israel, Deut 4:37; Ps 47:5) and righteousness and justice (Ps 33:5). He loves righteousness and hates wickedness (Ps 45:7). He loves the temple (Mal 2:11). The only place ’*ahab* includes the idea of intimacy is between a husband and a wife.

---

4. Absolute obedience on earth is not possible. Obedience is a sanctifying process of growth towards holiness and away from sin.

5. Bushell et al., "אהב."

6. Sakenfeld, "Love (OT)," 376.

7. Sakenfeld, "Love (OT)," 376.

8. Sakenfeld, "Love (OT)," 377.

God uses this imagery in Hosea to reveal his faithfulness and deep love to Israel, who has played the harlot and committed adultery by chasing after other lovers (other gods and the cultures that worship them).

The idea of intimacy in love is best found in the Hebrew word חסד (pronounced *ḥesed*), which is translated as steadfast love or unfailing love. This is the word for love used in Psalm 89:14 which we have encountered above. Sakenfeld understands "*ḥesed* and faithfulness almost as divine attendants" that stand before "the incomparable Creator of the universe, whose throne is founded on justice and righteousness."[9] She concludes that this *ḥesed* brings order and not chaos. We first encounter *ḥesed* in connection with Abraham's servant asking God to show steadfast love to Abraham by giving this servant success in finding a wife for Isaac (Gen 24:12, 14, 49). Abraham had previously entered into a covenant with God that he would have multitudes of descendants and that the whole world be blessed through him (he was blessed to be a blessing). In Genesis 39:21 (ESV) we read that "the LORD was with Joseph and showed him steadfast love and gave him favor in the sight of the keeper of the prison." In Exodus 20:6 (NIV), the second commandment against idols states, "but showing love [*ḥesed*, steadfast love] to a thousand generations of those who love me [the relationship of love to God as between family members] and keep my commandments." God uses it twice to describe himself to Moses in Exodus 34:6–7 (NIV), "The LORD passed before him and proclaimed, 'The LORD, the LORD, a God merciful and gracious, slow to anger, and *abounding in steadfast love* and faithfulness, keeping *steadfast love* for thousands, forgiving iniquity and transgression and sin, but who will by no means clear the guilty, visiting the iniquity of the fathers on the children and the children's children, to the third and the fourth generation'" (italics are mine).

Mounce describes *ḥesed* as "the special relationship God has with his covenantal people" that "denotes 'kindness, love, loyalty, mercy,' most poignantly employed in the context of relationship between God and humans as well as between one human and another—the former relationship using the word three times as often as the latter."[10] Harris downplays the covenant relationship and writes, "Ex 20 and Deut 5 simply [say] that God's love (*ḥesed*) to those who love him (' *ahab*) is the opposite of what he will show to those who hate him. The context of these commands is surely God's will for all mankind, although his special care, indeed his covenant, is with Israel. That *ḥesed* refers only to this covenant and not to the eternal divine kindness back of it, however, is a fallacious assumption." He sees God's faithfulness to his covenant only "because it is the loving God who speaks the oath."[11] Of course, it is presumed that God's steadfast love precedes his declaration of *ḥesed* because there never was a time that God did not exist prior to creation and was complete as he is today.

---

9. Sakenfeld, "Love (OT)," 379.
10. Mounce, "Love," 426.
11. Harris, "חסד," 305–7.

As Harris has identified, God shows love to those who love him and the opposite (judgment? He does not say) to those who hate him. Therefore, he could not love all people in the same way. It seems that Harris has narrowly focused on the Sinai Covenant of the Ten Commandments. God already had a covenant with Abram and his descendants when we first read about *hesed*. Additionally, a love primarily focused on an intimate covenantal relationship presupposes God's love for his creation and the desire to redeem it after the fall. Loving God by entering into his covenant is now and always has been the way to enter into the intimate relationship, like the covenant of marriage, reserved for those whom he calls his people.

This *hesed* love is always a matter of the heart. Those who love God also love God's righteousness and justice, hate evil and wickedness, follow his commands, and honor his truth. In the Old Testament, circumcision was to be the outward show of what was in the person's heart. Scripture tells God's people to circumcise their hearts so that they would love him with all their heart and soul. This means they would no longer be stiff-necked and deserving of God's wrath but would be alive in God (Deut 10:16; 30:6; Jer 4:4). Additionally, Jeremiah (31:33–34) prophesies a new covenant that God will make with people in which he will put his law in their minds and write it on their hearts, and their sins will be forgiven. He was talking of the covenant Jesus would make hundreds of years later.

Sakenfeld has identified three characteristics of *hesed*. First, it is never shown to inanimate objects or ideas. Second, the word never appears where a relationship has not already been established. Third, it refers to a specific action or an attitude conveyed by these specific actions.[12] Within the covenant relationship, God's *hesed* promises "commitment, provision for need, [and] freedom."[13] Sakenfeld finds one more aspect in *hesed* that is vital for a divine/human relationship to exist. Inherent in *hesed* is the cry to a superior power of a helpless person for deliverance from his or her enemies. Nothing is more needed in helpless humans than the deliverance from their sins. In God's self-revelation to Moses in Exodus 34, Sakenfeld notices that the phrase God's "abounding in love" is used only of God and frequently refers to his divine forgiveness. In this way it "moves beyond the normal parameters of *hesed* in human relationships."[14] Furthermore, "forgiveness springs from God's radical commitment to the relationship with Israel (and indeed with all humankind) . . . . [God's forgiveness] fulfills 'need' that is basic to all other need within the divine-human relationship—the very possibility of the continuation of the relationship."[15] Forgiveness comes as a freely offered act and gift from God.

Recall that since the fall of Adam and Eve, all humanity is separated from God because of its sin. God's *hesed* makes the way for that to change. Sakenfeld sees both

12. Sakenfeld, "Love (OT)," 378.
13. Sakenfeld, "Love (OT)," 378.
14. Sakenfeld, "Love (OT)," 379.
15. Sakenfeld, "Love (OT)," 379.

individual and corporate "forgiveness as an act of *ḥesed* that continues the divine-human relationship [and] is foundational to life itself and undergirds all other manifestations of *ḥesed*."[16] Without God's *ḥesed* as found in the covenants God made with Noah, Abraham, Moses, and David and culminating with Jesus Christ and the new covenant God made through his blood, sinful men and women could not be forgiven and reconciled to God and begin their new relationship with him. Therefore, *ḥesed* remains the loving relationship between God and his covenant people. All others are outside this relationship by virtue of their lack of love for God as shown through their unbelief in the One whom he sent. This clearly shows the origin of New Testament theology on forgiveness to have its roots planted firmly in the Old Testament.

Hence, we discover that *ḥesed* is similar to the ἀγάπη love we find in the New Testament. John 3:16–18 tells us that God so loved the world (everyone) that he sent his only Son to redeem them (John 14–16; 1 John). They were already condemned; Jesus came to provide the means for their escape from judgment. This salvation is only applied to those who believe in Jesus, the originator of the new covenant. These are the ones that love him. They will love and do his commandments (as discussed in previous chapters) and believe his truth as found in all of Scripture (not just the parts that agree with what they want to hear). In the Old Testament that covenant was based on law. In the New Testament it is based on the love, grace, and truth of Jesus, the cross, and his resurrection which does not negate the law but fulfills it and assigns it more of a tutorial role.

At the time Jesus walked this earth, there were many religious and philosophical ideas about love. Klassen reports that secular authors wrote "primarily about love as sexual technique." Citing Ovid' *Ars Amatoria* he notes, "True love must not be encumbered by ethical questions." While he attributes part of this to parody, he observes that "the main instructions (addressed to men) concern how to find, win, and keep a female lover [not wife]."[17] Citing the work of Epictetus, Klassen also notices that "it is a general rule that 'every living thing is to nothing so devoted as to its own interest. Whatever, then, appears to it to stand in the way of this interest, be it a brother, or father, or child, or loved one (*eromenos*) or lover (*erastes*), the being hates, accuses, and curses it. For its nature is to love (*phileō*) nothing so much as its own interest; this to it is father and brother and kinsmen and country and God.'"[18] I include this to describe the age in which the New Testament was written which sounds much like the popular thinking today. This personal freedom to which we aspire today indicates that we are not evolving as many would have us believe, but rather, *de-evolving* into a more primitive time before the good news of the gospel was given. Christian love is the evolution.

16. Sakenfeld, "Love (OT)," 380.
17. Klassen, "Love (NT and Early Jewish)," 382.
18. Klassen, "Love (NT and Early Jewish)," 383.

At the time of the writing of the New Testament and the LXX translation of the Old Testament into Greek, the common word for love was *eros*, which was understood as "a universal love, generous, unbound and non-selective."[19] Many in today's churches would identify this as God's love. Like today, in the first century, the application of universal, unbounded, and general meant "a general love of the world seeking satisfaction wherever it can [unbounded] . . . . *Eros* seeks in others the fulfilment of its own life's hunger [universal use of anyone and anything for its own pleasure much like we found in today's culture in chapter 1]."[20] "Passionate" and "impulsive" are frequently used to describe *eros*.

While *eros* seeks its own fulfillment, *agapē* "is a giving, active love on the other's behalf."[21] Biblical writers rejected *eros* because of its popular use and chose *agapē* for God's love "mainly because by reason of its prior history [infrequent and benign use] it is the best adapted to express the thoughts of selection, of willed address and of readiness for action . . . . [additionally] the whole group of words associated with ἀγαπᾶν is given a new meaning by the Greek translation of the OT."[22] First the Jews then the Christians took over *agapē* and redefined it to fit their own need for describing their God.

Therefore *agapē* love is the love of the Old Testament that is "the jealous love which chooses one among thousands, holds him with all the force of passion and will, and will allow no breach of loyalty . . . . It is a love which makes distinctions, which chooses, which prefers and overlooks. It is not a cosmopolitan love embracing missions."[23] This is why so many in churches today, without realizing it, identify more closely with *eros* than the *agapē* love of the Bible and want to make the God of the Old Testament something other than the God of Jesus. *Eros* agrees with our cultural understanding of love, which permeates the internet and social media and relentlessly invades our thinking until it becomes so familiar that Scripture sounds strange to us.

The third Greek word for love is *phileō*, which represents the love of a parent to a child or between a husband and wife. God's love for people is sometimes expressed by this term as well as a person's love of objects or ideas such as: "I love chocolate," or "I loved that movie." In the Bible it is used "to describe the tender affection that God the Father has toward his Son, Jesus Christ" in John 5:20, and it is used to express the love of a person to God in 1 Corinthians 6:22. It is used interchangeably with *agapē* by Jesus with Peter after the resurrection when he asked him three times if he loved him in John 21:15–27.[24]

---

19. Stauffer, "Ἀγάπη," 49–55.
20. Stauffer, "Ἀγάπη," 49–55.
21. Stauffer, "Ἀγάπη," 49–55.
22. Stauffer, "Ἀγάπη," 49–55.
23. Stauffer, "Ἀγάπη," 49–55.
24. Mounce, "Love," 428.

For John, the ultimate expression of God's love is that he sent his Son, Jesus, into the world, the divine being living a truly human life but without sin. God's love felt great physical pain on the cross with the cold harsh reality of nails and wood. God's love suffered spiritually and emotionally when Jesus cried out, "My God, my God, why have you forsaken me?" It was an act of selfless love in which Jesus willingly gave his life on the cross to pay the penalty that sin, yours and mine, exacts from us, which is death, not only physical but spiritual death of eternal separation from God.[25]

Jesus made atonement for our sins, but it can only be applied to those who believe in him. However, not everyone calling himself or herself a Christian accepts that God would condemn people or that a God of love could also hold wrath against sin, but a Holy God could and that is what the Bible tells us from beginning to end. God's love is holy love. Some people have chosen not to believe this about God because it does not fit their idea of love, and they cut out those parts of the Bible that talk about it.

When this happens significant breaches with other apostolic beliefs soon follow. The apostle John who tells us God is love also tells us that *genuine love begins with what we believe about God*. This is the biggest difference between God's love and human love. Genuine love believes that Jesus alone gives eternal life (1 John 1:2), that God sent him as the atoning sacrifice for our sins (2:2; 4:10), that there is no sin in Jesus (3:5), that he came to take away our sins (3:5), and that Jesus is the Son of God who came to destroy the devil's work (3:8). This leads to the condemnation of evil and of those not believing in Jesus (5:10–12), and to other doctrines such as the virgin birth. These are doctrines to which many calling themselves Christians do not subscribe because they do not see them as loving or think they are possible. However, John tells us that first and foremost holy love means Christians will believe in what the apostles taught, which included the Old Testament as interpreted by the New Testament. While individuals may come to believe these less popular biblical doctrines in varying degrees and change their understanding of them with time and maturity, the corporate church must hold unwaveringly to the biblical witness given by the prophets and apostles as the highest form of love.

Furthermore, only Jesus' act of love makes the way for people to be able to love God. When people love Jesus with all their heart, mind, soul, and strength, they will desire to follow his holy commands, for they have been made a new creation. This happens because the promised Holy Spirit is now living within them. He seals each one for God, guaranteeing that they have been redeemed and belong to God. He is the assurance that each one has a place in heaven and an inheritance there. Without him they are incapable of loving God.

Drawing from John, Mounce notes that *agapē*, which is holy love, is one characteristic that sets Christians apart from the world. The disciple is to give up his or her life in order to keep it for eternity. The one who tries to hold onto life in this world

---

25. For more on the doctrine of hell and eternal damnation, see Lewis's fantasy, *The Great Divorce*, and Keller, *Reason for God*, chapter 5, "How Can a Loving God Send People to Hell?"

"will ironically lose that which he loves." Because they have another worldly characteristic, Jesus' followers will be hated by the people infatuated with this world. Mounce concludes, "But the wonderful news is that God the Father himself loves those who love Jesus and believe that he came from God (16:27)."[26] Throughout history, men and women have been rejected by their families, lost their inheritance, and been forbidden to do anything but menial labor because of their faith in Jesus.

Summary

God's love looks vastly different from the concept of love commonly held in our culture and among many who call themselves Christians in this age. "All you need is love" and "love means you never have to say you're sorry" are beliefs made popular by the secular media. The human concept of love (which includes ecology and social justice) when separated from the gospel of Jesus Christ does not measure up to God's standard of love, which includes the wrath of God, his righteousness, justice, judgment, and hell along with his love, grace, peace, and mercy. The problem today is that many in the church believe these doctrines are negotiable, outdated, or obsolete, having been replaced by a supposedly new and better universal love and general acceptance of all people and things. However, we have seen how this is based on human understanding and represents a de-evolution to a pre-gospel age.

We have seen that the phrase "God is love" means he is the source of love and defines what it is. When we contradict Scripture and think, "But a God of love would never allow innocent people to get hurt" or "God would never judge a person or nation" or "God would never choose one person over another," we are adopting the wisdom of the world and not the wisdom of the word. We are saying Love is God; we are defining what that god must be like according to human reason, which asks, "Why can't we all just coexist?" The short answer is: Evil exists, and human nature is opposed to God whenever he disagrees with us even though he is love, grace, and truth. This enables evil to run rampant. I urge you to do as John commands. Test your beliefs about love to see from which spirit they come, to see if they measure up to God's standard.

Finally, anyone who tries to make God's love unconditional in the sense that all people are automatically saved apart from a personal relationship with Jesus is not thinking biblically. We are saved by grace through faith in Jesus Christ. Any doctrine or theology that demands God save all people (except for perhaps the very worst of humanity—although no one is willing to say who those people would be), regardless of what they believe and persist in doing, denies God's love, cheapens grace, and negates the sovereignty and truth of God. We will examine these in chapters 13 and 14. In the next chapter we will look at how love works itself out in the lives of Jesus' disciples.

26. Mounce, "Love," 428.

Chapter 12

Practical Concerns

As we live in God, our love grows more perfect.

—1 John 4:17a, NLT

LOVE REQUIRES OBEDIENCE TO God's holy ways. God's ultimate act of love, the atoning sacrifice of Jesus, was the result of his commitment to obey God's will no matter what the cost. Obedience requires a standard by which it can be measured. That standard is summarized by the Great Commandment, which says to love God with all your heart, mind, soul, and strength first and then to love people as you love yourself. The Jews knew this because it summarized the Ten Commandments. The law shows us what God expects of us and is the standard by which we are to live and by which all are disciplined and judged.

Holy love will never lie to his neighbor or slander her name. Godly love will never steal from her neighbor or covet her husband. Holy love always shows respect for people, for all are made in the image of God. Biblical love also respects the property of others. Holy love functions at a higher standard than the world's love. It is revealed to us through Scripture (the Law, the Prophets, and the apostles) and the Holy Spirit. Holy love draws us to God through Jesus' atoning sacrifice as the only way to salvation. Those who want to do away with these standards must remember that when Jesus was on earth, he actually raised the bar by interpreting the commands to include inward lusts, anger, and pride and not just the outward committing of adultery, murder, and the more obvious violations of the law (Matt 5–7).

Of this intensification of the law by Jesus, William Klassen believes Jesus was "more interested in people and relationships than in principles." If you truly love, you will be concerned for the welfare of other people; you will want the very best for them, which is God's holiness that brings beauty, wholeness, light, hope, life, peace, and joy. As such, Klassen believes "there is no evidence that he [Jesus] sought to do away with Torah when he summarized it in the double love command."[1] The continuation of the law along with the New Testament command to work out your salvation (Phil 2:13 and Heb 10:14) reveal a progressive work towards perfection in Christian love by

---

1. Klassen, "Love (NT and Early Jewish)," 387.

those who have already been perfected by faith in Jesus. Below we will examine some of the ways Christians grow in love.

Only God's People Are Empowered to Love Him

Jesus brought a new love, but not in the way many today expect. He radicalized love by making it possible for people actually to love God. Why is this so radical since many of us already assume that all people are capable of loving God? Initially, love for God is made possible because God's covenantal love brings forgiveness to those who believe in Jesus. This restores their relationship with God. Until the Age of Reason took over in the modern era, there was a general acceptance that without Jesus there is no relationship with God and no love to God (John 14–15; 1 John 5) which is why Ethelbert Stauffer calls it radical—the human race goes from no relationship to being sons and daughters of God through Jesus.[2] However, the "no relationship with God apart from Jesus" is rejected even by many Christians today.

God's holy love is radical in that it requires people to make an either/or choice: either they put their faith in Jesus and follow his ways, or they follow their own ways with maybe a mental assent to Jesus. But both cannot be love to God. Using the Sermon on the Mount in Matthew 6:24ff, Stauffer asserts that to love God is to be his slave: "It is to listen faithfully and obediently to His orders, to place oneself under His lordship, to value above all else the realization of this lordship (cf. Mt 6:33)."[3] Loving God means "to base one's whole being on God, to cling to Him with unreserved confidence, to leave with Him all care or final responsibility, to live by His hand."[4] Loving God means "to hate and despise all that does not serve God nor come from Him, to break with all other ties, to cut away all that hinders (Mt 5:29 f), to snap all bonds except that which binds to God alone."[5] Can American Christians understand this kind of love?

From Jesus' own mouth we discover that love faithfully obeys God's orders and forsakes, even hates, everything not of God. Furthermore, it does away with everything that tries to tether the person to anyone or anything that is not God. This is necessary because ultimately such things destroy God's good creation. How unlike the view of many Christians today who are more inclined to encourage a person to be faithful to himself or herself.

Additionally, Stauffer recognizes three "forces which man must renounce and fight against if he is to love God."[6] They are riches, pride/power, and fear of persecution. From the Sermon on the Mount, Stauffer deduces that "he who would heap up riches

---

2. Stauffer, "Ἀγάπη," 49–55.
3. Stauffer, "Ἀγάπη," 49–55.
4. Stauffer, "Ἀγάπη," 49–55.
5. Stauffer, "Ἀγάπη," 49–55.
6. Stauffer, "Ἀγάπη," 49–55.

is a heathen of little faith who is of no use in the kingdom of God (Mt 6:24b, 30ff)." Of power and pride he writes, "The love of prestige is incompatible with the love of God" as in the description of the Pharisees in Matthew 6.[7] These forces of riches, pride, and power correspond closely to 1 John 2:15-16 (NIV), which says, "Do not love the world or anything in the world. If anyone loves the world, the love of the Father is not in him. For everything in the world—the cravings of sinful man [lust of the flesh], the lust of his eyes and the boasting of what he has and does—comes not from the Father but from the world." But, few sermons are preached on this passage today.

The solution to the third force that keeps a person from loving God can also be found in the Beatitudes (Matt 5:10-12) where Jesus warns his disciples that there will be persecution for following his righteousness. Jesus acknowledges the fear it brings by telling the disciples they are blessed and share the same position as God's prophets of old. Jesus tells them to rejoice! It is human nature not to want to suffer "the assaults and afflictions, the insults and sufferings, which will necessarily break over the heads of His disciples." To Stauffer, persecution will be "a decisive fiery test of their loyalty to God . . . . the character of [their] love for God [will be] clear and conclusive. It is a glowing passion for God, the passion of a little flock which perseveres faithfully and unshakeably, in spite of every puzzle, power or threat, until He is manifested whom it loves."[8] Love will not result in unity and peace where the Spirit of God is not prominent. Do not be surprised by this but rejoice when you are persecuted for righteousness' sake. In all of this, be sure it is Jesus and not your pride, arrogance, critical spirit, or judgmental attitude that is offending people.

Love in God's Community and Love of Neighbor

Stauffer does not see rugged, "gut it out on your own" independence in Jesus' words on persecution; quite the contrary. He sees people of like mind coming together, loving God, loving one another, and encouraging one another to stay faithful to Jesus, and to remain firm and unshakeable in their faith. For John, love begins with the family of God. Klassen points out that in 1 John "there is not one reference to loving the neighbor," but he does see the love of the Christian community for each other as critical to being recognized as Jesus' disciples.[9] The love of the Christian community is essential for two reasons. First, their love brings unity that will witness to the world about the difference Jesus makes. Second, the love of the community is necessary for Christians to withstand persecution. However, when the church looks and sounds like the culture, there will be division and a weakened witness for Jesus. Consequently, there will be little persecution, and therefore, little need for Christians to gather to encourage one another in their faith.

7. Stauffer, "Ἀγάπη," 49–55.
8. Stauffer, "Ἀγάπη," 45–55.
9. Klassen, "Love (NT and Early Jewish)," 390.

Interestingly, for all the emphasis put on it today, Klassen observes that "one of the striking features of the Synoptic Gospels is that they say nothing explicitly about God's love. Jesus himself never speaks about it, except to point out concretely in parables how gracious and accepting God is, especially of people who fail or who are marginalized in other ways."[10] This is because people who have failed or have been marginalized by society are often open to a better way. This is not a mandate to the church that all who have failed or are marginalized will have hearts open to God. In our culture, often these very people have been taught they are entitled to more and have hearts just as hard as those who have all of the world's goods. In all of this, Jesus does command his disciples to love their neighbor and their enemy.

Indeed, love begins in the family of God. That family is now comprised of all who believe in Jesus as the Son of God and all that it means as we have been discovering. Furthermore, the love that God gave to them is also to be shown to their neighbor. In the parable of the good Samaritan, Jesus expands the definition of neighbor from a confined familial or national relationship to encompass anyone in near proximity in whom he or she perceives a need. However, Stauffer cautions that helping the neighbor in need as in the good Samaritan should not become "a system which applies schematically to all men and places. It consists only in absolute concreteness. It is built up from case to case around a man in need."[11]

God's universal love for all people is not I-centered but you-centered and is *always specifically identified*. Jesus ministered to individual people such as *a particular* tax collector, *a particular* prostitute, *a particular* woman being divorced without just cause, or *a particular* person in financial or physical need. As such he could enter into a relationship with individuals whose hearts were open to God's salvation or leave them until such time as they had a change of heart like he did in his hometown of Nazareth because of their unbelief. Congregations would be advised to do the same.

This does not preclude Christians working together to meet larger needs or to help in emergencies. Certainly, Christians should be at the forefront of giving care in the event of personal and national disasters such as hurricanes, earthquakes, forest fires, and the like. I have heard of Christian organizations that gave aid in Indonesia when that government would not allow them to mention Jesus or to have any indication on their supplies that they were Christian. Afterwards, despite that restriction, the people in the towns that had been helped asked the Christian workers to tell them about Jesus. Here, food pantries help millions of people. It is compassionate to help them. However, Christians must live in the tension and consider the long-term help of such organizations with an eye to the mission of fulfilling the Great Commission. Organizations that feed the body and neglect the soul are failing the people they serve if they do not offer salvation in Jesus along with the physical help.

---

10. Klassen, "Love (NT and Early Jewish)," 385.
11. Stauffer, "Ἀγάπη," 49–55.

Consider John 6 where we read that Jesus had performed many miracles and the crowd followed him and the disciples up a mountain. There he performed another miracle and fed a great multitude. That evening the disciples took boats and left for the other side of the Sea of Galilee. Jesus followed later by walking on the water to help the disciples who were in danger because of a sudden storm. The next day, the people followed Jesus on foot around the sea. When they found him, they asked when (not how) he had gotten there. His answer was (John 6:26–27, NIV), "I tell you the truth, you are looking for me, not because you saw miraculous signs but because you ate the loaves and had your fill. Do not work for food that spoils, but for food that endures to eternal life, which the Son of Man will give you. On him God the Father has placed his seal of approval." The crowd immediately wanted to know what these works are that God requires. Jesus' answer was, "The work of God is this: to believe in the one he has sent."

They responded by asking for still another miraculous sign that Jesus is this one. They brought up how their forefathers ate manna in the desert. Jesus reminded them that it was God who gave them the manna to sustain life and now God has sent "he who comes down from heaven and gives life to the world" (v. 33, NIV). They asked him to give them this bread. Jesus answered, "I am the bread of life. He who comes to me will never go hungry, and he who believes in me will never be thirsty. But as I told you, you have seen me and still you do not believe . . . . For my Father's will is that everyone who looks to the Son and believes in him shall have eternal life, and I will raise him up at the last day" (vv. 35–36, 40, NIV).

The next several verses record an extensive dialogue between the people and Jesus. Basically, Jesus is telling them he is the bread of life, anyone who believes in him will have eternal life, and he, alone, has seen God the Father. He informs them that his flesh is this bread that they must eat to have eternal life. Furthermore, they must also drink his blood. This is the way for eternal life. The people are offended and leave—all but the disciples. Jesus was concerned for the people's eternal wellbeing above their physical welfare. Christians must be careful about compromising the gospel in order to do good works, all the while thinking they are showing God's love. Test the spirits. If folks cannot tolerate a simple, straightforward message, prayer, or blessing, then perhaps their need is not so great after all.[12]

Another time Jesus left the crowds behind, thereby ignoring their physical needs, was at Peter's mother-in-law's house (Matt 8:14; Mark 1:30; Luke 4:38). She had been sick with a fever, and Jesus healed her. All that evening, the townspeople brought their sick to him, and he healed them also. The next morning while it was still dark, Jesus spent a lot of time in solitary prayer. By the time others were up and about, people

---

12. Do not take this as an excuse not to feed the poor or to help neighbors unless you can verbally give the gospel. You can always pray for the folks you are serving. Long term, you might consider putting your time and money into Christian-based programs and organizations that do both. In the secular world of government and politics we should always promote and support those things that provide dignity and respect for all people.

from the surrounding areas had gathered at Peter's mother-in-law's house to be healed by Jesus. The disciples went to look for him, and when they found him, they tried to get him back to her house because everyone was waiting for him. Surprisingly, Jesus said no; he took off for other parts to proclaim the good news of the kingdom of God. The primary goal was not to heal physically all who came but to give as many as possible the message of salvation in Jesus so that they would have eternal healing and life in him. The key to when to move on and when to stay is in having a deep and abiding prayer life (more about this in chapters 15 and 16). After much prayer, he knew what God his Father wanted him to do, and he did it.

I see three guidelines for the church in these two stories. First, she should not be overly worried about offending someone with the good news of the gospel (unless the offense is because of her being abusive and condemning). To give the gospel in a gentle and respectful manner is the most loving thing she can do for people. Second, she cannot meet every need of all the people all of the time. There are such things as enabling people to continue in sin and lack of responsibility for themselves. Third, and this is what directs the first two, she must pray without ceasing while abiding in Jesus. Then she will know God's mind, which will probably be different from human wisdom.

I want to offer more insight on the first and second guidelines above. Stauffer observes that neighborly love "does not imply emotional extravagance," but that "what is demanded is the most unsentimental imaginable readiness to help. The Samaritan does in all sobriety what the moment demands, taking care for the immediate future, no more and no less. He . . . neither throws everything aside nor wastes words on the duties or guilt of others. He . . . does what has to be done, and what he can do."[13] The emotional guilt trip to feel everyone's pain and to have deep emotional ties to every problem (promoted in many churches and by our culture) is unbiblical. Guilt is not to be confused with God's conviction given to the person who refuses to do what God is calling him or her to do. Conviction leads to godly sorrow, repentance, and restoration with God. Guilt constantly accuses you and continually makes you feel bad about yourself. Heed John's advice to test the spirits to see of what sort they are concerning loving your neighbor.

Holy Love and Discipline

Because of our aversion to law, one area in which we struggle with God's love is discipline. While the church may talk about parents disciplining their children, she rarely applies that admonition to her own children, those within her sphere of influence. Picking up on Proverbs 3:11–12 (NIV), "My son, do not despise the LORD's discipline and do not resent his rebuke," the writer of Hebrews 12 affirms that God disciplines those whom he loves, his children, those whose faith is placed in Jesus

---

13. Stauffer, "Ἀγάπη," 49–55.

and who abide in him. He takes it one step further and states that failure to discipline means that the child would not be God's.

Here we see that the lack of discipline is tantamount to giving up on your child and to removing your love from him or her. How contrary this is to today's interpretation of love as being a buddy who only encourages people to be true to themselves. What has largely been forgotten is that the purpose of discipline is to bring the person into a right relationship (reconciled) with God so he or she can be a whole person living in beauty, who will be brought into the dance and share in the feast.[14]

People in God's covenant of grace receive his discipline because he loves them, and the purpose of discipline is to make them holy. The saddest words in Scripture (after "be gone, I never knew you") are "and God gave them over" to their own wants and desires (he no longer strives with or disciplines them). It always leads to the person or culture spiraling down into sin and destruction. Tim Keller observes that "when we build our lives on anything but God, that thing—though a good thing—becomes an enslaving addiction, something we *have* to have to be happy. Personal disintegration happens on a broader scale."[15] This disintegration works itself out like a drug addiction. "As time goes on you need more and more of the addictive substance to get an equal kick, which leads to less and less satisfaction. Second, there is the isolation, as increasingly you blame others and circumstances in order to justify your behavior."[16] Unfortunately, this is what drives our consumeristic, materialistic culture. The solution is to recover this holy love that dares to face the difficult things in life and to pursue discipline and repentance that leads people to God and holy living, beauty, and wholeness.

Later in Hebrews 12 Paul summarizes the discussion of discipline leading to holiness without which no one will see God and writes (28–29, NIV), "Therefore, since we are receiving a kingdom that cannot be shaken, let us be thankful, and so worship God acceptably with reverence and awe, for our 'God is a consuming fire.'" God's kingdom cannot be shaken because he is immutable; his holiness endures, and anything not of him will perish as in a fire.

Peter helps us to understand this aspect of God as a consuming fire as a symbol of purification. First Peter 1:6–7 tells us that although we suffer all sorts of afflictions on this earth, the purpose is to refine or to purify our faith, similar to the process of refining gold.[17] It produces a Christian who is like porcelain as opposed to ceramics (see

---

14. This is not saying that every bad thing that happens is discipline (and certainly not punishment). Bad things do happen to good people. There are such things as natural disasters. Discipline is often given in the form of conviction rather than bad things happening to people unless it is the direct consequence of something they have done. The purpose of all suffering is to purify one's faith and to draw the person closer to God.

15. Keller, *Reason for God*, 81.

16. Keller, *Reason for God*, 80–81.

17. Not all suffering is the result of sin and the subsequent need for discipline. Sometimes God is simply refining a person's faith for greater service in his kingdom.

appendix 4 for details). Porcelain and ceramics are made from the same materials, but porcelain is fired hundreds of degrees higher than ceramics. Porcelain is more durable; ceramics are more porous and break more easily. When God turns up the heat, it is not to punish a person or because he enjoys making him or her suffer. He is fashioning strength and durability in the person. He is forging a holy man or woman, for the purpose of purifying his or her faith so that he or she can live like Jesus (1 John 2:6).

Even in the Old Testament, the God who sends suffering does so only for the purpose of restoring and reconciling people with himself as is witnessed in the Joel 2:12–14 passage (NIV), "'Even now,' declares the LORD, 'return to me with all your heart, with fasting and weeping and mourning. Rend your heart and not your garments.' Return to the LORD your God, for he is gracious and compassionate, slow to anger and abounding in love, and he relents from sending calamity. Who knows? He may turn and have pity and leave behind a blessing." In the difficult Hosea 5 reference above, the purpose of God tearing the Israelites to pieces and carrying them off was to bring them to the end of themselves so that they would stop relying on themselves and the wisdom and power of the world and seek God.

When suffering surrounds people, when they feel bent and broken in gale force winds, know that God is showing his love for them. He is prying loose the grip they have on the world and driving them to seek him so that they may grow in their faith and be like Jesus. Know also that he only does this after kinder and gentler ways have failed to get them on the right path. The goal of discipline is to produce holiness in a person so that he or she may be given the rewards of beauty and wholeness, which are great in this life but are without equal in the next. This is not usually preached in twenty-first-century America in favor of a gospel where God only wants people be healthy, happy, and well-off.

Love Divides and Unifies

This brings us to two more common misconceptions about love. Secular love is not the unifying force promoted by the culture; neither is biblical love the destructive force often portrayed by the culture. Christianity is selective and creates real differences between people. What we often fail to discern is how divisive secular love is. In the secular understanding of love that elevates personal truth over God's truth, there will always come a time when compromise is no longer an option apart from surrender to bullies. When my wants deny your wants, eruption is bound to follow.

Additionally, the world hates God and his people (John 7:7; 15:18–20; 17:14). There is no live-and-let-live here. Often when Christians try to live faithfully according to Scripture in love, the world reacts negatively and sometimes violently. This is how Jesus describes it (Matt 10:34–39, NIV; also Luke 10:51–53),

> Do not suppose that I have come to bring peace to the earth. I did not come to bring peace, but a sword. For I have come to turn 'a man against his father, a daughter against her mother, a daughter-in-law against her mother-in-law—a man's enemies will be the members of his own household. Anyone who loves his father or mother more than me is not worthy of me; anyone who loves his son or daughter more than me is not worthy of me; and anyone who does not take his cross and follow me is not worthy of me. Whoever finds his life will lose it, and whoever loses his life for my sake will find it.

The culture's concept of love is not as benign as the media would have us believe. The news testifies to this.

Neither is Christian love the destructive and divisive force that some claim it to be. Indeed, the wars that have been fought in the name of religion would seem to declare them correct. The truth is that without God's love all would be lost, and human self-interest under the guise of love would quickly destroy everything good. What matters is the degree to which people follow God's holy ways. God has a standard by which all can live in peace and harmony.

However, culture rejects biblical love with its exclusive claims of God on his people and grants freedom to do whatever a person wants while guaranteeing a universal love, forgiveness, and salvation for all people. Many Christians have followed this path, but we have seen that this is not holy. This is more closely associated with *eros*. It seems right to our human way of thinking because we hear it promoted nonstop by the media, but it will always end in destruction. It remains that "God so loved the world that He gave his only begotten Son, that *whosoever believes in him* shall have eternal life" (John 3:16, italics are mine). Jesus is the way, the truth, and the life. No one can reach God except through him. It is precisely because of this unique call that Christianity places on people that God has made the way for a hostile world to be saved from their willful self-destruction.

God's ways bring unity because they bring respect for people and their possessions and drive them to put others' needs on par with their own instead of putting self first. Few in this culture receive it. The church must realize that rather than being the force that divides this nation, Christian love, holy love, is the only hope for real and lasting peace in a world of individuals vying for their own way. Holy love is the only unifying force that can bring lost people to live together now in the beauty and wholeness for which they were created.

Holy love is the only thing that can fill the void in every person. Klassen makes a key observation, "Love as Jesus defines it aims first of all at unconditionally overcoming lostness; it does not begin with nobility, but with human misery . . . . Moreover, *love is a consequence of the rule of God*; it arises *out of the experience of salvation*" (italics are mine).[18] Notice that genuine love is not inherent in people because they are naturally good. It occurs only as a result of the experience of salvation and is the

---

18. Klassen, "Love (NT and Early Jewish)," 386.

consequence of God's subsequent rule in that person's life. Lack of holy love makes living peacefully with others difficult and creates enemies.

Love Your Enemy

Returning to the Sermon on the Mount, Jesus also commands his followers to love their enemies. In Matthew 5, Jesus overturns popular folk wisdom that directs people to love their neighbor but hate their enemy. Instead of talking about compassion and gentleness as we might expect, Klassen sees Matthew reminding his readers of "God's impartiality. The sun rises on good and bad alike, the rain is sent on the just and the unjust alike . . . . Both Luke and Matthew ask: 'If you love only those who love you, what credit is that?' (Matt 5:46; Luke 6:32)."[19]

To answer this question, Klassen connects Jesus' command to love your enemies with Paul's revelation in Romans 5:8–10 that while we were still sinners and enemies of God, he sent his Son, Jesus, to die in our place so that all who believe in him would be redeemed. Klassen writes, "The command to love the enemies is grounded ultimately in the patience and forgiveness of God and his compassion." The command to love one's enemy presupposes "the goodness of God promised in this message [of forgiveness and] on the human side presupposes a universal inclusion under the judgement of God [not under the universal love of God as many suppose today] . . . . If all are universally under judgment, then it is not their innate goodness which calls forth divine or human love."[20] Christians are to love those who have nothing worthy of love even as God has done for them. This also shows grace, which we will examine in the next chapter.

Love Your Enemy and Nonviolence

Today many find in Matthew 5 several verses that seem to imply that people, and especially Christians, should be pacifists. These folks cite "do not resist an evil person" (Matt 5:39) and combine it with "love your neighbor" (v. 42), "love your enemy" (v. 43), and "do not judge" (v. 7:1) to support their view of total nonviolence.[21] We live in an increasingly dangerous world, and it is essential that we understand what Jesus is saying and not read into it things that are not there. Our interpretation of passages like these has far reaching ramifications for the safety and welfare of our homes, schools, and nation. What does Jesus mean when he says, "Do not resist an evil person?"

At first glance, nonretaliation seems straight forward and obvious. What else could he possibly be saying other than his disciples must be pacifists? Keller and Volf

19. Klassen, "Love (NT and Early Jewish)," 386.
20. Klassen, "Love (NT and Early Jewish)," 386.
21. Some examples of this thinking can be found in Yoder, *The Politics of Jesus*, and works by Sider, *The Scandal of Evangelical Politics, Nuclear Holocaust and Christian Hope*, and *Nonviolent Action*.

agree but with a caveat. They insist that in order for God's people to take the path of nonresistance against evil, that a loving God must also to be a God of vengeance who *will* judge evil and do away with it. In witnessing the atrocities of communism firsthand, Volf sees our Western view of a God of passive love that never judges anyone or anything as the logical outgrowth of a safe and protected suburban outlook that has never had to deal with the rape of wives and daughters nor had their homes pillaged and burned while they watched. He writes,

> My thesis that the practice of nonviolence requires a belief in divine vengeance will be unpopular with many Christians, especially theologians in the West. To the person who is inclined to dismiss it, I suggest imagining that you are delivering a lecture in a war zone (which is where a paper that underlies this chapter was originally delivered).... Soon you would discover that it takes the quiet of a suburban home for the birth of the thesis that human nonviolence corresponds to God's refusal to judge. In a scorched land, soaked in the blood of the innocent, it will invariably die. And as one watches it die, one will do well to reflect about many other pleasant captivities of the liberal mind.[22]

Volf asserts that the belief in a God who loves but does not judge can only be found in an environment where evil has mostly been kept in check by God's love through its citizens following God's ways. Although far from perfect, especially in the area of racism, this was the general state of mid-twentieth-century America. This is what had impressed de Tocqueville a century earlier. Prior to the 1960s few Americans even considered locking their doors, so great was their sense of security. Contrary to the popular idea of a God of love that will never judge or condemn evil and those who promote it, Volf believes it is only the knowledge that God will one day judge evildoers and set things right that enables Christians not to seek vengeance and retaliation.

Keller agrees and writes, "If I don't believe that there is a God who will eventually put all things right, I will take up the sword and will be sucked into the endless vortex of retaliation. Only if I am sure that there's a God who will right all wrongs and settle all accounts perfectly do I have the power to refrain."[23] Furthermore, Volf acknowledges that "it may be that consistent nonretaliation and nonviolence will be impossible in the world of violence. Tyrants may need to be taken down from their thrones and the madmen stopped from sowing desolation" like Bonhoeffer's participation in the plot to kill Hitler, but Volf believes there is no support for it in Scripture.[24] I disagree. God's charge to the rulers, the shepherds of nations and families, gives them the responsibility (and therefore the right) to protect the people in their charge. If we look more closely at the Sermon on the Mount, we find that Jesus did not forbid resisting evil when gentler and reasoned attempts have failed to stop violence.

---

22. Volf, *Exclusion and Embrace*, 304.
23. Keller, *Reason for God*, 77.
24. Volf, *Exclusion and Embrace*, 306.

Many like Volf and Keller interpret Matthew 5 as a mandate for universal nonresistance, but on careful examination, we notice essential and substantial things in this passage that would indicate something different. Jesus opens with a reference to the law, "an eye for and eye and a tooth for a tooth" (v. 38) and then says, "Do not resist an evil person." He goes on to give examples. Charles Quarles has identified two major qualifications that must be placed on this passage that give it a different meaning from total pacifism as the way to express love. He writes, "First, Jesus' command prohibits acts of retaliation and revenge inspired by anger and resentment, [he does] not [prohibit] defensive or evasive action necessary to protect oneself or others from serious harm." He reminds us that Jesus defended himself verbally when he was slapped by the priests at his trial and withdrew from areas of hostility "in order to avoid being a victim of violence."[25] He actually took the offensive when he overturned the tables of the money changers in the temple area because they had used a place for prayer to steal from the poor. Jesus repeatedly confronted evil but never by using evil means, and never by vengeful violence.

Quarles identifies a second important qualification that is being ignored today, "The blow Jesus commanded His disciples to endure graciously was painful and insulting but not likely to cause permanent danger or be life-threatening."[26] He points out that Jesus did not say, "If someone gouges out your right eye, turn and offer him your left eye." He did not say, "If someone knocks out your right tooth, turn and offer to let him knock out another on the left, or if someone pierces your right side with a sword . . . or if someone pummels your nose with their fist."[27] None of the examples Jesus uses are life-threatening. They may be inconvenient, humiliating, and even painful but nothing that would do permanent harm or place someone in danger. Quarles sees this shift from dangerous and harmful actions such as an eye for an eye or tooth for a tooth to a mere slap or going an extra mile as "intentional and significant." Jesus is still allowing a person to "do what is necessary to defend himself in the case of a life-threatening or potentially dangerous attack."[28] This would be consistent with meekness, also found in the Sermon on the Mount, of great strength and power under equally strong self-control to be used sparingly and wisely. I acknowledge that there may be times when God is calling an individual or a group to make the ultimate sacrifice for their faith, but to love your enemy with total nonresistance to evil must be determined on a case-by-case basis and not be made an absolute and universal mandate. There may come times when nonviolence fails, and stronger actions are required to overcome evil. However, revenge and retaliation are inconsistent with love and are *never* to be a person's motives for resisting evil. What have we learned about holy love?

---

25. Quarles, *Sermon on the Mount*, 150.
26. Quarles, *Sermon on the Mount*, 151.
27. Quarles, *Sermon on the Mount*, 151.
28. Quarles, *Sermon on the Mount*, 151.

Summary

The biblical, unconditional love of God that we talk about today must be to accept into his kingdom everyone and anyone regardless of who they are or what they have done *on the condition* that they love his Son, Jesus, accept his death as the payment for the debt their sins owe, and follow his ways. This is for their sake. It is the loving thing to do. God's unconditional love can only be expressed in salvation through Jesus Christ. It makes distinctions that chooses one and overlooks others. This is why we find words like "chosen," "predestined," and "elect" in the New Testament.

Correspondingly, God's love separates his disciples from the world. In fact, the more Christians demonstrate the love of God in all its aspects (not simply by doing good works that anyone can do but by speaking the truth in love and proclaiming the gospel of peace), the world will hate them because they are no longer of this world. Love must begin in the household of faith, the church, so that Christians may encourage one another in the faith, support each other through persecution, and be God's witness to the world. In his high priestly prayer in John 17, Jesus prays that his disciples would be one in order that the world would see God's love for Jesus in them and learn that God had sent him. However, this is not usually the case; Klassen comments, "This interdigitation of the mission of the church and oneness is a very striking phenomenon; it is as if the world is kept from discovering the love of God by the brokenness of the church."[29] In observing the fighting among Christians, the world stays away thinking they have enough of this in the world. Why should they lose sleep on Sunday just to experience more of it? However, holy love calls Christians not only to love each other but to love their enemies and to pray for them. They must not seek revenge or retaliation but leave such things to God.

Finally, we have discovered that biblical love is based on a covenant relationship. Stauffer makes an amazing observation: love is a covenant relationship that "is an act of decision, like the basic act of love itself. In it there is fulfilled the covenant which God has concluded with His elect and which defies all the powers of heaven and earth . . . ἀγάπη [is] the measure and goal of freedom."[30] Far from being an emotion or feeling, love is a decision that involves a covenant of God with the elect, who become the new creation that is set free, liberated from sin, and given the ability to love God and others as God loves them.

The law is overcome because it is fulfilled—perfectly by Jesus and increasingly by the saints, the holy ones. Those who are newly created (born again, to use Jesus' words) reject the ways of the world to follow God's ways as laid out in Scripture. They fully realize they are not saved by works, and yet, they will want to work out their salvation (sanctification) with God, who is at work in them (because of justification) to will and to do his good pleasure and not their own (Phil 2:12–13). Additionally, one-by-one,

---

29. Klassen, "Love (NT and Early Jewish)," 389.
30. Stauffer, "Ἀγάπη," 49–55.

the objections they may have had against Scripture disappear, and it all begins to make sense. Oddly enough, they will find that surrendering their plans, wants, and personal freedom to follow God's holy ways brings the greatest pleasure and wholeness anyone can know in this world. This is biblical love. Next we will examine God's grace.

Chapter 13

Holy Grace

> Cheap grace is the preaching of forgiveness without requiring repentance, baptism without church discipline, Communion without confession, absolution without personal confession. Cheap grace is grace without discipleship, grace without the cross, grace without Jesus Christ.
>
> —Dietrich Bonhoeffer, *The Cost of Discipleship*

IN ADDITION TO HOLINESS, wholeness, and love, grace and truth are two more doctrines in the church which have been distorted by our culture. The essence of these doctrines comes directly from Jesus. John writes (1:14 and 17, NIV), "The Word became flesh and made his dwelling among us. We have seen his glory, the glory of the One and Only, who came from the Father, full of grace and truth . . . . For the law was given through Moses; grace and truth came through Jesus Christ." At first glance, these two characteristics might seem to be at odds with each other, like righteousness and love. In our culture, holding someone to the truth is not generally perceived as gracious. The truth is that God judges sin. The truth is that murder, slander, stealing, and adultery, to name only a few, are sin. However, telling someone he or she is a sinner who needs to repent does not feel very gracious. In this chapter we will examine the doctrine of grace, and in the next chapter we will examine the scriptural idea of truth in order to distinguish the biblical meanings from the current cultural use that has resulted from the paradigm shifts of Modernity, Postmodernity, and Technopoly so prominent in America today.

What Is Biblical Grace?

As with God's revelation of himself, beauty, wholeness, and love, there is a general sense and a specific sense inherent in God's grace. In the general sense, God loves everyone and shows grace to all people because he shows kindness and gentleness to all people and sustains all life. However, specific grace refers to his favor, his saving grace, and is bestowed only on those whose faith is found in Jesus, who is full of grace and truth. Spiros Zodhiates points out that we frequently confuse God's grace with his graciousness. He sees God's specific grace as "unmerited favor... which He sovereignly and efficaciously confers upon sinful men the blessings of salvation."[1] However he indicates that there is a more broad or general grace given to all life when he writes, "This [saving grace] is to be distinguished from His general goodness (*chrēstós* [5543], gentle, gracious), by which He shows favor even to the unthankful and wicked (Luke 6:35) in conferring on them common blessings such as the sun (Matt. 5:45)."[2] Our culture and many in our churches have taken God's general graciousness of his common goodness as saving grace discussed in detail throughout Scripture. They presume kindness and gentleness to equate to salvific grace. Therefore, we will look at a more detailed description of grace.

In the Old Testament, חֵן (pronounced *ḥēn*) is the word for grace. Edwin Yamauchi describes the action of giving grace as "a heartfelt response by someone who has something to give to one who has a need."[3] John Kselman elaborates on this and writes that "grace is characteristically a favor for a specific occasion given to an inferior by a superior, a person in authority."[4] Moreover, he sees grace as not simply a "positive disposition of someone toward another.... It is an undeserved gift or favor which can be requested, which is freely and unilaterally given and not coerced, and which can be withheld."[5] That it can and may be withheld is vital to the biblical understanding of grace. The means to "this uncoerced and unilateral favor is more than a disposition of passive benevolence on the part of God. It is action that is requested, God's action in aiding the poor, delivering the oppressed and the mortally ill ... and forgiv[ing] sin (Ps 41:5; 51:3; 103:8–10) *after repentance* (Isa 30:19; Joel 2:13)" (italics are mine).[6] Grace can be requested, but it cannot be demanded or coerced. Neither can it be presumed to be given automatically. Automatic grace is not grace because the giver no longer has the option to withhold it. When it is given it is the free and happy choice of the giver, the one with more authority, to bestow upon the needy person.

Grace can be profane (common or secular) when one person shows kindness and gentleness to another. Christians are to give this kind of grace to all people, for they are made in the image of God. However, when we consider God's divine or holy grace, we quickly find references to salvation and forgiveness of sins for repentance by the person in need. Unlike our popular use of grace, which accepts everything as the same, truth-wise, holy grace makes distinctions. In the Old Testament, the word "gracious" is almost always used of God in connection with his righteousness and judgment. Yamauchi observes that "grace is revealed together with his righteousness

---

1. Zodhiates, "χάρις," 1470.
2. Zhodiates, "χάρις," 1470.
3. Yamauchi, "חָנַן," 302.
4. Kselman, "Grace (OT)," 1085.
5. Kselman, "Grace (OT)," 1085.
6. Kselman, "Grace (OT)," 1085.

... [and] most of the passages ... speak ... of his judging evil, e.g. Joel 2:13."[7] Considering the one exception, Yamauchi writes, "In Psalm 112:4, the RSV supplies 'the Lord' as the one who is gracious, but the description is probably of the righteous man who shares the characteristics of his God."[8] He also observes that "in the final analysis the Lord is sovereign in acting graciously to those whom he selects (Ex 33:19)."[9]

This Old Testament word for grace is often translated with the word for mercy in the Greek. In fact, love, grace, and mercy are so closely related that they have been used interchangeably at times. We find this in God's proclamation of himself to Moses in Exodus 34:6, which we examined in chapters 11 and 12. In fact, it is here that Yamauchi finds "perhaps the most striking use of this word."[10] Interestingly, in this passage we also find *ḥesed*, the Hebrew word for steadfast love.

As Old Testament thinking progressed, *ḥen* and *ḥesed* became more interrelated. The meaning of God's steadfast love (*ḥesed*), his grace (*ḥen*), and χάρις (*charis*), the word for grace used in the Septuagint (LXX), the Greek translation of the Old Testament, became bonded together. As such, grace took on the qualities of *ḥesed*. Therefore, grace is to be understood as taking place in the covenant relationship of God and his people, or as Walther Zimmerli puts it, grace is "conduct in relation and in demonstration of this relation . . . . It presupposes an ongoing fellowship."[11] Not only is there an ongoing relationship, but this relationship is grounded in righteousness and the righteous judgment of evil and sin that Jesus and the apostles readily adopted. That is why receiving it is such a great deal. The slate is wiped clean and the person is enabled to live righteously in accordance with God's ways.

Moving to the New Testament, we find the same Greek word for grace, *charis*, as was used in the Old Testament LXX. William Mounce describes grace as "favor—the acceptance of and goodness toward those who cannot earn or do not deserve such gain." Furthermore, to "'find favor in the presence of God' (Lk. 1:30) means that God has an attitude of kindness toward someone, wishing to prosper them. Being 'highly favored' highlights God's decision to bless and use that person for his good purpose (of Mary, Lk. 1:28; even of Jesus 2:52; cf. also Stephen, Acts 6:8)."[12] While this is helpful, we must dig deeper in order to arrive at a more complete description.

Gerhard Kittel observes that the noun "grace" does not appear in Matthew, Mark, 1 John, or 3 John. In Luke he finds that *charis* was commonly used in the church to "characterize the message of salvation."[13] When we read the epistles, we find that grace is specifically connected with Jesus, his death on the cross, and the salvation that

---

7. Yamauchi, "חָנַן," 304.
8. Yamauchi, "חָנַן," 304.
9. Yamauchi, "חָנַן," 302.
10. Yamauchi, "חָנַן," 304.
11. Zimmerli, "χάρις," Old Testament," 381–82.
12. Mounce, "Grace," 303–4.
13. Kittel, "χάρις," 392.

comes through belief in him. Kittel observes that Paul "does not speak of the gracious God; he speaks of the grace that is actualized in the cross of Christ (Gal 2:21, cf. vv. 15–20) and that is an actual event in proclamation. If God's favour is identical with the crucifixion, then its absoluteness is established. We are saved by grace alone."[14] In the New Testament, grace is synonymous with the cross of Jesus, which led to the Reformation proclamation: Salvation is by grace alone through faith alone in Jesus Christ alone. This is biblical grace, but it is also one of the most misinterpreted doctrines both in biblical times and today.

Already in Paul's day, people used grace as an excuse to continue to sin. In Romans 6, Paul was compelled to write (vv. 1–2, NIV), "What shall we say, then? Shall we go on sinning so that grace may increase? By no means! We died to sin; how can we live in it any longer?" Thomas Schreiner understands this to mean that "sin is a power . . . . [and] sin's reign over people leads them to commit specific acts of sin . . . . such acts of sin reveal that one is still enslaved to the power of sin (cf. 6:16–23)."[15] Paul makes it clear that grace does not mean people can go on choosing to sin because that makes the person a slave to sin and evil instead of a slave to God, whom they should now be serving if they belong to him.[16] Christians are to always be in the process of becoming like Christ, and he never sinned.

Paul asks a second time and gives an emphatic "no!" (v. 15, NIV), "What then? Shall we sin because we are not under law but under grace? By no means!" Schreiner interprets "not under law" to mean not that believers "are free from the moral commands contained in the Torah. It means that they are free from the power of sin . . . . to say that believers are under grace means that they now have the power to keep the moral norms of the law (cf. 8:4; 13:8–10)."[17] He connects tangible actions to this power of sin. He comments that "those who live under grace show that they are under grace because they have a new master (God) and are liberated from their old master (sin). Paul refuses to accept any abstract understanding of grace separated from concrete daily living. Grace does not merely involve the forgiveness of sin. It also involves power in which the mastery and dominion of sin are broken."[18] Christians obey God from the heart as prophesized in the Old Testament (Jer 31:31–34; Ezek 11:19–20; 36:26–27) because God places his Holy Spirit in the hearts of all people who accept Jesus as their Lord and Savior. Their justification and sanctification are by God's grace through faith in Christ alone.

Paul continues by contrasting life under the law and life under grace (Rom 6:16, NIV), "Don't you know that when you offer yourselves to someone to obey him as slaves, you are slaves to the one whom you obey—whether you are slaves to

---

14. Kittel, "χάρις," 394.
15. Schreiner, *Romans*, 304.
16. John makes this same argument in 1 John 1–3.
17. Schreiner, *Romans*, 330.
18. Schreiner, *Romans*, 332–33.

sin, which leads to death, or to obedience, which leads to righteousness?" Just as the power of sin is advanced through specific actions, so, too, the "slavery to righteousness must be ratified by the decision to be God's slave in the particulars of life."[19] Schreiner reminds us that people do not submit to sinning against their will and writes, "Unbelievers are slaves to sin in that they always desire to carry out the dictates of their master. This does not mean that those with addictions (e.g., to alcohol, pornography, or gambling) never wish to be freed. It means that the desire for these things is ultimately greater than the desire to be freed from them. Sinning is what they want to do."[20] He understands from the biblical witness that the only solution to this is for God to "release them from such subjection, for new desires are necessary to escape the bondage of sin. Of course, this is precisely what God has done . . . . He has planted new desires within them."[21]

From this we understand that choosing to sin is never good and is without excuse. In this, Schreiner has exposed the sinister foundation of our culture that calls sin good and claims saving grace for those who continue to choose it. Schreiner confirms that "those who are free of righteousness are inevitably slaves of sin. We confront again the idea that no middle ground is possible."[22] There is no middle ground. We cannot be neutral. Either we are for God, or we are against him.

Notice that Paul does not allow for human independence and freedom so prevalent in our thinking today. James Dunn explains, "Paul poses two alternatives—slavery of sin, and slavery of God . . . . he characterizes *both* relationships as that of master and slave. Implicit therefore is the same conviction elaborated in 1:18–32: that man can*not* be independent; that the person who refuses God's mastery over him- or herself does not thereby achieve independence, but becomes instead a slave to sin."[23] Unfortunately, much of our culture thinks sin is fun and righteousness inhibits freedom, or we think we can pursue both—serve God and have our fun. Unfortunately, no one can serve two masters. Dunn continues, "Evidently for Paul there is no third alternative. The choice confronting everyone is the choice of being ruled by God or being ruled by sin."[24]

To Christians, Paul writes (v. 17), "But thanks be to God that, though you used to be slaves to sin, you wholeheartedly obeyed the form of teaching to which you were entrusted." Paul makes it clear that there is a particular set of instructions that Christians obey that was given to them through the apostles and entrusted to their keeping. It is not open for successive generations to decide for themselves what is or is not acceptable to them. He continues (v. 18, NIV), "You have been set free from sin

---

19. Schreiner, *Romans*, 337.
20. Schreiner, *Romans*, 337.
21. Schreiner, *Romans*, 337.
22. Schreiner, *Romans*, 338.
23. Dunn, *Romans 1–8*, 352.
24. Dunn, *Romans 1–8*, 353.

and have become slaves to righteousness." Dunn describes this as "liberation from the domination of self-indulgent desires and selfish habits. Where previously they had lacked real freedom of choice and sin's constraints were too powerful, now that state of affairs no longer pertains. The newly purchased slave who still acts on behalf of his old master is clearly being unfaithful to the new [God]."[25] Choosing God and his righteousness and holiness is the only way to have freedom. Grace always leads to righteousness as found in God and revealed in Scripture.

By contrast, slavery to sin always leads to impurity, which Paul calls freedom from righteousness. Paul describes it as (vv. 19–21, NIV), "I put this in human terms because you are weak in your natural selves. Just as you used to offer the parts of your body in slavery to impurity and to ever-increasing wickedness, so now offer them in slavery to righteousness leading to holiness. When you were slaves to sin, you were free from the control of righteousness . . . . Those things result in death!" This is what happened in the 1960s.

With the advent of Postmodernity, our culture threw off the shackles of doing what was right according to an external standard because it was perceived as restrictive and denying personal freedom and rights. We have been reaping the whirlwind ever since: rampant drug abuse and overdosing, riots in our streets, terrorist attacks, shootings in schools and malls, racial conflict, abortion, and the list goes on. These things have always existed. What is different is the degree and extent to which they happen today. Instead of being relegated to secrecy and kept in darkness, these things are now boldly paraded in daylight with the battle cry, "You shall not judge!" However, a Holy God does judge, and he has given this charge to his people, "Test the spirits to see of what sort they are." God rightly judges both the heart and the actions. His people may only judge the actions of people ("do not cast pearls before swine"; this also includes speech such as the false teachers of Matthew 7). They are forbidden to judge the heart and worth of a person; actions and speech must be judged based on their conformity to God's word, Scripture.

Paul concludes his argument with (Rom 6:22–23, NIV), "But now that you have been set free from sin and have become slaves to God, the benefit you reap leads to holiness, and the result is eternal life. For the wages of sin is death, but the gift of God is eternal life in Christ Jesus our Lord." Dunn calls this gift of God a "free gift" that begins the moment the person agrees with God to make Jesus his or her Lord and Savior. Unfortunately, some have interpreted the "free" gift to mean that it is owed and will be efficacious to all people regardless of what a person believes or does.

However, in accordance with Scripture, Dunn relates this "free gift" to the "conversion-initiation" experience which will control the entire life of the person. He writes that "conversion-initiation . . . is not an isolated and once-and-for-all event in its character of grace meeting obedience. Rather for Paul that first act characterized

25. Dunn, *Romans 1–8*, 354.

the whole of the believer's life as believer."[26] There must be a continual calling on and receiving grace in this life in obedience. For Dunn the Christian must identify "with Christ in his death" now and this identification "must be reaffirmed ever and again until death plays its last card and the believer can know identification with Christ in his resurrection. The obedience of first commitment must be repeated in every decision of any moral consequence so that it may increasingly be an obedience which results in righteousness, a righteousness which results in sanctification, a sanctification which results in eternal life."[27] Grace not only provides forgiveness of sins at the outset of the Christian life, but must be called upon for help in choosing to do God's will at all times and in every aspect of life.

Schreiner agrees and puts it this way: "The power of grace must lead to a transformed life, for holiness of life is necessary for life eternal . . . . Those who have been freed from the power of sin must be holy in order to experience eternal life. They cannot rely on . . . God's grace and shuck off the need for concrete obedience in the particulars of life."[28] Grace leads to righteousness and holiness and not to doing whatever gratifies you or gives you pleasure in the moment. Such a person is not living in grace; the Bible calls this living in the flesh.

Other New Testament writers felt compelled to elaborate on salvation by grace alone in order to prevent antinomianism. James writes that he will show you his faith by his good works, by which he means a lifestyle of righteousness as opposed to licentiousness. This lifestyle includes championing the oppressed and caring for the earth but is not limited to such things. Jude makes it perfectly clear (v. 4, NIV) that some folks have slipped into the church who have changed "the grace of our God into a license for immorality"; in doing so, they have denied "Jesus Christ our only Sovereign and Lord." The fact remains today that grace does not give permission to continue to pursue sin.

Current scholars agree. Kittel writes, "The power of grace . . . is displayed in its work, the overcoming of sin."[29] He takes it one step further and states that not only does the Christian overcome sin because of grace but asserts that grace is an impartation that destroys sin.[30] Charles Ryrie affirms that it was only at the coming of Christ that grace was fully understood, and that contrary to granting permission to continue in human wants and passions, grace "when it is received by the believer . . . governs his spiritual life by compounding favor upon favor. It equips, strengthens, and controls all phases of his life."[31] This control is never permissive to include what the Bible calls sin but is what empowers people to live holy lives.

26. Dunn, *Romans 1–8*, 357.
27. Dunn, *Romans 1–8*, 357.
28. Schreiner, *Romans*, 341.
29. Kittel, "χάρις," 395.
30. Kittel, "χάρις," 396.
31. Ryrie, "Grace," 726.

Gary Shogren understands the grace in the epistles as a "saving grace [which] also means that Christians may find power to live holy lives apart from legalistic structures."³² People will not need external rules because God will have written them on their hearts through the Holy Spirit. Furthermore, "sovereign grace is always purposeful, for the life under grace is a life of good works."³³ These good works go far beyond the good works commonly accepted by today's culture to include personal and corporate righteousness, confession and repentance of sins, and forgiveness through belief in Jesus Christ. Ryrie writes, "Sovereign grace is not an arbitrary display of God's grace. In order to receive it, man must believe. In order to enjoy it, the believer must be obedient."³⁴

Zodhiates expands on this view of grace and writes, "*Charis*, when received by faith, transforms man and causes him to love and to seek after the righteousness of God."³⁵ A new birth happens because "*charis* is initially regeneration, the work of the Holy Spirit in which spiritual life is given to man and by which his nature is brought under the dominion of righteousness."³⁶ Furthermore, "the maintenance of this condition requires an unbroken and immense supply of grace. Grace remains constant in, and basic to, a believer's fight without against the devil and his struggle within against sin."³⁷ Therefore, it is God's grace that empowers the person receiving it to emulate Jesus, to overcome sin and evil, and to persevere through suffering. Paul was not delivered, but God's grace was sufficient for him to continue his work as the apostle to the gentiles. God's grace enabled the Macedonians to give sacrificially to help the church in Jerusalem. "God's grace brings enablement to the helpless, especially the poor and persecuted."³⁸

Continuing with the work that grace does in the lives of believers, Mounce credits God's grace as the empowering force by which Christians have "the ability to obey the gospel from the heart (Rom. 6:17), the ability to work hard (1 Cor. 15:10), and [to have] an increase of joy in severe trials (2 Cor. 8:1–2)." He agrees with Zodhiates and Shogren about suffering and writes, "The Christian knows that no matter the level of suffering or weakness in life, Christ's grace toward them is sufficient (2 Cor. 12:9), allowing them to 'approach the throne of grace with confidence in order that we may receive mercy and find grace to help us in our time of need' (Heb. 4:16)."³⁹

---

32. Shogren, "Grace: New Testament," 1087.
33. Ryrie, "Grace," 726.
34. Ryrie, "Grace," 726.
35. Zodhiates, "χάρις," 1469.
36. Zodhiates, "χάρις," 1469.
37. Zodhiates, "χάρις," 469.
38. Shogren, "Grace: New Testament," 1087.
39. Mounce, "Grace," 304.

Grace for Today

"'Grace' is commonly connected with the preaching of the Word," for we find that "God's grace is extended where the gospel is preached and received (2 Cor 4:15; 6:1)."[40] Therefore, biblical grace is always associated with salvation through Jesus Christ and the proclamation of the gospel message. To receive grace, the person must believe in Jesus. To believe in him the person must hear about him through the clear proclamation of the gospel (see Rom 10:14–15, 17). The person then becomes a member of God's elect people.

To realize the power of grace in his or her daily life, the Christian must seek God's righteousness and obey God's commands as Jesus did (Phil 2). This is impossible apart from the grace which God gives to his elect in Christ. Of this life, Kittel states, "Election is a miracle" because it is "not the normal case on which we can count."[41] By this we understand that it is not generally applied to all people. "'Grace' in Romans 5–6 is a shorthand both for the gospel and for the liberty with which the Christian serves God apart from the Law (see Rom 5:2, 15, 17; 6:1, 14, 15)."[42] As we have seen, this freedom is the freedom from the slavery to sin and not simply a get-out-of-jail-free card to continue in sin.

Grace never leaves the person in the condition in which they were when they received it. Grace sets the person free from sin and brings them into a relationship with God through Jesus, thereby giving them hope. To remain in the sinful state is tantamount to falling from grace. However, today, some folks call on the name of Jesus and persist in claiming their freedom to continue sinning. Historically, this has been called antinomianism by the church, something to be avoided at all costs; today it is called grace in many circles. To these, Kittel writes that they fail "to see that grace is impartation, and that as such it is the destruction of sin."[43] Not only does grace enable the Christian to overcome sin and be set free from sinning, but it destroys sin in the believer. This is what John tells the church in his first epistle (1 John 1:8—2:3).

Robert Jeffress has identified four bad ways grace is commonly practiced today and follows each with the correct way to implement grace:

> Bad grace avoids the responsibility of discipline, resulting in an unhealthy congregation.
>
> Good grace applies scriptural discipline in love, resulting in a healthier, happier, and more peaceful congregation.
>
> Bad grace equates correction with condemnation.

---

40. Shogren, "Grace: New Testament," 1087–88.
41. Kittel, "χάρις," 395.
42. Shogren, "Grace: New Testament," 1087.
43. Kittel, "χάρις," 396.

> Good grace understands that sometimes the most loving thing we do for other believers is to confront them about their disobedience.
>
> Bad grace uses the "live and let live" philosophy as an excuse for ignoring a fellow believer who is held hostage by sin.
>
> Good grace recognizes that we have a responsibility to rescue believers who have been overtaken by sin.
>
> Bad grace rarely considers the effect that an individual's sin has on an entire congregation.
>
> Good grace recognizes our responsibility to protect the moral, doctrinal, and emotional health of the church.[44]

Holy grace will always bring renewal in the person's life, which can only be supplied by God as the person perseveres in holy righteousness.

Of this perseverance, Zodhiates writes, "Renewal is stimulated and impelled by God's illuminating and strengthening of the soul, and will continue and increase so long as the soul perseveres."[45] The churches in Revelation are told they must persevere and overcome evil. Each Christian is under that command. God's grace is the means by which they will do it. Zodhiates writes, "Grace insures that those who have been truly regenerated will persevere until the end of life. This entire work is called sanctification, a work of God 'whereby we are renewed in the whole man and are enabled more and more to die daily unto sin and to live unto righteousness' as is stated by the Westminster Shorter Catechism (Rom. 12:2; 2 Cor. 4:16; Eph. 4:23; Col. 3:10)."[46]

Corresponding to its sanctifying and persevering work, a true understanding of grace never minimizes the truth of the "guilt of sin." Bryan Chapell describes how the work of grace looks in the life of the Christian: "We know grace in its fullness when we are broken to the point of tears over the shame of our sin. We, in fact, strive to see our wrongdoing in all its horror and betrayal of our Savior; for when we do, the marvel of our God's grace becomes all the more profound and mobilizing.... we find strength to embrace him and his purposes in the joy made more real and more deep by our tears of shame."[47] Where grace is at work, Christians are horrified and ashamed of their sin because it is betrayal of the one who so deeply loves them and has given everything for them. But by that same grace they find the strength to persevere and to find acceptance and joy greater than the shame.

Chapell explains the purpose for this sense of shame and writes, "Such understanding denies us candy-coated perceptions of our lives. We really are the temptable

---

44. Jeffress, *Grace Gone Wild!* 199–200.
45. Zodhiates, "χάρις," 1469.
46. Zodhiates, "χάρις," 1469. The early creeds, confessions, and catechisms are important supplements to Scripture for understanding God's holy grace and the absolute truth on which it rests.
47. Chapell, *Holiness by Grace*, 35–36.

and tempted, the vulnerable and frail, the weak and wretched sinners that the Bible portrays us to be."[48] We find that God and Scripture are right, but he does not direct us to wallow in the self-condemnation that so many promote, but leads us to the complete work of grace, which is gratitude and holy living. He writes, "But we recognize at the same time that such honesty is neither helpful nor healthy if tears of remorse do not at the same time turn us in gratitude toward the One who has delivered us from our guilt. In this soul-deep thanksgiving is the power of new obedience for Christ's sake."[49] Chapell is describing the godly sorrow (2 Cor 7:10) that brings people to repentance and leads them to salvation and consent to being in general (God) which brings them beauty and wholeness. This is how grace functions.

Summary

Since people are saved *by* grace *through* faith *for* good works, it is vital that the church has a clear and accurate understanding of grace and the truth on which it is based. As we have seen above, grace can be defined as "the acceptance of and goodness toward those who cannot earn or do not deserve such gain."[50] Ryrie observes that while grace was evident in the Old Testament, it is only in the New Testament that we find its fullest expression: "Grace in its fullest definition is God's unmerited favor in the gift of His Son, who offers salvation to all and who gives to those who receive Him as their personal Saviour added grace for this life and hope for the future."[51] Grace is not something owed to everyone but is freely given to the person who believes in Jesus.

The apostle John tells us that Jesus was full of grace and truth, and that grace and truth come to us *through* Jesus (John 1:14 and 17). Furthermore, "*grace never lowers the standards of holiness. Jesus . . . raised it*" in the Sermon on the Mount, and grace enables us to meet that higher standard.[52] Notice that grace and truth are not *by* Jesus but through him, implying a relationship is needed in order to discern them.

Grace is not something owed to everyone but is freely given to the person who believes in Jesus. According to Ryrie, in order for a person "to receive [God's grace] man must believe. In order to enjoy it the believer must be obedient. Grace provides acceptance (Rom 3:24), enablement (Col 1:29), a new position (I Pet 2:5, 9), and an inheritance (Eph 1:3, 14)."[53] These are all things we attribute to salvation in Jesus Christ.

From Zodhiates we learn that this grace transforms the person in relationship with Jesus and causes him or her to reject sin and to seek and to live in righteousness which

---

48. Chapell, *Holiness by Grace*, 36.
49. Chapell, *Holiness by Grace*, 36.
50. Mounce, "Grace," 303–4.
51. Ryrie, "Grace," 726.
52. Alcorn, *Grace and Truth Paradox*, 66–67.
53. Ryrie, "Grace," 726.

EQUIPPED TO TELL THE NEXT GENERATION

requires "an unbroken and immense supply of grace."[54] The new person is under the control of righteousness because he or she is under the control of the Holy Spirit. From Ryrie we learn that where this grace is at work in a person, he or she finds favor with God, who also equips, controls, and strengthens every aspect of life.[55]

It is only in the context of holiness that we will understand God's grace, which must function in God's holy and absolute truth, which we will examine in the next chapter. This truth comes from Scripture and Christian history and not through individual revelation, which leads to relative truth. The early creeds are important and reliable guides to Christian truth.

---

54. Zodhiates, "χάρις," 1469.
55. Ryrie, "Grace," 726.

Chapter 14

Absolute Truth

God is, even though the whole world deny him. Truth stands, even if there be no public support. It is self-sustained.... Truth is superior to man's wisdom.

—Mohandas (Mahatma) Gandhi[1]

Grace and truth are like the cylinders of a two-stroke engine of a motorcycle. Both must be working well together in order to have a smooth ride. Jesus was full of both, and both come to us through him. The age-old question is, "What is truth?" Pilot asked Jesus that question, and it has been raised time and again throughout history. There have always been many different philosophies about truth, which has led people to think that truth is relative. The truth of an invading army is going to sound very different from the truth proposed by the vanquished people. Contemporary understanding of this has led most people in this culture to declare that all truth is relative; your truth may not be true for me (are you the invader or the vanquished?). We have confused perspective with truth. Perspective will usually contain some truth that will usually be surrounded by personal viewpoints and wishful thinking that may contain untruth, and in some cases intentional false statements and misrepresentation of the truth in order to deceive. Somehow, we are to accept this and believe it will enable us to live together in harmony.

However, what happens if someone murders a person or a group of people? You want to know the truth of who the murderer is and why. You do not want to condemn an innocent person. What happens if a thief steals your identity and destroys everything you spent a lifetime building? What about the food you eat? You want the truth about the ingredients being put into it. Is it GMO or non-GMO? Does it contain peanuts, soy, gluten, or other possible allergens? What pesticides might be in it? What about the processing plant? Is it clean, or might it breed E. coli or worse? These are questions for which relative truth is not enough. We want the actual truth in order to be healthy.

Truth in other areas of life is just as important. When you sign a contract for a new roof, you want the roofers to show up on time, to clean up after themselves, and

1. Quoted in "India's Christians: What Would Gandhi Do?"

to use the quality of materials for which you paid. Good enough to one person might not keep your roof from leaking and destroying your home. So it is in all areas of life. You do not want your friend to lie to you because you want to trust him. You want your children to tell you the truth for the same reason. Relative truth contains lies which lead to mistrust and walls being erected to protect self. Mistrust leads to isolation, brokenness, dissent, and fighting.

Relative truth will always contain partial lies, and lies cause people to be jaded. This is where we are as a nation. We are worn-out and weary of trying to navigate everyone's truth claims. We have become cynical of our politicians and most authority figures, whether it is the government, the church, or the family. We are bored and fed up with the way things are but have no means of changing them given the basic assumptions at work in our culture: all people are good, there is only relative truth; all people are the same, and God, if he or it exists, will only tell us what we want to hear. Thank God there is absolute truth!

Jesus came full of grace and truth, and through him, we have been given grace and truth. We can know the truth through Jesus. What is more, the Scriptures were given by him and reveal what God's truth is (John 17:17). It is by them that we are sanctified through the work of the Holy Spirit. Jesus claims to be the truth (John 14:6), but this is not some transient truth relative to different situations. It is the truth that when followed in all areas of life will set you free (John 8:32). Truth is one of the qualifications for being able to live on God's holy mountain and to dwell in his sanctuary (Ps 15:1–2). What is this actual truth of which Jesus speaks?

Some Issues Surrounding Truth

Jonathan Edwards understood truth as "the consistency and agreement of our ideas with the ideas of God." Consistency and agreement are synonyms for consent. Edwards defines beauty as consent to being. Seeing things as they really are may be thought of as beauty. Therefore, truth is beauty because it consents and agrees with God's law and order and represents reality. "In ordinary conversation," truth is to be understood as "the agreement of our ideas with the things as they are."[2] When interacting with things outside the mind, he identifies truth as "the consistency of our ideas with those ideas or that train and series of ideas, that are raised in our minds according to God's stated order and law."[3] When considering truth in abstract ideas, he also perceives consistency, but this time it is "consistency of our ideas with themselves, as when our idea of a circle, or a triangle, or any of their parts, is agreeable to the idea we have stated and agreed to call by the name of a circle, or a triangle . . . . Those ideas are false that are not consistent with the series of ideas that are raised in our minds by, according to, the

---

2. Edwards, "Scientific and Philosophical Writings," 341–42. (Hereafter cited as WJE 6:page number).

3. WJE 6:342.

order of nature."[4] We all agree the sky is blue. To call it any other color would be inconsistent and therefore not true. Therefore, according to Edwards, truth is consistent agreement with God's ideas placed into this universe at creation.

Allan Killen understands truth as something which "is known, in the sense [that] it is both believed and acted upon" and as consistency that must satisfy "three tests: logical consistency, factual consistency, and practical consistency."[5] First, he defines logical truth as something "that is empirically verifiable" meaning it can be examined scientifically. Logical truth denies metaphysical truth because it fails this test. The Christian response is "metaphysical and moral truth comes to man by revelation and cannot be known other than as *a priori* since it forms the very basis of knowledge and existence itself."[6] This is no different than the axioms upon which all mathematics and science are founded. Unfortunately, the lack of scientific proof has led some Christians to deny logic altogether in favor of revelation only. However, Killen states that "God is rational and logical, and the Bible proves not to be full of paradoxes and contradictions when accepted by faith as written. He [God] has given credible evidences of the truth and infallibility of His Word. This conclusion is the witness of believers of both Testaments (Ps 108:4; Jn 20:30–31; 1 Jn 1:1–3)."[7] Metaphysical truth is consistent like the truth given by credible witnesses in a courtroom trial.

Second, of factual truth, Killen writes, "Truth must fit the facts of life and existence. This means propositional correspondence to reality. Truth . . . must . . . fit the facts while organizing them correctly through the use of universals."[8] Note that having incomplete or inaccurate facts leads to false conclusions and not truth, and this is where relative truth thrives. Third, Killen describes practical consistency as "what Christ speaks of as the basis of salvation, namely, experiencing the truth by acting upon it (Jn 8:32). It entails a content of knowledge upon which the action is taken."[9] Furthermore, Killen asserts that "the Scriptures give all three their proper place. They expect faith to be based upon reasonable evidence and action to follow the reception of clear self-consistent revelation."[10] Christianity satisfies all three criteria for truth.

However, today's *a priori* assumption is that there is no absolute truth which in itself is a contradiction. Alister McGrath describes our postmodern world as "post-Enlightenment," by which he means there is a "loss of confidence in reason. . . . [that] has seriously eroded credibility of a universal rationality once regarded as central to 'liberal' theological method."[11] Eugene Borowitz observed at the close of the twentieth

---

4. WJE 6:342.
5. Killen, "Truth," 1751.
6. Killen, "Truth," 1750.
7. Killen, "Truth," 1750.
8. Killen, "Truth," 1750–51.
9. Killen, "Truth," 1751.
10. Killen, "Truth," 1751.
11. McGrath, *Evangelicalism and the Future of Christianity*, 102.

century that just as scholars had de-mythicized the supernatural, prophecy, miracles, and much of the Bible in the nineteenth and twentieth centuries, liberalism had de-mythicized "universal rationalism and science" and replaced them with only "*possible 'constructions of reality*,'" which has worked itself out in "ethical relativism" rather than in "necessary values and duties" among masses of people (italics are mine).[12] People feel free to make their own truth, and it need not conform to any known facts, neither does it need to be consistent. Today's mantra has become, "Things may be true for today but wrong for tomorrow." This is often defended by the claim that people should not limit God by claiming specific behaviors as truth.

Killen proposes that since God is truth in his being and if truth depends on God, "then absolute truth does not limit but rather reveals God. God is love, but love does not steal, lie, etc., and the commandments only state these truths which already exist in the character of God. They are not limiting but revealing statements which have their basis in His nature."[13] Therefore, "because God is truth, Christ is truth, both in His person and His revelation (Jn 1: 14, 17; 14:6). His Character and His words thus complement each other, and His teaching reveals His holy character and that of the Father (Mt 5:43–48)."[14] To those like the existentialists who promote "*being* the truth while denying that truth has a propositional content, i.e. a content which is contained in revealed statements in Scripture," he responds, "Their attempt fails when one realizes that Christ, using the language of the Schoolroom, maintains in Jn 8 that His record is true. He teaches only what He has heard (vv. 26, 40), seen (v. 38), and been taught by the Father (v. 28). He can confirm what He says because the Father has not left Him alone (v. 29)."[15]

Killen recognizes John 14:6 where Jesus clearly states he is the truth as referring "to the content of His teaching, showing that He is not merely the truth personally, but also teaches propositional truth."[16] Later in John 8 Killen understands Jesus as "defending the truth of His teachings, that He says, 'And ye shall know the truth, and the truth shall make you free' (v. 32). This makes it clear that He is not speaking of some mystical personal knowledge of Himself which will save a man, but a knowledge whose content is composed of what He teaches."[17]

Rather than limit God, truth reveals who God is. It is similar to Edwards who understands Scripture as the holiness of God in writing; Killen understands Scripture

---

12. Borowitz, "Enduring Truth," 230–47, 231. We see this at work in accusations against our political leaders. Someone is accused of "wrongdoing" without facts or with made-up facts, and it must be prosecuted as if it were true as in consistent with the facts. Think about the devastating impact this will have on our nation as this becomes the prominent way to process all legal cases.

13. Killen, "Truth," 1751.

14. Killen, "Truth," 1751.

15. Killen, "Truth," 1751.

16. Killen, "Truth," 1751.

17. Killen, "Truth," 1751.

as God's truth in writing.[18] It represents who he is. Therefore, Jesus, God's Son, is the truth, and he has conveyed that truth through his teaching, which all of Scripture reveals to us. Now that we are aware of the issues surrounding our pursuit of truth, let us turn our attention to the biblical meaning of truth.

Biblical Truth

The Old Testament word for truth is אמת (pronounced *ʾemet*). It is in the family of words from which we also get אָמֵן, which means "verily, truly," and has been adopted in English as the familiar word "amen." At the heart of the meaning of this family of words is "the idea of certainty," which "gives clear evidence of the biblical meaning of 'faith.'"[19] Scripturally, *ʾemet* "carries [the] underlying sense of certainty, dependability" and means "truth, faithfulness, verity."[20] "It is frequently applied to God as a characteristic of his nature" as in Genesis 24:27 and Exodus 34:6. We have encountered these two passages in regard to love and grace. Additionally this word is "fittingly applied to God's words (Ps 119:142, 151, 160; Dan 10:21)."[21] Biblically, God's truth is revealed to people, and "it therefore becomes the means by which men know and serve God as their savior (Josh 24:14; 1 Kgs 2:4; Ps 26:3; 86:11; Ps 91:4; Isa 38:3)," and it then becomes a "characteristic to be found in those who have indeed come to God (Ex 18:21; Neh 7:2; Ps 15:2; Zech 8:16)."[22] Therefore, God's truth is an essential part of salvation and is necessary to serve God. Relative truth does not serve God's purposes because he is always truth, and there is no lie in him.

Jack Scott concludes that "it becomes manifestly clear that there is no truth in the biblical sense, i.e. valid truth, outside God. All truth comes from God and is truth because it is related to God."[23] Be careful not to read into this our twenty-first-century biases. Humans are made in God's image. As such, elements of God's truth remain in us. However, just because a person agrees with God that murder is wrong, that we

18. While all truth (actual and not simply what we want the truth to be) reveals God, human perception through the filters of sin and personal wants will skew our perception of truth. Additionally, our ability to learn this truth is limited by natural ability and opportunity (both formal education and experience). No one has all the truth. We need each other and must do the difficult task of discerning what God is showing us. Along this line, Christians should be cautious about making absolutes of behaviors that are not specified in Scripture as has been done in the past, e.g., DeMoss warns about not watching television or playing cards or seeing movies.

19. Scott, "אָמֵן," 51–53. The truth found in science and mathematics comes from God because he created all that is. Scientists sometimes get it wrong and have to reverse themselves as they unveil some new truth that causes them to look fresh at something they thought they knew. Nevertheless, they are not able to make up their own truth but only to uncover what God has already placed into being.

20. Scott, "אָמֵן," 52.

21. Scott, "אָמֵן," 52.

22. Scott, "אָמֵן," 52–53.

23. Scott, "אָמֵן," 53.

should take care of the earth, or that honesty is the best policy, this does not indicate that the person has saving faith. All belief systems will have something in common with God's truth or they would not be believed. Only God is true in every way and at all times, and he has chosen to reveal himself in Jesus his only son, the Christ.

Furthermore, only as the Christian faith is believed and lived out do people walk in greater truth. Gottfried Quell elaborates on how the concept of God's truth in humans works when he writes, "The pious man, who is often juridically described as the righteous (→ δίκη), grounds his attitude to God on the incontestable fact of truth, and exercises truth, just as truth is the foundation in God's own acts and words. The truthfulness of God requires the truthfulness of man."[24] The Christian faith is founded on God's truth, and its practitioners will believe it and live it out in their lives. Truthfulness will be part of the foundation of their faith and the core of their being because Jesus is there by virtue of the Holy Spirit, and Jesus is grace and truth.

Furthermore, Quell links 'emet with ḥesed in Hosea's complaint that there is no truth in the land because there is no knowledge of God's will. Quell understands this connection as further evidence "that in every sphere of life truthfulness grows out of unerring knowledge of God's will, and that such knowledge is for its part an actualisation of truthfulness."[25] When people know God, they know truth. To support his assessment Quell cites numerous passages that we have examined above concerning Scripture, such as Psalms 15, 19, and 119. He points out that metaphors, like walking in God's truth, "may be reduced to solid rules of life which are called truth and which are the theme of divine instruction (cf. Ps. 86:11)."[26] Knowing God; walking with God; and living for God entail very concrete knowledge and behaviors which are not left to personal preferences.

This is the Old Testament view of truth. What does the New Testament have to say? Interestingly, the Greek word for truth, ἀλήθεια (pronounced *alētheia*), compares favorably with 'emet. It means the actual state of things, non-concealment, and is used to "denote real events as distinct from myths, and philosophers to indicate real being in the absolute sense."[27] Spiros Zodhiates describes "truth as evidenced in relation to facts, therefore, *alētheia* denotes the reality clearly lying before our eyes as opposed to a mere appearance, without reality (Mark 5:33; John 5:33; 16:7; Acts 26:25; Rom. 9:1; 2 Cor. 6:7) . . . . both in words and conduct."[28] In the same sense as 'emet, *alētheia* "has certainty and force" and is the "valid norm." It means "reliability" and "trustworthiness," "sincerity" and "honesty." It can be used as "the truth of a statement," meaning what is actual and real. It is also "used for 'truth teaching or faith.'" It is linked with

---

24. Quell, "ἀλήθεια," 232–47.
25. Quell, "ἀλήθεια," 232–47.
26. Quell, "ἀλήθεια," 232–47.
27. Kittel and Bultmann, "Ἀλήθεια," 232–47.
28. Zodhiates, "ἀλήθεια," 120.

righteousness to denote "judicial righteousness," but often "takes on the weaker sense 'uprightness.'"[29]

In the New Testament we find truth connected with the Christian faith and its teachings: "divine truth or the faith and practice of the true gospel is called 'truth' either as being true in itself and derived from the true God, or as declaring the existence and will of the one true God, in opposition to the worship of false idols. Hence divine truth is gospel truth, as opposed to heathen and Jewish fables (John 1:14, 17; 8:32; . . . 40, 45, 46; 16:13; 17:17, 19; 18:37)."[30] The Old Testament connection can be seen in passages like Galatians 5:7 and 1 Peter 1:22 to mean the "true faith" and "true teaching." Therefore, Kittel observes that "the way is thus prepared for the historical development which fashions the concept of dogma, in which truth and law are conjoined."[31] Hence, we have ample reason to eschew relativism and a sufficient basis for describing and adhering to theology and doctrines in the church such as the early creeds and confessions. They are the human attempt to understand the truth that is God. This precludes every path being equal and all roads leading to God. Jesus is the way, the truth, and the life. His road is the narrow way, the ancient path, the Highway of Holiness with specific instructions to show the way.

In his first epistle, John addresses the doctrines of love, sin, redemption, and evil, and relates them to truth. For John, truth, *alētheia*, reveals an actual embodiment of evil and the subsequent battle between Christians and the prince of this world (John 14:30). The Hellenic dualism between good and evil can be found in his writings with the distinction that for John, "ἀλήθεια [truth as 'divine reality' or 'divine power'] and ψεῦδος ['anti-divine' or falsehood from which we derive 'pseudo'] are understood as genuine possibilities of human existence rather than substances."[32] Additionally, John assures Christians that Jesus has already won the victory, and he lives in the believer through the Holy Spirit. Therefore, "He who is in you is greater than he who is in the world" (1 John 4:4, NIV).

Kittel notices that for John truth denotes "divine reality" in two ways: "1. This [divine reality] is different from the reality in which man first finds himself, and by which he is controlled, and 2. It discloses itself and is thus revelation."[33] Divine reality is not inherent in people and cannot be discovered by people apart from the revelation of God and the preaching and teaching of the true gospel. Kittel explains ἀλήθεια as "the reality of God which is . . . opposed and inaccessible to human existence as it has constituted itself through the fall from God, i.e., through sin."[34] God's revelation of truth is "beyond the reach of the being which is alien to God." That any receive it is a

29. Kittel, "ἀλήθεια," 232–47.
30. Zodhiates, "ἀλήθεια," 121.
31. Kittel, "ἀλήθεια," 232–47.
32. Kittel, "ἀλήθεια," 232–47.
33. Kittel, "ἀλήθεια," 232–47.
34. Kittel, "ἀλήθεια," 232–47.

miracle. Yet God's truth, his revelation, reveals to people the opportunity of discovering their true selves when they surrender to it. Therefore truth, ἀλήθεια, can be found "neither by rational or esoteric instruction on the one side nor psychical preparation and exercise on the other; it takes place in obedient faith."[35]

This is where Modernity failed in trying to reason its way to God. Truth is not something humans can discover on their own. It must be proclaimed and believed. I agree that we humans do still reflect some of the divine image and therefore will know some truth like the secondary beauty of chapter 8. It is meant to lead us to God's Absolute Truth, but in our post-Christian culture that has collectively put the Triune God out of our public life, it is not surprising that we flounder in relative truth and fall further and further from God's divine, holy truth. Truth, for John, requires speaking the truth so people can hear the revelation and know the truth and be brought to faith in Jesus.[36] But political correctness has conditioned Christians, including many evangelicals, to keep silent about their faith in obedience to cultural ideas. Mounce writes, "Thus, there is a close connection between one's knowledge of truth and godly activity; the two cannot be separated. In an age where truth is all too often shaded to obscure falsehood, there is no group of people who should be more dedicated to speaking the truth forthrightly and living by its holy standards than the followers of Jesus (cf. Phil. 4:8)."[37]

Grace and Truth Today

Our current culture tries to separate grace from truth and denies absolute truth, and the church is far too compliant. We take grace for granted (it is owed to everyone) and make truth relative (everyone makes his or her own truth). Consequently, several changes have occurred in Christian thinking that must be identified and replaced with biblical fact.

One of these corrections must be that relative truth does not cut it in the Christian life. This is why God calls his people the righteous ones. Christians are to live in the actual, verifiable truth of God. The God Christians worship is the true God (1 Thess 1:9) and must be worshiped in Spirit and in Truth (John 4:23–24). Jesus is truth (John 1:14, 17; 14:6), and the Holy Spirit is the Spirit of truth (John 14:17; 15:26; 16:13). In fact, John 14:6 tells us that not only is Jesus the way, the truth, and the life, but that he is the only way to God. The Scripture is truth (John 17:17). The Good News of Jesus is the gospel of truth (Eph 1:13; Col 1:5–6). Jesus' disciples will know the truth as they follow him (John 8:31–32). It is in this obedience to truth that they are set free.

---

35. Kittel, "ἀλήθεια," 232–47.
36. Kittel, "ἀλήθεια," 232–47.
37. Mounce, "Truth," 748.

Truth is consistency—something which is very rare in this culture. The church can engage people by challenging them to see their inconsistencies of their own belief systems, but Christians must be sure they are consistently living out their beliefs when they challenge others. It is not the Christians who have their heads in the clouds with pie-in-the-sky wishful thinking, but it is the secular world with its relative truth that has no solid foundation. It is wishful thinking to imagine that an entire culture can be based (not on truth but) on the lies inherent in relative truth and survive. Eventually it becomes as fragile as a house of cards and collapses just as easily.

The Christian life means conformity to God's truth, which is constant in all ages and for all people. This has not always been accepted in the church in the past sixty-plus years. Randy Alcorn helps us to understand why we need to live by truth when he compares it to guardrails that keep a driver from crashing down a mountain. An aware driver is thankful for a dented bumper rather than total destruction. Additionally, Alcorn connects bad behavior and lack of truth with bad grace when he writes, "The world's low standards, its disregard for truth, are not grace. The illusory freedom, however, feels like grace to someone who's been pounded by graceless truth—beaten over the head by a piece of the guardrail."[38] Alcorn explains what happens when Christians separate truth and grace: "Truth without grace breeds a self-righteous legalism that . . . pushes the world away from Christ. Grace without truth breeds moral indifference and keeps people from seeing their need for Christ."[39] Either way people are driven away from or kept from God, and evil wins. We have witnessed this in our culture and even in our churches.

As relative truth claimed this culture, the idiom "I don't know" has become a safe approach to everything that is commonly accepted and practiced in order to be politically correct.[40] "I don't know" is an escape from telling the truth to a person or about an event in order to avoid offending anyone. Many think this is humility, but it is not spiritual. It is pseudo-humility. It is like doubt (chapter 3); it stems from unbelief.

"I don't know" fits well with the relativism of the day and feeds the tolerance of everything but truth. This affects how the church understands Jesus and discipleship. Alcorn claims that "the modern, mythological Jesus comes full of tolerance and relativism"; and representing him "now . . . means 'making people like us [instead of submitting to Jesus].'"[41]

---

38. Alcorn, *Grace and Truth Paradox*, 37.

39. Alcorn, *Grace and Truth Paradox*, 18.

40. I am not talking about the times that we truly do not have an answer. At those times it is honest and truthful to say, "I don't know." However, it is advisable to pray and to study Scripture and the writings of mature Christians to find an answer. I also recommend seeking the counsel of a mature and Spirit-filled Christian.

41. Alcorn, *Grace and Truth Paradox*, 72–73.

Summary

Grace and truth are the two cylinders of a two-stroke engine. Both are needed to function smoothly and to have maximum power. Both are in Jesus and come to the people of the world through him, but we have drifted away from absolute truth and holy grace, and Christ has drifted out of the minds of most Americans. The church must recover holy grace and holy truth if she is going to proclaim Jesus to the people of Western culture. To appreciate grace, we must first understand truth.

Truth refers "to something that is accurate."[42] Truth denotes what is "real [and] actual, not counterfeit" that requires people "to act genuinely, truly."[43] Mounce reminds us that "truth is not only something that we believe; it is also something that we are called upon to speak and even to practice. This connection between truth and action is found throughout the NT.... Christians are expected to be truthful in this way, being honest and having actions that reflect the commitment to truth (1 Cor. 5:8; Eph. 4:24–25)."[44] Therefore, truth implies "conduct conformed to the truth [with] integrity, probity, [and] virtue; a life conformed to the precepts of the gospel."[45]

There is only one truth, God's truth, as found in the Scripture.[46] It is God's word to us for the healing of the world, but we persist in picking and choosing what we will believe and what we will follow. The church must let go of the aberrations of her major doctrines that have emerged in the past 150-plus years.

Do not despair; there is always hope because of what Jesus did. Alcorn writes, "Christ went to the cross because he would not ignore the truths of holiness and our sin. Grace never ignores or violates truth. Grace gave what truth demanded: the ultimate sacrifice for our sins."[47] This same hope is still active and offered today, but the church must consistently agree and accurately proclaim it for it to be effective. Unfortunately, most Christians are too politically correct to allow the clear proclamation of the gospel. Too often "I don't know" is the default setting on which they rely. It fits well with the popular relative truth. The solution is to recover the knowledge of the Holy God and all of his attributes according to biblical truth.

Grace and truth are two good places to begin. Alcorn challenges and reminds the church, "If you are not stunned by the thought of grace then you aren't grasping what grace offers you, or what it cost Jesus."[48] Those who take grace for granted or

---

42. Mounce, "Truth," 747.
43. Zodhiates, "ἀλήθεια," 121.
44. Mounce, "Truth," 747–48.
45. Zodhiates, "ἀλήθεια," 121.
46. As in all general revelation there are elements of God's truth that can be discerned naturally, such as the beauty of a sunset that is intended to lead a person to seek the beauty of the One who created it or that we are to take care of the earth or that it is wrong to murder and steal. As with beauty, this truth is designed to lead us to the greater truth of God himself.
47. Alcorn, *Grace and Truth Paradox*, 32.
48. Alcorn, *Grace and Truth Paradox*, 30.

presume grace will cover their chosen sinful lifestyle are of this mindset. Grace and truth are what we find when we pursue a relationship with Jesus Christ. When we seek to become like Jesus we are seeking to renew the image of God lost in the fall. We are seeking holiness which holds together all of God's characteristics and makes perfect sense of grace and truth found in Scripture. In the next two chapters we will examine prayer that God longs to hear.

Chapter 15

The Necessity of Prayer

> Few Christians have anything but a vague idea of the power of prayer; fewer still have any experience of that power . . . . This spiritual carte blanche on the infinite resources of God's wisdom and power is rarely, if ever used—never used to the full measure of honoring God.
>
> —E. M. Bounds, Purpose in Prayer

WE HAVE BEEN EXAMINING how generally God loves all people and is gracious towards them, but that he is a covenant-making God who invites everyone into the special relationship that is specified in that covenant. Prayer also falls into this design. I believe God hears every prayer uttered by every person. In his sovereignty, he chooses to answer some. To those who have given their lives to Jesus and follow him, God makes many promises not only to hear but to answer their prayers.

Perhaps you have heard that "prayer changes the world." E. M. Bounds explains how it works: "Prayer secures blessings, and makes men better because it reaches the ear of God . . . Prayer affects men by affecting God. Prayer moves men because it moves God to move men. Prayer influences men by influencing God to influence them. Prayer moves the hand that moves the world."[1] Prayer accomplishes all of this through faith in Jesus Christ. Bounds writes, "Prayer is absolutely dependent upon faith. Virtually, it has no existence apart from it, and accomplishes nothing unless it is its inseparable companion. Faith makes prayer effectual, and in a certain important sense, must precede it."[2] So then, how do we pray?

Perhaps you have heard about different kinds of prayers which may have confused you. Take heart, you do not have to know what label your praying should be given for your prayers to be effective, but just so you know, they are usually classified as petition and intercession. Richard Foster simply describes them as "when our asking is for ourselves it is called petition; when it is on behalf of others it is called intercession."[3] He goes on to tell us that petitionary prayer is usually our primary

---

1. Bounds, "The Possibilities of Prayer," 165.
2. Bounds, "The Necessity of Prayer," 22.
3. Foster, *Prayer*, 179.

kind of prayer because "we are forever dependent upon God. It is something that we never really 'get beyond,' nor should we even want to."[4] By "get beyond" he means that we should never stop praying petitionary prayers, not that we should not move on to intercession for other people and things. There is one more term often used in connection with prayer—supplication, which Foster describes as "to ask with earnestness, with intensity, with perseverance. It is a declaration that we are deadly serious about this prayer business."[5] This is what Jesus had in mind when he told his disciples to keep asking, seeking, and knocking.

Of course, the best-known prayer is the Lord's Prayer, given to the church by Jesus himself. We see elements of this prayer in the Westminster Shorter Catechism when it describes prayer as "an offering up of our desires unto God [our Father who art in heaven, hallowed be thy name], for things agreeable to his will [thy kingdom come, thy will be done on earth as it is in heaven; give us this day our daily bread], in the name of Christ [this came at a later time in Christ's ministry], with confession of our sins [forgive us our debts as we forgive our debtors], and thankful acknowledgement of his mercies [for thine is the kingdom, and the power, and the glory forever]."[6]

In another place, Jesus promises that those who believe in him will do even greater things than he did (John 14:12–14). This will be accomplished through prayer asked in his name. Additionally, Jesus promises that if they keep asking they will receive; if they keep seeking, they will find, and if they keep knocking the door will be opened to them (Matt 7:7; Luke 11:9). So, with these great promises, why is it that the church is not bursting with pray-ers filling the throne room of heaven to bring down God's blessings to change the world? My guess is that Christians have prayed and have had no discernable answers or received answers they could not or would not accept. It might be that somewhere along the way a pastor steeped in the modern ways of reason and science told them that prayer does not really change things or that they were not to bother God with their trivial troubles. God had much greater things on his mind than their petty problems. This is a form of deism, which was making its way into the educated elite as early as the eighteenth century. The reasons why we are reluctant to pray are many, but before we talk about unanswered prayer, we must examine what prayer is.

What Is Prayer?

Prayer is communication with God. In any good relationship there must be good communication, and this is true in covenant relationships as well. Think of a marriage covenant. When the couple ceases to communicate, the relationship becomes distressed. Unless communication is restored, they become distant from each other

---

4. Foster, *Prayer*, 179.
5. Foster, *Prayer*, 197.
6. Question 98 of "The Westminster Shorter Catechism," 185.

and may end up divorced or living together for convenience's sake. Perhaps this describes the relationship some Christians have with God. Perhaps you are in the "struggling to make it work" phase or the "everything is brand new and exciting" stage or somewhere in between. Wherever your relationship with God may fall, prayer is the key to making and to keeping the covenant relationship with God electrifying. Nothing is more electrifying than praise.

The Prayer of Praise

The prayer for which God is listening begins with praise and adoration of who he is. With all of our worldly knowledge and psychotherapy, this sounds awfully egocentric, and if he was not a Holy God, we would call him narcissistic. C. S. Lewis thought long and hard about this and concluded that praise is for our benefit, not God's. He noticed how human enjoyment of everything automatically overflows to joy, adoration, and praise. We need only look at our reactions to sporting events when our favorite team wins the trophy or at how excited we get when recommending a favorite book or painting. We can hardly stop praising the athlete, author, or artist.

Reflecting on Lewis's findings, Tim Keller writes, "If God is the great object of admiration behind all other beauties and magnificence, then to praise and admire him would be 'simply to be awake, to have entered the real world,' while not doing so would be to become far more profoundly crippled than those who are blind, deaf, and bedridden."[7] He concludes, "We must praise God or live in unreality and poverty. We cannot merely believe in our minds that he is loving or wise or great. We must praise him for those things—and praise him to others—if we are to move beyond abstract knowledge to heart-changing engagement."[8]

Lewis explains it as delighting "to praise what we enjoy because the praise not merely expresses but completes the enjoyment; it is its appointed consummation." Lovers tell each other how wonderful they are because their "delight is incomplete until it is expressed."[9] You know how unsatisfying it is to be captivated by a beautiful waterfall in the mountains, a new favorite author or artist, and not be able to talk about it with anyone "because the people with you care for it no more than for a tin can in the ditch." The greatest and most complete delight can only be realized when we "really and fully praise even such things . . . to perfection . . . [until it] almost bursts you."[10] Praising God maximizes and completes our joy of him.

We praise God because we have seen and experienced his holiness in beauty, grace, wholeness, love, truth, righteousness, peace, and justice, and we are so moved by him that praise just flows out of us for his goodness. If we do not have this appreciation

---

7. Keller, *Prayer*, 191.
8. Keller, *Prayer*, 192.
9. Lewis, *Reflections on the Psalms*, 111.
10. Lewis, *Reflections on the Psalms*, 111.

for God, then we are not seeing and living in reality but in the darkness of a world gone awry. Sometimes we must praise him anyway even when we do not feel that joy to remind ourselves of the truth. Many times it will break the grip that darkness has on us in the moment. Perhaps this is why Keller asserts that "praise and adoration are the necessary preconditions for the proper formulation and motivation of all the other kinds of prayer."[11] It is gets us in the right mindset for prayer.

Therefore, praise requires knowing something about that person. A baseball fan will be able to tell you the batting averages, ERAs, RBIs, and all the statistics of her favorite players and will delight to talk with anyone who will listen. The same is true of fans of authors, artists, and actors as well. Again, we find knowledge of God as a prerequisite for prayer. Therefore, Keller encourages Christians to "do everything possible to behold our God as he is, and prayer will follow. The more clearly we grasp who God is, the more our prayer is shaped and determined accordingly."[12] In this age of Bible illiteracy, this could explain a lot of why we do not see more dramatic answers to our prayers.

Prayer and Meditation

As we have just seen, one goal of the church is to educate her people so that she can live righteously and pray effectively. This education of God's people comes from the truth found in God's word, which represents reality and the Holy God in writing. A second goal for God's people is not just to study but to meditate on God's word. Keller uses Psalm 1 to understand meditation and writes, "Meditation is likened to tree roots taking in water. That means not merely knowing a truth but taking it inside and making it part of yourself. Meditation is spiritually 'tasting' the Scripture—delighting in it, sensing the sweetness of the teaching, feeling the conviction of what it tells us about ourselves, and thanking God and praising God for what it shows us about him."[13] Furthermore, he tells us that "meditation leads to stability . . . but not to complete immunity from suffering" and reminds us that there are seasons in our spiritual lives just as there are seasons in the physical world.[14]

Unfortunately, most Christians do not understand meditation. Keller asserts that is because of their consumeristic, fast-paced lifestyle that encourages them to "skim everything, picking and choosing on impulse, having no thought-out reasons for their behavior [it feels good at the time]. Following whims, they live shallow lives. The people who meditate can resist pressure—but those who do not go along

---

11. Keller, *Prayer*, 190. This does not mean we can never skip this to go directly to petition when needed.

12. Keller, *Prayer*, 62.

13. Keller, *Prayer*, 150–51.

14. Keller, *Prayer*, 147.

with the throng, chafflike, wherever it is going."[15] That the church has lost its ability to meditate is supported by the rush in the 1960s of Americans to learn meditation from Eastern religions and New Age.

The most common excuse given for not meditating is that we are too busy, but the number of people outside the church seeking this experience tells Christians they must relearn this part of the faith. Capitulation with the culture has cost the church dearly in the depth of her own walk with her Lord. So then, what is Christian meditation, and how does it differ from New Age and other religious meditation?

New Age and other religious forms of meditation teach you to empty your mind to receive whatever comes without discernment or concern of the source. There is great danger in this because as we have seen above, there is a real enemy who loves to lead folks away from God by suggesting good things that will keep you from God's best. Therefore, instead of emptying their minds, Christians are instructed to fill their minds with God's holy word. They are to sit still and think on God's character or a specific passage of Scripture. Foster describes the role of Scripture in meditation as "internalizing and personalizing the passage. The written Word becomes a live word addressed to us. This is a time not for technical studies or analysis or even the gathering of material to share with others. We are to set aside all tendencies toward arrogance and with humble hearts receive the word addressed to us . . . . Our rushing reflects our internal state, and our internal state is what needs to be transformed."[16]

Keller calls meditation "spiritually 'digesting' the Scripture—applying it, thinking out how it affects you, describes you, guides you in the most practical way. It is drawing strength from the Scripture, letting it give you hope, using it to remember how loved you are . . . . Meditation is taking the truth down into our hearts until it catches fire there and begins to melt and shape our reactions to God, ourselves, and the world."[17] The Holy Spirit is the one orchestrating the truth, guidance, love, and hope that you experience.

In this atmosphere of prayer and protection (the armor of God), Christians must quiet themselves and wait for God to respond. Sometimes, a verse of Scripture may come to mind or a deeper understanding of one. At other times, an impression of something may come to mind. Sometimes, I have received answers in the form of ideas as to how to proceed in a difficult situation or how to solve specific problems. One time I asked God if I should accept an invitation to lead a women's retreat. I was waiting for a "yes" or "no" answer. At this time the outline and the details of what I should present kept coming to me. I must have asked God several times if it was "yes" or "no." I finally figured it out that if the talk was formulating so easily in my mind, the answer was "yes"; I was to present it. At other times you might think of things you

---

15. Keller, *Prayer*, 147.
16. Foster, *Prayer*, 146.
17. Keller, *Prayer*, 151.

need to do or need at the grocery store. That is fine, keep paper and pencil nearby and simply jot it down for later and continue meditating on God.

During times of prayer and meditation, I have received some of the illustrations used in this book. Whatever happens, remember to test it with the totality of Scripture and ask: Who gets the glory? Is it scriptural? What are the fruits? When I have used the illustrations received in times of meditation, God's people have always responded with how powerful they were and how helpful they found them. Test the spirits.

These are only the basics of Christian meditation. Much more could be written. I hope I have introduced you to enough to whet your appetite to try this or to research it further. I will end this section with some thoughts from two of my favorite authors on prayer. Foster advises anyone who would meditate not to "manipulate God; just receive. Communion with him isn't something you institute. It's like sleep. You can't make yourself sleep, but you can create the conditions that allow sleep to happen. All I want you to do is create the conditions: open your Bible, read it slowly, listen to it, and reflect on it."[18] I would add that you also learn to sit in silence in God's presence. Keller reminds us that "meditation brings blessedness—a very fulsome idea in the Bible. It means peace and well-being in every dimension. It means character growth, stability, and delight (Ps 1:2). Meditating on the law of the Lord, the Scripture, moves us through duty toward joy. The biblical promises for meditation are enormous."[19]

Praying the Scriptures

What are the prayers God is waiting to hear and would gladly answer? Besides praise, confessions of sin, and repentance, I direct you to the prayers found in the New Testament. Paul opens most of his letters with prayers for the churches. For the Philippians he prays that their love would grow in knowledge (of God) and depth of insight so that they would be able to discern what is best and be pure, blameless, and filled with the fruit of righteousness (Phil 1:9–11). For the Colossians he prays that God would fill them with the knowledge of his will, all spiritual wisdom, and understanding. He prays this so that they would grow in knowledge of God, excel in good works, be strengthened with power, endurance, and patience, and be filled with praise and thanksgiving. In short, they would be living in God's kingdom of light (Col 1:9–14).

Paul's letter to the Ephesians is filled with prayer. He prays that the Father would give them the "Spirit of wisdom and revelation" in order for them to know God better and that "the eyes of your heart may be enlightened in order that you may know the hope to which he has called you, the riches of his glorious inheritance in the saints, and his incomparably great power for us who believe" (Eph 1:15–21, NIV). He goes on to explain that this power is the same power that raised Jesus from the dead, and he is praying for them to know that they have it. In chapter 3:14–19, he prays that God

---

18. Foster, *Prayer*, 144.
19. Keller, *Prayer*, 148.

would strengthen them with power from the Holy Spirit; that Christ would dwell in their hearts through faith (they are already Christians); that they would be rooted and grounded in love; that they would have power to grasp the height, depth, and width of God's love that surpasses knowledge, and that they would be filled with all the measure of the fullness of God. Does this sound anything like the prayers you or I pray privately or corporately at church? I urge you to incorporate these and other Scriptures into your prayer life. (See appendix 5: "Prayers of the New Testament.")

This is what is called praying the Scriptures. There are many books about the promises God has made, and the implication has been that you simply find one that will give you what you want, and God will deliver. This is similar to my sixteen-year-old son who wanted to pray for a Jaguar. You may on occasion receive such things, for God loves to delight his children, but more often I find greater help in searching Scripture for passages that pertain to *God's will* in any given situation and adapt that to prayer. Beth Moore has done an excellent job teaching and modeling this in *Praying God's Word*. She describes everyday struggles with suffering, grief, depression, and unforgiveness and then adapts specific Scriptures pertaining to those things into prayers and suggests others that you might try on your own.

The Possibilities of Prayer

Simply put, prayer is communicating with God, but oh, how understated that is. Bounds reminds us of the possibilities of prayer: "Prayer is no mere untried theory. It is not some strange unique scheme, concocted in the brains of men, and set on foot by them, an invention which has never been tried or put to the test."[20] Prayer has been tested and found trustworthy because "prayer is a divine arrangement in the moral government of God, designed for the benefit of men and intended as a means for furthering the interests of his cause on earth, and carrying out his gracious purposes in redemption and providence." He insists, "Prayer proves itself."[21] Furthermore, Bounds asserts that prayer is so successful because it "lays its hand on Almighty God and moves him to do what he would not otherwise do if prayer was not offered."[22]

Some people in the church struggle with this because they feel it is not in accord with Jesus' prayer, "nevertheless, not my will but thine be done," in Gethsemane just before his crucifixion. All prayer requires submission of the person's will to God's answer, but it must not stop us from asking what is on our hearts. At Mt. Sinai, Moses prayed for the rebellious Israelites whom God was going to wipe out (and start over with Moses) when they made and worshiped the golden calf. Moses prayed and changed God's mind. Moses could have reasoned that if God was willing to make him the head of a great nation, who was he to argue with God. After all, he was Abraham's

20. Bounds, "The Possibilities of Prayer," 162.
21. Bounds, "The Possibilities of Prayer," 162.
22. Bounds, "The Possibilities of Prayer," 162.

descendant. This would have had the added benefit of being rid of all the gripers and complainers who plagued him.

Bother Andrew, who smuggled thousands of Bibles into communist lands in the second half of the twentieth century, observes that "Moses, the true intercessor, doesn't accept *a* word from the Lord as *the* word from the Lord. He understands God's character; he knows God to be reasonable, merciful and true to His Word," so he reminds God of his word and his promises and that, from the human perspective, it would look like God is destroying the very people he just protected and set free.[23] God changed his plan because the circumstance changed; Moses prayed. Brother Andrew concludes, "So you see, in interceding for his nation instead of accepting God's plans as final, Moses changes history."[24] This is one area where the "I don't know" mentality that has crept into the church has done great damage. Most churchgoers do not know God's character or his will, much less have the courage to pray this way.

Fatalism and False Faith

A blind acceptance of events as God's will leads the church to the practice of fatalism so popular in our age. Fatalism is the belief that what happens is what was meant to be. Brother Andrew informs us that "the majority of the people on this planet today . . . belong to the fatalistic non-Christian religions, and their numbers are increasing at an alarming rate. And now the Christian Church is being infected as well with the paralyzing virus of fatalistic apathy."[25]

One reason fatalism is so popular is that "fatalists can relax because they are no longer responsible for anything. They don't have to obey God or actively resist evil; they can simply 'let it be' (as the Beatles recommended in their hit song of the '60s)."[26] It is the easy way; the broad way that leads to destruction. So we find that fatalism and the subsequent freedom from responsibility reduce the effectiveness of prayer.

Deceptively, this freedom from responsibility often comes cloaked as faith. Brother Andrew continues, "The fatalist's attitude seems to reflect tremendous faith: 'I refuse to question the will of God,' he will say with pious humility. . . . 'If God allows it, there must be a reason,' he will say, 'and I can't hope to understand God's reasons with my small mind, so I accept what He does by faith and 'praise the Lord anyway.'"[27] Many today see this as faith like Jesus' in the garden before the crucifixion.

The difference is that Jesus knew why he had come to earth—to be crucified for our sins, to satisfy God's righteous judgment, and to appease his holy wrath. He was asking if there was any other way God's will could be accomplished. Although he was hoping for

23. Andrew, *And God Changed His Mind*, 31.
24. Andrew, *And God Changed His Mind*, 33.
25. Andrew, *And God Changed His Mind*, 18.
26. Andrew, *And God Changed His Mind*, 19.
27. Andrew, *And God Changed His Mind*, 18.

something different, in the end he submitted to what he knew was the will of God. This is not what happens in the lives of Christians today. They do not claim to know the will of God, and then they ignore the commands to pray and to overcome evil with good, which leads them to a docile and "safe" acceptance of every evil under the sun.

Increasingly, this fatalistic mindset has become the automatic default setting of Christians. I hear, "it was meant to be" as if whatever happens is synonymous with God's will being done. This results in the church abdicating her responsibility, power, and authority that with prayer she can move mountains and turn back evil. As Brother Andrew writes, "We don't have to take life as it comes; we can have an earth-shaking impact on our world because God's mind and heart are open to us and His power is available to us."[28] Like Moses, we have the power to move God to change circumstances, but often we ignore prayer; then we wonder why God isn't doing more to change the world.

Instead of blindly accepting all events as being from God, recall that John commands Christians to test the spirits (1 John 4:1) of all things to discern the source. The discernment process is a series of questions that Christians should ask about whether something is really of God: Is it scriptural? Who gets the glory? Is God glorified in these events or teachings? Who benefits from such doctrines? What are the fruits?

In most of these cases of "what happens is what was meant to be," God becomes the bad guy who causes evil, and terrible things get attributed to him. Consequently, people want nothing to do with this god while the evil one (who is really behind it) is free to continue his wreckage in the world. I would think rather that it is Satan who benefits when Christians allow evil to run rampant and unchecked without serious prayer to the contrary because they are ostensibly submitting to God's will in a fatalistic manner.

Fatalism has gained popularity because of the church's general lack of knowledge of God, which we will discover below is another reason our prayers often fall short. Brother Andrew reminds us that "the people who change God's mind are the people who know two things about Him—His character and His will."[29]

Knowledge of God Improves Prayer

Keller helps us to see this more clearly when he describes prayer as a journey that "unites us with God himself,"[30] and defines prayer as "a personal, communicative *response to the knowledge of God*" (italics are mine).[31] From Romans 1:19–20 we know that all people have some knowledge of God. Keller connects this with prayer and writes, "At some level, they have an indelible sense that they need something or

28. Andrew, *And God Changed His Mind*, 17.
29. Andrew, *And God Changed His Mind*, 29.
30. Keller, *Prayer*, 30–31.
31. Keller, *Prayer*, 45.

someone who is on a higher plane . . . . Prayer is seeking to respond and connect to that being and reality, even if it is no more than calling out into the air for help."[32] He concludes therefore that "prayer is profoundly altered by the amount and accuracy of that knowledge."[33] Where there is only nebulous and unclear knowledge of God there may be attempts at conversation, "but it cannot be a real conversation because the knowledge of God is too vague."[34] In this age of Bible illiteracy (chapters 1–5), this is perhaps the main reason Christians find so little beyond personal problems to entice them to pray and why their prayers often seem to go unanswered.

The only place we can find more knowledge of God is in Scripture. The saints throughout its pages prayed powerful prayers: Moses interceded for Israel, reminding God of his words, and turned away God's judgment; Daniel prayed repentance on behalf of Israel and prayed God's words and covenant back to him based on what he understood from Scripture; and Nehemiah confessed the sins of Israel and himself and reminded God of his promise to restore the people from exile. Therefore, the solution for better praying begins with the study of God's word, the Bible. Keller warns the church immersed in the Western culture, "Without immersion in God's words, our prayers may not be merely limited and shallow but also untethered from reality. We may be responding not to the real God but to what we wish God and life to be like. Indeed, if left to themselves our hearts will tend to create a God who doesn't exist."[35] Keller reminds us that "people from Western cultures want a God who is loving and forgiving but not holy and transcendent. Studies of the spiritual lives of young adults in Western countries reveal that their prayers, therefore, are generally devoid of both repentance and of the joy of being forgiven."[36]

Powerful praying results when God's people know the powerful God who is holy. Keller surmises that "without prayer that answers the God of the Bible, we will only be talking to ourselves."[37] This would explain why we often do not get better answers to our prayers.

Bounds helps us to begin to understand the power in prayer when he writes that men and women "are to pray—to pray for the advance of God's cause. Prayer puts God in full force in the world."[38] Furthermore, he asserts that prayer "is the one condition God puts in the very advance and triumph of his cause."[39] What is his cause? Only knowledge of God's word can answer this. Moses had spent much time with God and knew him well. He prays and reminds God of his other characteristics, such as mercy,

32. Keller, *Prayer*, 45.
33. Keller, *Prayer*, 45.
34. Keller, *Prayer*, 45.
35. Keller, *Prayer*, 62.
36. Keller, *Prayer*, 62.
37. Keller, *Prayer*, 62.
38. Bounds, "The Purpose of Prayer," 300.
39. Bounds, "The Purpose of Prayer," 300.

and provides God with alternate justification for doing something different. Walter Brueggemann asserts therefore that Moses is able to be bold to stand before God and to pray for him to reconsider his actions based on additional input (Moses' prayer) "because he [Moses] knows the textual tradition, to pray the text back to God, and to call God to account," for God to back up his own words. Moses can do this because he is no stranger to God nor is he spouting his own ideas, but he "prays out of a long history as an old and well-established colleague and confidant of YHWH."[40]

You may argue that Moses was special; that he was the leader of an entire nation, and that you have nothing to recommend you to do such things. I remind you that if you believe in Jesus, you have God's own Spirit living in you. This is a New Testament reality. Scripture is clear on this. Jesus said that his disciples (Christians of all ages) would do the very things that he did and greater, and that they would ask the Father in his name, and they would have what they asked (John 14:12–14). Jesus said that he has given his authority to his disciples; all authority in heaven and earth is at their disposal (Matt 28:18; Luke 10:19) because he and the Father send the Holy Spirit to live in each believer. To refuse to use this power and authority is a lack of knowledge and understanding at best. At worst, it is false humility or outright rebellion. I believe most Christians fall into the first category. They do not know or understand the clear teaching of Scripture on God's will, his power, and the Holy Spirit.

God's Will and Prayer

Concerning his will, we know that it is God's will that all people come to a knowledge of the gospel and be saved by Jesus (1 Tim 2:4). It is God's will that you always be joyful, pray continually, and always give thanks (1 Thess 5:16–18). First Thessalonians 4:3–8 (NIV) gives a lengthy explanation of God's will: You should be sanctified and live holy lives avoiding sexual impurity. Be in control of your bodies and do not be passionate like the heathen. Be honest with all people and do not take advantage of any. It is also God's will that Christians tell people about the gospel of Jesus Christ (Matt 28:18-20). It is God's will that Christians live pure and holy lives and love God first and other people as they love themselves.

The problem is that too often people do not want to do what they know is right (they want a shortcut or want to pursue their comfort and pleasure), and then feel confused, disappointed, or angry when God does not answer their prayers. There is much in Scripture to instruct us of God's will if we really want to know. Too often, we are reluctant to study it because we fear that we might have to change something we dearly love to do. Therefore, our prayers become safe prayers so as not to interfere with what we really want.

---

40. Brueggemann, *Great Prayers of the Old Testament*, 21.

Additionally, we find that prayer not only requires knowledge of God but is the only way to truly know ourselves. Keller writes, "Prayer is the only entryway into genuine self-knowledge."[41] God is truth. Therefore, as a person grows in his or her knowledge of him, he or she grows in all truth, which naturally encompasses self. This could be an obstacle to prayer because we may not like what we discover there: darkness and emptiness. This emptiness exposes the popular philosophies of this age that tell everyone he or she is right and good. Keller observes that "we are so used to being empty that we do not recognize the emptiness as such until we start to try to pray."[42] This may keep some people from praying. Nevertheless, Keller affirms that "prayer is awe, intimacy, [and] struggle—yet the way to reality. There is nothing more important, or harder, or richer, or more life-altering. There is absolutely nothing so great as prayer."[43] Keller has discovered that in God there is no separation of "truth *or* Spirit, between doctrine *or* experience."[44] All exist in prayer.

Praying in Jesus' Name

Basically, praying in Jesus' name means praying for the things God wills. Here, then, is another way lack of knowledge of God inhibits prayer. Instead of struggling to know God's will in a given situation people tend to take the easy way out and pray a blanket "your will be done" to cover their bases. Few are willing to pray like Moses because we have taken a fatalistic approach to events in our day. When challenged to pray or to live out God's will, most people respond, "I wish I knew what that was."

Scripture will be your guide to knowing God's will. To begin, it means surrender to God's sovereignty. It starts with giving your life to Jesus in faith that through his sacrifice, your sins are forgiven. It means obeying all of his commands instead of following your personal wants. Foster describes it as "the complete laying down of human will. . . . In the school of Gethsemane we learn to distrust whatever is of our own mind, thought, and will even though it is not directly sinful. Jesus shows us a more excellent way. The way of helplessness. The way of abandonment. The way of relinquishment . . . 'my will, my way, my good' must yield to higher authority."[45] This is a surrendering of personal will for personal advancement of God's will that must precede the kind of prayer Moses prayed on behalf of the Israelites.

Bounds reminds us that the need for abdication of our own will and surrender to God's will comes from the life of "our Lord Jesus Christ [who] was preeminent in praying, because he was preeminent in saintliness. . . . Jesus learned obedience in the school of suffering, and at the same time, he learned prayer in the school of obedience

41. Keller, *Prayer*, 18.
42. Keller, *Prayer*, 24.
43. Keller, *Prayer*, 32.
44. Keller, *Prayer*, 15.
45. Foster, *Prayer*, 49–50.

.... A righteous man is an obedient man, and he it is, who can pray effectually, who can accomplish great things when he betakes himself to his knees."[46] He concludes that "if the will of God does not master the life, the praying will be nothing but sickly sentiment. If prayer does not inspire, sanctify and direct our work, then self-will enters, to ruin both work and worker."[47] Success in ministry and effectiveness in prayer are both dependent on knowledge of and obedience to God's will, which is the meaning of praying in Jesus' name. It is in surrender to the knowledge of God's character that the righteous person prays against the evil that is happening, reminding God of his promises and other characteristics that may not be active at that time, as in Moses' case.

Prayer and Righteousness

James tells us that we do not receive from God primarily because we do not ask him for things, and secondarily because when we do ask, we ask for the wrong things and in the wrong way (Jas 4:2–3). The reason he gives is that we are asking for things that enhance our own pleasure. One day my sixteen-year-old son asked me what John 14:13 meant—"Ask anything in my name, and I will do it." I explained God's will and James's clarification that we do not receive because we ask wrongly simply to give ourselves pleasure. He looked a little bummed and said as he walked away, "Then I guess I shouldn't ask for a Jaguar." It is okay to pray for whatever you want. Just determine to be content with what God gives you.

There is a way to pray and to get what you want. James tells us that the prayers of a righteous person accomplish great things. Elijah prayed that it would not rain because of the excessive evil in his day, and it did not rain for three and a half years until he prayed for the drought to end (Jas 5:16–17). Time and again in Scripture we find that God hears and delights in the *righteous* person. Christians must add righteous living to their loving to be effective in prayer. Personal righteousness is vital to effective prayer. Personal righteousness wants what God wants.

In a culture where all people are declared good and sin is either passé because truth is relative or automatically forgiven and grace is presumed, we find it difficult to confess and to repent of sins. Yet James commands Christians to do that very thing, and not just to God but to one another (5:16). Where confession is included in our prayers, it is usually offered only for generalized sin. Confessing and repenting of specific things is difficult because it pierces the heart of our pride and truly humbles us. How we deal with sin affects how we look at forgiveness. Forgiveness without confession and repentance is not automatic, no matter what the culture tells us. More importantly, forgiveness of others is a requirement for our own forgiveness (Matt 6:12, 14–15).

---

46. Bounds, "The Necessity of Prayer," 58–59.
47. Bounds, "The Necessity of Prayer," 59.

Because forgiveness is so pivotal to Christian living and prayer, it is vital that we understand what it is and what it is not. Foster writes, "Forgiveness does not mean that we will cease to hurt. The wounds are deep, and we may hurt for a very long time."[48] It does mean that "just because we continue to experience emotional pain does not mean that we have failed to forgive."[49] Additionally, it is not loving to tell people "forgive and forget." Foster writes, "Forgiveness does not mean that we will forget. That would do violence to our rational faculties."[50] It does mean that "we remember, but in forgiving we no longer use the memory against others."[51] Moreover, "forgiveness is not pretending that the offense did not really matter."[52] Foster counters, "It did matter, and it does matter, and there is no use pretending otherwise. The offense is real, but when we forgive, the offense no longer controls our behavior."[53]

Another misconception he identifies is that "forgiveness is not acting as if things are just the same as before the offense."[54] This might be possible for small offenses, but for things like rape, abuse, or character defamation, this might never be possible. It will take a long time for trust to be rebuilt, if it ever can be. Foster writes that in forgiveness "we must face the fact that things will never be the same. By the grace of God, they can be a thousand times better, but they will never again be the same."[55]

Foster describes forgiveness as "a miracle of grace whereby the offense no longer separates . . . . We will no longer use the offense to drive a wedge between us, hurting and injuring one another . . . . The power of love that holds us together is greater than the power of the offense that separates us."[56] In 2 Corinthians Paul writes about restoring the offending person back into fellowship, but this can only truly occur if there has been genuine repentance on the offender's part and not simply an "I'm sorry I got caught" or "I'm sorry you got hurt" attitude. In the case of abuse, the elders must monitor the situation to be sure the offense does not continue.

Praying for Your Enemies

In Scripture, unforgiveness presents an additional obstacle to Christian prayer—to pray for our enemies. This requires that we forgive and presumes that we understand what that is and what it is not. Moore identifies many strongholds (patterns of thinking built up in our minds, 2 Cor 10:4–5) associated with unforgiveness and writes,

48. Foster, *Prayer*, 187.
49. Foster, *Prayer*, 187.
50. Foster, *Prayer*, 187.
51. Foster, *Prayer*, 187.
52. Foster, *Prayer*, 187.
53. Foster, *Prayer*, 188.
54. Foster, *Prayer*, 188.
55. Foster, *Prayer*, 188.
56. Foster, *Prayer*, 188.

"Left untreated, unforgiveness becomes spiritual cancer. Bitterness takes root, and since the root feeds the rest of the tree, every branch of our lives and every fruit on each limb ultimately become poisoned. Beloved sister or brother, the bottom line is . . . unforgiveness makes us sick. Always spiritually. Often emotionally. And, surprisingly often, physically."[57] She also refers to 2 Corinthians 2:11 where Paul warns Christians to forgive so that Satan does not outwit them because they are not ignorant of his schemes. This presumes a specified set of knowledge.

Unfortunately, since the modern age of reason began, most Christians have relegated Satan to the realm of superstitions, and if they do acknowledge him, they generally ignore him, thereby giving him free reign to work against God and all humanity. Unforgiveness is one of the schemes he uses to divide the church and to make her ineffective. In fact, Moore describes "unforgiveness . . . as one of the most powerfully effective forms of bondage in any believer's life. We cannot tolerate it. Yes, this stronghold demands serious demolition, but the liberty you will feel when you finally let go is inexpressible! Forgiveness is the ultimate 'weight loss'!"[58] This is part of righteous living that affects your prayers.

Jesus includes our enemies in this forgiveness and tells his disciples to love their enemies and to pray for them (Matt 5:43–44). Paul extends this to blessing those who persecute you and commands Christians not to curse them. If you are like me, praying for and blessing my enemies is a really difficult thing to do. In my years of depression, I found it nearly impossible to wish for people who hurt me the very things that God had withheld from me. When most of us think of blessing, what usually comes to mind are things like health, wealth, success, happiness, and all the secular ideas of the good life that come from our culture. After I was delivered from depression and healed of cancer, I had time to study the word of God and my ideas on this changed. I began to look at God's will for people instead of the American dream people have.

God tells Abraham that he would bless him so that all the nations of the world would be blessed through him. That blessing was Abraham's descendant, Jesus, the Savior of the world. Abraham was blessed to be a blessing, and in the Sermon on the Mount, Jesus passed that same blessing on to every one of his children throughout the ages. Christians are blessed to be a blessing to the people of this world, and that includes their enemies. Material blessings may be part of that, but Jesus has in mind so much more.

Just as Jesus is the ultimate blessing to the world through Abraham, now his followers will bless the world with the message of salvation through Jesus. How might that look? Search the Scriptures. Matthew 28:18–20 commands, "Go into all the world and make disciples . . . teaching them to obey everything I have commanded you." Acts 1:8 instructs Christians to wait, "You will receive power when the Holy Spirit comes upon you, and you will be my witnesses in Jerusalem, in all of Judea and

---

57. Moore, *Praying God's Word*, 220.
58. Moore, *Praying God's Word*, 221.

Samaria, and to the ends of the earth." First Timothy 2:4 reveals that God wants all people to be saved and come to a knowledge of the truth. In 2 Corinthians 5:17–20 Paul reminds the church that each person who comes to Christ becomes a new creation and is given God's ministry of reconciling people to him in Jesus. God's people are his ambassadors to the people of the world for the purpose of reconciling them to God through Jesus. Without a doubt, it is God's will for the church to be taking the gospel to all people. Pray this!

With this in mind, how might Christians pray and bless their enemies? Search the Scriptures. One passage I use is 2 Timothy 2:24–26. It is an instruction on how to deal with people who oppose you in the faith. (Of course, this must be done with gentleness and respect.) I have taken the part that talks about the hope for this person and turned it into a prayer for people both inside and outside of the faith who do not understand God's truth. Sometimes I am that person. The prayer is, "Father, may you grant them/us repentance, that they/we will come to their/our senses, know the truth, and be set free from the trap of the devil, who has taken them/us captive to do his will" (adapted from the NIV). I turn it into a blessing simply by beginning it with "may they be granted repentance . . ." In this way, I find that I can genuinely pray for and bless my enemies in accordance with God's will. You may find other verses that apply to your situation.

Summary

We have had a *brief* survey of biblical prayer.[59] It is obvious that God looks for prayer from his people as an invitation to work on behalf of his kingdom and his people. Without it, people are exposed to being deceived and enslaved to the philosophies of this age and the evil one behind it. However, as with holiness, righteousness, and judgment, effective prayer has become a lost art among most Christians, but the Bible is clear: if we want God to extend his kingdom and to intervene to end terrorism and the senseless murder of children in our schools, and people of all ages in our malls, concerts, and workplaces, his people must pray.

Christians tend to look at the prayers of prophets like Moses and Elijah and think that they cannot pray like that, but that is where they are wrong. After Jesus went back to heaven, God sent the Holy Spirit to dwell in each Christian. Because of this, each Christian has the same power that raised Jesus from the dead residing in him or her. The church must begin to pray to recover this wonderful truth and to act on it. Bounds calls prayer "the keynote of the most sanctified life, of the holiest ministry. He does the most for God who is the highest skilled in prayer," and reminds us that "Jesus Christ

---

59. There is much more that could have been said. To begin, you might consider Brueggemann, *Great Prayers of the Old Testament*; Spangler, *Praying the Names of God*; and Lewis, *Reflections on the Psalms*.

exercised his ministry after this order."⁶⁰ He lived a sinless life and prayed long hours before making decisions or performing miracles.

The place to begin to recover this kind of prayer is to study the Scriptures in order to know God's character and will and then to use the knowledge found there to live a holy or sanctified life out of which will flow powerfully effective prayers. Bounds cautions, "Beautiful theories are marred by ugly lives. The most difficult as well as the most impressive point in piety is to live it."⁶¹ James tells us that the prayers of the righteous person are effective. This is found again and again in Paul and the Psalms (1, 15, 24, 27, etc.). So, a good place to begin to pray is with prayers of repentance for personal sin. Bounds reminds us that "repentance means to quit doing wrong and learn to do well. A repentance which does not result in pure conduct is a delusion," and he calls for prayer from "holy inflamed hearts" based on earnest desire and faith.⁶² Forgiveness and prayer for one's enemies are also essential to effective prayer. In the next chapter we will examine prayers that God desires for the revival and reformation of our culture.

---

60. Bounds, "The Purpose of Prayer," 300.
61. Bounds, "The Purpose of Prayer," 346.
62. Foster, *Prayer*, 346–47.

Chapter 16

Prayer for Revival and Reformation of the Culture

> The church seems almost wholly unaware of the power God puts into her hand. . . . Prayer is our most formidable weapon, but the one in which we are the least skilled, the most averse to its use. We do everything else for the heathen save the thing God wants us to do; the only thing which does any good—makes all else we do efficient.
>
> —E. M. BOUNDS, PURPOSE IN PRAYER

GOD'S WILL . . . THAT is the singular greatest prayer the church can pray. At the top of God's will is prayer for people's salvation. Jesus saw the lost people and had compassion on them, describing them as helpless and hurting, like sheep without a shepherd (Matt 9:35ff). He declared that the field was ripe for the harvest, meaning there were souls ready to enter God's kingdom, but there were not enough workers to bring them all in by telling them the kingdom of God was here in Jesus. He commanded his disciples to pray that the Lord of the harvest would raise up workers for this task.

In this passage, E. M. Bounds sees prayer as the key to growing God's kingdom and writes, "God's gospel has always waited more on prayer than on anything else for its successes. A praying church is strong though poor in all besides. A prayer-less church is weak though rich in all besides. Only praying hearts will build God's kingdom."[1] Jesus commanded the disciples to pray for the Lord of the harvest to send more laborers who will tell people the good news. If his disciples do not do their job in communicating the gospel, people will not hear and will not be saved from the consequences of their sins. It begins with prayer. But many Christians today are distracted by the things our culture offers them: entertainment, power, lust, and so on.

Since the fall, prayer has always gone before and made the way for God to work in the world. A hundred and twenty disciples spent the time between Ascension and Pentecost praying, and three thousand were brought into the kingdom of God in one day. Paul asks for prayer that the gospel would go forward and bear fruit and that he would be able to proclaim it as he should (Eph 6:19–20). Paul, who was imprisoned, beaten and left for dead, and run out of town on several occasions, attributes God's favor in

---

1. Bounds, "The Reality of Prayer," 293.

deliverance from the schemes of evil men to the prayers of the church (2 Cor 1:10–11). This has led E. M. Bounds to declare that "prayer became a settled and only condition to move his [God's] son's kingdom.... The secret of success in Christ's kingdom is the ability to pray.... The most important lesson we can learn is how to pray."[2]

This is not just his opinion; it comes from Scripture. When Israel wandered away from God and problems abounded, the way out was prayer. Second Chronicles 7:14–16 tells us that if God's people will humble themselves and pray and seek God's face, his favor, and repent of their evil ways, then he will hear their prayers and heal their land. What Scripture calls "healing the land" is today referred to as revival and reform.

R. C. Sproul helps us to understand the difference between the two. Revival brings "a renewal of spiritual life" in individual lives and perhaps local communities. Reformation describes "a renewal of the forms and structures of society and culture;" Sproul asserts that "it is not possible to have true reformation without first having true revival. The renewal of spiritual life under the power of the Holy Spirit is a necessary condition for reformation but not a sufficient condition for it."[3] Revival is a work of the Holy Spirit in a local group at a specific time, and there may be many. Revivals are necessary but do not constitute reformation, which is broader and affects the culture around it. Sproul views Jonathan Edwards's *Distinguishing Marks*, written to critique the Revival of 1734, as "a map to follow for all such periods of revival and for that reason is of abiding value for us today."[4]

As American congregations face declining numbers of attendees, any hope for a revival of the "good old days" when going to church was the thing to do has long passed. However, many continue to run the same programs offering the same propositions and arguments that worked sixty years ago. Increasingly churches are taking a new approach based on fellowship times and the new technology with some success. If you are looking for a program or steps to follow to bring revival and to reform the church and culture, this is not what you are going to get. Revival and reform cannot be reduced to rules and regulations of dos and don'ts. They are moves of God founded on the truth of Scripture, worked out in the power of the Holy Spirit, and set in motion by prevailing prayers of the saints.

We all want things to be better, but few are willing to change to bring it about. Is the church ready to humble herself, to confess and to repent of her sins, and to pray? Walter Kaiser claims that the need for repentance "has not grown any less in our day. It is still too easy to put off God's call for holiness of life in every sector of acting and thinking by pointing to a much more sensate and wicked culture than we as a believing community practice. But that never was the point: the measurement of holiness was the character of God."[5] The church must stop measuring her righteous-

---

2. Bounds, "The Purpose of Prayer," 300.
3. Sproul and Parrish, *Spirit of Revival*, 17.
4. Sproul and Parrish, *Spirit of Revival*, 19, 22.
5. Kaiser, *Revive Us Again*, 181.

ness by the world around her and see how it stacks up with God's holy standards in order to pray effectively.

Prayer and Revival

Prayer is one more example of how the Western church fails to live up to biblical standards. Prayer meetings are almost nonexistent, and if people do gather for prayer, it is more likely to be comprised of singing, Scripture reading, and preaching than actual praying. Each year National and World Days of Prayer are offered. They are poorly attended and look very much like what I just described. Kaiser identifies three characteristics that will be present in the church and the surrounding culture that reveal the need for revival prayer. First there will be a "consistent lack of obedience to the will of God among Christians." Second, when this happens specific events will be taking place in the culture that will signal the necessity for revival prayer: "When the wicked become bold, insolent, reckless, and arrogant in establishing new lows for morality and godlessness, righteousness has suffered a staggering blow because of the laxity of professing Christians. Such a time will be filled with terrorists, murderers, extortionists, crooks, thieves, whoremongers, and haters of God."[6] Third, he includes preaching as a sign in this need for revival and writes, "When the pulpit fails to declare the whole counsel of God and turns, instead, to pop psychology, self-realization talks, and identity types of searches in sermonettes, be sure that the populace, both inside the church and outside it, will see all hell break loose just as Moses witnessed after a mere forty-day hiatus of his presence and preaching while he was on Mount Sinai receiving the Ten Commandments."[7] Kaiser has one more criterion to assess the need for revival prayer and states, "Things had indeed become critical when the same evil that society was guilty of was also commonly reported in the household of faith . . . . This sign more than any other barometer of wickedness is the one that sounds the alarm, supposing there are any left who still have enough spiritual discernment to hear it."[8] This assessment will be difficult for many twenty-first-century Western Christians to hear because they have ignored God's holiness and righteousness and skewed their understanding of his love to accommodate Enlightenment philosophies.

In the previous section we examined the difference between revival and reformation as given by Sproul. Now we will examine more specifically what revival is and how to discern when you are in or have been in one. Kaiser describes it as a "time when believers witness an extraordinary work of God enlivening, strengthening, and elevating the spiritual life and vitality already possessed, but which life is now in a state of decline and is feeble, mediocre, and dull in its outworking. Revivals come as

---

6. Kaiser, *Revive Us Again*, 8–9.

7. Kaiser, *Revive Us Again*, 29. Walter Kaiser Jr. is not a hell-fire-and-brimstone Christian. He is a loving and fun grandpa-like man who loves Jesus and the church.

8. Kaiser, *Revive Us Again*, 62.

'times of refreshing from the Lord' (Acts 3:19)."[9] Bounds observes that "to look back over the progress of the divine kingdom upon earth is to review revival periods which have come like refreshing showers upon dry and thirsty ground, making the desert to blossom as the rose." Revivals always bring "new eras of spiritual life and activity just when the church had fallen under the influence of the apathy of the times and needed to be aroused to a new sense of her duty and responsibility."[10]

Richard Lovelace, commenting on Edwards's "Faithful Narrative," defines revival as "an outpouring of the Spirit which restores the people of God to *normal spiritual life* after a period of corporate declension" (italics are mine).[11] These "periods of spiritual decline occur in history because the gravity of indwelling sin keeps pulling believers first into formal religion and then into open apostasy. Periods of awakening alternate with these as God graciously breathes new life into his people."[12] Therefore, he surmises that "every major advance of the kingdom of God on earth is signaled and brought about by a general outpouring of the Holy Spirit."[13] And every outpouring of the Spirit is preceded by prayer and accurate preaching of the gospel of truth.

Prayer and accurate preaching must go forth hand in hand. Prayer empowers the preaching and changes God to change people. The gospel must be communicated clearly and accurately to the next generation or the love of the world settles in their hearts, and they are enticed by the comfort and entertainment they see there. The reality of heaven and the comfort, joy, beauty, peace, love, and righteousness found there can only be seen through a relationship with Jesus. Christians must reflect his joy, beauty, and the rest to reveal to people what they are missing, but only the Holy Spirit can change hearts.

Only prayer moves God's Spirit to move on our behalf. Bounds tells us why and writes, "All revivals are dependent on God, but in revivals, as in other things, he invites and requires the assistance of man, and the full result is obtained when there is cooperation between the divine and the human . . . . God and man unite for the task, the *response of the divine being invariably in proportion to the desire and effort of the human*" (italics are mine).[14] He continues, "All true revivals have been born in prayer. When God's people become so concerned about the state of religion that they lie on their faces day and night in earnest supplication, the blessing will be sure to fall"; then he adds, "Every revival of which we have any record has been bathed in prayer."[15] He goes on to mention Shotts, Scotland, in 1630, Mr. Moody, Charles

---

9. Kaiser, *Revive Us Again*, 21.
10. Bounds, "The Purpose of Prayer," 359.
11. Lovelace, *Dynamics of Spiritual Life*, 40.
12. Lovelace, *Dynamics of Spiritual Life*, 40.
13. Lovelace, *Dynamics of Spiritual Life*, 40.
14. Bounds, "The Purpose of Prayer," 360.
15. Bounds, "The Purpose of Prayer," 362.

Finney, and George Whitefield; additionally there were the first, second, and third Great Awakenings in America.

The mid-eighteenth century witnessed great revivals on both sides of the Atlantic that were preceded by great concerts of prayer. In Europe, the Moravians began a 24/7 prayer vigil in 1727 that lasted a hundred years. Out of this grew a great missionary movement that reached the American colonies and subsequently changed the course of the lives of John and Charles Wesley and George Whitefield, who were instrumental in revivals in both Great Britain and the American colonies (the Great Awakening was spearheaded by Whitefield). Lovelace attributes two additional movements occurring in the twentieth century to their prayer: "the Evangelicalism of Lausanne and the ecumenism of the World Council of Churches."[16]

Prior to and independent of the Great Awakening, Northampton, Massachusetts, and her pastor, Jonathan Edwards, experienced revival in 1734. He documented this revival and the Great Awakening that followed a few years later.[17] What he and his church found was that "they suddenly became aware that their problem was not isolated acts of conscious disobedience to God, but *a deep aversion to God at the root of their personalities*, an aversion which left them in unconscious bondage to unbelief, selfishness, jealousy and other underlying complexes of sin" (italics are mine).[18] You may not think of yourself as having an aversion to God, but consider what they discovered. It was not the conscious sins we usually identify. What had interfered with their faith and left them in *unconscious* bondage was that they had become "respectable, and they had a kind of rote orthodoxy . . . but their ultimate concerns were not God and his kingdom, but land and the pursuit of affluence."[19] Lovelace describes the condition of the church on both sides of the Atlantic at this time as having "a pattern of formal, moralistic, worldly 'churchianity' that was *steadily accommodating itself to the process of secularization*. Manners and morals seemed to be declining in both continents, and the Industrial Revolution was intensifying existing social problems and creating new ones" (italics are mine).[20] This condition is very much like what we find in twenty-first-century America and has been augmented by the technology available to us. It is entirely possible that just as superior as our current technology is over the technology of the Industrial Revolution, so is the greater depth to which manners, morals, and social problems, old and new, have fallen.

Concerning the Northampton revival and the Great Awakening, Edwards had much to say about the role of prayer: "There is no way that Christians in a private

---

16. Lovelace, *Dynamics of Spiritual Life*, 37.

17. See Edwards, "A Faithful Narrative"; *Distinguishing Marks*; and "Religious Affections." These may be found at The Works of Jonathan Edwards online, Jonathan Edwards Center of Yale University. Taking John's command to test the spirits to see what sort they are, he does an amazing job of discerning the work of God in revival that remains valid today.

18. Lovelace, *Dynamics of Spiritual Life*, 37.

19. Lovelace, *Dynamics of Spiritual Life*, 36–7.

20. Lovelace, *Dynamics of Spiritual Life*, 46.

capacity can do so much to promote the work of God, and advance the kingdom of Christ, as by prayer."[21] He writes, "There should be an agreement of all God's people in America . . . to keep a day of fasting and prayer to God." The purpose for this day (as in one day a month or one day a week, not simply a single day and done) of united prayer is threefold. First, God's people are to confess "our past long continued lukewarmness and unprofitableness." Second, they are "to address the Father of mercies, with prayers and supplications, and earnest cries, that he would guide and direct his own people, and that he would continue and still carry on this work [of revival and reconciliation]." Third, they are to petition God to "more abundantly and extensively pour out his Spirit; and particularly that he would pour out his Spirit upon ministers." In this petition for the Holy Spirit to be poured out they would ask "that he [God] would bow the heavens and come down [2 Sam 22:10; Ps 18:9], and erect his glorious kingdom through the earth."[22] Edwards believed these concerts of prayer would greatly encourage God's saints and would be the source of abundant rejoicing of all to be praying in unity and agreement. He cites Matthew 18:19, "Again I say unto you, that if any two of you shall agree on earth as touching anything that they shall ask, it shall be done for them of my Father which is in heaven."

Edwards believed the first responsibility of every Christian was to pray to advance God's kingdom and wrote, "[It] is God's will, through his wonderful grace, that the prayers of his saints should be one great and principal means of carrying on the designs of Christ's kingdom in the world."[23] With the advent of rationalism in Modernity, faith in prayer declined. As prayer declined, the power and the authority of the church gradually faded. God poured out his Spirit in isolated places like Azusa Street, the Evangelist Billy Graham's ministry, and the Charismatic movement, but mainline churches dramatically declined in the 1960s and continue the decline today. The decline is also being felt in some evangelical churches, but I am getting ahead of myself.

Despite the revivals, "by the end of the [eighteenth] century the evangelicals sensed an inner loss of power along with the challenge from the growing antichristian force of Enlightenment humanism."[24] This should sound familiar (see chapters 1–5). Could it be that during the Revolutionary War prayers were directed away from the pouring out of the Spirit for the advancement of God's kingdom? The solution was not people pulling themselves up by their bootstraps, reading self-help books, and simply working harder as Modernists would suggest. What was needed was an outpouring of God's Holy Spirit to bring conviction and confession of sin accompanied by genuine repentance, but the increasing influence of Modernity's emphasis on reason of the human mind and science gradually quenched the Spirit and the prayer for his being poured out on us.

21. Edwards, *The Great Awakening*, 518. (Hereafter cited as WJE 4:page number).
22. WJE 4:520.
23. WJE 4:516.
24. Lovelace, *Dynamics of Spiritual Life*, 46.

Volumes have been written about the Holy Spirit, and we cannot go into any great depth here other than to say that without the Holy Spirit's lead and work, the church becomes impotent, unable to reproduce, and certainly incapable of converting more than a handful of people to faith in Jesus Christ her Lord and Savior (and technically, these few are only by God's work). In John 14–16 Jesus speaks at length on the Holy Spirit's coming after his death and resurrection and says it is a good thing. It is the Spirit's job to convict people of sin, to teach them the truth, and to overcome the power in the world like he did at the resurrection. Paul prays for the Ephesians to know that the same power that raised Jesus from the dead is in them (Eph 1:13, 18–20). This is why Jesus could say that his disciples would do everything he did and greater.[25]

At the Ascension, Jesus commanded his disciples to wait for the promised Holy Spirit before they tried to take the gospel into all the world, making disciples and baptizing them (Acts 1:4–8; Luke 28:18–20). The hundred and twenty men and women spent those ten days praying. On Pentecost, the Spirit was poured out on the disciples and three thousand people came to saving faith in Jesus that day. It is not by accident that the fastest growing Christian movement today is global Pentecostalism, which operates in the Holy Spirit, while the mainline denominations that try to control the Spirit by allowing only what makes sense to human reason are dying. The move of the Spirit is always suspect to those who would be respectable and rely only on what makes rational sense. Behind this opposition is always the question of who is in control.

Lovelace attributes the Revival of 1734 and the Great Awakening to the work of the Holy Spirit and writes, "As the Holy Spirit opened the eyes of their hearts and illuminated theological concepts, the opaque orthodoxy of the laity suddenly became a transparent medium for vision through which they saw the glory of God. The gravity of covetousness which had drawn their hearts to earthly concerns was reversed . . . . The Word of God [Scripture] suddenly had free course in congregational worship"; sermons were alive, and hymn singing became a joy instead of a duty.[26]

God knew what he was doing when he jumpstarted the Great Awakening in a church with a pastor who did not stop the working of the Spirit but was able to discern what was and was not of God and was also able to communicate that to others. Essentially, the bottom line for the discernment of a work of God is not the excitement but the fruit that it bears.[27] What matters is changed lives! Edwards looked for the fruits of the Spirit (love, joy, peace, patience, kindness, gentleness, faithfulness, and longsuffering). He also included honesty, truth, and agreement

---

25. For more information on the Holy Spirit see Torrey, *The Person and Work of the Holy Spirit*; Spurgeon, *Holy Spirit Power*; Deere, *Surprised by the Power of the Spirit*; Long and McMurry, *Receiving the Power*; Brunner, *A Theology of the Holy Spirit*; and Graham, *The Holy Spirit*.

26. Lovelace, *Dynamics of Spiritual Life*, 38.

27. Edwards explained that revival often looked messy because when a sinful person comes into the presence of a Holy God, their reactions can be intense. His "Faithful Narrative," *Distinguishing Marks*, and "Religious Affections" are important reads for people interested in revival.

with Scripture. In short, what mattered was that the people were pursuing holiness in their everyday lives and that it lasted.

About a decade later, the same thing happened in Cambuslang, Scotland, with a pastor named William M'Culloch. Pastors John M'Laurin from Glasgow and James Robe from Kilsyth joined in support of the revival. M'Laurin wrote to the pastors in New England who had been involved in the 1734 revival in Northampton. Soon Edwards's "Faithful Narrative" was published and read in Scotland as a model of revival. M'Laurin's purpose in this "was to awaken praise in the godly, to allay prejudice and fears in others, and that posterity should also reap some benefit. He was concerned primarily with fact and a strict regard for truth and exactness."[28] Five years later, Robe documented that not one of the forty people in his church touched by the revival had returned to their former behaviors. Sanctification was still very much evident in their lives. Truth, honesty, and love persisted decades after the emotional events died away.

At this time Edwards was calling for "concerts of prayer," where people on both sides of the pond would pray at the same time for revival. In Scotland, "numerous societies for prayer were established, every member undergoing examination by the minister and some of the elders before being admitted. Almost every household practiced family worship."[29] John Sutherland, a pastor from Golspie, lamented his lack of success with revival in his church and was informed "that societies for prayer lay behind any good achieved." Sutherland established three such groups for prayer that met every Saturday, and soon he reported seventy people who had been spiritually awakened.[30] Many letters of encouragement crossed the Atlantic between New England and Scotland concerning revival; "notable amongst these inspirations was the concept of the Concert for Prayer."[31] The concurrent revivals taking place in England, Scotland, and New England were all outgrowths of prayer. (See appendix 6 for suggestions on how to organize this kind of prayer.) If you organize concerts of prayer, be careful not to quench the Spirit when God begins to pour him out on you. It may look different from what you are used to seeing. It might be a little messy. Learn to test the spirits using the discernment discussed here.

Prayer and Spiritual Warfare

However, not everyone agreed that it was God's movement. Edwards, Whitefield, the Wesleys, and others ran into stiff opposition by the well-established churches of Boston, England, Scotland, and elsewhere. Whitefield, the Wesleys, and others in England "were

---

28. Fawcett, *Cambuslang Revival*, 126.

29. Fawcett, *Cambuslang Revival*, 135. For additional information on how Christians can come together for spiritual awakening and world evangelization see Bryant, *Concerts of Prayer*; and Edwards, *A Call to United, Extraordinary Prayer*.

30. Fawcett, *Cambuslang Revival*, 137.

31. Fawcett, *Cambuslang Revival*, 142.

barred from Anglican congregations because the Reformation doctrine they preached had become so strange to the contemporary church [so they] began preaching outdoors to thousands of hearers in the coal-mining districts."[32] In America, pastors would travel to Northampton to observe for themselves what was happening with the intention of discrediting the revival but always went away excited that God was truly moving and wanting the same thing for their congregations. This brings us to an area of Christianity most churches today would rather ignore or outright deny in favor of the world's love and rational thinking. This is spiritual warfare.

Volumes have been written either promoting it or denying it. Some are balanced; many lean to one extreme or the other like people tend to do. Scripture is clear. Satan is the prince of this world, and although he was dealt a fatal blow at the resurrection, he is still at work in this world to steal, kill, and destroy the work of God and to take as many people with him to hell as he possibly can. He prefers to work unnoticed, building up strongholds of belief systems in the minds of people that contradict Scripture and holy living. He appears as an angel of light and is the master of deception by mixing some truth with as many lies as he can get you to believe. Those who do his bidding may appear to be morally good people, but Scripture labels them false teachers, false prophets, and false apostles because they mix false theology with truth and lead people away from the true gospel.

The devil is real. Jesus called the devil a murderer and the father of lies (John 8). As an outgrowth of these lies, Jesus warned (Matthew 24) that as his return approached deceptions would prevail so strongly that even God's elect children would be deceived, if that were possible. One way to avoid deception is to be aware of the devil's schemes. Paul tells the Corinthians that they know what these are, but I am not at all sure the twenty-first-century American church knows them. Too often unrepentance, unforgiveness, unholy living, and love for the world characterize her people. Too often she embraces ungodly deeds and criticizes those trying to follow Scripture. Too often she looks just like the un-churched, and Satan has a heyday destroying her unity, peace, and witness to the people of the world.

Edwards discovered this at the end of the Revival of 1734, which was why he was so determined to write *Religious Affections* to identify, to discern, and to defend the work of God in the Great Awakening. In these works, Lovelace finds that "revival involved a spiritual struggle in which every advance of renewal would involve severe conflict with fallen human nature and the powers of darkness." The reason for this is that "revival involves the displacement of the world, the flesh and the devil . . . [that brings] great spiritual agitation in which troop movements on both sides are dimly visible in the background. As the sun shining on a swamp produces mist, the rising of the countenance of God among his people may result initially in disorders and confusion."[33]

---

32. Lovelace, *Dynamics of Spiritual Life*, 39.
33. Lovelace, *Dynamics of Spiritual Life*, 41.

Lovelace reports the reason for this conflict and agitation is because "the devil, who is losing ground as the revival progresses, fights back in a number of ways." You can recognize his activity by the strategies he uses, such as accusation and infiltration. "He may attack the subjects of revival directly and internally with despair and discouragement; Edwards saw this happen at the close of the first Northampton revival in 1734." Additionally "he [the devil] may plant lies, caricatures or stereotypes in the minds of unbelievers or not-yet-revived Christians so that they will reject the work of God and attack its progress." Whenever possible, "he will set the leaders of the revival against one another in this way in order to divide and conquer. To create evidence to corroborate accusations he will overbalance the zeal of converts and cause them to run to extremes." "Finally, he will sow tares among the wheat in the form of counterfeit revivals, leading people to confound these with the real work which is in progress and to discredit it."[34]

To put it in more modern terms, the devil is a liar and the author of all crimes committed against children and everyone else. He is the accuser who keeps playing those tapes in your mind of all the bad things you have ever done. He is the discourager who tells you that you are worthless and will never amount to anything. He is behind school shootings and abuse of every kind, oppressive behaviors such as racism, and the destruction of family life. And if he can get people to turn against and to blame God, so much the better; he has won the battle. He doesn't stop there but works to bring division between people and especially God's children who are making progress in following Jesus. He will appeal to their pride or God working through them and their knowledge of God's truth so that they will exalt themselves or think they have a corner on God's truth or begin to take credit for the work God is doing.

For all of this, the church often claims to believe that Satan exists, but chooses not to acknowledge him with the excuse that she does not want to give him power by talking about him. However, by not dealing with him, he is allowed to exercise all his power unopposed over an unsuspecting church and culture. Again, Christians are on that pendulum of one extreme or the other when they should be doing the difficult work of acknowledging Satan and evil and taking an informed spiritual stand against him/it. What you do proves what you really believe.

Beth Moore along with many of us has learned the hard way that, "tragically, Satan has successfully duped the vast majority of our churches into imbalance regarding all things concerning or threatening him." She recognizes that "our human natures are drawn like magnets to polar points" and that "we unfortunately apply our fleshly extremes to our pulpits."[35] She applies this extremist tendency either to see a demon in every disorder or to ignore them altogether and writes, "I cannot say this strongly enough: it is imperative in the days in which we've been assigned to occupy this earth that believers walk in truth and soundness of doctrine. Just as Christ

---

34. Lovelace, *Dynamics of Spiritual Life*, 41.
35. Moore, *Praying God's Word*, 309.

warned in Matthew 24, we are living in days characterized by a rampant increase of deception and wickedness."[36] Moore points out that Satan knows the Bible far better than we do and knows Christ's return is near (Rev 12:12). She warns, "Therefore, he [Satan] has moved into comparative nuclear arms in his war against us while we're still using popguns in our war against him.... A war of unprecedented proportions is waging against the Church and the people of God." The solution is to "put on our armor, learn how to use our weapons, and fight with the confidence of those who know they are destined to win."[37] Moore calls the church to use the weapons she has been given, which we will examine below. She also charges Christians to pursue righteousness, which God's word makes clear is his primary will for their personal lives and the basis for all effective prayer.

Spiritual warfare is scriptural. Jesus took Satan seriously: he tempted Jesus in the wilderness; Jesus called him the prince of this world who orchestrated the crucifixion; and Jesus cast out demons who are part of Satan's entourage. Peter (1 Pet 5:8) warns that the devil, Satan, goes about like a roaring lion looking for people to devour. Paul warns the Roman Christians (chapter 10) that they were in a battle with the forces of evil (principalities and powers), but that the weapons they use are not the weapons of the world: fear, threats, fighting, brute force, name-calling, getting even, vengeance, and the like, but they have divine power to tear down strongholds.

Paul tells us what these weapons are and charges the Ephesian Christians (chapter 6) to put on the *whole* armor of God. This begins with salvation, which is worn as a helmet to protect their minds from deceptions. Next God's people are to live righteous lives and put it on as a breastplate, which will protect the body's vital organs. Christians are to wear truth like a belt around their waists into which they can tuck their long robes, enabling them to be ready for action. They are to have studied Scripture and be prepared with the gospel, which brings peace with God. They are to carry the shield of faith, which is to be used every day and not just at the moment of salvation. Additionally, it is not so much the amount of faith that matters. They only need to believe what God says even if their faith is the size of a mustard seed. Therefore, when they believe texts like Psalm 91 that tells them God's faithfulness to his people is their shield, their perception of the shield will go from a small round shield that covers very little of the body from the fiery darts of the enemy (Satan's attacks often in the form of lies and accusations) to a large, curved, rectangular shield that covers the entire person.

Scholars have noted that all of this equipment is defensive, and it is. Christians are given only two offensive weapons with which to wage the spiritual war in which they find themselves. The first is the word of God described as the sword of the Spirit. Hebrews 4:12 informs us that the word of God is "sharper than a two-edged sword" that can separate even the marrow from the bones. Scripture exposes falsehood and replaces it with truth. It judges the thoughts and attitudes of the heart.

36. Moore, *Praying God's Word*, 309–10.
37. Moore, *Praying God's Word*, 310.

When Jesus returns to reclaim the world he is described as having a sword coming out of his mouth. This is not a literal sword but portrays the power of the words he will speak and the means of his victory. On a smaller scale this is exactly what happens when Christians speak the word of Truth in the guidance and power of the Spirit of Truth who is released by God in response to the prayers of his people for the pouring out of the Spirit for revival. The people of the world will respond. Satan cannot defend against that. The only thing he can do is to try to obfuscate the message, to create fear and discouragement in the hearts of people, or to create distractions so that either the message does not go forward or is not heard. Such is the power of God's word, which is why Satan is so keen to have people believe it is full of errors, outdated, or unreliable so that it falls into disuse.

Many have claimed that the word of God is the only offensive weapon Christians have, but I would have to disagree. While Paul has ended his description of the armor, we have not yet uncovered the purpose for wearing that armor. In Ephesians 6:18–20 (NIV) Paul reveals what that is. He says put on the whole armor of God "and pray in the Spirit on all occasions with all kinds of prayers and requests. With this in mind, be alert and always keep on praying for all the saints. Pray also for me, that whenever I open my mouth, words may be given me so that I will fearlessly make known the mystery of the gospel.... Pray that I may declare it fearlessly, as I should." If Christians prayed like this for each other and their pastors, what a difference they would see in the power and effectiveness in their preaching and their own witness! (See appendix 7: "Put on the Armor of God.")

Summary

The purpose of these last two chapters is to equip the church for kingdom prayer that moves God to pour out his Spirit for revival and reformation. The best known prayer is the Lord's Prayer. It is a model for all prayer that usually begins with praise and adoration of God and moves to petitions, intercessions, and confessions in the middle. It will usually close with thanksgiving to and adoration of God. Much has been said about petitionary prayer and especially as it connects with illness and suffering, and rightly so—it is needed—but that is not the focus here. For a balanced treatment of suffering and prayer I would recommend to you Joni Eareckson Tada's book, *A Place of Healing*, and Jerry Sittser's book, *When God Doesn't Answer Your Prayer*. Both speak from a place of deep pain and healing and unanswered prayer and will answer your questions better than I could in these few paragraphs.

There are people who seem to have a genuine gift of praying, but do not let that deter you from praying if you are not one of them. Jesus said that "if two of you on earth agree about anything they ask for, it will be done for them by my Father in heaven" (Matt 18:19, NIV). This is why corporate prayer is vital. The bulk of prayer will most likely be done in the prayer closet (private prayer), but times must also be set aside for corporate prayer. Edwards and the pastors of the Great Awakening found this to be true. God has always worked in response to his people's prayers (Judges, 2 Chronicles 7:14–15). Learn to discern the work of God when he does respond so you do not shut down what God is doing.

So then, prayer is the only way to advance God's kingdom. Bounds affirms that "praying apostles make preaching apostles. Prayer gives edge, entrance, and weight to the Word."[38] Foster uses Ephesians to prove this position and writes, "Christ's heavenly position of authority (Eph. 1) gives us our heavenly position of authority (Eph. 2), which results in the ability to wage the warfare of the Lamb against all principalities and powers (Eph. 6). We exercise Authoritative Prayer from this heavenly position of authority."[39] The power behind this authority is the Holy Spirit, who is at work in God's people to will and to do God's pleasure, when they allow it. This is God's prescription for bringing in the harvest and advancing his kingdom. He has no other plan and no other means. The church must test the spirits and learn to discern what is of God and what is not, like Edwards and the New England and Scottish pastors did.

Foster defines authoritative (also called spiritual warfare) prayer as being "focused primarily upon coming against the principalities and powers of this present darkness [Eph 6:12]," which he feels is necessary because "underneath the organized structures of injustice and oppression are the principalities."[40] Foster believes the real power behind oppression, violence, and abuse today is the principalities and powers of which Paul speaks. He insists that "aiding and abetting the sexual violence and the race hate and the child molestation that are such a part of modern society are diabolical powers of destruction and brutality."[41] He concludes therefore that when we face oppression, cruelty, or opposition to the gospel, "we are also dealing with cosmic principalities and powers that are straight from the pit."[42]

Bounds would agree and writes, "Prayer . . . is a disinfectant and a preventive. It purifies the air; it destroys the contagion of evil . . . . It is a voice which goes into God's ear and it lives as long as God's ear is open to holy pleas, as long as God's heart is alive to holy things."[43] He claims that our prayers are eternal and reminds us that "God shapes the world by prayer. Prayers are deathless. The lips that uttered them may be closed in death, the heart that felt them may have ceased to beat, but the prayers live before God, and God's heart is set on them."[44] Prayer is never a waste of time but continues to bear fruit long after we have left this world.

---

38. Bounds, "The Reality of Prayer," 293.
39. Foster, *Prayer*, 239.
40. Foster, *Prayer*, 239.
41. Foster, *Prayer*, 239–40.
42. Foster, *Prayer*, 240.
43. Bounds, "The Purpose of Prayer," 299.
44. Bounds, "The Purpose of Prayer," 299.

I will leave you with Bounds's observation on the church and prayer, which I believe is still valid today. He reminds us that as partners in God's work Christians are "in not a little measure responsible for the conditions . . . around us." He asks, "Are we concerned about the coldness of the church? Do we *grieve* over the lack of conversions? Does our *soul go out to God in midnight cries for the outpouring of his Spirit*?" (italics are mine).[45] If the answer is no, then "part of the blame [for the way things are] lies at our door. If we do our part, God will do his. Around us is a world lost in sin, above us is a God willing and able to save; it is ours to build the bridge that links heaven and earth, and prayer is the mighty instrument that does the work."[46]

"And so the old cry comes to us with insistent voice, 'Pray, brethren, pray.'"[47]

---

45. Bounds, "The Purpose of Prayer," 363.
46. Bounds, "The Purpose of Prayer," 363.
47. Bounds, "The Purpose of Prayer," 363.

Chapter 17

Earmarks of Revival

> And we also thank God constantly for this, that when you received the word of God, which you heard from us, you accepted it not as the word of men but as what it really is, the word of God, which is at work in you believers.
>
> —1 Thessalonians 2:13, ESV

COULD THERE BE ANOTHER Great Awakening in America? In this chapter we will examine the earmarks of true revival and what the opposition to it might look like. Postmodernity has been influencing culture for fifty-plus years—at the pace of the Information Age that is the equivalent of centuries—certainly long enough to give people time to create a sense that "we have always done things this way." Is it becoming the "old way"? Could it be that people are beginning to realize this way of life leads to a dead end? Mark Shaw believes that the first indication of the death of the old way (in this case Modernity, Reason, Postmodernity, and beyond) can be seen in "bizarre, antisocial behavior" of younger generations in which "alcoholism, marital breakdown, and other signs of severe cultural stress become widespread.... There is a desperate need for a new paradigm, a new map of reality that will help people get unstuck."[1] To alcoholism, I would add drugs, pornography, abuse, the slave trade, and violence. Christians want God to bring the change that gets people unstuck. Historically it has been called revival; it is God's work, conducted by the Holy Spirit, and it always begins with his work in his people.

According to Shaw, Jonathan Edwards, in his writings on revival, offers us the map by pointing us to the essentials of Christianity.[2] Shaw writes that "in this vision of revival and its potential ... Edwards was way ahead of his time."[3] What will revival

---

1. Shaw, *Global Awakening*, 25–26.

2. We have seen in the last chapter how revivals in Scotland and Wales were influenced by Edwards's writings.

3. Shaw, *Global Awakening*, 214. God jump-started the Great Awakening in the town of Northampton, Massachusetts, in 1734–35. Jonathan Edwards was the pastor who is usually known only for his sermon "Sinners in the Hands of an Angry God." He is often called America's only true theologian who wrote extensively about Christian theology. His works on revivals were used both on this continent and in England, Scotland, and Wales. They are worth reading to this day: "Faithful Narrative," *Distinguishing Marks*, "Some Thoughts," and *Religious Affections* (these are the short titles). I will draw

look like? To begin, Edwards writes that the beauty of Christianity and the glory of the good news is that they are holy; it is a holy religion with holy doctrines, holy Scriptures, and a holy gospel.[4] Revival stirs up what he calls true religious affections, which he describes as the strong inclinations and will of the soul in a person. They discern and determine the things in which he or she delights and enjoys or finds grief and sorrow. They drive our likes and dislikes and decide what we choose or reject. It is these affections that tell us that we want what we want even if our minds cannot tell us why. They are different from passion, which he describes as "more violent, and the mind more overpowered, and less in its own command."[5]

Edwards's premise is "true religion [Christianity], in great part, consists in holy affections"[6] because they are true, pure, excellent, beautiful, loving, and joyful—all the things we have come to recognize as belonging to holiness. Therefore, reason alone is a servant to true religion and not the totality. Edwards asserts that just as there are holy (true) religious affections there are also natural, worldly affections that are the foundation of people's choosing and acting. Of the intellect he writes, "doctrinal knowledge and speculation only, without affection, never is engaged in the business of religion."[7] For him, the crux of true religion is that "everyone who has the power of godliness in his heart, has his inclinations and heart exercised towards God and divine things . . . that these holy exercises . . . prevail in him above all carnal or natural affections, and are effectual to overcome them."[8] He has captured Scripture's emphasis on the heart, including the commands for Christians to have changed hearts.[9] So then, what are the signs of a genuine move of God?

Recover the Authority of Scripture

The first sure sign of revival is that the Holy Spirit brings people into agreement with Scripture. Edwards observed that even those things that once were unacceptable to them, they now believe. Some of these are that "Jesus was born of the Virgin . . . was crucified . . . the truth of what the Gospel declares . . . his being the Son of God, and the

---

heavily from these in this chapter. They can be found in the online Works of Jonathan Edwards of Yale University. In this chapter I am using the printed copy of the online version for "Religious Affections."

4. Edwards, *A Treatise Concerning Religious Affections*, 259. (Hereafter cited as RA and the page number.)

5. RA 98.

6. RA 95.

7. RA 101.

8. RA 100.

9. Jer 29:13; also Deut 10:16; 11:13; 30:6, 17; 1 Kgs 8:61; multiple Pss; Jer 4:4; Matt 6:21; 12:34; 15:8, 19; 22:37; Mark 7:19, 21; 12:30-33; Luke 16:13; Rom 5:5; 8:27; 10:9-10; 2 Cor 1:22; 3:15; 9:7; Gal 4:6; Eph 1:18; 3:17; 4:18; 6:6; Col 2:11; 3:1, 15-16, 23; 2 Thess 3:5; 2 Tim 2:22; Heb 4:7, 12; 8:10; 10:22; Jas 3:14-16; 4:8; 1 Pet 3:15.

Savior of men."[10] Revived people are in agreement that Christ "appeared in the flesh, and that he is the Son of God, and was sent of God to save sinners, and that he is the only Saviour, and that they stand in great need of him."[11] This goes beyond intellectual consent to doctrine and puts actions to their words. He observes, "Words are cheap; and godliness is more easily feigned in words than in actions. Christian practice is a laborious thing."[12] What they agree to is the historical faith handed down to the saints from the apostles, attested to by Christians in all times and all places.

For Edwards Scripture is the ultimate source of understanding the holy affections essential for salvation because it is the word of God and is absolutely pure, perfect, and true. Today, many in our churches including some pastors would not agree. A practice that began with Modernity and Reason and found its fulfillment in late twentieth-century Postmodernity is the belief that Christian Scripture is obsolete, riddled with error, and cannot be trusted to be true. How are we to understand Scripture?

The Reliability of Scripture

For Edwards, the Scriptures are the only means of discerning what spirit people are following. Whatever enlightenment people receive, it must adhere to the plain teaching of the totality of Scripture if it is a move of God. A genuine work of God brings people to accept the truth of Scripture and removes prior prejudices they may have had against it. This means that along with Christians throughout the ages, they believe that God is the author citing passages such as 1 Timothy 3:16–17 and 2 Peter 1:19–21.[13] This acceptance of Scripture was supported by Jesus when he was on earth and by the apostles, who freely cited the Old Testament Scriptures. These were usually prefaced with "it is written," "God says," or the "Spirit says." This can be seen most clearly in Jesus' temptation in the wilderness, the Sermon on the Mount, and Peter's sermon at Pentecost. Jesus and the apostles drew on every part of the Old Testament and explained it in light of his coming. Jesus expanded it in the Sermon on the Mount, making it more encompassing and not less. He had no concern that the original autographs no longer existed or for the accuracy of the existing manuscripts. The apostles followed his lead.

James Packer explains that "God so controlled the process of communication to and through His servants that in the last analysis, He is the source and speaker not merely of biblical prophecy but also of the biblical history, wisdom, and doctrine, and also of the poems, whose giant-size delineations of adoration and devotion set worshipers of every age a standard for what their own praise and prayer should be."[14]

10. Edwards, "The Great Awakening," 249. (Hereafter cited as WJE 4:page number.)
11. WJE 4:250.
12. RA 411.
13. Other passages would include Pss 18:30; 19:7–11; 119:105. For a beautiful picture of the Christian life as it relates to the word of God (written), read all of Psalm 119.
14. Packer, "Adequacy of Human Language," 198.

Christians call the process of this communication inspiration that comes from the Holy Spirit. F. F. Bruce calls this "the distinguishing feature of the Old Testament collection [of books] when once it was reckoned to be complete."[15]

The same inspiration of the Holy Spirit is discerned in the New Testament. The same theme of salvation can be traced from creation, the fall of people into sin, and the redemption of them by God's Savior in both testaments. Bruce describes this as the unifying fact of the entire Bible. The Old and New Testaments must be taken together and no interpretation of any one part can stand apart from the whole.[16] Walter Kaiser Jr. agrees and explains how there would be no precedence for the salvation proclaimed in the New Testament if the Old Testament were removed. Without Acts and Revelation salvation would not have any use, for we would not see any way in which it was applied. Without the Gospels, the Epistles would have no anchor. As it is, each part is necessary and complements the other to make perfect sense when taken the way it was intended.[17] This raises questions of canon (which writings are to be included in the Holy Scriptures) and interpretation.

The Canon of Scripture

"Canon" comes from the Greek meaning a straight rod used as a rule much like we would use a ruler. From this we derive the meaning of "rule" or "standard." Early on, Christians used the phrase "rule of faith" or "rule of truth" to refer to "Christian teaching believed to reproduce what the apostles themselves taught, by which any system of doctrine offered for Christian acceptance, or any interpretation of biblical writings, was to be assessed."[18] Once the list of writings was formalized, "holy scripture came to be regarded as the rule of faith" for the Christian church as was expressed by Thomas Aquinas and attested to in the Westminster Confession of Faith.[19]

The Westminster Confession of Faith lists sixty-six books that comprise the Holy Scriptures. In them the early leaders discerned the work of the Holy Spirit in the message of salvation with authority, the same authority that Jesus had and had given to the apostles. It was life-giving and inspired hope and joy. The two criteria used by the early church to decide the canon were "antiquity and orthodoxy."[20] As centuries passed and writings began to emerge, some claiming to be from the apostles or those closely associated with them, they would be tested by two questions: "What does it teach about the person and work of Christ? Does it maintain the apostolic witness to

---

15. Bruce, *The Canon of Scripture*, 280.
16. Bruce, *The Canon of Scripture*, 280.
17. Kaiser, *Recovering the Unity of the Bible*, 18–20.
18. Bruce, *The Canon of Scripture*, 17–18. There is no space to do an in-depth discussion of the process by which the canon of Scripture came into being. Please see this work by Bruce.
19. Bruce, *The Canon of Scripture*, 18.
20. Bruce, *The Canon of Scripture*, 259.

him as the historical Jesus of Nazareth, crucified and raised from the dead, divinely exalted as Lord over all?"[21]

This is why some of the gospel accounts reemerging today did not find their way into the canon of Scripture. There was sufficient evidence that they did not conform to the apostolic teaching. Some examples are the Gospel of Peter, the Secret Book of John, the Secret Book of Thomas (the Gospel of Thomas), and many others, which include the works of the Gnostics that claimed secret knowledge and appealed to the spiritual elite but contradicted the known works of the apostles, Mark, Luke, James, Jude, and others in the New Testament.[22] Their messages contradict the "rule of truth," the "rule of faith," and orthodoxy of the canonical books of Scripture.

Remember that "in the canon of scripture we have the foundation documents of Christianity, the charter of the church, the title-deeds of faith. For no other literature can such a claim be made . . . . In the words of scripture, the voice of the Spirit of God continues to be heard."[23] This is what Edwards witnessed in revivals. People were brought to the historical truth and orthodoxy of the faith as attested in the creeds and confessions in all places and at all times.

Two Areas of Confusion

We have seen many ways in which our understanding of Scripture has been obfuscated. Before we look at interpretation, we will examine two specific ones. The first deals with the separation of Jesus from Scripture. The second misunderstands the work of the Holy Spirit in inspiration.

The Word of God

Historically, while Jesus was always viewed as the head of the church, he could only be known by what was written in Scripture (except for those with him during his days on earth). Today in some segments of the church, Jesus trumps Scripture, and direct communication from him negates anything in the written word even when it contradicts it. For the Reformers as for Edwards, "Word of God" usually referred to the written word, the Scriptures, as in the early written documents of the Westminster Confession. The church must realize that for the great majority of Christians prior to the second half of the twentieth century Jesus was the embodiment of the written word of God. Most used the phrase "Word of God" for the Bible and Jesus. Those who do are on solid ground because Jesus said, "You diligently study the Scriptures because you think that by them you possess eternal life. These are the Scriptures that testify about me" (John 5:39, NIV). The church throughout the ages accepted God as

---

21. Bruce, *The Canon of Scripture*, 260.
22. Bruce, *The Canon of Scripture*, 298–300.
23. Bruce, *The Canon of Scripture*, 283.

the author of them and that Jesus was the embodiment and fulfillment of them. D. A. Carson reminds us that "God's 'Word' in the Old Testament is his powerful self-expression in creation, revelation and salvation, and the personification of that 'Word' makes it suitable for John to apply it as a title to God's ultimate self-disclosure, the person of his own Son."[24]

Jesus as the "Word of God" comes from John 1:1-2 (NIV) where John writes, "In the beginning was the Word, and the Word was with God, and the Word was God. He was with God in the beginning." This designation spoke powerfully to both Jews and Greeks of Jesus' day. These opening words direct the Jewish person to God's creation and power of the spoken word. He spoke, and it was done. In Jewish thinking, "a word was something concrete, something much closer to what we would call an event or a deed. A word spoken was a deed done."[25] "Word," *logos*, had special meaning for the Greeks also. Nearly six hundred years before Jesus, the Greek philosopher Heraclitus spoke about a divine "reason" or "word" that ordered change so as to prevent random change which would bring chaos. Therefore, "logos became nothing less than the mind of God controlling this world and all men."[26] This was a formative idea for Plato, Socrates, and others.[27]

John is saying that like the Scriptures before him, Jesus as the "Word of God" is the self-revelation of God to people. The only difference is now he has taken on flesh to live among us, which was necessary for our redemption and reconciliation with God. Jesus is the God of creation and existed before it. If we want to know God we must come to Jesus only, for "if Jesus Christ is God, then . . . to know the Lord Jesus Christ is to know God. There is no knowledge of God apart from a knowledge of the Lord Jesus Christ, and there is no knowledge of the Lord Jesus Christ apart from a knowledge of the Bible."[28]

However, in Modernity scholarship began to distinguish between the Word of God, Jesus, and the word of God, Scripture. This has created confusion in the church because it tends to diminish the authority of Scripture, which is written, unchanging, and sound, and substitutes it with a nebulous inner guidance in which Jesus can tell people what he wants of them, and it need not conform to the written word. Edwards witnessed this and cautioned revivalists that this was not a genuine move of God.

He noticed that at times people would use passages from the Bible in a way that does not "properly come from the Scripture . . . [not] a right use of it, but from

24. Carson, *The Gospel According to John*, 116.

25. Boice, *The Gospel of John*, 34. Earl F. Palmer writes that understanding "Word" in this context is difficult but believes "the consensus among the most recent New Testament interpreters . . . is that John's vocabulary is influenced most heavily by the Old Testament and only secondarily by the Greek thought and philosophy" (Palmer, *The Book That John Wrote*, 16). Palmer's book was originally published under the titles *Salvation by Surprise* (1975, 1999) and *The Intimate Gospel*.

26. Boice, *The Gospel of John*, 34–35.

27. Boice, *The Gospel of John*, 35.

28. Boice, *The Gospel of John*, 23.

an abuse of it."[29] He noticed that frequently a verse or passage from the Scriptures would come to mind. He urges folks to discern the proper use of Holy Scripture in revival. In particular he mentions that some think God is giving them new revelation that may supersede Scripture. He heartily agrees with 1 John 4:1 to test the spirits to see of what sort they are.

If God is the source of their enlightenment, then it is not the reality of the experience or the strong desires, feelings, or wants resulting from it that make it holy affections but that it never contradicts the clear (and historic as explained in the creeds and confessions of the church) interpretation of the whole of Scripture. No one can pick and choose to which passages he or she will adhere or not. Jesus remains the fulfillment and the embodiment of the written word of God. You cannot know Jesus apart from the Scriptures, and you cannot rightly understand Scripture without a relationship with Jesus.

Inspiration of Scripture and Today

Inspiration is often confused with illumination. The books in the canon of Scripture are inspired by the Holy Spirit. God is the author. Bruce explains this inspiration in the Old Testament as "that operation of the Holy Spirit by which the prophets of Israel were enabled to utter the word of God. The vocabulary was theirs; the message was his. Only to certain individuals, and only occasionally to them, was this enablement granted."[30] This was eventually extended to include the law and the writings. In the New Testament, Jesus promised to all of his followers the Holy Spirit, whose role would be to lead them into all truth (John 14:26; 16:12–15). However, the church has always recognized the authoritative inspiration given to the apostles and those who knew them and wrote about them. "The divine inspiration of the Gospels of Mark and Luke is not to be denied, but these works were accepted, first as authoritative and then as canonical scripture, because they were recognized to be trustworthy witnesses to the saving events."[31]

In the early church as in this day and age, people are inspired by the Holy Spirit but not with the authority of the biblical writers; these voices "were helpful for the building up of Christian faith and life."[32] This would include the many wonderful books available to us today. Bruce points out that the early church continued to experience the work of the Holy Spirit in the role of "the witnessing and interpreting Spirit" of the Scriptures which "have been, and continue to be, one of the chief instruments which the Spirit uses."[33] This work of the Holy Spirit is like an inbreathing into God's people. Bruce

---

29. RA 143.
30. Bruce, *The Canon of Scripture*, 264.
31. Bruce, *The Canon of Scripture*, 266.
32. Bruce, *The Canon of Scripture*, 268.
33. Bruce, *The Canon of Scripture*, 281.

describes two different kinds of inbreathing. The "'inbreathing' into the authors is called inspiration and his 'inbreathing' into the hearers or readers is called illumination . . . at both stages it is one and the same Spirit who is at work."[34] Illumination is as essential for correct understanding of God and his holy ways by those who read or hear it as inspiration was for the accuracy of the messages of those who wrote the Scriptures.

Christians today can be assured that the Holy Spirit still teaches them and interprets Scripture to them as described in John 14:26 and 16:12–16. Bruce observes that "repeatedly new spiritual movements have been launched by the rediscovery of the living power which resides in the canon of scripture—a living power which strengthens and liberates."[35] Today, as in Edwards's day, God moves and quickens his people to recover the ancient meaning of the Holy Scriptures and to experience revival. People may hear from God or from some other spirit telling them about themselves, people, things, or the way they should go, but it must conform to Scripture and not negate, ignore, or do away with it. This has been the source of much confusion in our churches.

This supposed communication (illumination) may come in the form of visions, dreams, thoughts, or impressions on the mind giving them some new revelation. But sometimes, it permits people to do what they want, which conforms to the culture's morality and opposes Scripture. When this becomes prevalent, the church is left with no means of testing the spirits of what sort they are. This is very convenient for a culture where all truth is relative. Edwards cautions that true illumination by the Holy Spirit will lead people to the truth of Scripture and "give [them] a view of the spiritual divine excellency of Christ and his fullness, and of the way of salvation revealed in the gospel."[36] Test the spirits by the canon of Scripture attested by Christians of all times and all places as explained in the creeds and confessions. For Edwards, this was the concrete test of an authentic work of God in genuine revival. Jesus was speaking to today's church when he commanded, "Be wise as serpents and harmless as doves."

Interpretation of Scripture

Before we can talk about what Scripture means to us today, we must do the difficult work of uncovering what it meant to the human writer and the people to whom it was given. We miss the mark when we settle for "this is what it means to me." Contrary to many popular philosophies, the writers intended a particular meaning which we must identify before we can accurately interpret Scripture to see what it is saying to us.

That we can know the original meaning has come under attack first in Modernity as scholars "threw out" the supernatural such as prophecies, miracles, and Jesus rising from the dead. These things were considered to be impossible because they violated the natural laws of science. This led to some strange beliefs such as Jesus did not rise

---

34. Bruce, *The Canon of Scripture*, 282.
35. Bruce, *The Canon of Scripture*, 283.
36. RA 149.

in deed, but in our hearts only. This was followed by the postmodern claim that the meaning of words is whatever the reader or listener gives to them. The original meanings are impossible to know. However, with better archeological methods devised in the twentieth century there has been a plethora of knowledge gathered that helps us to understand the times, people, and events of long ago.

Test the spirits: who benefits from this modern and postmodern way of knowing—God or Satan? What fruit does it bear? Does it build Christian faith that overcomes the world or attempt to destroy it? Between the two ideologies of modern and postmodern thought, most Christians today have been left with only a surface knowledge of what the Scriptures teach. Often the church limps by on shallow beliefs based only on what seems right to those who attend. These beliefs are further limited to those things on which they can agree.

Over the centuries, the church has devised hermeneutical guidelines for reading, studying, preaching, or teaching Scripture that will help to overcome this deficit. "Hermeneutics" comes from a Greek word meaning "to interpret."[37] It covers three general areas: what it meant to the original writers, what it means for me, and how to apply it to others. We must study to learn as much as possible about the historical setting, the people, and the times in which a text was written and what was happening at that time. There are many valuable resources to help with this.[38] It is imperative that you keep in mind that there are different types of literature in Scripture: historical, poetic, prophetic, didactic, epistolary, and descriptive texts. Read them accordingly.

Another principle is how we approach unity and diversity found within the Scriptures. Paul talks about salvation by faith while James talks about works. Is there a deeper unity underlying the two that reconciles them? What message are the various writers communicating? What do we do with seemingly oddball statements like being baptized for the dead? Grant Osborne affirms that "Terry's dictum" remains valid to this day, "No single statement or obscure passage of one book can be allowed to set aside a doctrine which is clearly established by many passages."[39] Closely related to this is to let Scripture interpret Scripture and use the entire Scriptures. Osborne identifies a "basic evangelical fallacy" of our age, which is "proof-texting" or "proving" a "doctrine or practice merely by alluding to a text without considering its original inspired meaning."[40] Let context determine meaning and not your personal opinion.

---

37. Osborne, *The Hermeneutical Spiral*, 5.

38. A few of these are the IVP Dictionaries: *Dictionary of Jesus and the Gospels*, *Dictionary of the Later New Testament and Its Developments*, *Dicitonary of Paul and His Letters*, and *Dictionary of the Old Testament Prophets*, and the NIV Application Commentary series.

39. Osborne, *The Hermeneutical Spiral*, 11.

40. Osborne, *The Hermeneutical Spiral*, 7. John Jefferson Davis has identified several hermeneutical principles. They include: "a text is not to be interpreted in a way that contradicts the clear meaning of another text"; "the historical-grammatical meaning is the primary meaning of the text"; "the text is not to be interpreted in a way that excludes the supernatural"; "the New Testament is the normative guide to the meaning of the Old Testament"; "passages addressed to an individual should be

Another principle of hermeneutics is progressive revelation or communication, meaning that "God revealed himself in stages." Osborne asserts that "later passages do not replace the earlier; rather, they clarify the earlier passages and show that they formed a mere stage in the developing understanding of the people of God."[41] This can be seen in the understanding of the Savior that God would send, and why now that he has come we interpret the Old Testament in light of the events of the New, but we cannot ignore them.

Bruce cautions us against thinking that each stage of this progression is more advanced than the previous one or that we can receive communication today that supersedes Scripture. He reminds us that each Scripture contributes to the whole for our understanding the whole, but that it is impossible to understand the whole without understanding each part.[42] When the canon of Scripture was closed, all progression or evolution in thought would only be that which transforms us to agree with God, not to reject his word and to continue in sin. Edwards witnessed to the first and warned against the second in the revivals of his age.

Recover the Reality of Sin

In revival, along with turning people to the truth of God's Scriptures, Edwards notes change in the way a person views sin and their desperate need of a Savior. He understands sin as the result of the fallen human state, which is not simply opposed to holiness but is radically and fundamentally an absence of holiness. Sin leads to hardness of heart, which he identifies as a "want of pious affections of the heart" which delude people and lead them into error.[43] He observes that in revival the Holy Spirit makes people see the "dreadfulness of sin," "the displeasure of God against it," "their own miserable condition as they are in themselves, by reason of sin," and "their great need of deliverance from the guilt of them" for eternal salvation.[44] This leads to repentance from those sins and transformation in the way they live.

Subsequently they are led to "confirm their minds in the belief of the story of Christ, as he appeared in the flesh, and that he is the Son of God, and was sent of God to save sinners, and that he is the only Saviour, and that they stand in great need of him; and seems to beget in them higher and more honorable thoughts of him than

---

interpreted in light of passages written to the church"; "parallel passages in the epistles can shed light on difficult passages in the gospels"; "descriptive passages are to be interpreted in light of the didactic texts"; and "incidental references are to be interpreted in light of the systematic teachings." These can be found in Davis, "Lesson 6: Biblical Interpretation," 11–12.

41. Osborne, *The Hermeneutical Spiral*, 11.
42. Bruce, *The Canon of Scripture*, 297.
43. RA 118.
44. WJE 4:252.

they used to have."⁴⁵ The Holy Spirit changes their hearts, gives them discernment, and empowers them to avoid future sin.⁴⁶

How different it is today when in the name of love we try to eliminate hell, sin, and judgment. It should come as no surprise, then, that most churches have little need for evangelism. The church must remember that Jesus talked about these things more than anyone else and declared in John 3:18 that anyone who does not believe in him stands condemned already. Which is more loving, to tell people about their sin in order to bring them to repentance and salvation in Jesus or to tell them it's okay to do what they want and leave them to suffer the consequences both now and for eternity in separation from God? To use Edwards's analogy, if a house catches fire at night, is it the one who calmly assures people sleeping there that it will all be okay in the end or the one who yells "fire" and tries to arouse the sleepers from their slumber in order to get them out of the burning house?

Additionally, sin has consequences for individuals as well as organizations and culture. A man loses his temper and shakes a three-month-old baby too hard because she is crying and kills her. A CEO embezzles the pension fund of his employees and they have nothing on which to retire. A culture relegates truth to only what is true for the individual and reaps anarchy. It is the church's job to lead the people through the flames of conviction of God's condemnation for sin but not allow them to fall into self-condemnation that destroys. In that way she is like a therapist who reassures people in order not to revolt them with her judgmental and critical spirit. However, unlike many therapists, she can never change the truth of the reality of sin and hell in order to encourage them to be themselves and to assure them all is well—it will always be okay. She must bring them to see the gravity of their situation and help them to find rescue in Jesus.

Revival Brings Change and Revitalizes the Evangelical Spirit

The final sign of revival Edwards notes is that it brings about great love to God and to people. From 1 John 4 he observes that if the Holy Spirit is dwelling in them then divine love which is holy love will be growing in them also. Divine love awakens people to the seriousness of their sin, a sense of their "own utter unworthiness," and their enmity against God and Christ which brings real understanding of the "sovereignty of God's love to us in Christ Jesus."⁴⁷ They become the new creation in Christ, transformed in both mind (thinking) and actions (doing). Revival works into people a great love to God and to people, a genuine appreciation of the wonderful love of God in sending his Son to die in our place and the wonderful love of Jesus in carrying that out. The revived person longs for God and Christ, loves to

45. WJE 4:250.
46. WJE 4:252.
47. WJE 4:257.

meditate on God's divine attributes, and conforms to them in order to please him. The benefits of their salvation, like God's love for them, become the superstructure of the foundation which is God and Christ.

The hypocrites (Edwards's word) who are not truly in line with genuine revival have it reversed. They love to hear of Christ's great love *to them*; they are caught up in the beauty of their *own experiences* and not the glory of God, and they are pleased "in hearing how much God and Christ makes of 'em so that their joy is really a joy in themselves, and not in God."[48] In most twenty-first-century American churches God's love *for* people and what he will do *for them* is heavily emphasized, while the love of obedience and service to God receives a mere mention. Make God and Jesus your foundation. The things he gives you and the life you live become the structure by which people will see God. Love God for who he is and not for what you can get from him.

Additionally, revival changes people's attitudes and actions towards others. The world of the Holy Spirit "also quells contentions among men, and gives a spirit of peace and goodwill, excites to acts of outward kindness and earnest desire of salvation of others' souls; and causes a delight in those that appear as the children of God and followers of Christ."[49] In "A Faithful Narrative," Edwards described the changes in the town as a result of the 1734–35 revival. The effect of the conviction produced by the work of God was that the people "quit their sinful practices ... [being] done with old quarrels, backbitings, and intermeddling with other men's matters; the tavern was soon left empty, and persons kept very much at home ... and every day seemed in many respects like a Sabbath day."[50] They wanted to tell others about Jesus.

He gives several examples of changes in entire groups of people from youth, to social practices at weddings, and individual changes such as a young woman with a reputation for being one of the greatest "company keepers" who changed so dramatically that many others in town were awakened through her, like the woman at the well.[51] He includes two personal stories in his report.[52] He also reports that two years later "there is still a great deal of religious conversation continued in the town"; "a religious disposition appears to be still maintained"; there are "frequent private religious meetings," and "all sorts are generally worshipping God at such meetings."[53] The youth have their own meetings, and to his knowledge none returned to their former loose lifestyle.[54] Of the 1734–35 revival in Northampton, he

---

48. RA 251.

49. WJE 4:256.

50. Edwards, "Faithful Narrative," 161.

51. WJE 4:148–558.

52. You may read about Abigail Hutchinson, a young woman dying of an illness, and Phebe Bartlet, the four year old daughter of William Bartlet in WJE 4:191–205.

53. WJE 4:209.

54. WJE 4:209.

concludes, "There has been a great and marvelous work of conversion [justification] and sanctification among the people here."[55]

Edwards has given us much to consider in revival from prayer to the recovery of the historic Scriptures and Jesus as given in the canonical books and as interpreted in the creeds and confessions that have come down to us through the ages. Revival brings sanctification and the love for others in the form of what is best for them, which includes sharing the gospel of Jesus Christ with them.

The Narrow Way

We have seen how all of us miss the mark in one way or another. We all try to broaden the road to accommodate personal beliefs and practices. Edwards has identified marks of the narrow way which he calls "holy boldness." He tells us it is *not* "the exercise of any fiery passions . . . in fierce and violent speeches, and vehemently declaiming against, and crying out of intolerable wickedness of opposers, giving 'em their own in plain terms."[56] These he calls false affections. I think of how often we want to give people a piece of our minds. This is not holy boldness but carnal practice. Holy boldness is: "not opening [your] mouth when afflicted and oppressed, in going as a lamb to the slaughter . . . praying that the Father would forgive his cruel enemies . . . not shedding others' blood; but with all-conquering patience and love, shedding his own."[57] These are holy or religious affections. He connects this with the meekness blessed by Jesus in the Sermon on the Mount. How different this is from the all-too-common practice in which people argue their point, wag their heads in a superior attitude, and walk out of meetings, and where confession of faults is considered a weakness at best or grounds for rejection at worst.

Edwards helps us discern between these affections. False affections "trust [Christ] as the Saviour of their sins . . . . They make Christ the minister of sin and great officer and vicegerent of the devil, to strengthen his interest . . . so that they may sin against him with good courage, and without any fear, being effectually secured from restraints."[58] Furthermore, "they trust in Christ to preserve to 'em the quiet enjoyment of their sins, and to be their shield to defend 'em from God's displeasure . . . . some of these, at the same time, make a great profession of love to God and assurance of his favor, and great joy in tasting the sweetness of his love."[59] On the other hand, gracious (holy) affections make the heart soft and tender towards God and "fill it with a dread of sin, or whatever might displease and offend God" and comes from a heart "bruised and broken with godly sorrow" which is "much greater . . . than

---

55. WJE 4:209.
56. RA 351.
57. RA 351.
58. RA 358.
59. RA 359.

mere legal sorrow from selfish principles"[60] in which folks say they're sorry, but what they really mean is, "I'm sorry I got caught."

The more holy the affections, the more tender the heart. Holy affections banish "servile fear" and replace it with "reverential fear"; they remove fear of future punishment and God's displeasure and replace it with an "increase of fear of his displeasure"; they remove fear of hell and replace it with "an increase of the fear of sin."[61] People who have "more holy boldness" will have "less of self-confidence," will have more of a sense of the "desert" of hell, and will be "less apt to be shaken in faith."[62] These have the softest hearts and are the "poorest of all in spirit."[63] He continues that people of holy affections see God's excellence in Christ, "relish the divine sweetness of holiness," see their imperfections and great distance they are from God's perfection, "and so the more do they see their need of grace."[64] The greater the spiritual affections are in people, the greater their longing and appetite will be for grace and holiness.

True religious affections make holiness an inward and burning desire of the saints. "There is a holy breathing and panting after the Spirit of God to increase holiness as natural to a holy nature as breathing is to a living body. And holiness or sanctification is more directly the object of it, than any manifestation of God's love and favor."[65] The desire for holiness is higher than the desire for God's love or favor.[66] This challenges our thinking and our presentation of the gospel in the twenty-first century.

Scripture is always the rule for holiness, and Edwards affirms that the chief virtuous affection found there is love, but the readers must be careful not to understand love in the same sense as most understand it in the twenty-first century. Edwards is referring to holy love and also affirms "so that really, there is no place in the New Testament, where the declared design is to give signs of godliness, but that holy practice and keeping Christ's commandments, is the mark chosen out from all others to be insisted on."[67] Recall that righteousness and justice are the foundation of God's throne and love and faithfulness proceed out from it. If it is God's love, it will not oppose or try to change his righteousness. Edwards reminds his readers that everyone who has the hope of eternal salvation in Christ purifies himself, even as Christ is pure.[68]

He follows this with an appeal to understand the Scriptures in a proper way. For him, an unscriptural way would be "for us to make that great which the Scripture

60. RA 360.
61. RA 364.
62. RA 364.
63. RA 365.
64. RA 378.
65. RA 382-83.
66. RA 383.
67. RA 437.

68. First John 3:3, 6–11 tells us that if people do not do *what is right*, they are not God's children which includes *loving* others.

makes little, and that little which the Scripture makes, great." This "tends to give us a monstrous idea of religion; and (at least indirectly and gradually) to lead us wholly away from the right rule, and from a right opinion of ourselves, and to establish delusion and hypocrisy."[69] Making the Bible say what we want it to say brings consequences. This is especially true where grace is concerned.

Edwards credits the evidence of grace in a person as being "perfected or finished in holy practice"; just as the practice of sin begins in the lust of the heart, moves to the mind, and is worked out in evil actions, so it is with grace."[70] It begins in the heart, moves to the mind, and will be worked out in holy actions. Grace never excuses or condones sin. To him, holy practices are the proper evidence of "a gracious love both to God and men," "humility," "true thankfulness," "a gracious hope," "Christian fortitude," "the truth of grace," and "a cheerful practice of our duty and doing the will of God," which are "the proper evidence of a truly holy joy."[71] To the charge that holy practices as the chief *evidence* of grace is legalistic, he replies that it is not holy practices *being a sign* of grace that is legalistic but it is making those actions the *"price* of god's favor" (italics are mine) that makes them so.[72] He describes holy practices as grace in practice. He contends that Scripture insists on them as "the most importance in the evidence of our interest in Christ," and claims it is "greatly to the hurt of religion" that people "neglect the exercises and effectual operations of grace in practice and insist almost wholly on discoveries . . . from philosophy or experience."[73] Examine your ideas of grace to be sure they are holy grace and not just the opinions of people.

This human wisdom and discernment bring turmoil to the church. Edwards writes that if the church were to follow these principles that he has so diligently laid out, many problems could be avoided, and many good things would happen. It would convict "those whose hearts were never brought to a thorough compliance with the strait and narrow way which leads to life . . . [and] deliver us from innumerable perplexities arising from . . . inconsistent schemes that are about methods and steps of experience."[74] It would also "promote their engagedness and earnestness in their Christian walk."[75] The people of God living holy lives individually and corporately would remove stumbling blocks. People would not be hardened by the hardheartedness of those professing to be Christians. By their loving actions Christians would "convince people that there is a reality in religion, and greatly awaken them and win them, by convincing their consciences of the importance and excellency of religion.

---

69. RA 438.
70. RA 435.
71. RA 447–49.
72. RA 455.
73. RA 459.
74. RA 461.
75. RA 461.

Thus the light of professors would so shine before men, that others seeing their good works would glorify God in heaven."[76]

The way of revival is the narrow way. Do not try to broaden it in order to gain a hearing in our society. Christianity remains a highway of holiness, and the unclean, those still in their sins, will not be on it. This is the ancient path Jeremiah advises us to take, where the good way is, and we will find rest for our souls.

Summary

Christians in all ages and places are commanded to go into the world and proclaim the gospel, making disciples for Jesus by teaching them to live according to all that he has taught us. In the revivals he witnessed, Edwards attested that God's people are changed to reflect him. This includes love for him, acceptance and agreement with his word (written) and his Word (God's Son). This includes the Old Testament as well as the New Testament because God, the Holy Spirit, is the author of it all, and all of it testifies of Jesus. Without an authoritative Scripture, there is no mandate for the evangelical spirit. There is no truth, and error becomes only what we can perceive doesn't work. There is little reason to respect people you do not like or to be grateful and thankful for the things you have—you deserve them. Sin runs rampant and discipline declines. People are inclined to live for themselves in the immediate present. In short, what follows the deterioration of the authority of Scripture is what we see happening in twenty-first-century America.

Revival brings transformation (sanctification) and love for God, self, and others. But in twenty-first-century America, we try to have salvation (justification) and still hold on to our right to do whatever pleases us. But Christians are called to live the life Jesus laid out in the Sermon on the Mount and in all of Scripture and to build the church based not on individualized, personal beliefs but on a relationship, both individually and communally, with the thrice-Holy God through Jesus Christ his Son. This is accomplished only by the power of the Holy Spirit as revealed in the totality of Scripture found in the canonical books as interpreted throughout history by the church in the creeds and confessions. Christians must be careful to reflect the biblical Jesus. This means living a holy life: know the Scriptures, not just your favorite parts, and practice what you find there (Matt 10:1); be ready to have an answer for the hope in you (1 Pet 3:15), and spend quality time with God in prayer (1 Thess 5:17).

This love for others includes sharing the message of salvation through Jesus with those who do not have a personal relationship with him. God has revealed himself to us in Scripture and has rescued, redeemed, and reconciled to himself everyone who comes to him through faith in Jesus. He has given his people the ministry of rescuing, redeeming, and reconciling others to him through the clear proclamation of the gospel. The

---

76. RA 461.

psalmist commands God's people simply to tell the next generation all the great things God has done for his people. Right now, the church is not reaching the vast majority of people caught in this culture. We have looked at many of the social, historical, and biblical reasons why this is happening. In the next chapter we will use this knowledge to examine what we might do to work with God towards revival.

Chapter 18

Final Thoughts on Telling the Next Generation and Revival

> A necessary pre-cursor of any great spiritual awakening is a spirit of deep humiliation growing out of a consciousness of sin, and fresh revelation of the holiness and power and glory of God.
>
> —John R. Mott, *Spiritual Awakening*

Revival is needed when people fall away from following God's ways and plunge society into chaos and destruction. This is not the intended or stated goal; it is the natural consequence of following humanity's conventional ways. It is both individual and corporate. Biblically, all revivals come when God's people cry out (supplication prayer) to him for deliverance from their terrible situation. For that to happen, there must first be at least some leaders with the necessary understanding to direct them in such prayers. These leaders will have an evangelical heart set on the rescue of people from sin, the redemption of people through Jesus, and their reconciliation with God. They will also be able and willing to apply godly discipline when needed to help God's people live holy lives. In the Old Testament they were called prophets or judges. In the New Testament, they were called apostles. Sadly, today they are often called fanatics.

Much of what today's church calls justice, forgiveness, love, mercy, and grace as well as her interpretations of the doctrines of holiness, righteousness, sin, hell, judgment, conviction, repentance, and redemptive suffering strongly imply the need for revival and reformation. God always has his people who will call the larger church back to him. Look around. Who is this person in your congregation or denomination? It will most likely not be the most popular person or the one with the most charisma.

Edwards observes that in a true revival the pleasure saints find in God will always come down to specific things: the joy they find in God for his perfection, Christ's beauty, the way of salvation by Christ, and the "holy doctrines of the gospel by which God is exalted and man abased, holiness honored and promoted, and sin greatly disgraced and discouraged and free and sovereign love manifested."[1] The things that used to bother people about Christianity now seem perfectly reasonable.

---

1. Edwards, *Religious Affections*, 250. Hereafter referred to as RA with the page number.

Another effect of revival is wholeness. Conrad Cherry's assessment of Edwards's view of a move of God is "if a revival promotes that wholeness, it is to be encouraged; if it fragments the person, it is to be brought under the severest criticism."[2] Unfortunately the revivals of the postmodern era have only sporadically persuaded people to stop compartmentalizing every segment of life: work, family, marriage, friends, and church, let alone the recovery of major doctrines that have been lost in recent times. Christians are to become whole with the Holy Spirit having access to every chamber of their hearts, but too often they have been ingrained so deeply with compartmentalizing that they usually do not look significantly different from the culture around them. Christians, be whole. Let God have every part of you!

This is no more evident than in their view of condemnation for sin and the need for Jesus alone for salvation. Edwards believed and acted on the biblical truth that people are condemned already (John 3:18) and that only belief in Jesus (John 14:6) can save them from that judgment, and the church must do the same. This means more than bringing people to Christ for salvation. Michael Frost and Alan Hirsch remind us that redemption means not just buying something back that was lost, but to "clean it up, and put it back to its original intended use,"[3] which for God is a holy purpose. This is true love. As C. S. Lewis writes, "It would be cruel not to say it" and especially the more so because we are afraid to say it. Know that you are truly loving people when you *share* the gospel. Do not berate or criticize them for not acting like Christians. Share the hope that is in you because of Jesus. Who knows; you might start a revival!

While we want things to get better, not everyone welcomes revival. One reason churches resist revival is that it often looks messy: people crying and agonizing over their sins or enraptured with a view of the beauty of a Holy God. Richard Foster shares how John 14:12, where Jesus says that those who believe in him will do all the things he did and greater, scared him because he was afraid that people might move outside the sovereignty of God and try to do things in their own strength. He shares his anxiety "about the pride and presumption in all of this authoritative talk. Most of all, I was afraid people would fall off the deep end . . . afraid I would fall off the deep end. But quickly I saw that the danger of superficiality is clearly as perilous as the danger of excess, perhaps more so. In my concern over falling off the deep end, I realized that I just might fall off the shallow end."[4] Like Edwards and others in the revivals on both sides of the Atlantic, he discovered that wanting to be seen as respectable was interfering with his ability to pray and to evangelize. He writes, "My desire to maintain religious respectability could easily result in a domesticated faith. I knew that I dare not let this happen. I must be willing to step out even if the waters looked deep. *There are precious people who desperately need help*" (italics are mine).[5]

2. Cherry, "Imagery and Analysis," 27.
3. Frost and Hirsch, *Shaping of Things to Come*, 172.
4. Foster, *Prayer*, 235.
5. Foster, *Prayer*, 235.

We see the pendulum of extremes at work here also. Christians tend to play it safe and stay in the shallow end, or they go for total abandonment (without discernment) and go off the deep end. Either extreme plays into Satan's schemes, which will always try to keep the church off balance even if he cannot keep her from heaven. Foster urges Christians in each age to pray for this authority to do the things Jesus did. Holiness is worth whatever the cost may be. Today, because of respectability, reason, and caution, most Christians are in far more danger of falling off the shallow end than the deep.

Answering the Critics

At least some of this imbalance and hesitation comes from external criticism either from within the church or from the culture. Throughout history intellectuals and groups, from Gamaliel to Marx, and from communism to the American media, have claimed that Christianity must adapt to the culture or become extinct. These are voices of the world that claim Christianity is archaic and has outlived its relevancy and usefulness. Test the spirits! Recognize that this is the *opinion* of naysayers trying to preserve their sins and to discourage Christians in order to destroy their faith that overcomes the world (1 John 5:4–5). Remember that Christians have been told this from the first century to our present age. Who receives the glory from such ideas? What are the fruits of their beliefs?

In examining these claims, Mark Noll concludes that Christianity is flexible enough to appeal to all cultures in all times and writes, "Christianity by its very character is poised to meet individuals, families, clans, groups and societies where they are. It is by its nature a religion of nearly infinite flexibility because it has been revealed in a person of absolutely infinite love."[6] Christianity does not simply give people dos and don'ts to follow, but their individual and corporate lives model the love in their personal relationship with the Holy God.

The church's response to these charges of irrelevancy must be a clear proclamation of the gospel that flows out of "a longing to share the good news of God with a world that sorely needs hope and forgiveness," but this must rest "on a fundamental conviction of the truth of the gospel."[7] The foundation of this conviction is a Holy God who equips them with a holy lifestyle. Alister McGrath reminds the church that "*Evangelism springs from deep feelings of love and a heartfelt desire to share something wonderful and trustworthy, something that would be selfish and irresponsible to keep to oneself*" (italics are mine).[8] This was Edwards's motivation for preaching "Sinners in the Hands of an Angry God," which set in motion the Revival of 1734. It was not to make people feel badly about themselves but to produce godly sorrow so that they would see their situation and be saved from eternal death and torment. Apart from

---

6. Noll, *New Shape of World Christianity*, 192.
7. McGrath, *Evangelicalism and the Future of Christianity*, 163.
8. McGrath, *Evangelicalism and the Future of Christianity*, 163.

Christ, the situation of people never changes no matter how good they look or claim to be because they are all descended from Adam. Only the holiness of God can fill the emptiness in the human soul. Christians, take heart; in spite of what the media, intellectuals, and culture tell you, the gospel of Jesus Christ is just as relevant and sorely needed today as it ever was.

Preaching for Revival

Biblical preaching is essential to revival and the advance of God's kingdom. Reflecting on Edwards and the 1734 revival in Northampton John Piper writes, "With Edwards's view of the reality of heaven and hell and the necessity of persevering in a life of holy affections and godliness, eternity was at stake every Sunday. This sets him off from the average preacher today."[9] To support this he reasons, "Our emotional rejection of hell and our facile view of conversion and the abundant false security we purvey have created an atmosphere in which the great biblical intensity of preaching is almost impossible."[10] Edwards's power did not come from "rhetorical flourish or ear-splitting thunders. It was born in brokenhearted affections."[11] Piper urges preachers to be like Edwards in knowing their brokenness: "The spirit we long to see in our people must be in ourselves first. But that will never happen until, as Edwards says, we know our own emptiness and helplessness and terrible sinfulness. Edwards lived in a kind of spiraling oscillation between humiliation for his sins and exultation of his Savior."[12] The church cannot present to the world something that she does not believe herself or has never experienced. Edwards "stood in continual awe at the weight of the truth he was charged to proclaim."[13]

How unlike much of the preaching today that has accommodated the culture with amusing stories and psychological self-help. Thank God for pastors who give more and the congregations who want more. Unfortunately, too often just as "producers are chopping up their products to fit the shorter attention spans of online consumers, as well as to raise their profiles on search engines,"[14] so preaching has been shortened and often reduced to entertainment, self-help, and what God will do for them, and many churchgoers prefer it this way. This may be a good way to attract people initially, but the church must work on developing the length and depth of the message her people are equipped to comprehend and to uphold.

---

9. Piper, *Supremacy of God*, 103.
10. Piper, *Supremacy of God*, 103.
11. Piper, *Supremacy of God*, 102.
12. Piper, *Supremacy of God*, 101–2.
13. Piper, *Supremacy of God*, 103.
14. Carr, *The Shallows*, 94.

The Pothole of Losing the Message in the Exegesis

Preachers have been trained to exegete a passage to learn what it means, and they must do that. I have heard forty-five-minute sermons on the meaning of one verse. Familiarity with the Scripture passage is vital. However, if that is all pastors give their congregations they could be missing the greater message. An example of how to preach a difficult passage in the face of the challenges of the postmodern, politically correct mindset might be found in Matthew 10. This is rarely preached in its entirety today because it sounds like judgment to our postmodern ears. Let's examine what Jesus is saying. He has just seen the people harassed and thrown down like sheep without a shepherd and has compassion on them. He brings in the spiritual interpretation saying the harvest is ripe (people are ready to receive the salvation message) but there are not enough workers to tell them about it. He turns to the disciples and tells them to pray that the Lord of the harvest would send out laborers to bring in the harvest.

Jesus then commissions them to go out two-by-two and to do the very things he has been doing: preaching and teaching the kingdom of God, healing the sick, and casting out demons. When they come to a home, they should greet the people with something like, "The kingdom of God has come in his son Jesus." If people want to know more, they are to stay and share the faith with them, thereby letting their peace with God through Jesus rest or abide in that place. They are "deserving" simply because they have chosen to want to know more about Jesus. It is the people listening who make that determination.

However, not everyone will want to hear about Jesus. Jesus allows for this contingency and tells the disciples that if folks want nothing to do with the message, then they are undeserving. The disciples are to leave and shake the dust off their shoes. To say someone is undeserving is not politically correct. It sounds harsh to us today, but we must realize that in these cases the people have chosen not to know about Jesus and are "not deserving" because of their own preference.

Jesus is saying that if people decide they do not want to know about him, do not force the gospel on them. Do not use your limited resources of time, money, and energy where they are not wanted. Jesus is looking for followers who are committed and loyal to him, not large numbers of people who have an intellectual knowledge and remain committed to the cultural beliefs. Leave and take nothing of theirs with you: not money, not provisions, and especially not their beliefs, doctrines, and theology. Shake the dust off your shoes.

Some things to note about this are that the disciples are never to judge who is worthy or not worthy to be presented with the gospel. It is offered to all. The people decide for themselves if they want to know more. The disciples are to abide by the people's own decisions. Once they decide, the disciples are to spend their time and resources on the folks who respond positively. They should leave where they are not welcomed. There will be consequences for rejecting Jesus, but God will decide, not the disciples. However, this does not mean that the disciples cannot continue to pray for these folks to become part of the harvest at some later time.

The Pothole of Losing Sight of the Larger Picture

Closely related to losing the message in the details is losing sight of the landscape of what is happening in Scripture. It is like missing the forest for the trees. Put each section in the context of the whole. See appendix 8 for an example of missing the overall picture by dissecting each section from the other. Context decides meaning, and contrary to popular thought, we can and do know much about the ancient civilization in which the Bible was written.

Congregational as Well as Pastoral Responsibilities

Edwards's preaching and writing got people to look at themselves through the lens of Scripture. He brought them into encounters with the Holy God in both the intellect and the emotions. To reach people today, the congregations must also learn how to put the gospel in context for the postmodern/technological world without capitulating to it. Hirsch and Frost help us to understand contextualization as "the dynamic process" in which the unchanging gospel message interacts with the relative human situation so that it becomes meaningful to the one to whom it is given.[15] For them the goal of evangelicals is "to communicate the gospel in word and deed and to establish churches in ways that make sense to people within their local cultural context.... in such a way that it meets people's deepest needs and *penetrates their worldviews*, thus allowing them to follow Christ and remain in their own cultures."[16]

All Christians Proclaim the Gospel of Jesus

This cannot be left to pastors only. The entire congregation must model the beauty, joy, and unity of their relationship with the thrice-Holy God through Jesus. Out of this holy lifestyle they "proclaim the profound attractiveness of faith to the world, in the full and confident expectation that the gospel is inherently attractive and relevant."[17] This includes all the doctrines of holy righteousness, justice, judgment, condemnation, sin, and hell as well as holy love, forgiveness, grace, and mercy.

Leonard Sweet has considered this and recommends the "EPIC model of doing church that is *biblically absolute* but *culturally relative*: Experiential, Participatory, Image-driven, Connected" (italics are mine). Churches in the twenty-first century are

---

15. Frost and Hirsch, *Things to Come*, 109.
16. Frost and Hirsch, *Things to Come*, 109.
17. McGrath, *Evangelicalism and the Future of Christianity*, 164.

to be "like the church of the first century . . . [and] learn to measure success not by its budgets and buildings but by its creativity and imagination . . . . built on God's grace where the 'top things' . . . in life are given freely, tended and tilled conservatively, and distributed liberally."[18] He recommends that we recover our storytelling capabilities and use of metaphors without changing the message.

Above all, worship is more about the Spirit than about style. "If the spirit is there, presentation also means little . . . . Metaphors do the heavy lifting. Metaphors generate a spirit that quickly captures and charges space. That is why Jesus' method of communication was not the exegesis of words but the exegesis of images: 'the kingdom of heaven is like . . .'"[19] Sweet reminds us that all of these things are for one purpose only—to bring people into God's presence. When that happens, the Holy Spirit moves mightily, and all the technology, food, and coffee become unimportant. God's presence is more than enough to satisfy people.

Jesus used metaphors constantly, such as the kingdom of God is like the pearl of great price or yeast or a mustard seed. In his time, Edwards was a master of imagery, from spiders suspended by a web over a pit of fire to God's light being the sun, to little white flowers swaying in the breeze of his Spirit. Metaphors and the images they produce make the message vivid in the listener's mind. Whether it is fair or not, the church is in competition with the imagery that technology produces.

Frost and Hirsch agree with Sweet and report, "Nonbelievers are not coming to our churches at all precisely because of the perceived boredom factor."[20] They recommend including dialogue in the message. This is something to consider as long as it does not deteriorate into nothing more than personal opinions and preferences. Metaphors still do the lifting because stories dominate our minds and communication. The stories that are memorable are the ones that move us and not the ones that simply entertain.

Find Points of Connection with the Christian Story

James Smith reminds the postmodern church that Christians have "The Story" to tell the world, and they should recapture their storytelling roots that come from Jesus and the parables.[21] Be clear about this: the story of the gospel is not made up; it is a record of actual events and people. Smith also calls Christians to support their storytelling "by [their] story living" and reminds them that "seekers are looking for something our culture can't provide. Many don't want a religious version of what they can already get at

---

18. Sweet, *Post-modern Pilgrims*, xxi.
19. Sweet, *Post-modern Pilgrims*, 95.
20. Frost and Hirsch, *Things to Come*, 189.
21. Lucado is especially gifted in this area—see *No Wonder They Call Him the Savior*; *Six Hours One Friday*; and *Tell Me the Story*, among many others. Similar offerings come from McKnight, *The Story of the Christ*; and Eldredge, *Epic: The Story God Is Telling*.

the mall."²² People may not understand your message, but they will understand that your lifestyle is different in a positive way from what they find elsewhere.

Living in God's holiness may open doors to tell people about Jesus. In a culture obsessed with beauty, health, and pleasure, the beauty of holiness and the wholeness and joy it brings is a powerful way to connect with folks in twenty-first-century America. Some points of contact with our culture might be care of the earth (Gen 1), delight (Ps 37), beauty (Pss 29, 96), and enjoyment.²³ You might gently and naturally comment on a beautiful sunset as something God makes for us to enjoy. You might let the person know that you believe that God wants us to care for the earth and see if it leads to an open discussion of God. If offense is given, it must be "for the right reasons"; the church must "affirm those aspects of every culture that agree with God's purposes and that predispose members of that culture to comprehend the gospel."²⁴

While we look for good things through which we can connect with the culture, Frost and Hirsch remind us that not everything in the culture has its counterpart in what Scripture affirms that we believe and do. They remind us that "the gospel also comes to judge the evil elements in every society that are contrary to God's will. The creation of humankind in God's image means that there is no culture that lacks virtuous elements in terms of which the gospel can be expressed. At the same time the fall of humankind from grace means that no culture is completely virtuous."²⁵

In every culture there is good and bad, but just because there is some good does not mean that the people of the culture are good to go to heaven. The bad that coexists with the good separates them from God for eternity apart from faith in Jesus. Always remember the three Rs: rescue, redemption, and reconciliation. It is imperative that Christians identify what it is in culture that is part of God's truth and what is not. Connect with them in the things that do correspond favorably with Scripture and gently move into how Jesus rescues and redeems the bad and makes them a new creation—gives them a do-over.

Watch Out for the Potholes

The Pothole of Elevating the Good

A tendency common to all of us is to take a good thing and to make it the ultimate thing (elevating it above God). In contextualization there is always the chance that Christians can over-identify with culture (see chapters 4 and 5). One way churches have used the consumerist approach of the culture to make their worship more inviting is by offering coffee bars prior to, after, or between services. They have used the entertainment aspect

---

22. Smith, *Who's Afraid of Postmodernism*, 78–79.
23. Question 1 of "The Westminster Shorter Catechism," 175.
24. Frost and Hirsch, *Things to Come*, 113.
25. Frost and Hirsch, *Things to Come*, 113.

so prominent in this culture by incorporating more technology during the service such as the use of PowerPoint and videos to supplement the message. Most churches have web pages. Some have movie night and invite the community.

All of these things are good when used as means to reach people in culturally relevant ways as long as churches *communicate the gospel without changing the message.* Don't let them become ends in themselves. McGrath reminds us that not only must our message be relevant and attractive to today's culture, but it must be "securely grounded in God's self-revelation, not invented yesterday in an effort to get a hearing in the marketplace."[26] God's self-revelation can be found only in Scripture.

The Pothole of Relying on Human Reason and Beliefs over Scripture and Christian Beliefs

Scripture and not human reason is the only reliable criterion by which to sort this all out. The gospel the church proclaims must reach people in a way they can understand, but Christians must also challenge those things that fall outside the bounds of Scripture. Some of these are the ways people pursue pleasure, what they do for entertainment, or how they manipulate people, because such things destroy health, happiness, and life. "Everybody's thinking/saying/doing it" is not a good enough reason to adopt an idea or action.

Human reason usually results in faulty ideas about God that may need to be addressed before people are ready to hear the gospel of Jesus. You might try challenging a person's beliefs with the same arguments they level against Christianity. Challenge them to apply the same scrutiny to their own principles that they use to dissect Christianity.[27] Remember always to be as gentle as possible and always treat people with respect.

You might try to get them to see, as McGrath has observed in today's consumeristic culture with its fast-paced, image-driven advertising, that "the attractiveness of a belief [what they believe today] is too often inversely proportional to its truth." Today, the media makes things that lead to destruction look very attractive. Too often the more truth is in a thing, the less attractively the media portrays it. It often makes truth the object of derision, such as is portrayed in the pro-life movement. Move out into the community in the assurance that Christianity rests secure in millennia of truth.[28] Move out and meet the real needs in our culture and be wise as serpents and harmless as doves showing them what these genuine needs are. The church is God's force

---

26. McGrath, *Evangelicalism and the Future of Christianity*, 103.

27. Keller shares some of his conversations with people in *The Reason for God*. For the charge of narrowmindedness, see chapter 5. To the charge that there is no God, see Keller's argument in chapter 9 of the same book.

28. McGrath, *Evangelicalism and the Future of Christianity*, 103.

for good in this world *provided* she does not change the message to accommodate society's perceived needs by looking, sounding, and acting just like them.

The Potholes of Accommodation and Human Tradition

As the church moves into the community she must make sure that she is not using "wooden repetition of yesterday's ideas [which] may alienate today's people from the gospel—not because the *gospel* is alienating, but because *a particular presentation of the gospel* is seen as out of touch, out of date and out of place. Advance [of the gospel] involves adaptation—but *adaptation need not involve change*" (the second italics are mine).[29] Contextualize; don't capitulate.

The church's approach to this culture must accommodate where people are in order to engage with them on a meaningful level. It does not mean that she rewrites the Bible to accommodate their behaviors and beliefs. Her goal is to be peacemakers (helping people to find peace with God through Jesus) and not merely peacekeepers compromising everything to maintain an absence of conflict which encourages the bullies of this world to demand even more. It does mean that she proclaims the gospel with "all the power and persuasiveness at [her] disposal."[30] Preachers need to take this to heart and courageously proclaim all the word of God and not just the popular parts. But this must be done out of a holy life or it will be hypocritical.

Sweet agrees with McGrath and warns church leaders not to "strive to replace the 'modern consciousness' with a 'postmodern consciousness'"; they are to "help replace the 'modern consciousness' with a 'Christ consciousness' that can live and move and have its being in the postmodern culture."[31] Furthermore, he points out that "there are certain presuppositions in the postmodern worldview that are opposed to the Christian worldview as revealed in the biblical texts and traditions of our faith. I want us to become not worldly wise but worldly unwise."[32] The ways of the natural person only dimly reflect God's ways, similarly to primary and secondary beauty. Always test the beliefs and practices of people to discern which sort they are. Ask: Is it scriptural? Who gets the glory? And what are the fruits? There is a way that seems right to people but ends in death and destruction.

The Pothole of Plurality as an Excuse Not to Tell People about Jesus

There is one more consideration. Plurality cannot be used as an excuse not to proclaim the good news of Jesus' atonement and the joy of facing our sin, repenting,

---

29. McGrath, *Evangelicalism and the Future of Christianity*, 114.

30. Michael Green, as quoted by Alister McGrath, *Evangelicalism and the Future of Christianity*, 162.

31. Sweet, *Post-modern Pilgrims*, 48.

32. Sweet, *Post-modern Pilgrims*, 48.

and being forgiven. McGrath reminds us that "the Christian proclamation has always taken place in a pluralistic world, in competition with rival religious and intellectual convictions."[33] Christians, take heart! *Pluralism was rampant in the world in which the first disciples lived.* If they could do it, you can too. God's arm is not any shorter today or his power any less than it was two thousand years ago.

Revival Prayer Revisited

Concerted prayer for preaching and revival is often missing in the church. Piper reminds us that "good preaching is born of good praying."[34] However, too often, the church relies on programs to advance her cause. God does work through means, but his primary plan for advancing the gospel is the witness of his people. E. M. Bounds recognizes this and writes, "We are constantly on a stretch . . . to devise new methods, new plans, new organizations to advance the church and secure enlargement and efficiency for the gospel. This trend of the day has a tendency to lose sight of the man or sink the man in the plan or organization . . . . The church is looking for better methods; God is looking for better men."[35]

For Bounds the answer "is not more machinery or better, not new organizations or more and novel methods, but men whom the Holy Spirit can use—men of prayer, men mighty in prayer. The Holy Spirit does not flow through methods, but through men. He does not come on machinery, but on men. He does not anoint plans, but men—men of prayer."[36] He cautions pastors to remember that "if prayer be left out of account, the preacher rises to no higher level than the lecturer, the politician, or the secular teacher. That which distinguishes him from all other public speakers is the fact of prayer. And as prayer deals with God, this means that the preacher has God with him, while other speakers do not need God with them to make their public messages effective."[37]

Bounds also reminds the church that "the Reformation of the sixteenth century owes its origin to prayer. In all his lifework . . . Martin Luther was instant in prayer. The secret of his extraordinary activity is found in this statement: 'I have so much work to do that I cannot get along without giving three hours daily of my best time to prayer.'"[38] A little more than two centuries later, William Wilberforce echoes this sentiment, "I have been keeping too late hours, and hence have had but a hurried half hour to myself. I am lean and cold and hard. I had better allow more time, say two

---

33. McGrath, *Evangelicalism and the Future of Christianity*, 162.
34. Piper, *Supremacy of God*, 100.
35. Bounds, "Power through Prayer," 447.
36. Bounds, "Power through Prayer," 447.
37. Bounds, "The Weapon of Prayer," 413. Hereafter referred to as Book 6.
38. Martin Luther, as quoted by Bounds in "The Weapon of Prayer," 441.

hours, or an hour-and-a-half, daily to religious exercises."[39] The people that God uses mightily are mighty people of prayer.

Prayer was common to the revivals of Edwards's day and preceded every known revival. Before the Revival of 1734, the Moravians had established a 24/7 prayer vigil in Europe that lasted for a hundred years, during which time we see the Great Awakening and the Second and maybe Third Great Awakenings in America. This prayer includes the private prayers of pastors and people and corporate prayer of clusters of people gathered together to petition God for revival in what Edwards called concerts of prayer inspired by "Some Thoughts." He was in touch with pastors as far away as Scotland, such as William McCulloch and John McLaurin, who promoted his writings in that country. They coordinated prayer groups that met for two years at first and then decided to go for another seven.

In this concert "nearly one thousand individuals were praying for universal revival in the church."[40] Arthur Fawcett identifies thirty societies in Edinburgh and another forty-five in Glasgow.[41] The groups were comprised of pastors and laymen who covenanted to pray once a week, once a month, or once a quarter. Edwards hoped that prayer for the outpouring of the Holy Spirit would sustain the Scotland revival for years rather than months as it had in New England and would reduce the "disruptive and divisive" elements of the American revival.[42] Edwards wrote to the Rev. John McLaurin,

> I hope the time is hastening, when God's people in all the different parts of the world . . . . shall become . . . one family, one holy and happy society, and all brethren, not only all united in one head, but in greater affection, and in more mutual correspondence, and more visible and sensible union and fellowship in religious exercises, and the holy duties of the service of God; and so that . . . the church on earth will become more like the blessed society in heaven.[43]

Fawcett notes that prayer and unity go hand-in-hand. John Wesley had recommended Edwards's plan of prayer to the Scottish pastors, and Fawcett writes, "So it was that an English Episcopalian recommended to Scottish Presbyterians the inclusion of an American Independent within the comprehension of united intercession!"[44] Unity brought about by prayer equaled a mighty move of God. George Marsden asserts that the "prayer societies . . . were essential parts of the evangelical awakenings."[45]

---

39. William Wilberforce, as quoted by Bounds in "The Weapon of Prayer," 441. Wilberforce was a member in parliament who was instrumental in ending the slave trade in the British Empire.
40. Batzig, "Transatlantic Concert," 84.
41. Fawcett, *Cambuslang Revival*, 224.
42. Kimnach, "Transatlantic Brotherhood of Preachers," 14.
43. Edwards, "Letters and Personal Writings," 183.
44. Fawcett, *Cambuslang Revival*, 227.
45. Marsden, *Jonathan Edwards*, 334.

To get your church started praying for great preaching and revival, I recommend that each Sunday, the congregation be given a brief prayer (just a sentence or two) that petitions God for the main idea of the sermon. I call these "Prayers that Will Change the World." See appendix 9 for an example of a Scripture passage used in a sermon and the prayer that the people would pray that week. Tell them to pray it as they get dressed in the morning, or make meals, or mow the lawn, or even when driving (especially while sitting at red lights). They should pray it as many times during the day as they thought of it. The following Sunday, ask for a show of hands of who actually did it. When I did this, at first only about a quarter of the congregation participated, but eventually at least two-thirds of them got into it, so much so that one week I forgot to give them a prayer, and they asked for one. It may not be exactly what Edwards called a concert of prayer, but it is a start. I urge you to consider it for your congregation.

Summary

We all want things to be better in this country, but that means things must change. For the Christian this is formally called revival. For revival there must be powerful, spirit-filled preaching, but such preaching is only the result of powerful and effective praying. Effective prayers result from righteous, holy living. Both righteous, holy living and effective, holy prayer require accurate knowledge of God. Accurate knowledge of God can only be found in Scripture, which instructs people on the grievousness of sin, the need for discipline, and the process of discernment of right and wrong, and explains the gospel of Jesus. The church must be confident that her understanding of the word of God is accurate as Jesus and the apostles were.

Change requires the complete package, not just the things you want. This change is doable because Jesus has sent his Spirit, who lives in everyone who believes in him. This is the same Spirit who raised Jesus from the dead, and he works in each of God's redeemed children to bring about all that is needed to accomplish his will. Be holy because God is holy: trust him, joyfully obey him, call on his name, allow him to work through you, and watch him accomplish the things Jesus did and greater.

The Wrap-Up

> Resolution One: I will live for God.
> Resolution Two: If no one else does, I still will.
>
> —Jonathan Edwards, "Resolutions"

LIFE IS A JOURNEY for which we must be equipped spiritually as well as physically and mentally. Just as a mountain climber would not begin the climb without the proper clothing, training, and trustworthy equipment including survival gear, so too it is vital that Christians be equipped for their journey through life. The path we choose determines the life we will live here on earth and in the life to come. God asks each person to choose the Ancient Road, the one he created and intended humanity to travel. Isaiah calls it the Highway of Holiness. Jesus calls it the Narrow Way. In each case, the implication is that there is a right way, God's way, and a wrong way, our cultural biases that go against God's truth. Since no culture is perfect, the ancient path is just as relevant to us today as it was for the people to whom it was written. The human condition never changes apart from salvation in Jesus. Finding God's way requires testing the spirits to discern God's truth from human reason, wants, and relative truth.

There will always be some truth in culture because people are made in the image of God and retain at least some of God's attributes in them, but this is not enough to grant anyone access to heaven or to enable them to enter into God's presence. Even one sin separates an individual from God who is perfectly holy. Each person since Adam and Eve naturally travels the world's way which Scripture calls the broad road that pursues anything under the sun, and while it may feel like freedom and love, it is really bondage to sin and leads to death. Herein lies the problem: discerning the Ancient Way/road/path in the midst of the clamor around us.

The Road We Are on

Historically, Alexis de Tocqueville credited the greatness of the 1830s United States to the powerful and unified preaching in the pulpits of every church regardless of denomination. He also understood that the problems of democracy were solved by the strong religious influences which taught moderation in all things and constantly worked to direct people's focus towards heaven and others. For de Tocqueville, the spirit must prosper so the material world can be well. The soul must be elevated so that the body, individually and corporately, can prosper. In the early nineteenth century, the same unifying morality and basic belief system was present everywhere.[1] For these reasons, he urged "lawmakers in democracies and all decent and enlightened men who live in them . . . [to] apply themselves unstintingly to the task of uplifting souls and keeping them intent on heaven. All who are interested in the future of democratic societies must unite and together make constant efforts to spread a taste for the infinite, a sense of greatness, and a love of immaterial pleasures."[2]

He also warned that if ever this system was to be removed, there would be dire consequences. While people were ripping away from the established faith, which was undeniably Christian, so, too, the people would be ripped apart as they tried to establish something new. About 130 years after his visit, the Supreme Court would remove God (the Judeo-Christian God) from our public consciousness by banning prayer and Scripture from our schools. Self-appointed watchdogs and enforcers would bring lawsuits and test just how extensively that ban could be expanded into all areas of our society. God and his moral code would be removed from our public life, and political correctness would be promoted and imposed by the media with self as the moral center.

The result has been to submerge much of Western culture into a controlled way of thinking that has made mini police out of all of us in micromanaging everything we say or do. Freedom of speech is disappearing.[3] Much of television and social media has conditioned Americans to talk and think in certain ways but without giving them a moral code by which to live. Neil Postman has pointed out how it is leading us into a path of constant entertainment in which we are *Amusing Ourselves to Death* (see chapter 2). Not only have we lost genuine freedom, but everyone is making his or her truth, and anarchy is at our doorsteps just as de Tocqueville foretold.

Since the 1960s, religion has become a matter of private preference; materialism and consumerism are growing, and each successive generation has rejected much of the wisdom and authority of their parents, teachers, and pastors and is seeking pleasure at unprecedented rates. Our pursuit of pleasure has been accelerated by our fast-paced technology, first by the advent of the television, then the computer, and most recently the internet. We have each become a quintessential consumeristic, materialistic, autonomous self. Our concept of independence now demands relative

---

1. This unity would change as North and South isolated Scripture passages and adapted them to justify their particular economic and political agendas instead of letting the word of God change them. This practice contributed to the Civil War and subsequent splits of God's word in its aftermath. See chapter 9 and Noll, *The Civil War as a Theological Crisis*.

2. de Tocqueville, *Democracy in America*, 635.

3. Take a stand on some idea contrary to the media's agenda like gun control, immigration, or health care and see how quickly they try to silence you by vilifying your character instead of discussing the facts.

truth, privatized morality, and not just extravagant tolerance but also acceptance of most things including sin.

Nevertheless, a Holy God still governs the world, and the same power that worked in Jesus' day is available today. God is able to turn a stone-cold heart to a heart of flesh and the mind that wants no part of him to adore him. God works through means, and the means he chooses to use in most cases are his people. God calls Christians to be his arms, hands, feet, and mouth. He calls them to stand firm, but this requires that they know how to stand and for what they are standing, and too often they look, think, talk, and act just like the culture. One way this happens according to Timothy Tennent is when people obscure the truth by changing the meaning of words in order to gain control over people and situations and writes, "The only remaining arbiter for truth is the sole perspective of an autonomous, vacillating individual.... [whose] personal interpretations of meaning are equally valid or, for some, equally meaningless."[4] If this is done by enough people, the original meaning is lost, or if a person does remember, he or she may not be aware that others are using the same words but applying different meanings to them (more on this below).

Tennent looks to the future and the logical outcome of individuals determining their own truth and asserts that such a position is "intellectually vulnerable and difficult to sustain.... because it would mean the end of all moral discrimination."[5] We see the effects of this throughout our nation if we have the courage to look. Without moral discrimination anarchy will come as everyone pursues his or her own truth, which can only result in a generalized lack of self-discipline, rejection of external authority, breakdown of commitment to anything outside of self, and increased human trafficking, sexual promiscuity, and use of mind-altering drugs to name a few.

Whenever someone tries to point out how a society is falling apart, there are always people who scoff at them, citing how similar statements have been made in every age. Be aware that each age feels this way because each generation must be told about God and his truth. Additionally, the current generation is encouraged to rebel at unprecedented rates through our advanced technology which constantly urges them to do things their way. Test the spirits to discern if their rebellion is legitimate, such as being opposed to racism, human trafficking, or pollution, but be sure you are using biblical standards and not the culture's criteria by which you test it. The culture's take on morality, love, grace, truth, and holiness may seem right but will often not agree with God's actual love, grace, truth and holiness. Whenever youth rebel against authority and the established rules of behavior in any society, there will be struggle and possibly disintegration of that civilization if the rebellion becomes broad enough.

When people rebel against God the results carry greater consequences. The short answer to why these cycles of obedience and rebellion happen is that God has no grandchildren. Each person must come to him personally—a parent's faith does

---

4. Tennent, *Religious Roundtable*, 242.
5. Tennent, *Religious Roundtable*, 242.

not automatically carry over to the next generation. Every person in every generation must hear the gospel of Jesus anew in order to be brought to salvation and to meet the Holy God.

To Be or Not to Be on the Ancient Way

For the Christian, the rules of behavior come from God himself as given in Scripture. There are definitely some dos and don'ts as the law teaches us what holiness looks like, but primarily the genuine Christian life is to be in a close relationship with God through Jesus and traveling his Highway of Holiness where there is beauty, wholeness, healing, love, grace, unity, purity, and peace as well as truth, righteousness, justice, and judgment. The alternative is not to be in this relationship with God and traveling the broad road, your own way. The greater the gap is between the last generation when a significant number of folks experienced God's holiness and the present generation, the greater is the need for revival and reformation. The greater the distractions are that keep us from thinking about God, the greater is the opportunity to be pulled away from him. The faster the access to information becomes, the less time we have to process what it means and the easier it becomes to be deceived.

Whatever the situation may be, God's truth must be passed on to each successive generation. The primary way to do this is through holiness, but we have forgotten what that means. We considered creation and what it meant to be made in the image of God and found that God's holiness constitutes the major part of what was lost of that image in the fall of humanity. We considered the relationship between holiness and sin and found they cannot coexist. God is holy; sin is not. Sin severed the relationship Adam and Eve had with God, and that chasm persists to this day. People still need to be rescued and redeemed in order to be reconciled to God and made holy.

But God's holiness is naturally foreign to us. It is a mystery; yet his holiness affects us at our innermost core. When humans enter his presence they are "undone" (Isaiah 6:1–6), and because God is holy, he is *numinous*;[6] he is the *mysteruim tremendum*.[7] As much as we can understand of holiness, we find it to be God's essential characteristic which holds together in perfect balance all of his other characteristics. God's holiness is the ultimate beauty humans can know, the greatest enjoyment they can experience, and the definitive word on love. His holiness brings meaning to our existence and wholeness to our lives.

People must be brought to realize that the emptiness they are feeling can only be satisfied by God who is holy. Only holiness can fulfill them because that is what has been missing in each person since the fall. Therefore, in order to reach the next generation for Jesus, Christians need to recover God's holiness, plow the ground with

---

6. Otto, *Idea of the Holy*, 8.
7. Otto, *Idea of the Holy*, 12.

revival prayer, and sow righteousness, making an environment ready for revival and reform (Hos 10:12). In short, live holy lives because God is holy.

One of the means God uses to bring about this transformation is powerful preaching like de Tocqueville witnessed (but contextualized to this culture) that filled the pulpits of American churches and unified Christian beliefs and morals. However, powerful preaching only happens where there is powerful praying, and effective praying is the result of accurate knowledge of God, which teaches people how to live righteous and holy lives. The only place to find this knowledge of God is in Scripture, whose author is the Holy Spirit.

Unfortunately, even when we study the Bible, we do so through the cultural lens that has been implanted in us so firmly that we often miss the truth found in Scripture. It began with the attack on the trustworthiness of Scripture launched by scholars in the eighteenth-century Enlightenment who rejected everything supernatural (including the resurrection). It was followed by the split among Christians over the doctrines of love or righteousness and the issue of slavery, selecting the parts of Scripture to support an economic, political, and often racist agenda. These things opened the door for the reemergence of ideas rejected long ago by the early Christians such as Jesus was not God but only a good person, or the opposite: he was so holy that he was not human.

Another idea rejected by the early Christians was that Jesus did not rise from the dead. The extra-biblical ideologies pursued in the twentieth century were mostly the resurrecting of the ideas long ago rejected by the church. Familiarize yourself with Scripture and the information in this book and learn to discern what is of God and what is not. Examine current teachings of the church and compare them against Scripture and the major doctrines of the church that have come under attack throughout the past 250 years. Test the spirits about a particular belief or behavior to discern its source (1 John 4:1).

In every case where they do not match up, people may not consciously have set out to undermine Christianity, but their human nature that is inherently opposed to God will ultimately lead to rebellion against him. Some will look kind and gentle while doing this, which makes them seem right; others may be outright belligerent, making what they are doing easier to identify. Either way, the result is always the same: ultimate rejection of Jesus and hence, God. What a belief system does with Jesus reveals its truth and efficacy and whether it is of God or not. You will find that along with each twisting or denial of the ancient truths, the church has lost something that has rendered her impotent and less able to tell the next generation about Jesus. These must be identified and the truth recovered if she is to live in to the role of being God's witness and ambassador to the world in order to rescue, to redeem, and to reconcile people to him.

In addition to powerful preaching, revival praying, living righteous and holy lives, trusting Scripture, and testing the spirits, Christians must learn to identify how the meanings of words have changed since they were used in Scripture or by the church throughout the ages. Since Postmodernity, spin is liberally applied to all language as per Foucault's suggestion to gain power over people. Combine this with the media's ever-present push for personal comfort and continual entertainment and the result is pernicious. Do the hard work of recovering what the Bible means.

Use the knowledge of the two, Bible and culture, to communicate the gospel clearly in this age. When you engage someone in conversation, you may have to probe for the meaning of the words he or she is using. Some examples are "gentleness," "peace," "unity," and "freedom." Gentleness means meekness, but unlike the culture's idea of "roll over and acquiesce" to everyone and every idea and become a doormat, Scripture identifies gentleness as great power under equally great self-control. God's freedom means freedom not to sin; our culture's meaning of freedom is to be free to do whatever seems right to you and includes sin. For Christians, peace means making peace with God. For our culture it means both absence of conflict and compromise of anything in order to acquire temporary personal peace and affluence. But what happens when you compromise truth and sacred principles? You will eventually run out of the very things that bring meaning, peace, and unity to your life.

What people mean when they talk about Jesus can be the most difficult to pin down. If a person claims to believe in Jesus, you might want to pursue exactly what that person has in mind. It could simply be an acknowledgment that Jesus was a good person. Not pursuing these things may be politically correct and let you off easy—you have done your duty; you talked about Jesus. There was no conflict and all are content—but the person may remain unchanged, lost in their sin, and not reconciled to God.

We can see the obfuscation of God's biblical truth clearly in the way cultural understanding of love influences the church. This love often rejects discipline and encourages self-autonomy: be yourself and do what feels right in the moment regardless of who gets hurt. This view of love is now viewed as God's ultimate characteristic, which just happens to reject all judgment and allows whatever the person believes is right for him or her. We have discovered that this comes to us through the social media and not from the Bible.

Jesus teaches his disciples (Matt 6:33) to "seek first the kingdom of God and his *righteousness* [not his love], and everything you need for a beautiful and healthy life will be added to you" (my paraphrase and also italics are mine). Of course, this will look very different from what the world tells you that you need. When you seek God, you will often find righteousness first which then produces love (Ps 89:14). When you come to faith in Jesus, God declares you righteous, not loved. God's love for you is already present as revealed in Jesus, his Son, whom he gave so that you may be *put in right standing* with God. Then you are in a position to experience the extravagant love we read about in Scripture. It is certain that God's love will never violate his righteousness. The culture has it backwards, and the church has often followed its lead. Scripture tells us there is a way that seems right to people (the culture's way), but in the end it leads to death and destruction (Prov 14:12; 16:25).

Hosea (10:12, NIV) tells God's people that if they *sow righteousness*, they will *reap* God's unfailing *love* and faithfulness. He calls on them to seek God "until he comes and showers righteousness on you." The fruit or result of righteousness is love. If the righteousness you pursue does not lead to love, you are not following God's holy righteousness. Conversely, if the love you claim to have does not correspond with God's holy righteousness and allows you to pursue sin as identified in Scripture, you are not living in God's holy love.

Contrary to cultural thinking, it is God's holiness, and not his love, that holds everything together in perfect balance. It is holiness that brings ultimate beauty, wholeness, love, peace, pleasure, enjoyment, hope, and unity. To pursue love without God's righteousness is just as hurtful to humanity as to pursue righteousness without God's love. The first leads to licentiousness, and the second leads to legalism. Both are destructive. God calls each person to himself through Jesus Christ and requires each to be holy even as he is holy.

Because God is holy, his righteous requirement of the death sentence that sin deserves cannot be ignored. In his compassion and holy love, God sent his Son, Jesus, to pay the penalty we owe. He died on the cross to fulfill the holy commands of the law and satisfied God's holy justice, holy judgment, and holy wrath. Because of Jesus' sacrifice, anyone who puts his or her faith in him will be justified (being declared holy because of Jesus' righteous act) and will begin the process of sanctification of actually becoming holy in their inner thoughts and outer words and deeds.

If you know people who focus on how terrible God is because he does not allow everyone into heaven, you might try turning it around by asking if they lock their doors and then point out how they do not allow just anyone into their house who might harm them, steal their possessions, or destroy their home. You might use it as an opportunity to talk about the gravity of sin. Most definitely you could point out that instead of being upset that not everyone goes to heaven, they should focus on the miracle that anyone gets there at all—this is the true meaning of holy grace. They need to realize that it is totally due to God's love, mercy, and grace in sending his Son, Jesus, to die in our place that any of us make it there. Those who do are those who believe in Jesus and trust him with their lives. It is God's house and his rules. He is sovereign.

In order to tell the next generation about this gospel message, Christians must recover their voices in the marketplace and the boldness to speak their convictions. However, the culture has conditioned people to keep their thoughts to themselves when advocating for Jesus. Discern the spirit behind such thinking. Christians must recover their freedom to let their light shine in the world (which includes talking about the one claim to love) and keep their voices from degenerating into merely human impressions of what God is like, similar to what has been done with love and truth. They will ground their convictions in the authoritative Bible and the truthfulness of all it teaches.

The church will recover the doctrines of sin, repentance, redemption, justification, and sanctification held in balance by holiness. She will recover her storytelling skills and be sure to portray accurately "The Story" given by the Law and the Prophets, the apostles, and Jesus. However, while recovering her stories, the church must guard against the story of the teddy-bear god (who *only* wants comforts you) and the glory story (God only wants to make you great). Both are attractive to our culture but will be ineffective and bring harm because they misrepresent the truth.

Additionally, Christians will stop separating God, the Scriptures, and his commands into those things that are approved and disapproved according to culture and adopt God's holy love, grace, and mercy. This includes recovering his holy truth, righteousness, justice, and judgment and understanding the necessity for God's wrath. The church will value God and his holy ways and let God validate her life and ministry. She will begin deferring to the One who made her and not rely primarily on her human wisdom, reason, strength, money, and programs.

Moreover, Christians will overcome their conditioning to accommodate the world and begin asking the world to accommodate Christ. They will present to the world a Holy God who is the source of all ultimate beauty and complete wholeness. They can only do this by knowing what the Bible actually teaches as opposed to what they *think* about it. They will recover the biblical meaning to their words and be able to communicate the difference. They will invite people around them to the divine dance because they will live a holy lifestyle because the One who calls them is holy.

Timothy Keller shows us how this might look when he describes conversations with people who have judged Christianity to be wrong and harmful to others. To the complaint "that belief in a God of judgment will lead to a more brutal society" he responds, "A loss of belief in a God of judgment can lead to brutality. If we are free to shape life and morals any way we choose without ultimate accountability, it can lead to violence . . . . the doctrine of God's final judgment is a necessary undergirding for human practices of love and peacemaking."[8] This is totally opposite of the culture's thinking but accurate both biblically and in practice. Not only have we seen the atrocities of the godless regimes of the Nazis and Communism, but we have also seen killings in our schools since the close of the twentieth century.

The culture has removed much discipline and many consequences for harmful behavior and constantly tells all children how good they are. Yet bullying, made easier by our technology, continues to damage our children to the point that goes well beyond low self-esteem. It has been called "the faceless evil," and about 34 percent of our students experience cyberbullying in their lifetime.[9] In Florida, one study showed that 70 percent of their students claimed rumors about them had been spread

---

8. Keller, *Reason for God*, 78. See Volf's observation on Nazism and Communism quoted in chapter 12.

9. Cook, "Cyberbullying Facts and Statistics," paras. 6, 26.

online.[10] Increased rates of suicide are attributed to cyberbullying. Bullied "victims are more likely to engage in substance abuse and nonviolent delinquency."[11] Cyberbullying causes students to be more likely to suffer sleeplessness and depression; it affects their grades and contributes to them not feeling safe in school and adversely affects their motivation and overall success.[12] Bullying behavior is often a precursor to violent behaviors such as school shootings.

However, no one is asking whether if children knew they were made in God's image and loved by him, it would provide the self-worth they need to resist the urge to destroy those who hurt them. No one is asking if belief that God judges people for the hurtful things they do might help alleviate their feelings of desperation and the need for revenge. No one is asking whether if children understood that God vindicates them, it could prevent them from trying to vindicate themselves. Few children today have been told that God created them in his image and that he loves them, values them, and has great plans for them. If they knew, perhaps they would not feel that they need to take matters into their own hands. If they knew, perhaps the bullies could be persuaded that their actions are wrong and would then refrain from denigrating their peers and learn to respect them instead. Removing God's judgment of wrong and hurtful behaviors and telling children how good they are has not stopped the damage to our youth; we have actually seen it accelerate since God was removed from our schools and culture. It is the responsibility of the church to tell this message. Find your voice. It is greatly needed.

Another way to reach people today is to look for where the certainty of the uncertain is beginning to crack. Christians must equip themselves with the reality of the beauty, joy, and wholeness of God's holiness and be ready and willing to give the gospel to people who are ready to hear it, perhaps for the first time. Never assume that anyone accurately knows who Jesus is or what the Bible says. Moreover, never assume that people will automatically reject what you have to say if you approach them in gentleness and respect. Model for them and tell them why God is important to them and meets their deepest needs.

Additionally, our congregations must make people aware that not only do they have choices but that their choices have consequences. Os Guinness reminds us that "it is not up to us to turn our culture around, or to turn this country back to God, but we can highlight our generation's choices and their consequences. Choices always have consequences, and Americans must be challenged to face the logic of their choices and the responsibility of their consequences."[13] This is a truth not faced (on any large scale) by this nation in decades, but it is the gracious, loving, and compassionate thing to do. It must be done in humility with grace and truth. To be effective, Christians must have pure motives and not be eager to point out the faults of others

10. Cook, "Cyberbullying Facts and Statistics," para. 29.
11. Cook, "Cyberbullying Facts and Statistics," para.18.
12. Cook, "Cyberbullying Facts and Statistics," paras. 20, 28.
13. Guinness, "Found Faithful," 107.

in order to make themselves look superior. You can work long and hard with minimal results if you are not living holy lives: living righteously, loving significantly, and praying effectively. People need to see the message as well as hear it.

This way of life will be different from the world because the Christian God is holy. He is utterly different than us in the quality of the things for which we settle. "We care about success; he cares about holiness. We care about temporary pleasures; he cares about eternal consequences. We covet others' experiences like teenagers longing to taste more of the world; he longs for a closer embrace like a parent seeking to keep a family together."[14] Furthermore, a holy life brings together in perfect balance all the qualities we attribute to God: the fruits of the Spirit with the gifts of the Spirit, love and peace with righteousness, mercy with justice, grace with judgment, and discipline with healing, wisdom, knowledge, miracles, evangelism, and prophecy. God accomplishes this with ultimate beauty bringing us into the wholeness, joy, pleasure, and delight for which we are created. He rescues, redeems, reconciles, and sets us on the right path to his glory. This is the message Christians bring to the world, and they must model it in their lives. This life comes only through faith in the work of Jesus on the cross, which made the way for our sins to be forgiven and for holiness to be restored to us.

So then, the message Christians must give to Western society is this: the thrice-Holy God did not *do* away with the penalty and seriousness of sin; He *made* the way through Jesus for it to be forgiven to all who enter the narrow way, the Highway of Holiness, by choosing the ancient path of belief in Jesus (justification). This is much more than an intellectual agreement with certain beliefs about Jesus. It is a life commitment to become like him, to love God and his truth, his word—the Scriptures—and to obey God's ways in humility with love for God and others, concern for lost souls, and all the other characteristics we read about in Scripture (sanctification). The bond of this commitment is the Holy Spirit. It is primarily God's work from beginning to end, but living out the holiness Jesus won for us depends on the cooperation of the person or group. Live holy lives because God is holy.

In Closing

We are all on a journey. We have seen how holiness sets you free to become whole, to dance again, and to become the person God created you to be. This book is not a "how-to" manual. It is a guide for recovering the essentials of the Christian faith—those things that have been forgotten or compromised to Modernity, Postmodernity, Technopoly, and culture. It is a guide to equip you to melt away the false beauty of this world (like the frozen window in the preface) and to see through it to the beautiful reality beyond that lasts for eternity. It is an attempt to help you to visualize an ocean when you have only ever seen a pond. In this age of self-help and therapeutic religion, the greatest inroads

---

14. Chapell, *Holiness by Grace*, 177.

THE WRAP-UP

Christians have with our culture are through beauty, enjoyment or pleasure, and wholeness (health and well-being), all of which are the direct result of holiness and will lead to deeper appreciation of God and the historic gospel.

Evil is accelerating. Our culture has sown the wind and is reaping the whirlwind (Hos 8:7), and the church has capitulated. The church in the twenty-first century is facing a never-before-experienced phenomenon that does not allow for thoughtful reflection because of its speed of light communication through our media and internet. Guinness describes what she is up against as "powerful . . . pressurizing, and . . . pervasive . . . [with] speed, scope, and simultaneity . . . acceleration, compression, and intensification."[15] He cites three things essential to the church's mission: "we need deep biblical convictions"; "we need a sure grasp of the history of ideas"; and "we need a skillful use of the sociology of knowledge."[16] The last two of these three are not well understood in the minds of most Christians; even the first is rapidly fading from the minds of those who attend church regularly. I have tried to supply at least some of the historical and social aspects (chapters 1–5) as well as the biblical knowledge needed (chapters 6–11) in order to recover the deep biblical conviction and commitment required to be holy and to be equipped to tell the next generation about Jesus (chapters 12–18).

This is not a once-and-done event in the life of a Christian. It is a journey lived out every day on earth, and like every journey there will be choices to make about which path to follow. God tells us we are at a crossroads (Jer 6:16). We must choose which road we will take. Unfortunately, the options and attractiveness of the alternatives increase daily. That means a lot of discernment will be needed to follow Jesus. Once we are on the Highway of Holiness, we must examine ourselves daily and make adjustments to our thoughts, attitudes, and actions to conform to God's ways like the builders of the transcontinental railroad who surveyed daily to make sure they were on course. Although there will still be suffering on earth (no one is exempt from that) God's way leads to a life of beauty, delight, joy, happiness, singing, and wholeness now (in spite of circumstances) and ultimately filled with those things to perfection in heaven where suffering is forever ended. At the giving of the law, Moses told the people that they had a choice to follow the law or not, which would then determine whether they would receive blessings or reap curses. Hosea instructs us to choose God's way, which is to sow righteousness that will reap God's steadfast love. This is excellent advice in any age.

The New Creation: You Must Be Born Again

Moses challenged the Israelites to choose life, God's holiness, so that they might live. It is a challenge to us as well. If the law could bring life to Israel by following it, how

15. Guinness, "Found Faithful," 102.
16. Guinness, "Found Faithful," 102.

much more glorious and powerful is the promise of life to those who choose Jesus! Jesus compared it to being born again. Paul translated that into becoming a new creation. When you were born, your DNA determined much of your personality and whether you would have blond, black, or red hair and blue, brown, or green eyes as well as tendencies toward certain diseases. When you give your life to Jesus, believe on him and make him your Lord as well as Savior, you are given a new DNA by the Holy Spirit. This is why Jesus called it being born again. If he had told them they would get new deoxyribonucleic acid, they would have looked at him like he had a demon. He simply said, "You must be born again." In the new birth, the Spirit sets up residence in you and begins the process of rewriting your DNA, but he does not force the changes on you.

Think of it like a bone marrow transplant. Twenty-plus years ago, I had one of these to fight cancer. After the chemo killed my bone marrow, I had no way of producing the blood I needed to keep me alive. I compare this with the natural state of all people. Nurses gave me transfusions of red blood cells and platelets to keep me going, but I no longer had any white cells to fight off diseases and to keep me healthy. Just about every antibiotic known to medicine was pumped through my body to keep me from getting sick.

After the strong chemo was flushed from by body, the medical staff infused me with new bone marrow. In theory, this would take up residence in my bones and begin to produce all the blood and antibodies my body needed to live. However, this is never guaranteed to happen. The body might reject the bone marrow and prevent it from taking over. The body may think it is doing the right thing, but death inevitably follows. I was so thrilled the first day I saw 11 white cells had been found in my blood test. The nurse told me rather dourly that I had a long way to go because I needed thousands of them to live. Nevertheless, I was ecstatic because I knew the bone marrow was doing its thing and settling in my bones, making new blood for me.

The same thing is true of the gift of the Holy Spirit, whom God gives to each of his children through belief in Christ. He is in you, but you must cooperate with him and let him set up residence and take over rewriting the way you think, talk, and act. He will work in you to will and to do God's good pleasure (Phil 2:12–13). You may reject his working in you, but if you cooperate with him, he will rewrite your DNA to look like God's Son's DNA. If you fight him and remain unchanged, you may continue for a while, but genuine life that satisfies will be greatly diminished. If you reject him completely, you will die in your sins and be separated from God forever. To choose God's way is to choose life. Whenever Jesus talks about life, he always means something more than just living a life of comfort and pleasure here. He is concerned for eternal life. Choose life in Jesus; choose the cross; choose holiness as the way to have abundant life that tells the next generation about Jesus and the great things he has done.

Summary

Finally, have confidence that many people want the things God has to give: beauty, wholeness, peace, joy, pleasure, happiness, and to be loved. They were created to need what Christianity alone can give, God, and he is holy. They are seeking the holiness lost in the fall, but they do not realize it. The catch is that they want it on their own terms instead of God's way. They have been told that they deserve what they want when they want it, and they expect God to acquiesce to them and to bless their efforts. They want to be part of the dance, the incredible feast God throws, but on their terms instead of his. It is the task of the church to show and to tell them why their way does not work and to point them to the way, the truth, and the life who is Jesus and through whom they must pass (he is the door and the way/path) if they are to enter heaven.

God calls *each* of his children to live holy lives and to partner with him in the process of bringing the people of this world into the light of his truth and grace found only in Jesus, the Christ, God's Son. Equip yourself with God's holiness and pass along to the next generation the good news of salvation in Jesus Christ and the great doctrines of justification and sanctification. Tell them and equip *them* with holiness for life's journey so that they can, in turn, equip the generation that follows them with the holiness without which no one will see God.

Appendix 1

Timeline

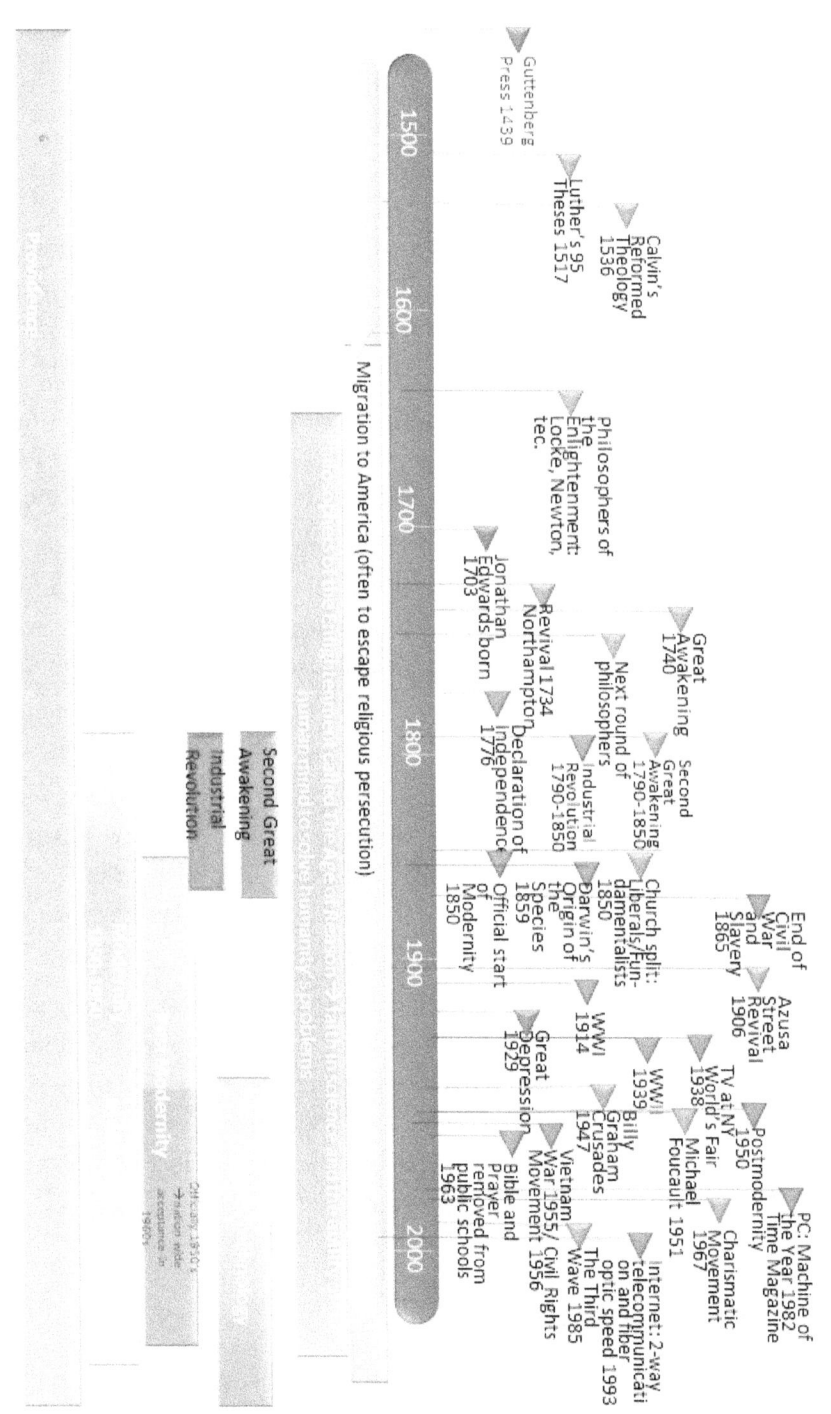

287

Appendix 2

Joni's Wisdom

WE MET JONI IN chapter 10 where I condensed her thoughts on healing and wholeness. Below is a more detailed report of these ideas taken from her book *A Place of Healing: Wrestling with the Mysteries of Suffering, Pain, and God's Sovereignty*. I urge you to read this book for a more complete understanding of who she is and her life and ministry.

- "We are healed by Jesus wounds, but not necessarily immediately"—there is a tree in an acorn, but it may take a century before it can be made into furniture; so it is with Jesus' salvation: it is complete and the outcome settled "but the application of salvation to God's people was anything but finished."[1]
- "Suffering restores a lost beauty in Christ.... It isn't the hurts, blows, and bruises that rob us of the freshness of Christ's beauty in our lives. More likely, it is careless ease, empty pride, earthly preoccupations, and too much prosperity that will put layers of dirty film over our souls."[2]
- "God isn't asking you to be thankful. He's asking you to give thanks. There's a big difference. One response involves emotions, the other your choices, your decisions about a situation, your intent, your 'step of faith.' .... Trusting God has nothing to do with following your feelings. Give thanks that He is sovereign. Give thanks that He is in control. Give thanks that He's planning it all for your good—for your family's good—which ultimately will be all to His glory."[3]
- "The fact is that the God who loves us doesn't allow distressing medical reports in our lives to send us down worry-choked side roads of medical minutia. No, any such crisis is meant to awaken us to the reality of God, His nearness, His care, His presence, and His ever-present help. As with all of life's disappointments and heartaches, it's meant to put force behind the directive in Hosea Chapter 6, where it says, 'Let us know; let us press on to know the LORD.'"[4]

1. Eareckson Tada, *A Place of Healing*, 64–65
2. Eareckson Tada, *A Place of Healing*, 86.
3. Eareckson Tada, *A Place of Healing*, 140.
4. Eareckson Tada, *A Place of Healing*, 142.

- Jesus is the ultimate fulfillment: after forty years in a wheelchair, she sometimes has memories of what it was like to play the piano, to dive through waves, to peel an orange, or to hold the hand of someone she loves. Drink into your soul her words, "Whatever it is I have lost here on earth, whether it be the ability to hold things or feel things, or to run or to walk—whatever it is I have lost, it will all be regained in heaven. And not just 'regained'! Even the best memories of walking and running and swimming and riding a horse—why, these are whispers and faded newspaper images of how much more I will have in heaven.

  "And our relationship with our Savior? Oh, it will be much, much, more. It had better be! Because the whisper of every good thing on earth will find completeness and fulfillment in heaven. I will do so much more than peel an orange or touch a flower or run across a meadow. Those are good things and treasured memories. But they are only hints and promises of more wonderful things yet to be fulfilled. Yes, I certainly love the Lord Jesus on earth. But in heaven? In His physical presence? Wow. I will love him as purely and perfectly and as completely as He loves me. I can't even begin to imagine how wonderful that will be, but the Bible promises me that one day in heaven, the earthly Joni will step into the glorious Joni God intended me to be . . . . The best thing about heaven will be a pure heart no longer weighed down by sin and selfishness. And I can say *that* from this wheelchair."[5]

These are her questions followed by her personal answers.

- "What do I have?" Her answer: "According to the Lord, that's all I need."
- "Am I using what I have?" Her answer: "Well, I will admit it's been more difficult lately . . . . but I will still show up for work, offering what I have to the Lord for His use, and asking for His help. And I know that I will have that help, because He never gives a task without supplying the need. His command never comes without empowerment."
- "Am I prepared to lose what I have?" Her answer: Ah, this is the litmus test of contentment. This one scares me a little . . . . To be honest, it frightens me to think about the future sometimes. What if my pain never goes away—or gets even worse? What if my paralysis becomes even more profound and I lose the few abilities I now possess? Well, deep down I know the answer: My calling isn't only to abandon my future wants, but to trust in God and hand over what I already possess."
- "Am I ready to receive what I don't have?" Her answer: "What would that be? What might it look like? I have no idea. More responsibility? More open doors?

---

5. Eareckson Tada, *A Place of Healing*, 167–68. I highly recommend this book to everyone who is looking for a practical application to the material found in this book.

More suffering for His name's sake? . . . . I'd just be happy if God would simply make my heart larger to receive more of His peace and joy."[6]

I urge you to use her questions to examine yourself. Take a personal inventory of what you have and how you are using it to God's glory.

---

6. Eareckson Tada, *A Place of Healing*, 202–4.

Appendix 3

Images of Love from Our Culture Vs. Scripture

Images of Love from Our Culture

LOVE IS AN ESSENTIAL part of the Christian life. Therefore, it is vital that Christians can identify and separate what is biblical love from the secular understanding of love. To help us to do this, we will look at a few popular secular songs on love. Then we will consider one contemporary Christian song and a few Scriptures that many Christians today might find problematic. This is intended to be used with chapter 11.

Think of the lyrics to some of the songs mentioned in the opening of chapter 11 and discern from what spirit they are:

- Frank Sinatra sang "Love Is a Many Splendored Thing," where the splendor of love is a touch that results in strong physical emotions—the world stands still and the heart sings.
- Burt Bacharach (writer) and Jackie DeShannon (performer) gave us "What the World Needs Now Is Love, Sweet Love," which was written as a sort of prayer in which God supposedly does not know or care that all people need love and as if he had not already given love and offered it to everyone.
- Perry Como told us "Love Makes the World Go Round" but depicted that love as a strong emotion that raises your pulse, overpowers your heart, and moves the world.
- The Righteous Brothers, in "You've Lost That Lovin' Feeling," told us, first, that love stutters and, second, that love is a *feeling* we cannot live without.
- The Beatles, in "All You Need Is Love," taught us to use actions associated with love to play the game of life, to be who you are (without input from higher authority), and to go and to do whatever you want. The title says it all—use "love" to manipulate others in order to get what you want.

Today the emotional aspect of these songs has degraded to animalistic behaviors enhanced by the visual aspect of scantily clad women making suggestive movements and postures. Beyoncé's "Crazy in Love" portrays this with the addition that love makes you so crazy that you burn cars and destroy fire hydrants. The video for

APPENDIX 3: IMAGES OF LOVE FROM OUR CULTURE VS. SCRIPTURE

Mariah Carey's hit "We Belong Together" shows her in bed and then getting ready for her wedding to one man as she sings these words about another. In the end she leaves the fiancé at the alter and runs away with the other man. These are two of Fox's *best* picks for love songs of this century.[1] There are the thousands of messages about love that we take in from the secular media every week. For a more detailed analysis of this please see chapter 11.

Images of Love from Scripture

One hour in church on Sunday is no match for the hours of indoctrination we receive the rest of the week from the media. This is a large part of why Scripture sounds strange and God is not whom we expect to find there. To see where you fall in this continuum, test your reactions to these descriptions of biblical love:

- Solomon talks about love being as strong as death. Its jealousy is like fire. It is more precious than all the wealth of the world. Love cannot be bought. In fact, if a person would try to buy love he or she would be *utterly despised* (Song 8:6–7).

- Mark McMillan writes in "Oh, How He Loves Me" that God is jealous for each of us and his love is a hurricane. We are the trees that get bent or broken in the gale-force wind. Additionally, if God is an ocean, then we are all sinking down (drowning) into his mercy (Isa 30:27–29; Amos 2:5; 5:27; 8:11; 2 Chr 7:11–22; Hos 5:14–15; Joel 2; 1 Pet 1:6–7; 2 Cor 2:15–16; 7:8–11; Matt 5:10–11).

- The writer of Hebrews 12 tells us that God disciplines those whom he loves, and this discipline is not pleasant at the time. He assures us that this discipline is not capricious but is designed for the purpose of enabling us to share in his holiness because without holiness no one will ever see God. Then he closes the passage with a statement that sounds very unloving to our ears. There will be shaking to get rid of the temporary things of this earth so that only the eternal things that are of God remain, "for our God is a consuming fire."

The images of the Christian life found in songs like "Oh, How He Loves Me" may make you feel uncomfortable. In this song, God is a hurricane and people are trees being bent and broken by the gale-force winds. God is an ocean in which we are drowning in his mercy (to die to self?). Oh, how he loves us. How familiar are you with a God who is jealous and judges people and breaks people? Most Americans are uncomfortable with such a God and might outright reject him. If you are one of them, then you will have missed genuine love. To find out why read chapters 11 and 12.

---

4. "The Best Love Songs of the 2000s."

APPENDIX 3: IMAGES OF LOVE FROM OUR CULTURE VS. SCRIPTURE

Scriptural Images of God That Christians Often Reject

In some passages of Scripture, God's breath is like a rushing torrent that shakes evil nations in the sieve of destruction; God will send a fire to consume the fortresses of wicked people; he will send famine; and he holds back the rain and sends the locusts and the plagues. This does not fit well with the twenty-first century understanding of love. Many people have noticed that all of these references are from the Old Testament and have claimed that the God found there is not the God of Jesus. They feel free to ignore this god, and some have rejected the Old Testament entirely.

Therefore, let us now look at New Testament references. Jesus expects his followers to give up their lives, to deny themselves, and to take up their crosses and follow him. He warns that there will be suffering for those who follow him, but that those who persevere are blessed. Peter likens this suffering to a refining fire. The author of Hebrews calls it a consuming fire. Paul talks about godly sorrow whose purpose is to bring restoration and reconciliation with God.

Christians in America struggle with these images of God's love because they do not fit with their idea of God's comfort (which includes all of the latest commodities, an air conditioned house and car, and endless entertainment so they can feel good about themselves) and peace (which becomes freedom from hardships and absence of conflict).

Appendix 4

Refining Gold and the Firing of Porcelain and Ceramics

THE BIBLE TALKS ABOUT refining fire and our faith being refined as gold. Often the trials of life feel like fire trying to destroy us, but God sees it differently. Peter talks about faith being refined as gold through the things we suffer. "In ancient times, this form of refining involved a craftsman sitting next to a hot fire with molten gold in a crucible being stirred and skimmed to remove the impurities or dross that rose to the top of the molten metal" with flames that reached temperatures in excess of one thousand degrees Celsius.[1] The heat of suffering and the effect it has on your faith may also be compared to porcelain which is fired in a kiln. "The average firing temperature for high-fire stoneware is 2381°F (1305°C) . . . . High-fire stoneware becomes hard, vitrified, and non-absorbent. It is extremely durable, especially compared to both low-fire and mid-range ceramics."[2] The Christian who endures the heat of God's refinement is more impervious to the culture's enticements, false teachings, and persecutions. He or she is equipped for lasting and greater service in God's kingdom.

1. "How to Refine Gold."
2. "Guide to Kiln Temperature Ranges for Pottery."

Appendix 5

Prayers of the New Testament

CHRISTIANS WHO WANT TO pray the will of God can begin by using Paul's prayers for the church. Paul is speaking on behalf of himself and the Christians who are with him. His prayers varied depending on to whom he was writing and the events happening there. Notice how often he uses "may." At this time in the Greek language blessings often began with "may."[1] Many of these prayers can easily be turned to blessings. I have structured these passages to help you to pick out the prayer/blessing and the purpose for which Paul prayed them. The purpose should be considered part of the prayer—as in praying for an outcome consistent with God's will. It is my hope that you will begin to pray in this same way and search the Scripture for other prayers such as those mentioned below and in chapters 15 and 16 on prayer.

---

1. Wallace, *Greek Grammar Beyond the Basics*, 447, 462–63. Wallace writes, "Mood is not always in line with its general force. For example, in the language of prayer, when pronouncing a blessing . . . the optative is virtually required. Yet this does not mean that the speaker thinks of such a blessing as less likely to occur than if he had used the subjunctive" (447). In NT times he asserts that the optative was dying out and being replaced by the subjunctive because of the number of people using Greek as a second language who were unable to adjust to the subtleties (462).

Colossians 1:9–12

. . . we have not stopped praying for you and asking God [BL 1–6]
- to fill you with the knowledge of his will through all spiritual wisdom and understanding.

. . . in order that (purpose)
- you may live a life worthy of the Lord
- and may please him in every way:
- bearing fruit in every good work,
- growing in the knowledge of God,
- being strengthened with all power according to his glorious might

so that (purpose)
- you may have great endurance
- and patience,
- and joyfully giving thanks to the Father

Ephesians 1:15–19a

. . . ever since I heard about your faith in the Lord Jesus and your love for all the saints, I have not stopped giving thanks for you, remembering you in my prayers. I keep asking that the God of our Lord Jesus Christ, the glorious Father, may

- give you the Spirit of wisdom and revelation,

so that you may (purpose)

- know him better.

I pray also that (purpose)

- the eyes of your heart may be enlightened

in order that you may (purpose)

- know the hope to which he has called you,
- the riches of his glorious inheritance in the saints

APPENDIX 5: PRAYERS OF THE NEW TESTAMENT

Ephesians 3:14–19

I kneel before the Father,

from whom his whole family in heaven and on earth derives its name.
I pray that out of his glorious riches he may

- strengthen you with power through his Spirit in your inner being,

so that Christ may (purpose)

- dwell in your hearts through faith.

And I pray that you, being rooted and established in love, may

- have power, together with all the saints, to grasp how wide and long and high and deep is the love of Christ,
- and to know this love that surpasses knowledge—

(so) that you may (purpose)

- be filled to the measure of all the fullness of God.

APPENDIX 5: PRAYERS OF THE NEW TESTAMENT

Philippians 1:9–11

And this is my prayer: that

- your love may abound more and more in knowledge and depth of insight,

so that you may (purpose)

- be able to discern what is best and
- may be pure and blameless until the day of Christ,
- filled with the fruit of righteousness that comes through Jesus Christ—to the glory and praise of God.

Other suggestions of prayers or passages that could be turned into prayers: the Psalms; Exodus 32:7–14; 2 Chronicles 7:13–15; Nehemiah 1 and 9; Job 42:8–10; Isaiah 38:2–6; Daniel 9; Romans 8:26; 10:1; 12:12; 15:30–33; 2 Corinthians 1:8–11; 13:7–9; Ephesians 6:18–20; 2 Thessalonians 1:11–12, and Philemon 1:3–6.

Appendix 6

Start Your Own Concert of Prayer

JONATHAN EDWARDS AND THE Scotland pastors took to heart what Zechariah tells us (8:20–21, NIV), "This is what the LORD Almighty says: 'Many peoples and the inhabitants of many cities will yet come, and the inhabitants of one city will go to another and say, "Let us go at once to entreat the LORD and seek the LORD Almighty. I myself am going."'" They were moved to organize thousands of people to pray for revival.

Sadly, most of us struggle to pray a few minutes each day. Often our concept of prayer is more of drudgery than joy or something more of a duty than something delightful. But praying in the Spirit is delightful, joyous, and uplifting. I am not thinking primarily of praying in tongues (although please use that gift if you have it). I am referring to the ancient practice of *lectio divina*, the practice of meditation on God's word and listening for his prompting on what is on his heart, listening for the prayers he wants to hear.

When I tell people how life-giving and enjoyable prayer is, they usually do not believe me. When they join me to give it a try, the usual comments I hear are, "Wow! I never thought I could pray an hour, let alone an hour and a half!" "How fast the time went!" "I never knew that prayer could be like that!" When you begin to see specific answers to prayer, your faith is stirred to pray more. A woman whose knee was injured in a softball game and further by a subsequent fall down steps was healed. Another woman was set free from emotional bondage. One time we were about to end the meeting when I discerned intense evil at work. We continued to praise God and to pray against evil. About an hour later we found out that a teen we knew had tried to take her life and had reached out for help at the exact time we were praying this way. She survived. Things happen when God's people pray.

Jonathan Edwards understood the wisdom of corporate as well as private praying. He based his call for concerts of prayer coordinated on both sides of the Atlantic on the Zechariah passage opening this appendix. He sees in this a visible unity among the people of God. He also notices that the approach of the people going to pray is speedily. It is something they can't wait to do. He gives the literal translation as "Let us go on going," and reminds us that the Hebrew language repeats a word in order to give strong emphasis to its importance.[1]

Edwards also saw the need for the Holy Spirit in such prayer efforts primarily because he is the Spirit of promise of which Jesus spoke in John 14–16 and prayed for in John 17 saying it is better that he leaves so that the Holy Spirit could come. At his ascension Jesus told his disciples to wait and pray until the Holy Spirit came upon them. Paul makes it clear that this same Spirit is in each one who believes in Christ and that because of this they have the same power at work in them that raised Jesus from the dead.

Edwards describes the Holy Spirit as "the great blessing Christ purchased by his labours and sufferings on earth . . . . This is the sum of those *gifts* which Christ *received for men, even for the rebellious* at his ascension, and . . . obtains for men by his intercession."[2] Edwards concludes therefore that if Christ suffered so much and died to obtain the Holy Spirit for us, then "surely his disciples and members should also earnestly seek it, and be much in prayer for it."[3] Since all revival is God's work and God works through the Holy Spirit and chooses to work through people as they open themselves to his leading, then the church must learn to test the spirits and to discern the Holy Spirit's work from other spirits at work in our age.

In addition to revival, or perhaps because of it, there would be many benefits of these concerted prayer efforts. It would display the unity of the body of God's people and the beauty that comes out of it. It would promote unity and love "between distant members of the church." Furthermore it would "promote mutual affection and endearment . . . [and] it would naturally tend . . . to awaken in them a concern about things of this nature, and more of a desire after such a mercy."[4] People would live in the beauty of holiness and the wholeness, love, joy, peace, mutual respect for one another, respect for the things of God, gratefulness, and thankfulness that accompany holiness.

How to Begin

David Bryant is helpful here. In his book *Concerts of Prayer*, he uses Edwards's work as a jumping-off place and then proceeds to lay out very practical steps to achieve it. In the same Zechariah passage he identifies four hallmarks of concerted revival prayer: an attitude of urgency that "presses as far as it can go, even into the very Holy of Holies"; an agenda that "spiritual awakening was the greatest need for the remnant"; an impact that makes God's salvation available to the world and begins at home as unsaved people see Christians living together in unity and in godliness; and an ignition through those who seek God and get others to "go" with them.[5] In a spiritual

1. Edwards, *Humble Attempt*, 50, 52.
2. Edwards, *Humble Attempt*, 90.
3. Edwards, *Humble Attempt*, 93.
4. Edwards, *Humble Attempt*, 127–28.
5. Bryant, *Concerts of Prayer*, 34–37.

awakening the Christian says, "I am committing all I can see of myself to all I can see of Christ for all I can see of His global cause—at this moment."[6] In spiritual awakening the Holy Spirit is poured out, enabling God's people to see and to embrace all they have in Christ and to respond "in love to all He tells us to do."[7] In this outpouring of the Spirit, "the Church is reintroduced to the consuming Fire from heaven and tastes His holy love with trembling obedience" and is revived in a "corporate sense of Christ's intimate direction of both our inward and outward life."[8]

The ultimate goal of spiritual awakening is "decisive devotion to Christ." This occurs in five natural phases: the Spirit moves people for corporate prayer; "the Church receives an intensified vision of Christ's fullness"; she is then "led into a deep unity of love for one another and resolve to serve the purposes of Christ"; there is a pruning of existing ministries and revitalization of ministry in general; and "all this flows into an expansion of Christ's Kingdom."[9] As Christ's lordship is acknowledged, often divorce rates drop, crime rates go down, people are more prone to take care of the environment and to respect each other, etc., but sometimes things may get worse before they get better. A key mark of spiritual awakening is that the spiritual gifts are "set free." He surmises, "Concerted prayer for spiritual awakening is the most critical step the church can take for the sake of the nation."[10]

If this sounds like something you would like to have happen, Bryant gives you three steps to begin. The first is repentance. The pray-ers must repent for "lack of faith," "lack of desire for the kingdom," our "indifference," our "indulgences," our unwillingness to reconcile with people, our "spiritual pride," our national sins, our acceptance of the status quo, and our "disobedience to the Great Commission."[11] These confessions along with repentance make room for the Spirit's work. After repentance comes unity as we pray for the same thing with our eyes focused on Christ. The third is to practice daily disciplines for getting in shape spiritually in which Christians prepare themselves for God's answers. These include prayer, discipleship, and ministry. This means to live into all that we understand of Christ and what he wants of us, to study Scripture daily, and to develop daily discipline that "integrates a vision for the world into daily discipleship within the environment of prayer."[12] According to Boyer, this can be done in just fifteen minutes a day: five to study Scripture on the Great Commission; four to study other resources on evangelism; three to pray for the world based on what you have just studied; two to share with another Christian what God has shown you in this; and one

---

6. Bryant, *Concerts of Prayer*, 42.
7. Bryant, *Concerts of Prayer*, 43.
8. Bryant, *Concerts of Prayer*, 43.
9. Bryant, *Concerts of Prayer*, 47.
10. Bryant, *Concerts of Prayer*, 49.
11. Bryant, *Concerts of Prayer*, 77–81.
12. Bryant, *Concerts of Prayer*, 84.

to be still and to listen for what God might want to say to you.[13] However, he cautions that "prayer without discipleship and ministry can turn into a powerless pietism. But discipleship and ministry without prayer can become formal and dead."[14] This explains why so many of our efforts today bear so little results.

Bryant points out several common problems people have with prayer: we have not had our prayers answered in the past; we lack understanding of God's ways; every person has an "aversion to God who is holy and sovereign"; "we may be afraid of his answers"; and day-to-day logistics and problems that get in the way of our praying.[15]

To mobilize people for prayer he recommends that you keep it biblical, begin even if you are the only one, and be humble. Set an agenda of spiritual awakening by praying for it in every situation you encounter. Start small. Look for folks who are like-minded. Be enthusiastic. Identify barriers to prayer and help people to overcome them. "Help people to see that concerted prayer is compatible to who they are, relevant to what they need, and desirable in achieving God's life and objectives for them." Give people a new vision of God. Show them that concerts of prayer are manageable: twenty minutes once a week for seven weeks or an hour once a month for seven years (as Edwards initially proposed). Provide information to help get them involved in the praying. His book is a great tool to motivate and to train folks. Get connected with other groups with similar goals. Finally, realize you are entering the battlefield. "Satan's greatest concern, next to preventing the gospel from reaching those who haven't heard, is to sabotage prayer movements that call for God to revive His Church and advance His Kingdom. He will try to discourage you" with dwindling numbers, interruptions, or accusations of spiritual elitism by those unwilling to pray.[16]

Edwards urges Christians of every age to be aware of the season in which they live and "to go on in united prayers for the advancement of Christ's kingdom with increasing fervency."[17] Concerning the Zechariah passage, he asks, "Will it not become us readily to say, *I will go also*?"[18] I hope you will be moved to begin concerted prayer in your congregation or study group and hopefully with churches in your area or around the world. Bryant has many concrete suggestions and examples of what to do and is a great resource for things to pray, the format to follow, and lessons to use to help you get started. May you find spiritual awakening happening in your life and the life of your congregation.

---

13. To me this sounds ambitious and rather forced, but this may help busy people to begin a concert of prayer.
14. Bryant, *Concerts of Prayer*, 83.
15. Bryant, *Concerts of Prayer*, 87–88.
16. Bryant, *Concerts of Prayer*, 88–90.
17. Edwards, *Humble Attempt*, 137.
18. Edwards, *Humble Attempt*, 131.

Appendix 7

Put on the Armor of God

CHRISTIANS ARE ENGAGED IN spiritual warfare whether they want to be or not. If you want to expand God's kingdom by growing deeper in your walk with God or by telling others the gospel, you have entered the battle. Satan will always push back; he does not give up territory uncontested (he is the prince of this world; he pretty much has full reign except where God's people take their stand). Unfortunately, many Christians have been deceived in this area of spiritual warfare. Like most things in life, people tend to go to one extreme or the other.

Spiritual warfare is one more area where Christians tend to polarize into two camps. Either they deny Satan or refuse to talk about him so as not to give him any recognition and power, or they see him under every bush and behind every event and often get very loud when they come against him. Either they are soldiers waging God's war for people's souls, or they are prisoners of war. Satan is real, and ignoring him only gives him carte blanche to do whatever he wants. Furthermore, he is not deaf; there is no need to yell when commanding him.[1] Paul tells us the weapons God gives are spiritual, meaning they are different from the things people of this world use when they fight.

In the armor God gives in Ephesians 6, notice that it talks about salvation, righteousness, truth, and faith. These are all the things we have come to connect with a holy life. It is in living the Christian faith that Christians find their authority, and it is the knowledge of God found in Scripture under the guidance of the Holy Spirit that makes it effective. Notice that the only armor they have for offense is the sword of the Spirit, which is the Scriptures of both Old and New Testaments and prayer. Knowledge of the Bible is essential for living a holy life, praying effectively, and advancing God's kingdom.

Paul claims that all of these parts of the holy life are needed in order to pray effectively when he tells them to put on the armor and then immediately writes, "And pray

---

1. If you would like to read more, I recommend the Dunamis workshop manuals: Long, "Gateways to Empowered Ministry"; Long et al., "In the Spirit's Power"; Long et al., "The Healing Ministry of Jesus"; and Long et al., "Spiritual Warfare." Long has also written several books on Holy Spirit–led prayer that may help you to grow in prayer. They are Long and McMurry, *Receiving Power*; *The Collapse of the Brass Heaven*; Long, *Passage through the Wilderness*; and *Prayer that Shapes the Future*.

APPENDIX 7: PUT ON THE ARMOR OF GOD

. . ." Therefore, Christians, put on the whole armor of God each day and pray realizing that this is a lifestyle that you are putting on and wearing. Below you will read how I put on the armor of God every morning.

I searched the Scriptures to find passages that I felt pertained to the area of the body which that piece of armor protected. For the helmet of salvation, it was the mind, and I thought of Jesus' warning about deceptions (Matt 24). The breastplate of righteousness covers the heart, which in biblical terms is the center of the will (Phil 2:12–13). The sword of the Spirit being an actual offensive weapon, I connected it with Psalm 18:32–36 and God directing its use in the warfare in which we find ourselves. Always remember that the word of God was given by the Spirit of God and directs its use (John 14:26; Rom 8). The rest of it is fairly self-explanatory. After praise and adoration of God I pray,

> I put on the helmet of salvation. Protect my thinking from deception and lies. Give me your wisdom and discernment. Put your words in my mouth and your thoughts in my mind.
>
> I put on the breastplate of righteousness which is your righteousness in me. Lord Jesus, work in me to will and to do your good pleasure (grow your righteousness in me). Keep my heart soft and pure and malleable in your hands alone.
>
> I put on the belt of truth. Let me speak your truth in love.
>
> I put on my feet the gospel of peace. Lead me to where I should go, when I should be there, and let me stand firm on the Rock which is Jesus.
>
> I take the sword of the Spirit which is the word of God. Holy Spirit, teach me your word and bring to my remembrance what I need, when I need it that I may bend a bow of bronze. Teach my hands to war and my fingers to do battle that I may bend bow of bronze.
>
> I take the shield of faith which is your faithfulness. Cover me with your feathers; surround me with your wings. Be my strength, my refuge, my high tower. Keep me by your power that the fiery darts of the enemy cannot reach me. I place your protection on . . . (name your family and friends for whom you are praying—be sure to include your church, your pastor, and church officers and their families).

In recent years I have begun to add the following for my grandchildren, the spouses God has chosen for them, and the spouses, parents, grandparents, children, grandchildren, great-grandchildren, siblings, their spouses, and their children for all for whom I pray (friends, relatives, denomination, pastors, etc.). Since none of us is free from error, I include myself in this as well.

> Lord, be the hound of heaven going after us until we are safely in your kingdom and walking mature in every way fully persuaded that your ways are perfect and your word is flawless. May we be pure in body, mind, spirit, and soul; may our hearts be fully in love with Jesus, attuned to his ways and following them every

APPENDIX 7: PUT ON THE ARMOR OF GOD

day of our lives. And if in any way we are otherwise minded please convict us and grant us repentance that we may come to our senses, know the truth, and be set free from all the schemes Satan uses to keep us captive to do his will.

All of this takes about five minutes. The words that I use are not important for it to be effective. Let the Holy Spirit lead you to do this in your own way. This is offered to help you get started. May you walk in God's powerful and effective praying!

Appendix 8

An Overview of Matthew 18–20

MATTHEW 18–20 IS ONE passage in which we might miss the bigger picture by separating and examining the individual parts. It begins with the disciples asking who is greatest in the kingdom of heaven. "We get it" when Jesus immediately points them to little children and tells his disciples they must become as they are. We focus on those few verses, and *maybe* we include the part about woe to the people who bring offenses that hurt them, although this last part violates political correctness, which says not to judge and all people are good. Then the next passages are split into the parable of the lost sheep, discipline, unforgiveness, and divorce and are usually preached as isolated and disconnected topics. What we often miss is that Matthew has arranged his material for a specific purpose.

Earlier in his gospel he grouped chapters 4:23 through 9:35 together about Jesus' ministry by telling his readers that Jesus went all around the area preaching and teaching the kingdom of heaven, healing, and casting out demons. Here, he does a similar thing. In 18:2, Jesus calls the children to him to illustrate the greatest in God's kingdom. In 19:13–14 the disciples try to keep the children away from Jesus, but he calls them to himself and blesses them, reminding them again that the kingdom of heaven belongs to such as these.

If we take our cues from Matthew, then those seemingly disconnected passages in the middle become examples of things Jesus had in mind when he said a very politically incorrect thing: "But if anyone causes one of these little ones who believe in me to sin, it would be better for him to have a large millstone hung around his neck and to be drowned in the depths of the sea" (18:6, NIV). He follows this with another scandalous statement (by current accepted cultural etiquette) on the seriousness of sin: "Woe to the world because of the things that cause people to sin!" (18:7, NIV). Suddenly, this section becomes a teaching on some major ways children (God's elect people) can be helped or hurt. If the greatest in the kingdom of heaven must be like a little child, then we should look at why this is and what happens to most people to change this as they grow into adults. The "why" Matthew informs us is the great importance and value Jesus places on each one of these little ones (the parable of the one lost sheep). The "what" follows first with the proper way to handle discipline and offenses (18:15–20). He closes this discussion on proper discipline with "where two or three agree." Could this be because Matthew had in mind the family where family members agree that they will have what they ask for their errant children?

Matthew then moves into the hurtfulness of unforgiveness and gives the parable of the servant who is glad to receive forgiveness but is unwilling to extend it to others. Jesus warned in the Sermon on the Mount that we are forgiven when we forgive. The final thing Matthew mentions that hurts children is divorce. In our age, I do not need to spend much time on the wounding the children experience when parents get divorced. Children often feel they are to blame for their parent's failure to love. Additionally, they have to watch a parent lavish attention on other children that should rightfully be theirs and much more could be said. How much better would life be in the home and in the church if God's people were to take seriously the destruction that sin causes, the great value God places on of each of his little ones (each other), the proper dealing with offenses and discipline, the need for forgiveness, and the necessity of working out differences and learning how to get along and to love one another. How differently might pastors preach this part of Matthew when viewed in this way, but Matthew has only begun to answer the question that began it all: "Who is greatest in the kingdom of heaven?"

He returns to this question with the story of the rich young man. In Jesus' day, wealth was always considered to mean the person was right with God. Indeed, this young man claims to have kept all of the commandments. Jesus tells him if he wants to be perfect, he should sell all that he has and follow Jesus. Matthew was not trying to make this a universal doctrine for all people, in all places, and for all time. It was to make the point that wealth means nothing when it comes to being first in God's kingdom, and he follows this with the parable of the laborers being hired at different times of the day and receiving the same payment. Again, we tend to make this a universal doctrine and interpret it as if everyone in heaven gets exactly the same rewards. That is not the purpose when taken in context.

Keep in mind the question, "Who will be first in the kingdom of heaven?" The world's way of recognizing who is first is not usually God's way, which is, "The first shall be last, and the last shall be first." Those who have power and riches here will mostly likely not be first in God's kingdom. Moreover, God, the Lord, and he alone, reserves the right to make that determination. God's sovereignty is the point, and the church is to stop looking at it from the world's perspective of who is first. How do I know this?

Matthew returns us to the original question immediately after the story of the laborers in the vineyard by recording the mother of the sons of Zebedee asking if her two sons will be given the privilege of sitting on Jesus' right and left hands. This leads to ill feelings among the disciples, and Jesus telling them, "Whoever wants to become great among you must be your servant, and whoever wants to be first must be your slave—just as the Son of Man did not come to be served, but to serve, and to give his life as a ransom for many" (20:26–28, NIV).

This pericope ends with Jesus and the disciples passing two blind men in a large crowd. Like the children who were considered insignificant in Jesus' day, the blind men represent the insignificant people of that time who are at the opposite end of the social status from the rich young man. The blind men keep crying out, "Lord, Son of David, have mercy on us!" This time it is the crowd and not the disciples who try to keep them from Jesus, but the blind men persist. When Jesus asks them what they want, they answer, "Lord, we want our sight." Jesus has compassion on them and restores their vision. Matthew closes this section on who will be first with this statement: "Immediately they received their sight and followed him" (20:34, NIV).

For Matthew, the answer is not to be concerned with who is first in God's kingdom; God is sovereign and can do whatever he wants. It is his to determine. What people should be concerned about is that they have received spiritual sight and are following Jesus and trusting him completely like little children trust their parents. It is not the money, gifts, and talents that you give to God that matter as much as what he does in you and how you respond to it. Matthew is now finished with this subject and directs our attention to Jerusalem and Jesus' final days on earth.

Appendix 9

Prayers That Will Change the World

TAKE THE PASSAGE OF Scripture being preached or studied and turn it into a prayer for revival of the church. Keep it to one sentence (two at most) that each person can pray during devotions, sitting at a red light, brushing their teeth, vacuuming, mowing, at mealtimes, etc. I have given twenty examples below.

1. **Ephesians 4:1–32:** Lord, may my life, and the life of this congregation do what Jesus would do and reflect your new DNA in missional living of righteousness, holiness, and truth. Amen.

2. **1 Peter 3:8–18:** Lord God, give us the courage, wisdom, and words to step through the doors of opportunity you open to share our hope in Jesus.

3. **Matthew 9:35—10:1:** Holy Father, the harvest is ripe; please send workers to bring it in, and may I be willing to be one of them.

4. **1 John 4:1–17:** Holy God, be gracious to me and this congregation and give us eyes to see the difference between your love and what the world tells us it is, minds to discern the truth of your love, and courage to live it to your glory.

5. **Multiple passages for Pentecost:** Jesus, send your Holy Spirit upon me and this congregation for prayer that will change the world.

6. **Psalm 22:1–11; Matthew 28:1–10; John 20:1–9; Hebrews 12:1–3:** Lord, I believe. Help my unbelief.

7. **John 12:12–13; Romans 8:16–18; John 14:12; Ephesians 1:13–14; Hebrews 12:1–3:** Gracious Lord, give me and this congregation the courage to follow your truth and righteousness every day, whatever that may require.

8. **Matthew 10:24–30:** Dear God, grant us wisdom to live in your light and to follow in the way of your beloved Son, Jesus Christ. Amen.

9. **Psalm 34:7–22; 1 John 4:13–18:** Gracious God, help me and this congregation to understand what it means to fear you.

10. **Proverbs 29:18; 2 Corinthians 4:4–11, 16–18:** Help me/us to identify and to live into your vision for me/us.

11. **Joshua 1:5–9; Matthew 10:1, 17–26, 37–39:** We renounce fear of people and ask that you release into me/us fear of you.

12. **Ephesians 6:10–19:** Dear God, may I speak truthfully, live righteously, follow your path of peace, be set free from the world's deceptions, be protected by your faithfulness, speak your word powerfully, and pray unceasingly to demolish the strongholds of evil where I live. Amen.

13. **Joel 2:28–29; John 16:4–15; Acts 1:1–11:** Jesus, send your Holy Spirit upon me and this congregation that we may be your ambassadors to the people around us.

14. **Matthew 5:43–48 and Leviticus 19:** Gracious God, I pray for those who oppose me and your church that you would bring them to repentance and to knowledge of the truth and that they would be set free from all the schemes of the enemy that he uses to hold them captive to do his will. (Adapted from 2 Tim 2:24–26.)

15. **Matthew 5:38–42; Romans 13:1–10; 1 Timothy 2:1–6:** Lord, we pray for our president, Congress, governors, mayors, councils, and legal systems at every level of this nation that they may know your truth and have the courage and boldness to work for it so that your people may live holy lives in peace.

16. **Hebrews 11:1–6; 1 John 5:1–12:** "I believe; help my unbelief." Gracious God, pour out your gift of faith that I and this congregation may trust you implicitly in Spirit and in Truth so that you may work your power and love through us. Amen

17. **1 John 5:13–15; James 5:13–18; John 14:12–13:** Father God, work in me and [the name of your congregation] to make Spirit-led prayer of faith a priority in our lives.

18. **Romans 5:1–11; James 5:13–16:** Father God, give us the gift of faith to come to you in prayer for everything that we may obey your word and pray without ceasing.

19. **Hebrews 10:16–25:** Heavenly Father, grant me and this congregation the will and gifts to stand in the gap and to pray the prayers you desire that will change the world.

20. **Ephesians 3:7–21:** Gracious Lord, grant me the will and determination to praise you in the storms of life and to trust you with my life, the lives of those whom I love, and the life of [the name of your congregation].

Appendix 10

Equipped to Tell the Next Generation Study Guide

Be Equipped

Chapter 1

Personal Equipping

1. What is a paradigm? In your own words, describe the paradigms discussed in this chapter.
2. Commercials have great effect on people. You are told to be sexy and their product will make you appear that way. You deserve every good thing, and their product will give it to you. Identify ways that you have been trapped by advertising to desire things that you really did not need and how you felt if you could not obtain or achieve those desires. Identify the source of those desires. How did you overcome the pull to always want more?
3. What in this chapter impacted you the most? Identify why it/they was/were important to you.
4. According to de Tocqueville, mid-nineteenth-century Americans believed that their religion was essential if they were to remain free. What does this convey to American Christians in the twenty-first century?

Equipping the Community

1. How might understanding the paradigm shifts in thinking and processing information that have taken place in this nation help you to talk more effectively with people about Jesus?
2. De Tocqueville claims that "when a society really reaches the point of having . . . a government equally divided between contrary principles, either revolution erupts or society dissolves." Give specific examples of how this is or is not happening in this nation.

3. De Tocqueville saw the Christian faith as the deterrent to tyranny and that Christianity was strong precisely where democracy was weak. He also claimed that Christianity was needed to maintain freedom. How does Christianity do these things? How does this impact the way you view the church's role in our culture and the way you look at the Great Commission being worked out in this nation?

4. Postman talks about how the telegraph and pictures of faraway places brought news and introduced folks to people and places free of context and meaning in place of real situations the people were facing. Its primary function became entertainment. Notice that our news today is context-free. We cannot place the information we are being given in a context to determine its truth or significance. In Postmodernity where context alone determines truth, discuss what being immersed in a context-free culture means for our people in general and the church's mission to take the gospel to her neighbors.

5. How do you determine what is true?

6. Identify several key Christian words and how their meanings have been changed. How does this challenge the way you share Jesus with people?

Be Equipped

Chapter 2

Personal Equipping

1. Change always happens. Identify some changes in your life: physical, emotional, relational, material, and technological. How have they impacted your spiritual life?

2. Identify specific ways your life reflects the American dream to be comfortable, to consume more, to possess more things, and to experience more pleasure. Then think about things you would be willing to sacrifice for the name of Jesus. Think about the things you are holding back.

3. What have you observed that either supports or refutes Carr's claim that the computer is "a concentration-fragmenting mishmash" and "an interruption system, a machine geared for dividing attention?"

4. Are you hooked on Facebook and "likes" from people as a means to find acceptance, self-worth, or meaning? How would going without technology for a day, a week, or a month affect you and change your life? Try it.

5. Have you considered seemingly opposing points of view to be pieces of a puzzle that may be needed to see the big picture? How might this change your attitude towards people who disagree with you? Might there be times when the piece is

truly "out there" and must be discarded as not belonging to this puzzle? How might you know?

Equipping the Community

1. How has technology replaced God?

2. Identify some of the ways Postman and Carr claim people have changed in the way they think and process information. Are they valid observations? Why or why not? How might this affect your approach to people with the gospel?

3. Do you trust information from the internet to be true? How might you verify it?

4. Is the "social media" really social? How has technology influenced our youth?

5. Postman describes Technopoly as "*progress without limits, rights without responsibilities, and technology without cost . . . .* [and] *without a moral center*" (italics are mine). He also claims it "*promises heaven on earth through . . . technological progress. It casts aside* all *traditional narrative and symbols that suggest stability and orderliness*, and tells, instead, of a life of skills, technical expertise, and ecstasy of consumption." How do you see this working out in our culture? Contrast this with the message of the Bible and the role of the church.

6. Gregory believes that the glue holding our pluralistic culture together is a continued conforming to consumerism and states (rather sarcastically) that "no matter what, individuals must be left free to be selfish . . . . In a world pullulating with so many incompatible truth claims, values, priorities, and aspirations, what else could do the trick?" Is he correct? Why? If you do not agree with him, what would you propose as the glue holding us together? Give evidence to support your opinion.

7. Discuss ways in which you can identify Huxley's Brave New World, Orwell's "Big Brother," de Tocqueville's dissolving society, and Bellah's "culture of separation" leading to an authoritarian state in our culture. How can the church use this to motivate her to fulfill the Great Commission?

8. Discuss how looking at apparently dissimilar ideas as pieces of a puzzle to be put together to make a unified whole instead of a pendulum of exclusively opposite concepts might make a difference in your life and the life of your church. How might you discern if a piece (idea) truly does not belong?

APPENDIX 10: EQUIPPED TO TELL THE NEXT GENERATION STUDY GUIDE

Be Equipped

Chapter 3

Personal Equipping

1. Which of these areas where culture has changed the church do you find in yourself?
2. How comfortable are you with the doctrines of holiness, righteousness, judgment, sin, hell, and condemnation? In your own words how would you tell someone what they are? In your own words describe redemption and reconciliation.
3. What is the therapeutic approach to life, and how do you use it in your everyday life?
4. Identify ways propaganda is used to sway people's opinions.
5. How do you describe the good life? Have you ever thought about holiness as the good life? Why?
6. Do your morals align with culture or the Bible?
7. To what extent does doubt influence your life?
8. When does self-help truly help, and when does it hinder you?

Equipping the Community

1. Explain the difference between contextualization and capitulation. Which church and personal actions and beliefs come under these two categories? Why is it important to identify these?
2. What was at the heart of the Conservative/Liberal split in the church? How do you see it being worked out today?
3. How often have you attended sermons or Bible studies or had conversations about judgment, condemnation for sin, holiness, hell, or the heart is deceitful above all else? Explain why this is true. How does the information in this chapter challenge or clarify your thinking about these things?
4. Identify ways you see the therapeutic approach at work in your church and in your personal life. Think about preaching, Bible studies, and conversations. How does McKnight's thought about Jeremiah's calendar challenge you?
5. Ellul claims people are looking for myths to replace the beliefs on which this nation was founded and that television, movies, and the internet are providing them. Why do you agree or disagree?

APPENDIX 10: EQUIPPED TO TELL THE NEXT GENERATION STUDY GUIDE

6. What is mysticism and who are most vulnerable to it? How does it pair with propaganda? How has deception and propaganda influenced the thinking in this country? In the church?

7. How do advertising and consumerism work together? How is consumerism like a religion? Have you ever thought of consumerism as a church? How has the Christian church been converted to the church of consumerism? How does this affect the way you might approach people who criticize your beliefs?

8. Why does Gillquist claim that "holiness is not some extra accessory added on to the Gospel. It is part and parcel of our salvation, not something separate from it"?

9. How does morality today differ from biblical morality? Explain how your view of sin affects the way you think about morality and goodness. Explain how the statement "all sin is the same" is both true and false.

10. Identify some of the strong convictions people have today. Now identify ways in which this nation and the church are drowning in a sea of doubt. How does doubt interfere with faith? How do you see it in relation with the Great Commission?

11. How has the emphasis on self-help changed the gospel?

Be Equipped

Chapter 4

Personal Equipping

1. What is your personal belief about Scripture? How has this chapter challenged or supported that belief?

2. How would you describe your knowledge of the Bible? Have you read it through cover to cover? How might you improve your knowledge (be specific)?

3. How have you noticed the victim mentality described in this chapter? How have you thought of yourself as a victim? What were the circumstances surrounding it? How does this affect your faith in what God has said?

4. How has this chapter challenged your understanding of love?

5. What has challenged you concerning unity, judgment, and discipline? Why?

Equipping the Community

1. Discuss Jesus' warning about deception in Matthew 24 and why it is important for today.

2. Discuss the confessions mentioned in this chapter and why these documents are or are not important today.

3. Some churches rely on the Spirit but are loathe to do serious study. Others swing to the opposite end of the pendulum and pride themselves on their study but want little to do with the Holy Spirit. Where would you place yourself and your church? Why have both camps missed the mark?

4. Kirsopp Lake asks, "How many were there, for instance, in Christian churches in the eighteenth century who doubted the infallible inspiration of all Scripture?" He affirms that there were very few and that the majority was right. The only defense he could offer for why he didn't agree with them was simply because he did not believe it. How does this shed light on the accepted views of Scripture today? How does this affect your view of Scripture? How does it inform an answer to people who do not believe it (like Lake)?

5. How does the victim mentality affect the faith and mission of the church?

6. Explain in your own words how the victim mentality affects a person's understanding of love and how it leads to Jesus' death seeming like a cruel waste.

7. In *The Great Divorce*, C. S. Lewis writes, "There is but one good; that is God. Everything else is good when it looks to Him and bad when it turns from Him . . . .The false religion of lust is baser than the false religion of mother-love or patriotism." He asserts that real love has not been talked about in a long time because people are afraid to speak it. Then he claims, "That is why sorrows that used to purify now only fester." Discuss what Lewis means and if he is right or not. Support your answers with Scripture and current events. How does this change the commonly held view that people are basically good and the way the church tells the next generation about Jesus?

8. How important is unity to your church? How does your church identify unity? How does this affect what you believe and the mission of the church?

9. What does your church teach about judgment? How does it compare with what is in this chapter? Explain what Jesus meant when he said, "Do not judge" in Matthew 7:1. How does this chapter change the way you understand judgment?

10. Christians are told not to discipline people who sin, but the culture disciplines the church all the time to conform to its ways. Do you agree or disagree? Support your answers with specific events and Scripture.

Be Equipped

Chapter 5

Personal Equipping

1. Explain the difference between guilt and conviction. Do you struggle with guilt? What is the solution?

2. What keeps you from confessing your sin and repenting of it?

3. Who receives forgiveness? Have you repented of your rebellion against God and asked Jesus to forgive you and to be your Lord and Savior? Have you experienced his forgiveness? If not, why not?

4. What part do good works play in salvation? How does this change your understanding of salvation?

5. How has tolerance, diversity, and inclusiveness affected your life?

6. How does Nancy DeMoss's comparison of sin to a sewer line break affect your view of sin?

Equipping the Community

1. In chapter 3 you were asked about whether consumerism has become a religion in this nation. In light of these last two chapters, has your thinking changed? What practices can you identify in the culture that would support this? How does this affect your thinking about Christian doctrines, beliefs, and practices?

2. Explain how the church's view of love and compassion might actually prevent people from coming to saving faith in Jesus. Why is it sometimes important to let people struggle for a little while as they do business with God concerning their sin?

3. N. T. Wright describes evil as "the force of anti-creation [and] anti-life, the force which opposes and seeks to deface and destroy God's good world of space, time and matter, and above all God's image-bearing human creatures." How does this change your view of evil and your stand against it?

4. What is the connection between evil and sin? Why is it not loving to be soft on sin?

5. What is your response to DeMoss's question, "Why are we so prone to defend our choices that take us right to the edge of sin, and so reluctant to make radical choices to protect our hearts and minds from sin?"

6. How does pandering to the victim mentality interfere with forgiveness? How does your church capitulate to this mentality? Is forgiveness automatically granted to everyone and everything? Which of the views of forgiveness presented in this chapter are held by you and the people in your church?

7. How does forgetting an offence equate to forgiveness, or does it? Why is a proper understanding of forgiveness crucial for salvation?

8. If the Christian faith is the only thing that can overcome the world, does it follow that the people of the world and Satan would work against the church to get her to deny her faith and to do mission in her own strength and wisdom according

to the world's terms? How does this affect the way you process the world's truth against Scripture? Which would you be more inclined to act upon?

9. Describe the difference between biblical justice and the culture's view of justice. What part do good works play in salvation (Eph 2:8–10)? How does this correspond with the understanding of the majority of people sitting in the pews of your church on Sunday morning? How often do you hear, "I hope I'm good enough to get to heaven"?

10. Why is the Old Testament law necessary?

11. How do tolerance, diversity, and inclusiveness preclude a strong stand against evil and sin and influence the doctrine of hell, or do they?

12. Read again the list of prayers promoted in Scripture. How does it differ from the prayers commonly prayed in your private life and in the life of your church? Begin to pray this way in your private prayer time and in your services and prayer meetings.

13. How does the strong American independent spirit affect the faith and practice of individuals and, by extension, the faith and practice of the church?

14. Nancy DeMoss takes a strong stand against sin, comparing it to a sewer line break. Is she justified? Why or why not? What connection might there be between the state of the church today concerning sin and her ineffectiveness in bringing people to faith in Jesus?

Be Equipped

Chapter 6

Personal Equipping

1. Before reading this chapter, how would you have explained God's holiness to someone? How has this information changed your understanding of holiness?

2. What surprised you about holiness?

3. How has your view of the law been challenged or changed?

4. Before reading this chapter, how would you have described love? What, if anything, in this chapter has changed that? Why?

5. Which section had the most impact on you? Why?

Equipping the Community

1. Share with each other the view(s) of holiness commonly held by yourself and your church prior to reading this chapter. Why is it significant that both Isaiah

APPENDIX 10: EQUIPPED TO TELL THE NEXT GENERATION STUDY GUIDE

and John depict God on the throne and the seraphim circling above crying out, "Holy, holy, holy?"

2. Give your favorite quote from this chapter and tell why it meant so much to you. Why do we need a holy God?

3. Tozer and Edwards argue for the immutability of God's holiness. Why is this important? What are the dangers or pitfalls of both sides of the argument?

4. Why must the people who serve God be holy? Discuss some of the passages from Psalms (15; 24; 85:10; 89:14) and Isaiah 32:15–17 about holiness. How does this affect your idea of holiness?

5. How does the Sermon on the Mount inform us about holiness?

6. What role does the law have in holiness? What prevents this from becoming legalistic on God's part?

7. Why is it significant that love is not specifically mentioned in either of the two throne room scenes? How do love and righteousness relate to each other?

8. Contrary to popular belief, righteousness produces peace. Explain why this is so and why people making their own truth and doing what seems right to them will not bring peace. Or will it? (Think about the world situation.)

9. What is the purpose of discipline and how does it contribute to a person getting to heaven? What do you think are the consequences of the lack of discipline so prevalent in this nation?

10. As is typical in this culture of pursuing one extreme or the other, Christians are often divided between the reasoned control of the life in Christ on one hand and the more emotive aspects of the faith on the other. With which group would you place yourself and your church? Why is it important to have balance? How might you achieve it?

11. O'Brien identifies two kinds of holiness. Describe them. How do they connect with the Christian faith? Describe justification and sanctification and tell how they relate to holiness. What implication does this have for you and your congregation?

Be Equipped

Chapter 7

Personal Equipping

1. What is your personal belief about Adam and Eve and the apple? What does it have to do with you?

2. Can you see yourself as holy? Why or why not?

3. Think about what the Bible calls the new creation in a person. How does that change your answer to question 2? What role does Jesus have in this new creation?

4. Have you ever made Jesus the Lord and Savior of your life?

5. Are you aware of one or more times when the Holy Spirit was at work in you? What was that like? What happened?

Equipping the Community

1. In your own words explain original sin.

2. What constitutes the image of God? What part of the image of God was lost to humankind in the garden of Eden after the fall from God's grace? What parts remained? How might we see them in the world today?

3. Why is the loss of holiness important? Explain total depravity in your own words. How might you explain this to friends who scoff at total depravity and believe in the basic goodness of people (the doctrine of the Enlightenment, not from Scripture)?

4. What or who is the "new self" people must put on? Calvin sees this as a catalyst for change in that all people recognize they are not what they should be and are dissatisfied with themselves. How might you use this to direct people's efforts to seek God (using the information uncovered this far in the book)?

5. How does the new person recover the image of God? Discuss the ideas of Lloyd-Jones, Westley, and Owen.

6. How does the Sermon on the Mount inform this "new creation?" How might you use your answers from question 4 and this one to talk with a person about their need for salvation?

7. Everyone in the church is familiar with the call to love one another. Discuss the passages of Scripture found here that call Christians to holiness and to be without blame. How does this speak to the morality commonly accepted in many churches today?

8. Do you agree with Lloyd-Jones's assessment that walking in the truth of the new creation is the way to revolutionize the church? Why or why not? Justify or debunk his lament that all of our failures and sins can be traced to Christians' lack of this holy nature of the new creation.

9. Owen calls the new creation a "new obedience" and writes, "without it, there is nothing but darkness and wandering, and confusion." What does he mean? Is he justified? Support your answer.

10. In your own words, explain why only Jesus can bring salvation. How might this be helpful in talking with people about Jesus?

11. How would you answer someone who protests that they are not good enough to enter heaven and never could be? What might you say to the person who believes he or she will go to heaven because he or she is a good person?

12. Explain the two kinds of grace identified by Owen.

13. According to Ryle, growing in grace means that a person's "sense of sin is becoming deeper, his faith stronger, his hope brighter, his love more extensive, his spiritual-mindedness more marked. He feels more of the power of godliness in his own heart. He manifests more of it in his life. He is going on from strength to strength, from faith to faith, and from grace to grace." How does Ryle's view differ from the commonly held view of grace in many congregations and the culture at large? Why is the correct understanding of grace important to the mission of the church?

14. What does Ryle mean when he talks about both the private and the public means of grace? Ryle writes, "I firmly believe that the manner in which these public means of grace are used has much to say to the prosperity of a believer's soul . . . . It is a sign of bad health when a person loses relish for his food; and it is a sign of spiritual decline when we lose our appetite for means of grace." How does this challenge your ideas on prayer, meditation, self-examination, and church attendance and the practice of the first three by the church as a means to grow? How would you use this to talk with other Christians about these things?

Be Equipped

Chapter 8

Personal Equipping

1. Recall a time when you were particularly close to God. Describe your thoughts and feelings at the time.

2. Was there any aspect of commitment associated with that experience? Explain.

3. Does your view of worship correspond more with the stoicism of the Age of Reason or the beauty of holiness? How does this differ or agree with your experience of question 1?

4. Why is it not wrong to desire pleasure and beauty?

5. Lewis and Dekker talk about a banquet where nothing spoils and then explain that we are on the outside looking in with a longing to belong in it, to be united

with it at the deepest level. Explain how we get into the eternal banquet. How might this help you talk to friends, family, and neighbors about Jesus?

Equipping the Community

1. What did Lewis mean when he wrote, "It would seem that Our Lord finds our desires not too strong, but too weak.... We are far too easily pleased?"

2. How does Lewis's idea of our weak desires and being "too easily pleased," connect with Edwards's idea that Christians glorify God the most when they testify to God's glory with both mind and delight?

3. For Lewis, what is the strongest desire a person on earth has? How does this lead to understanding two sources of pleasure? Why is it important to realize eternal pleasure is more than merely meeting departed loved ones? What is it the world's pleasure cannot deliver, and why is it import to know that? How does this and Dekker's analogy of the banquet of pleasures help in presenting the gospel of Jesus to others? Write a brief narrative of what you might say.

4. How does holiness answer the emptiness left in us by our technology? How does Lewis connect holiness, pleasure, and delight with the image of God?

5. Eldredge observes that "the heart does not respond to principles and programs; it seeks not efficiency, but passion" such as found in the arts. Why would you agree or disagree? What is the connection with Otto's "*mysterium tremendum*" in chapter 6?

6. In your own words, describe how Edwards views holiness in his "Miscellanies." How has this changed your concept of holiness?

7. Explain "consent to being," "consent to being in general," "universal," "universe," "primary beauty," and "secondary beauty." What is the significance of each? How does beauty defined as "consent to being" open doors for communicating the gospel to people?

8. Edwards distinguishes "between having an opinion that God is holy and gracious, and having a sense of the loveliness and beauty of the holiness and grace." Then he compares it with "having a rational judgment that honey is sweet, and having a sense of its sweetness." Using these terms, how would you describe your understanding of or relationship with holiness? Do you and your congregation identify more closely with "having an [rational] opinion" that holiness is excellent and beautiful, or it is "sweet and pleasant to [your] soul"?

9. Explain the role of the intellect and the role of the affections in Edwards's statement in question 8.

10. For Edwards, the opposite of beauty is not ugliness but nothingness. Explain what he means. What role do harmony and proportion play in beauty? Reflect on the observation of how, as the culture increasingly controlled Christian doctrines, the arts became less concerned with harmony and proportion. How do you see the downward spiral (degradation) from beauty to nothingness today? Or do you?

11. Combine Edwards's premise that "what disagrees with being must necessarily be disagreeable to being in general [God] .... Disagreement or contrariety to being is evidently an approach to nothing, or a degree of nothing, which is ... the greatest and only evil" with Delattra's interpretation, "Beauty is to being as deformity is to nothing. Good and evil are measured on this same scale running from the fullness of being and beauty toward nothing." What is the significance concerning good and evil for the church and culture where everyone makes his or her own truth? How does this inform your approach to tell someone about Jesus?

12. Why does Edwards argue for the highest beauty being objective and not subjective? Where do you and your church align with this? How do light and darkness play into this?

13. Think about someone you know who does not have a relationship with Jesus and is all about living a life of pleasure and beauty. Use the ideas presented here and write out how you might talk with this person about Jesus. Share these with the group.

Be Equipped

Chapter 9

Personal Equipping

1. What surprised you the most about this chapter?
2. Before reading this chapter how would you have explained wholeness? What, if anything, has changed your view of wholeness?
3. How do you determine what is valid? Why is it important to value what Scripture says is valid?
4. How has this chapter challenged or changed your understanding of love, righteousness, and holiness?
5. How does sin rob you of wholeness?
6. How would you use the information about sin and the law to talk with your friend who believes Christians are trying to earn their salvation by keeping the moral instructions found there? How would you connect this with wholeness?

7. Rate your time spent with God on a scale of 1–10. How does this compare with time you take to watch television, shop, play games, or otherwise spend on yourself? Do you know the beauty and joy of God that you have been reading about? Make a plan to change/improve that.

Equipping the Community

1. How would you explain wholeness to a non-believer? Include what it is; where it comes from; and how you get it.

2. How does wholeness connect with beauty (chapter 8) and holiness (chapters 6 and 7)?

3. Why is it important for things that are valid to determine values and not vice versa? Make an honest evaluation of yourself and your congregation. How do you align with these two ways?

4. How does thinking of obedience as consenting to God's being and beauty versus a duty or love owed to God change the way you talk with folks about Jesus?

5. How does building your own kingdom lead to brokenness and sin? How do you see it being played out where you live and work? Do you agree or disagree with Edwards's description of sin as a cruel tyrant? Why or why not?

6. Have you witnessed the great divide in this nation between love and righteousness? Give examples. Explain why people doing their own thing leads to chaos and anarchy.

7. Eldredge writes, "We must repent our sins; brokenness must be healed." How does this distinction make a difference in the way you talk to people about Jesus?

8. Explain the two graphs in your own words. Do you see the licentiousness of love and the legalism of righteousness and the hurt both cause when divested of the other? Most people quickly identify righteousness and legalism with a works-based religion of earning your way to heaven. How does love the way it is practiced today become works-based?

9. Reflect on Keller's statement that "belief in a God of pure love—who accepts everyone and judges no one—is a powerful act of faith. Not only is there no evidence for it in the natural order, but there is almost no historical, religious textual support for it . . . . The more one looks at it, the less justified it appears." How does this impact your understanding of love and Christianity?

10. Why are both love and righteousness needed for wholeness?

11. Why is the moral law in Scripture important to wholeness and the Christian life? Think about sin, unity, peace, beauty, and morality. What is your favorite Bible passage about the law?

12. Imagine that you are in a Bible study and you hear a member of the class say, "All you need is love. Just give me a God of love only." How would you respond to the person?

Be Equipped

Chapter 10

Personal Equipping

1. What have you heard from pastors, teachers, or others about healing? How does this chapter correspond with or challenge those ideas? Why is healing such an emotionally charged topic?

2. How have you encountered the four kinds of healing discussed in this chapter? Name them and describe them in your own words. Give examples where you can.

3. Have you ever recognized in Scripture that Jesus did not always heal everyone (apart from the lack of faith in his hometown)? How does this affect your thoughts about why God does not heal everyone today? How does this make you feel about your personal responsibility to help everyone who asks you?

4. If you are sick for a long period of time and someone tells you that you do not have enough faith or you would be healed, how might you answer them? How would you answer them if they tell you not to pray because God knows your needs, and you are not to bother him?

5. How do you receive wholeness, and how will it change you? Do you have an eternal perspective or are you living for right now?

6. How does Joni's story help you? Use Joni's questions to do an honest and thoughtful examination of yourself to determine if you believe God is all you need. What impact did the real-life stories of suffering and wholeness have on you?

Equipping the Community

1. What ideas about God healing people today are commonly accepted in your congregation? These might range from going to doctors and using modern medicine only to using prayer only to combat disease and disability or somewhere in between. What would a balanced theology on healing and wholeness look like?

2. Explain *shalom* and how Jesus is the fulfillment of this Old Testament concept.

3. Discuss the four kinds of healing mentioned in this chapter. Give examples if you can. How does healing relate to wholeness?

4. How do the concepts of the beauty of holiness connect with wholeness and healing? Think about primary and secondary beauty, harmony, and proportion.

5. How does the fact that Jesus did not always heal everyone affirm or change your ideas on healing and the mission of the church?

6. Discuss the source of sickness and the relationship sin has to healing. What role does faith play in healing?

7. What is Jesus' priority when it comes to healing? How does this change the way you might answer someone who struggles with why some people are healed and others are not? How do God's sovereignty and an eternal perspective affect your view of healing?

8. Explain wholeness and how we can get it. Describe how it changes a person.

9. Discuss Joni's experiences and how that impacts you when you read her solutions. Do your own thoughtful and honest self-examination using Joni's questions. What does it reveal?

10. What are some of the potholes that might keep you from wholeness?

11. How does your Christian walk and the life of your congregation match up with Merton's quote in the summary? What are you willing to change to make the difference smaller?

Be Equipped

Chapter 11

Personal Equipping

1. What single word or phrase would you use to describe love? How does sin affect love? How has sin prevented you from showing love?

2. In figure 11-1 which column best explains your thoughts on love? How has this chapter challenged your understanding of love?

3. What are some of the false assumptions you have had about God's love? How has the culture influenced this thinking?

4. Do you believe that God loves everyone the same? God deals with people in covenants. How might this change your view of universal love? Who makes the decision not to participate in God's great promises? How does this change your view of sharing Jesus with people?

5. Think about the difference between *eros* and *agape* love. Which one have you been living? How does this affect the way you share Jesus with others?

APPENDIX 10: EQUIPPED TO TELL THE NEXT GENERATION STUDY GUIDE

Equipping the Community

1. Before reading this book, what would you have said is the greatest characteristic of God? Has that changed?

2. Explain why love is so important to us and the effects rebellion and sin have had on it. In this chapter the example of the transcontinental railroad illustrates how sin causes us to miss the mark. What examples do you see in your own life, the life of your congregation, or the culture?

3. Which concept of love in figure 11-1 best describes your thinking about love? Which is prevalent in your congregation? What is the popular thinking about the salvation of people who do good works and are kind? Explain in your own words why these folks may not have salvation. How does this influence your approach to mission? What might you say to the person who believes she is not good enough to be in God's heaven? What might you say to the person who believes he has done enough good things to outweigh the bad and is therefore qualified for heaven?

4. Describe the four false assumptions discussed in this chapter. Can you identify others? Identify specific ways the culture influences Christians to believe these. How do these affect the mission of the church?

5. Describe the concepts of love contained in the Greek and Hebrew words for love. Make the connection between the Hebrew word *Ḥesed* and the Greek word *agape*. Do you and your church operate in *eros*, which was understood as "a universal love, generous, unbound and non-selective"? Why is this not biblical? What else surprises you about the biblical understanding of love? How does this influence your view of sharing the gospel of Jesus with others?

6. Explain covenant love and how it is unconditional but with a condition. Include in this discussion the cry to a superior power for deliverance from enemies and the necessity of obedience. How does this affect your everyday decisions? What implications does this have for your church's life and mission?

7. Do you see de-evolution happening in people and this culture as human love replaces God's love on an ever-increasing scale? Support your answer with examples.

8. How does having the *agape* view of love as opposed to the *eros* view of love affect your beliefs? What difference will it make in how you pursue the Great Commission?

9. Explain why living out holy love may cause conflict and bring persecution. What is the biblical answer to this?

APPENDIX 10: EQUIPPED TO TELL THE NEXT GENERATION STUDY GUIDE

Be Equipped

Chapter 12

Personal Equipping

1. How does God's moral law impact love?

2. Why is it loving to hate the things God hates? Why does he hate them?

3. How do wealth, pride, and fear of what others will think or say about you influence what you say and do? What does the Bible have to say about this?

4. Are you the person who deeply feels the needs of others and cannot say no when asked to help, or are you the person who always says no with no twinge of conscience? What is the biblical response? How did you respond to the examples of Jesus leaving people to preach the gospel? Why? Does this change your view of doing good works?

5. What is your personal choice of discipline? What is God's goal for all discipline? How does your personal preference fit in with God's goal for discipline?

6. What does it mean to love your enemy? What is your position on nonviolence? Do Keller and Volf or Quarles make the stronger argument?

7. Do you truly believe that telling someone about Jesus is the most loving thing you can do? If yes, what is keeping you from doing it?

Equipping the Community

1. How does the moral law inform godly love?

2. Stauffer calls godly love radical. Explain what he means. Why is it loving to hate the things God hates?

3. What are the three things that keep Christians from living in holy love? What is the biblical response? How do they manifest in your life and in the life of your congregation? What might be done to change this?

4. Why is Christian community vital to the health and well-being of Christians' faith? Why might attendance be dropping?

5. When Christians reach out to their neighbors, why is it important not to make helping all people "a system which applies schematically to all men and places"? How should such determinations be made? Using Jesus' examples, discuss what the most important work is and how that defines the good works of Christian mission.

6. Why is discipline necessary? Do you and your church practice consistent godly discipline, or are you more likely to allow folks simply to do what they believe is

right? Why are the words "and God gave them over" so sad? Why does God allow suffering or, in some cases, actually cause it? Where discipline is not needed (not a direct result of sin), why does God allow or perhaps actually cause suffering? How is this loving?

7. Explain why the culture's love is divisive. Explain why godly love sometimes divides. What will bring unity and peace? Explain what Klassen means when he writes, "Moreover, love is a consequence of the rule of God; it arises out of the experience of salvation."

8. In the Sermon on the Mount, Jesus commands his followers to love their enemies. Instead of compassion, he talks about God's impartiality. How is the church to understand the reason behind that command?

9. What is your personal view of nonviolence? According to Volf what is needed in order for Christians not to retaliate when evil destroys loved ones? He concedes that there may come a time when consistent nonviolence will be impossible but that there is no scriptural evidence for that. How would you answer him? How has Quarles challenged or encouraged your thinking about nonviolence and not resisting evil?

10. Why is telling people about Jesus the most loving thing you can do? Think of a specific person in your life who has resisted Jesus. How might you communicate the gospel to him or her?

Be Equipped

Chapter 13

Personal Equipping

1. How do you understand God's grace? Do you tend towards the belief that all are saved and going to heaven? How has this chapter challenged that? Write your definition of grace as understood throughout this chapter.

2. Why must God be allowed to withhold specific grace? Why is automatic grace not grace?

3. Zimmerli writes that saving grace presupposes a relationship with God and an ongoing fellowship. Why is this important to actualize grace in your life?

4. Why is confession and repentance of sin necessary for the actualization of grace in your life? How does grace change you?

5. What are the lifelong effects of saving grace? What changes take place? Do you see them in your life? How might you experience more grace in your life?

APPENDIX 10: EQUIPPED TO TELL THE NEXT GENERATION STUDY GUIDE

Equipping the Community

1. Distinguish the difference between general grace and specific grace. Use Zodhiates's observations to explain the difference between God's grace and his graciousness. Why is this important? How might you use this information to answer a person in your church who tells you that God's grace covers everyone and all are going to heaven?

2. In the Old Testament, grace is understood as unmerited favor and must be given by a superior to an inferior. According to Kselman, why is it necessary that grace can and may be withheld? What is the significance that grace must be requested? Grace is the free gift of God; so why is there a requirement attached? What is it?

3. Why does grace always refer to righteousness and righteous judgment in the Old Testament? How does this connect with mercy and love? What is the significance of the connection of grace with *Ḥesed*, steadfast love that we studied in chapters 11 and 12? What role do relationship and fellowship have in God's grace?

4. Grace means favor. According to Mounce, what does that mean? What does it mean to be "highly favored?"

5. According to Kittel, what does the New Testament connect with grace? Does this differ from the view of grace held by most people in your congregation? If so, how does it differ? How do we know that while saving grace is offered universally to all, it is not universally given to all?

6. What are the effects of grace on the person who has specific (saving) grace? Discuss slavery to sin versus slavery to righteousness. Why are righteousness and grace so closely connected? How does this differ from our postmodern way of thinking? Which paradigm, biblical, modern, or postmodern, dominates your thinking or the thinking of your congregation? How might you use the information in this chapter to answer the person who believes that the Bible is restrictive of people's rights and freedoms to choose?

7. According to Dunn, God's free gift of grace must be linked to the "conversion-initiation" experience. What does he mean? How does this affect the ongoing life of the recipient? How does this inform your preaching and teaching on the gospel of grace?

8. Discuss Jeffress's dichotomy of bad and good grace. With which parts does your congregation identify more closely?

9. What role does perseverance in suffering have to do with grace? To which doctrine does this point us? What role does this play in revival and renewal?

10. Alcorn states, "*Grace never lowers the standards of holiness. Jesus . . . raised it.*" What does he mean? Do you agree or disagree? Why? How might this influence your response to the person who tells you that "God loves everyone the same and

his grace covers all sin [meaning without confession and repentance]. There is no need to change behaviors. It's all good"?

Be Equipped

Chapter 14

Personal Equipping

1. What are your thoughts on absolute and relative truth? Have you considered the effects relative truth is having in your life or in the lives of your friends and family? Compare relative truth with consistency and agreement of what actually is. How does relative truth match up?

2. What would you say to someone who tells you she believes that what is true for you may not be true for her, or that what is true today may not be true tomorrow and that to think otherwise limits God?

3. What does the New Testament say about truth? How does this differ from relative truth?

4. What is the connection between truth, grace, and love? Why is it significant that "steadfast love" is used?

5. Why can "I don't know" be a cop-out? Why is this false humility?

6. How might you use Alcorn's metaphor of guardrails to help someone understand the biblical meaning of truth?

Equipping the Community

1. Discuss the consequences of relative truth in personal lives, the church, and our culture. Why is it important that truth comes to us through Jesus and not simply that he is truth?

2. Discuss Edwards's view of truth as consistency and agreement with God's ideas as well as things as they actually are. Why is this important?

3. Describe Killen's "three tests [of truth]: logical consistency, factual consistency, and practical consistency." Do you agree that "absolute truth . . . does not limit but rather reveals God"? Why?

4. Scott concludes "that there is no truth in the biblical sense . . . outside of God." What does he mean?

5. How does Old Testament truth become part of the believer? What is the connection of truth with righteousness and steadfast love, Ḥesed?

6. What meaning does the New Testament ascribe to truth? How does relative truth affect reliability, trustworthiness, sincerity, and honesty? Which value system provides greater stability? Cite specific examples to support your answer.

7. Why must truth embody specific teachings and beliefs? How does this support the historical documents (creeds, catechisms, and confessions) and the need for theology?

8. If truth is revealed in Scripture, why must all individual revelation today be subjected to a discernment process? What is that process?

9. It has often been said that Christians are so heavenly minded they are of no earthly use. Today, I have heard it said that Christians are so earthly minded they cannot be used for heavenly purposes. What does the biblical understanding of truth have to say to these two statements? How does relative truth relate to wishful thinking? As a corollary why is "I don't know" sometimes an unspiritual cop-out?

10. Alcorn proposes truth as guardrails that keep people from careening down a deadly cliff. Truth is the difference between a dented bumper and total destruction. Explain what he means and discuss the extremes Christians and/or culture tend to pursue in regard to truth.

11. How is truth related to conduct, and why must it be that way? What would you say to the person who comes to your Bible study and tells you, "That may be okay for you, but it is not truth for me"?

Be Equipped

Chapter 15

Personal Equipping

1. What is prayer? What are the three kinds of prayer? Can you identify each of these in your prayer life? Have you experienced John 14:12–14 (you will do what Jesus did and greater) answers to prayer in your life? What were they?

2. What holds you back from praying more? Does thinking of prayer as conversation make it easier for you to pray? Try talking to God like you would talk to your best friend.

3. Do you remember to praise God on a regular basis? Do you praise him in the difficult times of life such as illness, death, financial problems, or wounds inflicted by friends?

4. When Christians meditate, they fill their minds with God's characteristics and/or Scripture. It is also good to practice waiting for God to respond. Try this, and

try keeping a notebook nearby to jot down things that come to mind: either as things to do so you can put it out of your mind and focus on God or as things to be discerned as being from God for you.

5. When you pray God's word, do you tend to look for promises that will give you what you want, or do you seek to know God's will and pray to move him to move people to accomplish that?

6. Are you or your friends Christian fatalists? Why is this damaging to your faith and witness to those outside the faith?

7. How do you know God's will? Why are you able to pray as powerfully as Moses and Elijah? What does it mean to pray in the name of Jesus?

8. How does prayer teach you about yourself and fill the emptiness in your life?

Equipping the Community

1. How are the three kinds of prayer expressed in your congregation? How are you seeing answers to prayer like Jesus promised in John 14:12–14? Identify areas where you might improve and the things that keep you from praying in general and supplication in particular. What might you do to overcome the obstacles to prayer?

2. Why is praise important in the prayer life of your congregation? How would you answer a member of your Sunday school class who thinks God must be narcissistic to want us to praise him?

3. What is meditation, and how might you implement it in your church? Be sure to distinguish between Christian meditation and that of New Age or other religions. Create an atmosphere where it is safe for folks to share their experiences.

4. What are the ways you see people praying the Scriptures? How does this differ from what is presented in this chapter? Are you and your congregation more apt to pray promises to give you what you want or to search the Scriptures to determine God's will and then pray to move God to move people to make it happen? Organize prayer teams to pray God's will as seen in Scripture (appendices 5 and 6 will help you get started).

5. What erroneous teaching have you heard that inhibits your prayer life and the prayer life of your congregation? What would you say to the man in your Bible study who believes we are not to ask boldly for specific things in God's will but should always be cautious to pray "not my will but yours be done?"

6. What is Christian fatalism, and why is it dangerous to the faith and witness of the church? Why does it seem like genuine humility and strong faith? What feeds fatalism, and what is the greatest way to overcome it? What would you say

to a Sunday school teacher who always says, "It was meant to be," for everything good or bad?

7. Keller writes, "Prayer is profoundly altered by the amount and accuracy of that knowledge [of God]." Do you agree or disagree and why? How would you describe the accuracy of the knowledge of God and God's will among your church attendees? Are you individually and corporately praying to advance God's cause in the communities surrounding your church and homes or are you more likely to expect God to be "loving and forgiving but not holy and transcendent," requiring very little of you?

8. What does Keller mean when he writes, "Without prayer that answers the God of the Bible, we will only be talking to ourselves"? How are we to immerse ourselves in God's word (Scripture) enough to overcome the immersion in the culture that takes place as we go about our daily lives?

9. What role does righteousness have in prayer?

10. How does forgiveness affect your prayers? How might God's blessings differ from the culture's view of blessing? What comes to mind when you think of blessing others? How does this affect your willingness or ability to bless your enemies? What are some ways you can bless and pray for your enemies?

Be Equipped

Chapter 16

Personal Equipping

1. How important is prayer to you? How important is prayer to God? Evaluate your time spent in entertainment versus prayer. Try keeping a log of time spent in each. Evaluate the things you pray for as to whether they are petition, intercession, or supplication (all prayer is valid). What might you do to expand and deepen your prayer life?

2. What is revival? Have you ever experienced one personally or known someone who has? What was it like? What changed and did it last? According to Edwards and the experts on revival what is the distinguishing mark of revival?

3. Begin to pray intentionally for the salvation of people that they would be reconciled to God through faith in Jesus. Pray for God to send his disciples to tell the good news. Pray that you would be equipped and willing to be one of those workers as God sees fit.

4. How would you answer a friend who scoffs when you talk about how desperate times are and that sin is rampant and says, "Every generation thinks that of the generations that follow. Nothing is new"?

5. Have you ever stopped to consider how nearly everything promoted in this culture (personal choice and freedom, relative truth, lack of discipline, love that never judges anything, the emphasis on consuming, comfort, pursuit of pleasure, busyness, constant bombarding of music, videos, electronics, etc.) works contrary to the Christian faith? Can you identify specific strongholds in your own life that keep you from serving God with all your heart, mind, body, and strength? How has this chapter challenged your personal beliefs about spiritual warfare (the devil, demons, principalities)? Begin to pray and put on the armor of God (feel free to develop your own prayer).

6. Using the material found in this book and Scripture, identify schemes the devil uses to keep you captive to do his will. How has your understanding of blessing and praying for your enemies changed? Pray for them and bless them.

Equipping the Community

1. What is the scriptural evidence for prayer? Evaluate the prayer of your ministry and congregation according to what you find. If Scripture, Paul, Bounds, and Foster are right, what is getting in the way of more effective prayers for revival and reform in your ministry and in the ministry of your congregation?

2. Explain the difference between revival and reformation. Examine yourself and the ministry of your congregation or study group. Which is more important: the numbers of people attending and being in the black financially or people being transformed and forever changed to look increasingly like Jesus. Why do programs often fail to bring about the desired results of changed lives? What role does holiness have?

3. Examine your personal ministry and the ministry of your congregation or study group using Kaiser's four criteria that reveal the need for revival prayer. What do you find (be sure to use the biblical standard and not the culture's standard when evaluating)? What changes might you make as a result of this evaluation?

4. What are the earmarks of revival—how are you to recognize when revival is happening? Discuss the views of Edwards, Lovelace, Kaiser, Bounds, and the Scottish pastors. What did they all have in common? The Northampton congregation found that "their problem was . . . a deep aversion to God at the root of their personalities, an aversion which left them in unconscious bondage to unbelief, selfishness, jealousy and other underlying complexes of sin." They had become "respectable, and they had a kind of rote orthodoxy . . . but their ultimate concerns were not God and his kingdom, but land and the pursuit of affluence." Evaluate your personal life and the life of your congregation or study group in light of the things presented in this book. In what ways are you like the Northampton congregation?

5. Where do you see supplication happening in your personal life or in the life of those to whom you minister? Discuss the role of supplication in the revivals mentioned in this chapter. Have you personally witnessed such events? How are supplication and respectability related? Identify things that cause prayer, and specifically supplication, to decline. Do you want to change that? How might you go about it?

6. What do you and the members of your congregation or study believe about the devil, principalities, and spiritual warfare? What are the schemes of the devil, and how do you see them at work in your life and the life of fellow believers? Have you thought about opposition to the gospel in these terms? How does this change your determination and participation in bringing the harvest of people into God's kingdom?

7. Explain each piece of God's armor and why we need it. What are the offensive weapons and how do we use them? What role does holiness play in this warfare?

8. My prayer is that you have been convicted to begin concerts of prayer in your life and ministry and to pray God's will and knowledge of his character according to the truth of Scripture in the power of the Holy Spirit. Will you join me?

Be Equipped

Chapter 17

Personal Equipping

1. How has this section on the reliability of Scripture challenged and/or encouraged you?

2. What might you say in a Bible study when a neighbor asks how you can believe a book written thousands of years ago? How can it be relevant for us today?

3. How would you answer a friend who accuses you of worshiping the Bible because it means so much to you?

4. How can you tell if you are an evangelical or not? Why is it important? What is keeping you back from telling the next generation about Jesus? What might you do to change that?

Equipping the Community

1. In your own words explain the two kinds of affections Edwards describes. How can you identify which is which?

2. According to Edwards, what is the first sign of true revival? Why is it so important?

APPENDIX 10: EQUIPPED TO TELL THE NEXT GENERATION STUDY GUIDE

3. How was the Bible formed?

4. Explain the difference between inspiration and illumination.

5. How would you respond to a person in your small group or church who tells you that she had a powerful experience with God and that he told her she could have an adulterous relationship with a man whom she has grown to love?

6. What are some of the criteria we should use to understand what the text means for us?

7. What would you say to a member of your congregation or small group who says he can't believe the Bible because it is full of errors, contradictions, and only the writings of people expressing what the events of their day meant to them? What would you tell him if he presses further that it is a dead book not valid for our technological age?

8. What is Edwards's view of sin? Why is this important to our understanding of holy grace?

9. Describe gracious affections.

10. According to Edwards what makes a person a hypocrite? How does this affect you? Your congregation?

11. What are some positive signs of revival?

12. Discuss what it means to be evangelical. What are the three Rs of evangelicalism?

13. Edwards asks which is more loving: to calmly assure the sleepers that all will be well when the house is on fire, or to yell "fire" and to try to arouse them and get them out of the burning building? How would you answer him when it is applied to sin and its consequences? Does this change your view of the need to talk about sin in today's culture? How might you begin?

Be Equipped

Chapter 18

Personal Equipping

1. Have you ever seen or experienced revival? Have you ever been to a Billy Graham crusade or watched one on television? What were your thoughts and feelings? How does your experience connect with information in this chapter?

2. How has the media (television, internet, videos, music, games) influenced the way you perceive Christianity? Identify differences promoted in media and Scripture.

APPENDIX 10: EQUIPPED TO TELL THE NEXT GENERATION STUDY GUIDE

3. Think back over the things mentioned in this book that may stand in the way of total commitment to God: political correctness, consumerism, materialism, comfort, pleasure, beliefs that have been capitulated to the culture, etc. What is keeping you back from telling the next generation about Jesus? What might you do to change that?

4. What is the discernment process for testing the spirits to see what sort they are?

Equipping the Community

1. How do you recognize revival? What are the earmarks of all revivals?

2. After reading about revival, what, if anything, holds you back from praying and working for it?

3. Test the spirits of the reporting you hear on news networks and programs you watch on television. Are the messages they give consistent with Scripture or do they conflict (I am not talking about factual reporting of murders for example, but the spin that is placed on an event, situation, or program to sway your thinking about truth)?

4. McGrath writes, "Advance [of the gospel] involves adaptation—but *adaptation need not involve change.*" What does he mean?

5. Explain Sweet's EPIC model of doing church. How does this or other things in this chapter or book help you to contextualize the gospel without capitulating to the culture?

6. Why is storytelling important, and what role do metaphors play? What dangers might be inherent in this method of sharing the gospel?

7. Why is it imperative to back up your storytelling with story-living? Why is a serious view of sin and discipline important to sharing the gospel?

8. Smith tells us that people "are looking for something the culture cannot provide" and that they cannot get at the mall. Think back over the chapters in this book. What does Christianity provide that the culture cannot? How might you begin to communicate that to people who see no need for Jesus?

9. Some areas in which this culture reflects God's love are in concern for the earth, helping the poor and needy, and standing up for the rights of those too weak to help themselves. How might you use these or others to present the gospel?

10. Pastors, do you preach the entire word of God or only those parts that are popular today? Piper claims that in "Edwards' view of the reality of heaven and hell and the necessity of persevering in a life of holy affections and godliness, eternity was at stake every Sunday. This sets him off from the average preacher today." I

believe his is the scriptural way. How would having this view change the message you give? When was the last time you preached on holiness? Lay people: how will you support your pastor to the people who complain if he or she does step out and boldly proclaims the entire gospel?

11. I have recommended praying the Scriptures and prayers that will change the world. Will you do it or something similar? What other ways might you grow in your personal and corporate life of the church in holiness and prayer that will prepare the way for revival?

Be Equipped

The Wrap-Up

1. In order to see how far along your DNA has been rewritten by the Holy Spirit ask yourself, "Is my personal comfort or telling another person about Jesus more important to me?" If you are honest, most of you will have to admit that your personal comfort trumps sharing the good news of Jesus. That can change, and it will be easier than you might think because most individuals are not as hostile to talking about Jesus as the media makes out if it is done in humility with grace.

2. Additionally, the Holy Spirit is in you working to show you how. Learn to co-operate with him. It could be as simple as saying, "God bless you," or, "You look tired (or you look like you're having a bad day); I'll pray for you."

3. Look for people in whom God may be creating an opening for you to share Jesus in gentleness and respect.

4. Pray for God to open opportunities and for the courage to step up and answer when he does.

Bibliography

"The Age Gap in Religion around the World." *Pew Research Center: Religion and Public Life* (Jun 13, 2018) 1–6. https://www.pewforum.org/2018/06/13/the-age-gap-in-religion-around-the-world/.

Alcorn, Randy. *The Grace and Truth Paradox.* Colorado Springs: Multnomah, 2003.

Andrew, Brother. *And God Changed His Mind.* Grand Rapids: Chosen Books, 1999.

Asrar, Shakeeb. "Suicide Rate on the Rise in U.S." *USA Today*, Apr 22, 2016. https://www.usatoday.com/story/news/2016/04/22/suicide-rate-rise-us/83284568/.

Barclay, William. *The Letter to the Hebrews.* The New Daily Study Bible. Louisville, KY: Westminster John Knox, 1976, 2002.

Barth, Karl, et al. "The Theological Declaration of Barmen (1934)." Translated by Arthur Cochrane. In *Creeds and Confessions of Faith in the Christian Tradition*, edited by Jaroslav Pelikan and Valerie Hotchkiss. New Haven: Yale University Press, 2003.

Batzig, Nicholas T. "Edwards, McLaurin, and the Transatlantic Concert." In *Jonathan Edwards and Scotland*, edited by Kelly Van Andel et al. Edinburgh: Dunedin Academic, 2011.

Beeke, Joel R., and Sinclair B. Ferguson, eds. "Second Helvetic Confession." In *Reformed Confessions Harmonized.* Grand Rapids: Baker, 2002.

———. "Westminster Larger Catechism." In *Reformed Confessions Harmonized.* Grand Rapids: Baker, 2002.

Bellah, Robert N., et al. *Habits of the Heart: Individualism and Commitment in American Life.* Los Angeles: University of California Press, 1996.

Berry, Wendell. *The Art of the Commonplace: Agrarian Essays of Wendell Berry.* Edited by Norman Wirzba. Berkeley: Counterpoint, 2002.

"The Best Love Songs of the 2000s." *Fox40*, Feb 12, 2016. https://fox40.com/2016/02/12/the-best-love-songs-of-the-2000s-2/.

Blackaby, Henry. *Holiness: God's Plan for Fullness of Life.* Nashville: Nelson, 2003.

Blomberg, Craig L. *Matthew.* The New American Commentary 22. Nashville: Broadman, 1992.

Boice, James Montgomery. *The Gospel of John.* Vol. 1, "The Coming of the Light." Grand Rapids: Baker, 1999.

Bonhoeffer, Dietrich. *The Cost of Discipleship.* New York: Touchstone, 1995.

"Book of Confessions." *The Constitution of the Presbyterian Church (U.S.A.)* vol. 1. Louisville, KY: The Office of the General Assembly, 1967.

Boring, M. Eugene. "The Gospel of Matthew." In *New Interpreter's Bible.* Nashville: Abingdon, 1995.

Borowitz, Eugene B. "The Enduring Truth of Religious Liberalism." In *The Fundamentalist Phenomenon: A View from Within, a Response from Without*, edited by M. J. Cohen. Grand Rapids: Eerdmans, 1990.

Bounds, E. M. "Book 1: The Necessity of Prayer." In *The Complete Works of E. M. Bounds on Prayer*. Grand Rapids: Baker, 1929.

———. "Book 3: The Possibilities of Prayer." In *The Complete Works of E. M. Bounds on Prayer*. Grand Rapids: Baker, 1923.

———. "Book 4: The Reality of Prayer." In *The Complete Works of E. M. Bounds on Prayer*. Grand Rapids: Baker, 1924.

———. "Book 5: Purpose in Prayer." In *The Complete Works of E. M. Bounds on Prayer*. Grand Rapids: Baker, 1920.

———. "Book 6: The Weapon of Prayer." In *The Complete Works of E. M. Bounds on Prayer*. Grand Rapids: Baker, 1931.

———. "Book 7: Power through Prayer." In *The Complete Works of E. M. Bounds on Prayer*. Grand Rapids: Baker, 1912.

Bridges, Jerry. *The Pursuit of Holiness*. Colorado Springs: NavPress, 2006.

Brown, Dan. *The Da Vinci Code*. New York: Doubleday, 2003.

Bruce, F. F. *The Canon of Scripture*. Downers Grove: InterVarsity, 1988.

Brueggemann, Walter. *Great Prayers of the Old Testament*. Louisville, KY: Westminster John Knox, 2008.

Bryant, David. *Concerts of Prayer*. Ventura, CA: Regal, 1988.

Bullinger, Heinrich. "The Second Helvetic Confessions (1566)." Translated by Arthur Cochrane. In *Creeds and Confessions of Faith in the Christian Tradition*, edited by Jaroslav Pelikan and Valerie Hotchkiss, vol. 2. New Haven: Yale University Press, 2003.

Bushell, Michael S., et al. "אָהַב." *BibleWorks*, LLC, 2009.

Calvin, John. *Commentary on a Harmony of the Evangelists, Matthew, Mark, and Luke*. Translated by William Pringle. Calvin's Commentaries 16. Grand Rapids: Baker, 2005.

———. *Commentary on the Book of Psalms*. Translated by Henry Beveridge. Calvin's Commentaries 4. Grand Rapids: Baker, 2003.

———. *Commentaries on the Epistle of St. Paul to the Hebrews*. Translated by John Owen. Calvin's Commentaries 22. Grand Rapids: Baker, 2005.

———. *Institutes of the Christian Religion*. Translated by Henry Beveridge. Vol. 2 of 2. Peabody, MA: Hendrickson, 2009.

Carr, G. Lloyd. "שָׁלֵם." In *Theological Wordbook of the Old Testament*, edited by R. Laird Harris, Jr. et al., 2:930–32. Chicago: Moody, 1980.

Carr, Nicholas. *The Shallows: What the Internet Is Doing to Our Brains*. New York: Norton and Company, 2011.

Carson, D. A. *The Gospel According to John*. Pillar New Testament Commentary. Grand Rapids: Eerdmans, 1991.

Chapell, Bryan. *Holiness by Grace: Delighting in the Joy That Is Our Strength*. Wheaton: Crossway, 2001.

Cherry, Conrad. "Imagery and Analysis." In *Johnathan Edwards: His Life and Influence*, edited by Charles Angoff, 19–28. Cranbury, NJ: Associated University Presses, 1975.

Christensen, Duane L. *Deuteronomy 1:1—21:9*. Word Biblical Commentary 6A. Dallas: Word, 2003.

Clark, Jason. "Consumer Liturgies and Their Corrosive Effects on Christian Identity." In *Church in the Present Tense*, edited by Kevin Corcoran, 39–58. Grand Rapids: Brazos, 2011.

Cockerill, Gareth Lee. *The Epistle to the Hebrews*. New International Commentary on the New Testament. Grand Rapids: Eerdmans, 2012.

Cook, Sam. "Cyberbullying Facts and Statistics for 2016–2019." Comparitech, Nov 29, 2019. https://www.comparitech.com/internet-providers/cyberbullying-statistics/.

Danaher, William J., Jr. "Beauty, Benevolence, and Virtue in Jonathan Edwards's *The Nature of True Virtue*." *Journal of Religion* 87.3 (2007) 386–410.

Davis, John J. "Lesson 6: Biblical Interpretation." Printed lecture from Semlink class Theology Survey I. South Hamilton, MA: Gordon-Conwell Theological Seminary, 2000.

de Brès, Guido. "The Belgic Confession (1561)." Translated by Ecumenical Creeds and Reformed Confessions 1988. In *Creeds and Confessions of Faith in the Christian Tradition*, edited by Jaroslav Pelikan and Valerie Hotchkiss, vol. 2. New Haven: Yale University Press, 2003.

Dekker, Ted. *The Slumber of Christianity: Awakening a Passion for Heaven on Earth*. Nashville: Thomas Nelson, 2005.

Delattre, Roland A. "Aesthetics and Ethics: Jonathan Edwards and the Recovery of Aesthetics for Religious Ethics." *Journal of Religious Ethics* 31.2 (2003) 277–97.

———. *Beauty and Sensibility in the Thought of Jonathan Edwards*. New Haven: Yale University Press, 1968.

DeMoss, Nancy Leigh. *Holiness: The Heart God Purifies*. Chicago: Moody, 2005.

de Tocqueville, Alexis. *Democracy in America*. Translated by Arthur Goldhammer. New York: Library of America, 2004.

Derrida, Jacques. "Signature, Event, Context." Chicago: University of Chicago Press, 1982. http://hydra.humanities.uci.edu/derrida/sec.html.

Douglas, J. D., and Merrill C. Tenney, eds. "Sanctification." In *New International Bible Dictionary*, 894–95. Grand Rapids: Zondervan, 1987.

Dunn, James D. G. *Romans 1–8*. Word Biblical Commentary 38. Nashville: Thomas Nelson, 1988.

Eareckson Tada, Joni. *A Place of Healing: Wrestling with the Mysteries of Suffering, Pain, and God's Sovereignty*. Colorado Springs: David C. Cook, 2010.

Edwards, Blake. "Fighting, Family and Finding Peace." *Relevant*, Sep 14, 2011. https://relevantmagazine.com/life5/relationships/26757-fighting-family-and-finding-peace-2/.

Edwards, Jonathan. "A Divine and Supernatural Light." In *Sermons and Discourses, 1730–1733 (WJE Online)*, edited by Mark Valeri, 17:406–27. New Haven: Jonathan Edwards Center at Yale University, 1730. https://bit.ly/2EPeVaZ.

———. "Ethical Writings." In *Works of Jonathan Edwards (WJE Online)*, edited by Paul Ramsey, vol. 8. New Haven: Jonathan Edwards Center at Yale University, 1749. https://bit.ly/35Q2EPt.

———. "A Faithful Narrative of the Surprising Work of God." In *Works of Jonathan Edwards (WJE Online)*, edited by C. C. Goen, 4:97–212. New Haven: Jonathan Edwards Center at Yale University, 1758. https://bit.ly/2SjwJDs.

———. "The Great Awakening." In *Works of Jonathan Edwards (WJE Online)*, edited by C. C. Goen, vol. 4. New Haven: Jonathan Edwards Center at Yale University, 1758. https://bit.ly/2PLZBCo.

———. *An Humble Attempt*. Ross-shire: Christian Focus, 2003.

———. "Letters and Personal Writings." In *Works of Jonathan Edwards (WJE Online)*, edited by George S. Claghorn, vol. 16. New Haven: Jonathan Edwards Center at Yale University, 1758. https://bit.ly/2ZkaCOr.

———. "The Miscellanies." In *Works of Jonathan Edwards (WJE Online)*, edited by Harry S. Stout, vol. 13. New Haven: Jonathan Edwards Center at Yale University, 1722. https://bit.ly/2EKDd65.

———. "Original Sin." In *Works of Jonathan Edwards (WJE Online)*, edited by Clyde A. Holbrook, vol. 3. New Haven: Jonathan Edwards Center at Yale University, 1758. https://bit.ly/2PQRTap.

———. "Religious Affections." In *Works of Jonathan Edwards*, edited by John E. Smith and Perry Miller, vol. 2. New Haven: Yale University Press, 1746.

———. "Religious Affections." In *Works of Jonathan Edwards (WJE Online)*, edited by Paul Ramsey, vol. 2. New Haven: Jonathan Edwards Center at Yale University, 1754. https://bit.ly/390Fbx8.

———. "Resolutions." In *Works of Jonathan Edwards (WJE Online)*, edited by George S. Claghorn, 16:754–59. New Haven: Jonathan Edwards Center at Yale University, 1716. https://bit.ly/2Qat8EL.

———. "Scientific and Philosophical Writings." In *Works of Jonathan Edwards (WJE Online)*, edited by Wallace E. Anderson, vol. 6. New Haven: Jonathan Edwards Center at Yale University, 1714. https://bit.ly/2ZlvIMr.

———. "Some Thoughts." In *Works of Jonathan Edwards (WJE Online)*, edited by C. C. Goen, vol. 4.289–529. New Haven: Jonathan Edwards Center at Yale University, 1758.

———. *A Treatise Concerning Religious Affections*. New Haven: Yale University Press, 1746.

———. "The Way of Holiness." In *Works of Jonathan Edwards (WJE Online)*, edited by Wilson H. Kimnach, 10:466–80. New Haven: Jonathan Edwards Center at Yale University, 1720. https://bit.ly/2QdWEJJ.

Eldredge, John. *The Sacred Romance*. Nashville: Thomas Nelson, 1997.

———. *The Utter Relief of Holiness: How God's Goodness Frees Us from Everything That Plagues Us*. New York: Faith Words, 2013.

Ellul, Jacques. *Perspective on Our Age*. Toronto, Ontario: House of Anansi, 1997.

———. *Propaganda: The Formation of Men's Attitudes*. New York: Vintage, 1973.

———. *The Technological Society*. Translated by John Wilkinson. New York: Vintage, 1964.

Erickson, Millard J. *Christian Theology*. Grand Rapids: Baker, 1998.

———. *Postmodernizing the Faith: Evangelical Responses to the Challenge of Postmodernism*. Grand Rapids: Baker, 1998.

Estes, Clarissa Pinkola. *Women Who Run with the Wolves*. New York: Ballantine, 1997.

Fasching, Darrell J. *The Thought of Jacques Ellul: A Systematic Exposition*. Lewiston, NY: Mellen, 1981.

Fawcett, Arthur. *The Cambuslang Revival*. Edinburgh: Banner of Truth Trust, 1971.

Foster, Richard J. *Prayer: Finding the Heart's True Home*. New York: HarperCollins, 1992.

Frost, Michael, and Alan Hirsch. *The Shaping of Things to Come: Innovation and Mission for the 21st-Century Church*. Grand Rapids: Baker, 2013.

Gillquist, Peter E. *Why We Haven't Changed the World*. Old Tappan, NJ: Fleming H. Revell, 1982.

Gregory, Brad S. *The Unintended Reformation: How a Religious Revolution Secularized Society*. Cambridge, MA: Harvard University Press, 2012.

Grenz, Stanley J. *A Primer on Postmodernism*. Grand Rapids: Eerdmans, 1996.

Grudem, Wayne. *Systematic Theology.* Grand Rapids: Zondervan, 1994.

"Guide to Kiln Temperature Ranges for Pottery." SoulCeramics, 2017. https://www.soulceramics.com/pages/guide-to-kiln-temperature-ranges-for-pottery.

Guinness, Os. "Found Faithful." In *Renewing the Evangelical Mission*, edited by Richard Lints, 90–108. Grand Rapids: Eerdmans, 2013.

Harris, R. Laird. "חסד." In *Theological Wordbook of the Old Testament*, edited by R. Laird Harris et al., 1:305–7. Chicago: Moody Bible Institute, 1980.

Herbert Spencer. PBS American Experience. n.d. https://www.pbs.org/wgbh/americanexperience/features/carnegie-herbert-spencer/.

Hodgson, Robert, Jr. "Holiness (NT)." In *The Anchor Bible Dictionary* 3, edited by David Noel Freedman, 249–54. New York: Doubleday, 1992.

Horton, Michael. *Christless Christianity: The Alternative Gospel of the American Church.* Grand Rapids: Baker, 2008.

"How to Refine Gold." Gold Traders, n.d. http://www.gold-traders.co.uk/gold-information/how-to-refine-gold.asp.

Howe, Frederic R. "Perfect, Perfection." In *Wycliffe Bible Dictionary*, edited by Charles F. Pfeiffer et al. Peabody, MA: Hendrickson, 1975.

Huxley, Aldous. *Ends and Means: An Inquiry into the Nature of Ideals and into the Methods Employed for Their Realization.* New York: Harper and Brothers, 1937.

"India's Christians: What Would Gandhi Do?" *Beliefnet News.* n.d. https://www.beliefnet.com/columnists/news/2012/07/indias-christians-ask-what-would-gandhi-do.php.

Jeffress, Robert. *Grace Gone Wild!* Colorado Springs: WaterBrook, 2005.

Jenkins, Philip. *The Next Christendom: The Coming of Global Christianity.* 3rd ed. New York: Oxford University Press, 2011.

Kaiser, Walter C., Jr. *Recovering the Unity of the Bible: One Continuous Story, Plan, and Purpose.* Grand Rapids: Zondervan, 2009.

———. *Revive Us Again: Biblical Principles for Revival Today.* Ross-Shire: Christian Focus Publications, 2001.

Keener, Craig S. *A Commentary on the Gospel of Matthew.* Grand Rapids: Eerdmans, 1999.

Keller, Timothy. *Generous Justice: How God's Grace Makes Us Just.* New York: Penguin, 2010.

———. *Prayer.* New York: Penguin, 2014.

———. *The Reason for God: Belief in an Age of Skepticism.* New York: Riverhead, 2008.

Killen, R. Allan. "Truth." In *Wycliffe Bible Dictionary*, edited by Charles F. Pfeiffer et al., 1750–51. Peabody, MA: Hendrickson, 1975.

Kimnach, Wilson H. "'Unfearing Minds': A Transatlantic Brotherhood of Preachers." In *Jonathan Edwards and Scotland*, edited by Kelly Van Andel et al., 3–20. Edinburgh: Dunedin Academic, 2011.

Kittel, Gerhard, ed. "χάρις." In *Theological Dictionary of the New Testament*, edited by Gerhard Friedrich, 9:387–402. Grand Rapids: Eerdmans, 1974.

Kittel, Gerhard, and Rudolph Bultmann. "Ἀλήθεια." In *Theological Dictionary of the New Testament*, edited by Gerhard Kittel and Gerhard Friedrich, 1:237–47. Grand Rapids: Eerdmans, 1964.

Klassen, William. "Love (NT and Early Jewish)." In *The Anchor Bible Dictionary*, edited by David Noel Freedman, 4. New York: Doubleday, 1992.

Knox, John, et al. "The Scots Confession (1560)." Translated by James Bulloch. In *Creeds and Confessions of Faith in the Christian Tradition*, edited by Jaroslav Pelikan and Valerie Hotchkiss, vol. 2. New Haven: Yale University Press, 2003.

Kselman, John S. "Grace (OT)." In *The Anchor Bible Dictionary*, edited by David Noel Freedman, 2:381–96. New York: Doubleday, 1992.

Lake, Kirsopp. *The Historical Evidence for the Resurrection*. Eugene, OR: Wipf & Stock, 2004. Kindle.

———. *The Religion of Yesterday and Tomorrow*. New York: Houghton Mifflin, 1926.

Lane, Belden C. "Jonathan Edwards on Beauty, Desire, and the Sensory World." *Theological Studies* 65.1 (2014) 44–72.

Latourette, Kenneth Scott. *A History of Christianity*. Vol. 2: "Reformation to the Present; A.D. 1500—A.D. 1975." Peabody, MA: Prince, 1975.

Lewis, C. S. *The C. S. Lewis Index: A Comprehensive Guide to Lewis's Writings and Ideas*. Edited by Janine Goffar. Wheaton: Crossway, 1995.

———. "The Great Divorce." In *The Complete C. S. Lewis Signature Classics*. New York: HarperCollins, 2002.

———. "Mere Christianity." In *The Complete C. S. Lewis Signature Classics*. New York: HarperCollins, 1980.

———. *Reflections on the Psalms*. New York: HarperCollins, 1958.

———. *The Weight of Glory and Other Addresses*. New York: HarperCollins, 1980.

Lints, Richard. "Introduction." In *Renewing the Evangelical Mission*, edited by Richard Lints, 1–10. Grand Rapids: Eerdmans, 2013.

Lloyd-Jones, D. Martyn. *Darkness and Light: An Exposition of Ephesians 4:17–5:17*. Grand Rapids: Baker, 1982.

———. *God's Ultimate Purpose: An Exposition of Ephesians 1:1–23*. Grand Rapids: Baker, 1978.

———. *God's Way of Reconciliation: An Exposition of Ephesians 2*. Grand Rapids: Baker, 1972.

———. *Life in the Spirit: In Marriage, Home and Work, an Exposition of Ephesians 5:18–6:9*. Grand Rapids: Baker, 2000.

Long, Zeb Bradford, et al. *The Healing Ministry of Jesus*. The Dunamis Project. Black Mountain, NC: Presbyterian-Reformed Ministries International, 2000.

Lovelace, Richard F. *Dynamics of Spiritual Life: An Evangelical Theology of Renewal*. Downers Grove: InterVarsity, 1979.

Lyon, David. *Postmodernity: Concepts in Social Thought*. 2nd ed. Minneapolis: University of Minnesota, 2005.

Marsden, George M. *Jonathan Edwards: A Life*. New Haven: Yale University Press, 2003.

Martin, Ralph P. *2 Corinthians*. Word Biblical Commentary 40. Waco, TX: Word, 1986.

Mastin, Luke. "Age of Enlightenment." The Basics of Philosophy. http://www.philosophybasics.com/historical_enlightenment.html.

McClymond, Michael J., and Gerald R. McDermott. *The Theology of Jonathan Edwards*. New York: Oxford University Press, 2012.

McComiskey, Thomas E. "קָדַשׁ." In *Theological Wordbook of the Old Testament*, edited by R. Laird Harris, Jr. et al., 2:786–89. Chicago: Moody, 1980.

McGrath, Alister. *Evangelicalism and the Future of Christianity*. Downers Grove: InterVarsity, 1995.

McKnight, Scot. "Scripture in the Emerging Movement." In *Church in the Present Tense: A Candid Look at What's Emerging*, edited by Kevin Corcoran, 105–22. Grand Rapids: Brazos, 2001.

Meade, Michael J. *The Genius Myth*. Seattle: GreenFire, 2016.

Merton, Thomas. *No Man Is an Island.* Boston: Shambhala, 1955.

Moncrieff, Chris. "Interview for Press Association (10th anniversary as Prime Minister)." *Margret Thatcher Foundation,* May 3, 1989. https://www.margaretthatcher.org/document/107427.

Moore, Beth. *Praying God's Word: Breaking Free from Spiritual Strongholds.* Nashville: B&H, 2009.

Mott, John R. *Spiritual Awakening in a University.* Asia Pacific Campus Challenge, 1997. At https://xapinas.files.wordpress.com/2012/06/spiritual-awakening.pdf.

Mounce, William D. "Grace." In *Mounce's Complete Expository Dictionary of Old and New Testament Words,* edited by William D. Mounce, 303–4. Grand Rapids: Zondervan, 2006.

———. "Love." In *Mounce's Complete Expository Dictionary of Old and New Testament Words,* edited by William D. Mounce, 424–29. Grand Rapids: Zondervan, 2006.

———. "Truth." In *Mounce's Complete Expository Dictionary of Old and New Testament Words,* edited by William D. Mounce, 747–48. Grand Rapids: Zondervan, 2006.

———. "Whole." In *Mounce's Complete Expository Dictionary of Old and New Testament Words,* edited by William D. Mounce, 785. Grand Rapids: Zondervan, 2006.

Noll, Mark A. *The New Shape of World Christianity.* Downers Grove: InterVarsity, 2009.

O'Brien, Peter T. *The Letter to the Hebrews.* Pillar New Testament Commentary. Grand Rapids: Eerdmans, 2010.

Olsen, Roger E. *How to Be Evangelical without Being Conservative.* Grand Rapids: Zondervan, 2008.

Ortlund, Dane C. *Edwards on the Christian Life: Alive to the Beauty of God.* Wheaton: Crossway, 2104.

Osborne, Grant R. *The Hermeneutical Spiral: A Comprehensive Introduction to Biblical Interpretation.* Downers Grove: InterVarsity, 1991.

Otto, Rudolf. *The Idea of the Holy: An Inquiry into the Non-Rational Factor in the Idea of the Divine and Its Relation to the Rational.* 2nd ed. Translated by John W. Harvey. New York: Oxford University Press, 1950.

Owen, John. *Communion with God.* The Works of John Owen, edited by William H. Goold, 2. East Peoria, IL: Versa, 2009.

———. *The Holy Spirit.* The Works of John Owen, edited by William H. Goold, 3. East Peoria, IL: Versa, 2009.

———. *The Nature and Beauty of Gospel Worship.* Adobe PDF eBook. N.p.: Still Waters Revival Books. Orig. published 1721.

Packer, James I. "The Adequacy of Human Language." In *Inerrancy,* edited by Norman L. Geisler, 197–228. Grand Rapids: Zondervan, 1980.

Palmer, Earl F. *The Book That John Wrote.* Vancouver, B.C.: Regent College, 2002.

Piper, John. *The Dangerous Duty of Delight.* Sisters, OR: Multnomah, 2001.

———. *The Supremacy of God in Preaching.* Grand Rapids: Baker, 2004.

Postman, Neil. *Amusing Ourselves to Death: Public Discourse in the Age of Show Business.* New York: Penguin, 2005.

———. *Technopoly: The Surrender of Culture to Technology.* New York: Vintage, 1993.

Priestley, Theo. "Why Every Tech Company Needs a Chief Evangelist." *Forbes,* Aug 28, 2015. https://www.forbes.com/sites/theopriestley/2015/08/28/why-every-tech-company-needs-a-chief-evangelist/.

Procksch, Otto. "ἅγιος." In *Theological Dictionary of the New Testament*, edited by Gerhard Kittel and Gerhard Friedrich, 1:88–115. Grand Rapids: Eerdmans, 1964.

Quarles, Charles. *Sermon on the Mount: Restoring Christ's Message to the Modern Church*. Edited by E. Ray Clendenen. Nashville: Broadman, 2011.

Quell, Gottfried. "ἀλήφεια." In *Theological Dictionary of the New Testament*, edited by Gerhard Kittel and Gerhard Friedrich, 1:232–47 as found in Logos 7, electronic ed. Grand Rapids: Eerdmans, 1964.

"Religion." Electronic ed., 25 charted surveys. Gallup, 2019. https://news.gallup.com/poll/1690/religion.aspx.

Rorty, Richard. "Introduction." In *Pragmatism: From Peirce to Davidson*, by John P. Murphy. Boulder, CO: Westview, 1990.

Ruis, David. "Spirit Is on Me." *When Justice Shines*. Compact Disc. Vinyard Songs Canada, 2006.

Russell, Emmett. "Holiness, Holy." In *New International Bible Dictionary*, edited by J. D. Douglas and Merril C. Tenney, 445–46. Grand Rapids: Zondervan, 1987.

Ryle, J. C. *Holiness: Its Nature, Hindrances, Difficulties, and Roots*. Moscow, ID: Charles Nolan, 2001.

Ryrie, Charles C. "Grace." In *Wycliffe Bible Dictionary*, edited by Howard F. Vos et al., 725–26. Peabody, MA: Hendrickson, 1975.

Sakenfeld, Katherine Doob. "Love (OT)." In *The Anchor Bible Dictionary*, edited by David Noel Freedman, 4:375–81. New York: Doubleday, 1992.

Schleiermacher, Friedrich. *The Christian Faith*. 2nd ed. Edited by H. R. Mackintosh and J. S. Stewart. New York: T. & T. Clark, 1999.

Schreiner, Thomas R. *Romans*. Baker Exegetical Commentary on the New Testament. Grand Rapids: Baker Academic, 1998.

Scott, Jack B. "אָמַן." In *Theological Wordbook of the Old Testament*, edited by R. Laird Harris, Jr. et al., 1:51–53. Chicago: Moody Bible Institute, 1982.

Senior, Donald. *The Gospel of Matthew*. Interpreting Biblical Texts. Nashville: Abingdon, 1997.

Shaw, Mark. *Global Awakening: How 20th-Century Revivals Triggered a Christian Revolution*. Downers Grove: InterVarsity, 2010.

Shogren, Gary S. "Grace: New Testament." In *The Anchor Bible Dictionary*, edited by David Noel Freedman, 2:1086–88. New York: Doubleday, 1992.

Sider, Ronald J. *The Scandal of the Evangelical Conscience: Why Are Christians Living Just Like the Rest of the World?* Grand Rapids: Baker, 2005.

Sittser, Jerry. *When God Doesn't Answer Your Prayer: Insights to Keep You Praying with Greater Faith and Deeper Hope*. Grand Rapids: Zondervan, 2007.

Smedes, Lewis B. *Forgive and Forget: Healing the Hurts We Don't Deserve*. New York: HarperOne, 1996.

Smith, Colin. "A Critical Assessment of the Graf-Wellhausen Documentary Hypothesis." Alpha and Omega Ministries, Jun 1, 2002. http://www.aomin.org/aoblog/2002/06/01/a-critical-assessment-of-the-graf-wellhausen-documentary-hypothesis/.

Smith, James Bryan. *The Good and Beautiful God*. Downers Grove: InterVarsity, 2009.

Smith, James K. A. *Who's Afraid of Postmodernism? Taking Derrida, Lyotard, and Foucault to Church*. Grand Rapids: Baker, 2006.

Spock, Benjamin. *Baby and Child Care*. New York: Pocket Books, 1957.

Sproul, R. C. *The Holiness of God*. Wheaton: Tyndale House, 1985.

Sproul, R. C., and Archie Parrish. *The Spirit of Revival: Discovering the Wisdom of Jonathan Edwards.* Wheaton: Crossway, 2008.

Stauffer, Ethelbert. "Ἀγάπη." In *Theological Dictionary of the New Testament*, edited by Gerhard Kittel and Gerhard Friedrich, 1:35–55. Grand Rapids: Eerdmans, 1964.

Stone, Kathlyn. "The Most Prescribed Medications by Drug Class: Prescriptions Being Filled at an All-Time High." *The Balance*, Nov 6, 2019. https://www.thebalance.com/the-most-prescribed-medications-by-drug-class-2663215.

Sweet, Leonard. *Post-modern Pilgrims: First Century Passion for the 21st Century World.* Nashville, TN: Broadman, 2000.

Tennent, Timothy. *Christianity at the Religious Roundtable: Evangelicalism in Conversation with Hinduism, Buddhism, and Islam.* New York: Baker Academic, 2002.

Thompson, Marianne Meye. *1–3 John.* IVP New Testament Commentary Series. Logos electronic version. Downers Grove, InterVarsity, 1992.

Tozer, A. W. *Knowledge of the Holy.* New York: HarperOne, 1961.

Volf, Miroslav. *Exclusion and Embrace: A Theological Exploration of Identity, Otherness, and Reconciliation.* Nashville: Abingdon, 1996.

———. "Human Flourishing." In *Renewing the Evangelical Mission*, edited by Richard Lints, 13–30. Grand Rapids: Eerdmans, 2013.

Wallace, Daniel B. *Greek Grammar Beyond the Basics.* Grand Rapids: Zondervan, 1996.

Weisstein, Eric W. "Geometry." From *MathWorld*—A Wolfram Web Resource, n.d. http://mathworld.wolfram.com/Geometry.html.

Wellhausen, Julius. *Prolegomena to the History of Israel.* ZuuBooks, 2011.

Wesley, John. *A Longing for Holiness.* Edited by Keith Beasely-Topliffe. Nashville: Upper Room, 1997.

———. *A Plain Account of Christian Perfection.* Peabody, MA: Hendrickson, 2007.

———. "Sermon 44: Original Sin." In *The Sermons of John Wesley*, edited by George Lyons with corrections by Ryan Danker. Nampa, ID: Wesley Center for Applied Theology, 1999. http://wesley.nnu.edu/john-wesley/the-sermons-of-john-wesley-1872-edition/sermon-44-original-sin/.

"The Westminster Confession (1643–1647)." In *Creeds and Confessions of Faith in the Christian Tradition*, edited by Jaroslav Pelikan and Valerie Hotchkiss, vol. 2. New Haven: Yale University Press, 2003.

"The Westminster Shorter Catechism." In *The Constitution of the Presbyterian Church (U.S.A.).* Part I: "Book of Confessions." Louisville, KY: The Office of the General Assembly, 2007.

Wolf, Justin. "Impressionism." The Art Story: Modern Art Insight, 2014. http://www.theartstory.org/movement-impressionism.htm.

Wright, N. T. *Evil and the Justice of God.* Downers Grove: InterVarsity, 2006.

Yamauchi, Edwin. "חָנַן." In *Theological Wordbook of the Old Testament*, edited by R. Laird Harris, Jr. et al., 302–4. Chicago: Moody, 1980.

Zimmerli, Walther. "χάρις, Old Testament." In *Theological Dictionary of the New Testament*, edited by Gerhard Friedrich, 9:376–87. Grand Rapids: Eerdmans, 1974.

Zodhiates, Spiros, ed. "ἀλήθεια." In *The Complete Word Study Dictionary: New Testament*, 120–21. Chattanooga: AMG, 1992.

———. "χάρις." In *The Complete Word Study Dictionary: New Testament*, 1469–71. Chattanooga: AMG, 1992.

BIBLIOGRAPHY

Additional Resources for Further Study

Ahlstrom, Sydney E. *A Religious History of the American People*, 2nd ed. New Haven: Yale University Press, 2004.
Albright, William Foxwell. *Yahweh and the Gods of Canaan*. Garden City, NY: Doubleday, 1968.
Baker, Frank, ed. *Letters*. The Works of John Wesley, vol. 25. Nashville: Abingdon, 1987.
Bichell, Rae Ellen. "Suicide Rates Climb in U.S., Especially Among Adolescent Girls." *NPR's Morning Edition*, Apr 22, 2016. http://www.npr.org/sections/health-shots/2016/04/22/474888854/suicide-rates-climb-in-u-s-especially-among-adolescent-girls.
Boda, Mark J., and J. Gordon McConville, eds. *Dictionary of the Old Testament Prophets*. Downers Grove: InterVarsity Press, 2012.
Brands, H. W. *American Colossus: The Triumph of Capitalism, 1865–1900*. New York: Doubleday, 2010.
Bridges, Jerry. *Respectable Sins*. Colorado Springs: NavPress, 2007.
Brunner, Frederick Dale. *A Theology of the Holy Spirit*. Grand Rapids: Eerdmans, 1970.
Canedy, Ardel B., et al. *Four Views on the Historical Adam*. Grand Rapids: Zondervan, 2013.
Cardozo, Nathan Lopes. "On Bible Criticism and Its Counterarguments." *Torat Emet*, 1995. http://www.aishdas.org/toratemet/en_cardozo.html.
Collins, Kenneth J. *John Wesley: A Theological Journey*. Nashville: Abingdon, 2003.
Cook, Jeff. *Seven: The Deadly Sins and the Beatitudes*. Grand Rapids: Zondervan, 2008.
Crouch, Andy. *Culture Making: Recovering Our Creative Calling*. Downers Grove: InterVarsity, 2008.
———. *The Tech-Wise Family: Everyday Steps for Putting Technology in Its Proper Place*. Grand Rapids: Baker, 2017.
Darwin, Charles. *On the Origin of Species*. London: Macmillan Collector's Library, 2017.
Davies, Stevan, trans. *The Gospel of Thomas: Annotated and Explained*. Woodstock, VT: Skylight Paths, 2002.
Deere, Jack. *Surprised by the Power of the Spirit*. Grand Rapids: Zondervan, 1993.
Eareckson Tada, Joni, and Joe Musser. *Joni*. Grand Rapids: Zondervan, 2001.
Edwards, Jonathan. *A Call to United, Extraordinary Prayer (An humble Attempt . . .)*. Ross-shire: Christian Focus, 1748.
———. *Distinguishing Marks*. Jonathan Edwards Center Online. New Haven: Yale University Press, 2007.
Eldredge, John. *Epic: The Story God Is Telling*. Nashville: Thomas Nelson, 2004.
Fairbairn, Donald. *Life in the Trinity*. Downers Grove: InterVarsity, 2009.
Foucault, Michel. *Discipline and Punish: The Birth of the Prison*. Translated by Alan Sheridan. New York: Vintage, 1977.
———. "Nietzsche, Genealogy, History." In *Language, Counter-Memory, and Practice: Selected Essays and Interviews*, edited by Donald F. Bouchard, 139–64. Ithaca, NY: Cornell University Press, 1997.
Graham, Billy. *The Holy Spirit*. Nashville: Word, 1988.
Green, Joel B., et al., eds. *Dictionary of Jesus and the Gospels*. Downers Grove: InterVarsity, 2013.
Guinness, Os. *The Dust of Death*. Westmont, IL: InterVarsity, 1973.
———. *Fit Bodies Fat Minds: Why Evangelicals Don't Think and What to Do about It*. Grand Rapids: Baker, 2003.

Hatch, Nathan O. *The Democratization of American Christianity.* New Haven: Yale University Press, 1989.

Hawthorne, Gerald F., et al., eds. *Dictionary of Paul and His Letters.* Downers Grove: InterVarsity, 1993.

Howe, Daniel Walker. *What Hath God Wrought: The Transformation of America, 1815–1848.* New York: Oxford University Press, 2007.

Huxley, Aldous. *Brave New World.* New York: Harper, 1932.

Latourette, Kenneth Scott. *A History of Christianity.* Vols. 1 and 2. Peabody, MA: Prince, 1975.

Leloup, Jean-Yves, trans. *Gospel of Philip: Jesus, Mary Magdalene, and the Gnosis of Sacred Union.* Translated into English by Joseph Rowe. Rochester, VT: Inner Traditions, 2004.

Lewis, C. S. *The Screwtape Letters.* New York: HarperCollins, 1942.

Long, Zeb Bradford. "Gateways to Empowered Ministry." The Dunamis Project. Edited by Douglas McMurry. Black Mountain, NC: Presbyterian-Reformed Ministries International, 1997.

———. *Passage through the Wilderness.* Grand Rapids: Chosen, 1998.

———. *Prayer That Shapes the Future.* Grand Rapids: Zondervan, 1999.

Long, Zeb Bradford, and Douglas McMurry. *The Collapse of the Brass Heaven: Rebuilding Our Worldview to Embrace the Power of God.* Grand Rapids: Chosen Books, 1994.

———. *Receiving the Power: Preparing the Way for the Holy Spirit.* Grand Rapids: Chosen, 1996.

Long, Zeb Bradford, et al. "In the Spirit's Power." The Dunamis Project. Black Mountain, NC: Presbyterian-Reformed Ministries International, 1994.

Long, Zeb Bradford, et al. "Spiritual Warfare." The Dunamis Project. Black Mountain, NC: Presbyterian-Reformed Ministries International, 1999.

Lubell, K. M. "Suicide Trends among Youths and Young Adults Aged 10–24 Years—United States, 1990–2004." CDC Morbidity and Mortality Weekly Report (MMWR), Sep 7, 2007. https://www.cdc.gov/mmwr/preview/mmwrhtml/mm5635a2.htm.

Lucado, Max. *No Wonder They Call Him the Savior.* Nashville: Thomas Nelson, 2004.

———. *Six Hours One Friday.* Nashville: Thomas Nelson, 2004.

———. *Tell Me the Story.* Nashville: Thomas Nelson, 1992.

Martin, Ralph P., and Peter H. Davids, eds. *Dictionary of the Later New Testament and Its Development.* Downers Grove: InterVarsity, 1997.

McKnight, Scot. *The Story of the Christ.* Grand Rapids: Baker, 2006.

McPherson, James M. *Battle Cry of Freedom: The Civil War Era.* New York: Oxford University Press, 1988.

Miller, Steven P. *The Age of Evangelicalism: America's Born-Again Years.* New York: Oxford University Press, 2014.

Mounce, Robert H. *Matthew.* New International Biblical Commentary 1. Peabody, MA: Hendrickson, 1991.

Noll, Mark. *The Civil War as a Theological Crisis.* Chapel Hill, NC: University of North Carolina Press, 2006.

Orwell, George. *1984.* New York: Signet Classics, 1949.

Outler, Albert C., ed. *Sermons I.* In The Works of John Wesley. Nashville: Abingdon, 1984.

———. *Sermons II.* In The Works of John Wesley. Nashville: Abingdon, 1984.

———. *Sermons III.* In The Works of John Wesley. Nashville: Abingdon, 1984.

———. *Sermons IV.* In The Works of John Wesley. Nashville: Abingdon, 1984.

Shuster, Marguerite. *The Fall and Sin: What We Have Become as Sinners*. Grand Rapids: Eerdmans, 2003.

———. "The Mystery of Original Sin." *Christianity Today* 57.3 (2013) 38. https://www.christianitytoday.com/ct/2013/april/mystery-of-original-sin.html.

Sider, Ronald J. *Nonviolent Action*. Grand Rapids: Brazos, 2015.

———. *Nuclear Holocaust and Christian Hope*. Downers Grove: InterVarsity, 1982.

———. *The Scandal of Evangelical Politics*. Grand Rapids: Baker, 2008.

Soulen, Richard N., and R. Kendall Soulen. *Handbook of Biblical Criticism*. 4th ed. Louisville, KY: Westminster, 2011.

Spangler, Ann. *Praying the Names of God*. Grand Rapids: Zondervan, 2004.

Spurgeon, Charles. *Holy Spirit Power*. New Kensington, PA: Whitaker House, 1996.

Stanley, Charles F. *Landmines in the Path of the Believer*. Nashville: Nelson, 2007.

Toffler, Alvin. *Future Shock*. New York: Bantam, 1970.

Torrey, R. A. *The Person and Work of the Holy Spirit*. New Kensington, PA: Whitaker House, 1996.

Tracey, Patricia. *Jonathan Edwards, Pastor: Religion and Society in Eighteenth-Century Northampton*. Eugene, OR: Wipf & Stock, 1980.

Walton, John H., et al. *NIV Application Commentary Series*. Grand Rapids: Zondervan, 1994.

Wood, Gordon S. *Empire of Liberty: A History of the Early Republic, 1789–1815*. New York: Oxford University Press, 2009.

Yoder, John Howard. *The Politics of Jesus*. Grand Rapids: Eerdmans, 1994.

www.ingramcontent.com/pod-product-compliance
Lightning Source LLC
Chambersburg PA
CBHW080725300426
44114CB00019B/2489